THE WORLD OF ARCHAEOLOGY
General Editor: GLYN DANIEL

A History of American Archaeology

GORDON R. WILLEY and JEREMY A. SABLOFF

A History of
American Archaeology

with 124 illustrations

THAMES AND HUDSON · LONDON

To Philip Phillips, to whom archaeology has
always been anthropology

1 (*Frontispiece*) Catherwood's
drawing of a stela at Copan.
(From Catherwood, 1844)

© 1974 Thames and Hudson Ltd,
London

Printed and Bound in Great Britain
by Jarrold and Sons, Norwich

ISBN 0 500 78002 1

16

Contents

The present state of archaeology cannot be divorced from its past state.

Glyn Daniel

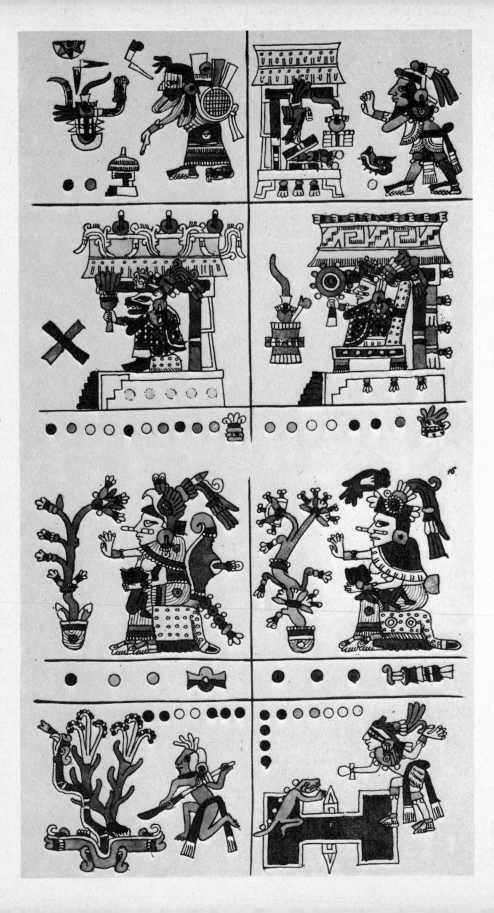

AMERICAN ARCHAEOLOGY – as all archaeology – is now in a phase of critical self-appraisal. Recent innovations in method and theory have aroused interest and argument in a way that has never occurred before within the discipline. This is the occasion, we believe, for a review of the full course of its development. In this way we can appreciate new developments in relation to those that have gone before; and from this historical perspective we may also see more clearly the significance of the new directions in which the field is moving. Being a pioneer effort, this book was not conceived of as definitive in any sense. Rather, it is hoped that it may be the first of a genre which will stimulate further critical reflections and writings on the intellectual history of the subject.

It is inevitable in a work of this sort that the authors draw not only upon formal writings but upon the informal conversations and interchanges with professional colleagues dating back over a period of a good many years. Our debts to many of these people will be made clear throughout the text and footnotes; to the others we offer our general, but nonetheless grateful, thanks. For his special efforts in calling our attention to numerous, but not well-known, references that bear upon the early history of North American archaeology we wish to express our special appreciation to Stephen Williams. It should also be noted that some of the ideas of the book were first launched and discussed in a Harvard seminar on the history of American archaeology which was offered by one of us (Sabloff) in the fall of 1969, and we acknowledge the aid and interest of the students of this seminar group.

A word should be said about the extensive system of notes and the bibliography. This is not undue pedantry. Although we have attempted to write a text that can be read without necessary reference to the notes, the latter are a very integral part of the book, especially for the student. It is obviously impossible to describe in detail the various examples of archaeological operations or ideas of interpretation with which we are dealing. Recourse to the source material undoubtedly will be desirable for many readers. We have gone to some pains to make this possible with our notes and references.

We take this opportunity to thank Katharine W. Willey and Paula L. W. Sabloff for their critical readings of the manuscript and Maria von Mering Huggins for the final typing. The bibliography was put in final form by Isabelle Center. Maps and charts are the work of Symme Burstein of the Peabody Museum staff.

2 (*Opposite*) Scenes from the Mexican Codex Féjerváry. (From Kingsborough, 1831–48)

9

Finally, it is our pleasure to thank Glyn Daniel, archaeologist, editor, and instigator of various series of archaeological publications, for his invitation to us to prepare such a book. His encouragement, together with the patience and help of the editorial staff of Thames and Hudson, have, in very large measure, made the book possible.

GORDON R. WILLEY
JEREMY A. SABLOFF

Chapter One

Introduction

'*Archaeology: 1. Ancient history generally; systematic description or study of antiquities. 2. spec. The scientific study of the remains and monuments of the prehistoric period.*' (The Oxford Universal Dictionary, *1955 ed.*)

The Nature of Archaeology

FEW dictionary definitions are ever wholly satisfactory in capturing the substance and meaning of complex subjects. This is certainly true for the discipline of archaeology. The one cited above is adequate, although only in a general way. It is true that most devotees of the subject, amateur or professional, would agree that archaeology is concerned primarily with the prehistoric past, that in the consideration of this past the emphasis is upon material or artifactual remains, and that the data are approached systematically, as regards description, classification, and comparison. But our principal objection to such a definition is that it does not specify the basic goals of the discipline, at least as we conceive them. Accordingly, we offer a modified definition to begin this historical account of the development of archaeology in the Americas. Archaeology[1] – in our view – is the study of the human cultural and social past whose goals are *to narrate* the sequent story of that past and *to explain* the events that composed it. The discipline attempts to achieve these goals by excavating and analyzing the 'remains and monuments' of past cultures and the contexts in which they are found.

Given such a definition, archaeology has an obvious alliance with history, for both history and archaeology deal with the human past. Both are concerned with the narration of that past and with its explanation. Their differences are primarily those of method rather than philosophical outlook. History orders and presents the past with the aid of textual references that were co-existent with that past; archaeology relies, as the dictionary definition informs us, on material 'remains and monuments' and, further, it relies on the distinctly archaeological methods and techniques of their excavation and preservation. There are, of course, instances where the two disciplines converge to contribute to an elucidation of the human past, as in those cultures where contemporary written records are few in number, selective in subject matter, or imperfectly translated, and where it is necessary to supplement them with the archaeological recovery and interpretation of artifacts and monuments.

Archaeology is also allied with anthropology. Anthropology is fundamentally a generalizing and comparative discipline. It begins with the particulars of human societies and cultures, but its most distinctive characteristic is its comparative point of view. The purpose of this comparison is, ultimately, an explaining of the ways in which cultural and social forms come into being, function, and change, or, more briefly, an understanding of process. At this point there is, by tradition, some philosophical distinction between archaeology as history and archaeology as anthropology. That is, most historians have dealt with the past in particularistic or idiographic terms while in archaeology there has been a somewhat greater trend toward comparative generalization. On the other hand, Spengler or Toynbee, historians by training and method, were interested in explaining the past in general comparative or nomothetic terms. Conversely, archaeologists often have been and are concerned with the specific event rather than the generalization that may be drawn from a comparison of events.

It is, thus, our definition and conception of archaeology – whether in its American version or elsewhere – that its objectives are both narration and explanation, that it is both allied to history and to anthropology, and that its procedures are particularizing (idiographic) and generalizing (nomothetic).[2] For although all of these dualities are conceptually separable, they are not mutually exclusive. On the contrary, they are inevitably related. This interrelationship is to be recognized in the simple fact that to explain past events it is necessary to describe and to plot them in space and in time and that, conversely, such events cannot be described satisfactorily until they are to some extent understood.

Archaeology in World Historical Perspective

Although man's interest in the past is very old and virtually universal, archaeology as a discipline is a western European development.[3] It has its traceable roots in the humanistic antiquarianism of the Italian Renaissance. This antiquarianism was founded on the discoveries of the monuments of Classical antiquity. The Renaissance findings, for the first time, gave western European man a comparative point of view about other cultures. This was the seed idea for both archaeology and anthropology. It was now known that another way of life, another civilization that rivaled and, in many ways, surpassed that of 14th and 15th century Italy, had once existed in the distant past. The conception of cultural difference in time (the essence of archaeology) was extended to the acceptance of contemporaneous cultural differences in geographic space (a primary tenet of anthropology).[4]

After the Renaissance, archaeology as humanistic antiquarianism took two courses. In northern Europe, especially England, France, and Scandinavia, such antiquaries as William Camden (1551–1623), John Aubrey (1626–97), William Stukeley (1687–1765), and Rasmus Nyerup (1759–1829) studied the local mounds and monuments of their countries and set down the accounts of their observations. The other course was followed by men like Giovanni Belzoni (1778–1823) who journeyed to the Classical world and the Near East and brought the treasures of these lands back to rich patrons in northern Europe. Belzoni was, perhaps, more romantic grave-robber than scholar; but towards the end of the 18th century and the beginning of the 19th more serious students followed such dilettanti. For example, a valuable by-product of Napoleon's Egyptian campaign was the introduction of French scholars to Egyptian antiquities, an event which led eventually to the work of men like Denon and Champollion and the truly archaeological achievement of the decipherment of the Egyptian hieroglyphs.

It was, however, the first of these two courses of humanistic antiquarianism that led more directly to what can be rightly called the first systematic archaeology. This occurred in Denmark where in 1819 J.C. Thomsen (1788–1863) followed up the work of Nyerup by organizing the national museum of that country along the lines of the 'Three-Age' system. This system was predicated on the belief that the ancient inhabitants of Europe (and probably other parts of the world as well) had passed, successively, through ages characterized by the use of stone, bronze, and iron implements and weapons in that order. The idea itself was not new. Greek and Roman historians and philosophers of Classical times had suggested it, and various European antiquarians of the late 17th and the 18th centuries referred to it. By the early 19th century it was in historical accounts and school books available in Denmark. Thomsen, however, was the first to apply the stone-bronze-iron classification to substantial collections of actual specimens, to insist that the classification corresponded to a sequence of chronologically defined periods, and to go on from the identification of stone, bronze, and iron materials to stylistic differences in weapons and tools that could be correlated with the three ages.[5]

Thomsen's work was continued by his younger colleague, J.J.A. Worsaae (1821–85), who enunciated some of the first important principles of archaeology, including the notion that objects accompanying the same burial are generally things that were in use at the same time and that were usually placed in burial association at the same time.[6] This is the basis of grave lot segregation and of the chronological seriation of such lots.

At about this time another line of investigation was beginning that was to merge with the Danish advances in the development of archaeology. For many years flint artifacts had been observed in geological strata, but their significance was not appreciated until Lyell revolutionized geology with his fluvial or depositional theories of that science in his *Principles of Geology* (1830–33). Then, in 1836–37, the French scholar, Boucher de Perthes, announced discoveries of man-made artifacts in deep geological strata, claiming for them great antiquity. The idea that man and his artifacts could be of such great age aroused a storm of opposition, both religious and scientific; however, the idea proved to be the beginning of Paleolithic archaeology. By 1860, with the support of Sir John Evans and others, the scientific world had accepted Boucher de Perthes's discoveries. The dimension of time, which had begun to transform antiquarianism into archaeology with the Danish Three-Age system, was now seen in all its implications for man's history and prehistory. Moreover, the presence of archaeological materials in different geological strata, and in strata which were found superimposed one over the other, introduced the vital concept of stratigraphy to the emerging archaeological discipline.

Still another intellectual force appeared in the mid 19th century to aid in the growth of archaeology – as well as anthropology. The year of 1859 was the year of Darwin's *The Origin of Species*. The book, together with Huxley's impassioned stand in its favor, had a revolutionary impact on all science and learned thought. From biological evolution the idea of progress was extended to the history of human societies and cultures; and two of the founders of anthropology, E. B. Tylor (1832–1917) and L. H. Morgan (1818–81), saw in this principle of cultural evolution, and in the findings of archaeology with its Three-Age system and its demonstrated great antiquity of man, the data from which to construct a model of the human social and cultural past. This model – the sequence of 'Savagery,' 'Barbarism,' and 'Civilization' – had, in turn, a profound effect upon archaeology, as well as upon all philosophies of history and society.[7]

Finally, and less specifically, there were other influences converging to aid in the development of archaeology in the early and middle 19th century. There was the general rise and appreciation of science in general, a trend that had begun in 18th century rationalism and had gathered momentum from that time forward. Closely interrelated with this was the rising industrialism of western Europe and America and the expansion of the power of these regions to what had been unexplored and exotic parts of the world. Industry had an obvious, direct alliance with fields like geology and the physical sciences; together with the exploration and exploitation of far corners of the world, it also had a more subtle, but nevertheless real, conditioning effect in bringing about an intellectual climate in which anthropology and archaeology could flourish.

The latter part of the 19th century and the first part of the 20th, up to the time of World War I, saw great progress in archaeology. Schliemann, Petrie, Sir Arthur Evans, and others conducted long-term operations in the Classical World and the Near East; Stephens, Catherwood, and others explored the Maya ruins of the New World; in England, General Pitt-Rivers set new standards of professional excavation; and in the United States Putnam began the training of a generation of professional archaeologists. After World War I archaeologists became more aware of the importance of chronology – not simply as the great developmental span of man's passage through the Three-Age system or the levels of 'Savagery' to 'Civilization' but as the means of ordering culture units or culture complexes in regional archaeological sequences. Problems were conceived of as more strictly historical in the sense of spatial-temporal relations between cultures and in the tracing out of diffusion. Generally, this was carried out within the limits of a regional framework, for this was a time of intensive regional specialization, but there were some outstanding broader historical syntheses, of which V. Gordon Childe's *The Dawn of European Civilization* (1925) and *The Most Ancient East* (1934) are of primary importance.

From preoccupation with strict historical schematics came a gradual shift towards an interest in the more detailed reconstructions of prehistoric life-ways within individual sites and culture units and in the workings or functionings of cultures. This began with a consideration of cultural-natural environmental relationships but spread from there to other aspects of culture, especially those of social structure. These trends began even before World War I but have grown in importance, in both Europe and America, since then.[8] They have led to attempts to understand culture process, to explain the past; and in these attempts archaeologists have called more and more upon other sciences – mathematics, physics and chemistry, geology, biology, and botany – and have designed research projects of an interdisciplinary nature.

American Archaeology: A Definition

In American usage the term 'archaeology' is applied to both the discipline itself and to the subject matter. That is, archaeology and prehistory are employed interchangeably. In Europe archaeology is more apt to be reserved for the discipline while prehistory refers to the substance. This is not a matter of great moment, but it is mentioned here to avoid confusion or misunderstanding in later contexts.

There is still another distinction about this same pair of words which the reader should keep in mind. In the New World the whole range of the prehistoric past may be referred to as either prehistory or archaeology, without reference to chronology or to level of cultural development. This contrasts, again, with European usage where earlier or simpler cultures are assigned to prehistory and terms such as 'Classical archaeology' or 'Egyptology' designate the study of later or more advanced cultures.[9]

With these few preliminary observations, we can now go on to say that American archaeology, as the name implies, refers to the practice of archaeology on the New World scene. The subject matter of this practice is, for the most part, the prehistoric or Pre-Columbian past of this New World. More specifically, this means that the peoples under consideration are the ancestors of the American Indian and the Eskimo-Aleut. The geographical range includes both major continents and the islands of the Arctic, Greenland, and the Antilles. The chronological span is from the first inhabitation of these lands, certainly as far back as 20,000 B.C. and quite likely earlier, down to the coming of the Europeans in A.D. 1492.[10] Now, while American archaeology is largely concerned with the Pre-Columbian inhabitants of the New World, it may also pertain to the historic European period. Thus, the establishment of a European trading post among the Indians of interior Georgia in the 18th century may be an event that is now known only, or principally, from what has been found in the ground by archaeologists. Nor does American archaeology have to be restricted to an involvement with the New World aborigines. Historic site archaeology may pertain wholly to European-derived Americans, to, for example, Colonial Williamsburg or to an American Civil War battle site.

In brief, and by widest definition, if archaeology is the telling and/or explaining of the past through archaeological methods and techniques, the American version of archaeology simply limits the field geographically.

3 Map of the Americas showing the three major divisions, North, Middle, and South

As we have already implied, the practice of archaeology in the Americas did not develop in isolation from that of Europe.[11] There was first a long period of antiquarian interest, much as there was in the Old World. It began with the European conquests and continued into the 19th century. As in Europe, this American antiquarian interest was also channeled along two courses. Count Waldeck and Lord Kingsborough, with their studies of the Aztecs and the Maya, can be seen as the counterparts to the dilettanti who traveled to the ancient world of Greece and Rome, while others, such as Thomas Jefferson or Caleb Atwater, digging in the Indian mounds of the Eastern United States, remind us more of the English or Danish antiquaries. The mid-19th century synthesis of the Danish Three-Age system, the realization of the geological antiquity of man, and Darwinian evolutionism made itself felt in the Americas very soon after it did in Europe. Subsequent American developments, again, show parallels to the European ones. The archaeology of the 'high civilizations' of Mexico and Central America tended to focus on the humanistic concerns of art, iconography, and documentary materials; that of the simpler cultures of North America was more in the natural science tradition with interests directed toward artifact typology, geological stratigraphy, and even digging techniques. But this divergence was by no means complete, even in the 19th century; and in America, as in Europe, these lines have been converging in the 20th century.

The Present Book

It is the purpose of this book to provide a history of the development of the discipline of archaeology as it has been, and is being, practiced in the Americas. Thus, our emphasis will be on the *doing* of archaeology. We will be concerned with the way problems of culture history have been conceived by the archaeologist and how these conceptions have changed through time. In pursuing this theme we will examine research strategies and methods employed in carrying them out – how data have been obtained, analyzed, and conclusions drawn therefrom. In other words, what is projected is an intellectual history of the subject. This should be more than a listing of new methods and discoveries as these have appeared from time to time. We will attempt to give the reader an appreciation of the intellectual climate of the various times under consideration and of the influence of other disciplines and philosophies upon American archaeology. What we will be arguing is that American archaeology is as good as its concepts and that the history of its development is related very directly to the addition of new and better concepts as these apply to the dimensions of form, space, and time and to the circumstances of context, function, and process. In so doing, we will be discussing and emphasizing those people and works which are most closely linked with the introduction and uses of new and important concepts. Even with these criteria, we cannot be encyclopedic but, on the contrary, consciously selective.

This history is in no way intended as a summary of substantive results. While archaeological strategies and methods cannot be entirely separated from archaeological data, we will be involved only in a limited way with substantive findings.[12]

To date, there have been no modern full-scale histories which embrace all of American or New World archaeology.[13] It is only proper to add, however, that we have been influenced in the organization and treatment of the present work by various shorter works and unpublished lecture courses which foreshadowed what we are trying to do here. In point of time, the earliest of these was a lecture course given by the late W. D. Strong, at Columbia University, in 1940 – 'Method and Result in American Archaeology.'[14] Strong was a student of Kroeber's, and he took from Kroeber an anthropological outlook with a definite historical bias; nevertheless, Strong conceived of archaeology as a science, which was, in his words, 'part history, part anthropology.' He was interested in the specifics of history and in the way these might be viewed in more general schemes of cultural evolution. In one of his lectures he made the statement that 'only a trained anthropologist could be a good archaeologist.' Of published works which deal wholly or in part with the history and development of method and theory in American archaeology, we should mention Walter W. Taylor's *A Study of Archaeology*, which appeared in 1948. Primarily a critique of current theoretical orientations and practices in American archaeology, it also offered an historical perspective on the development of the discipline. A long article, more historically oriented, is J. B. Griffin's 'The Pursuit of Archaeology in the United States,' which was brought out in 1959. It follows the course of archaeological research from early times to the mid-20th century in North America. A third work which has influenced us is D. W. Schwartz's 'North American Archaeology in Historical Perspective,' prepared in 1965.[15] Finally, a fourth paper, 'One Hundred Years of American Archaeology,' which to some extent anticipates the present book, was written by one of us.[16]

The Strong lectures and all of these writings share a common outlook in that all tend to view American archaeology as passing through more or less similar periods of development. The organization of the present book follows such a period scheme. This is clearly laid out in our chapter headings. It should be noted, however, as Schwartz has argued in his paper, that we are dealing with intellectual attitudes and that while the history of these attitudes can be usefully conceptualized into periods or eras they must also be appreciated as trends through time for there is a considerable overlapping of them from one period to the next.   4

Our first period and trend is designated as the *Speculative* (Chapter Two). This follows the terminology of Schwartz's article, and we believe it to be appropriately descriptive of the basic attitude toward the antiquities and aborigines of the New World during this period. The opening date for the period can be set at the 'discovery' of America in 1492. After this event European soldiers, explorers, priests, settlers, and savants indulged in speculative writings and discussions over the meaning of the New World and its inhabitants. We bring the period to a close at a date which we set, somewhat arbitrarily, at about 1840. By this

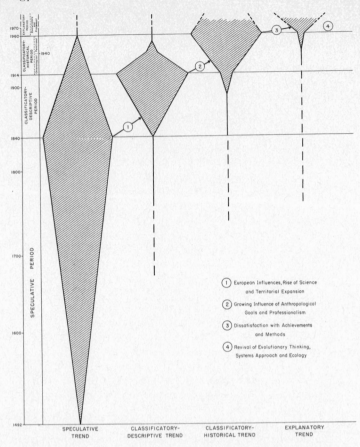

① European Influences, Rise of Science
and Territorial Expansion

② Growing Influence of Anthropological
Goals and Professionalism

③ Dissatisfaction with Achievements
and Methods

④ Revival of Evolutionary Thinking,
Systems Approach and Ecology

SPECULATIVE TREND	CLASSIFICATORY-DESCRIPTIVE TREND	CLASSIFICATORY-HISTORICAL TREND	EXPLANATORY TREND

4 Chart showing periods and trends in the development of American archaeology

time the world was moving into the beginnings of a scientific era, and in the Americas the decade of the 1840s marked the appearance of the first major archaeological writings in which systematic description outweighed speculation. There had been precursors to this kind of factual, descriptive archaeology in the years before, but from this time on it came increasingly to the fore.

We have applied the name *Classificatory-Descriptive* to this trend of factual archaeology and to the new period (Chapter Three). The title signifies the emphasis on systematic description of archaeological remains and monuments and on the classification of these data in accordance with formal typologies. The American archaeological publications which herald the period are the important monographs by Stephens and Catherwood, *Incidents of Travel in Central America: Chiapas and Yucatan* (1841) and *Incidents of Travel in Yucatan* (1843), and in the notable book by Squier and Davis, *Ancient Monuments of the Mississippi Valley* (1848). The period, defined as running from 1840 to 1914, saw a continued increase in classificatory-descriptive work at the expense of the sheerly speculative – not that the latter disappeared entirely from the scene. The period was also marked by the first professionalization of the American archaeological discipline, with the establishment of museums and university departments in the latter third of the nineteenth century. It was also the age of Darwin, Huxley, and Spencer in England, and the time of the spread of the theory of evolution from there to other parts of the world. Such influences were felt as early as the 1860s and 1870s on the American side of the Atlantic. Evolutionism was, in effect, the first process to be evoked or used by American archaeologists, in however naive a manner.

The threshold of World War I may be taken to mark the inception of our third period in American archaeological development, the *Classificatory-Historical*. The year 1914 is taken as a mean date for the first carefully controlled archaeological stratigraphy in the New World, a credit which should be shared by Gamio, with his Valley of Mexico excavations (1911–13) and by Nelson with his work in the Galisteo Basin of New Mexico (1914–16).[17] The name for the period, Classificatory-Historical, was selected to emphasize the historical or chronological interests which dominated it. The classificatory objectives of the preceding period were combined with archaeological chronology building, and the results were regional or areal chronologies, or space-time charts, of culture units or complexes. This, of course, was related to refinements in culture unit definitions, in stratigraphic and seriational procedures, and to the introduction of absolute dating techniques. It was to be a period in which American archaeology's ties to ethnology and social anthropology were continued and made even closer than before. This came about administratively, through departmental organization in universities, and ideologically, in the transfer of concepts from ethnology-social anthropology to archaeology. The 'direct-historical approach,' or the working from the ethnographic present to the archaeological past, and the uses of ethnographic analogy in archaeological interpretation, both of which flowered in this period, are examples of this interdisciplinary stimulation. Less felicitously, the strong anti-evolutionary bias of American social anthropology of the period was also passed on to archaeology. As we have defined the period it spans the years between 1914 and 1960, and, as such, it embraces almost the entire history of what still must be called 'modern archaeology' in the Americas. Because of this we have devoted two chapters to the Classificatory-Historical Period. The first (Chapter Four) is concerned with the earlier years, from 1914 until 1940. Most of the archaeology done in these decades was historically oriented only in the rather limited sense of being the geographical-chronological plotting out of monuments and remains. There were certain exceptions, however; some archaeologists attempted to go beyond this and to 'reconstruct' and narrate a story of the past which had more semblance to life. Between 1940 and 1960 there was a very definite shift of interest in this direction. Attempts were made to recover cultural contexts, as well as to erect space-time frameworks of artifact types, and to place artifact types and complexes into prehistoric patterns of behavior and to explicate function. All of this involved more intensive studies of the remains themselves, especially in conjunction with their natural environmental settings and with the inferences as to ecology that could be drawn from these conjunctions. It also involved an increased interchange of ideas between archaeologists and social anthropologists. These developments are treated in a second chapter devoted to the Classificatory-Historical Period (Chapter Five).

Our final period, the *Explanatory*, we see as emerging after 1960 (Chapter Six). Some hints of it can be seen earlier, especially in the latter half of the preceding period, but it is not until after 1960 that concerted attempts were made to understand culture process and thereby *explain* the human cultural and social behavior of the past. It is our opinion that American archaeology – and world archaeology – has turned an important corner in the last few years. It has begun to fashion a methodology that will enable it to understand prehistoric cultures as well as to describe and date them.

Chapter Two

The Speculative Period (1492–1840)

'We must not lose sight of the fact that modes of thought at any given time were firmly rooted in the ethos of that time and were severely circumscribed by the extent of knowledge then current.' Edwin N. Wilmsen

A Definition of the Period

THE Speculative Period is really a prelude to our story. The collection of virtually all the archaeological data uncovered during this period, with a few notable exceptions, was incidental to other pursuits. Archaeology was not established as a vocation or a discipline until well after 1840 and did not even become a popular avocation until the beginning of the 19th century. However, there were mounds and artifacts and a wide variety of antiquities, as well as the native American population, which could not be ignored, and speculation about all of these was rife. We can only sample the fascinating multitude of written comments and discourses on American antiquities and the American Indian from 1492 to 1840.[1] Hopefully, though, we will succeed in conveying some of the flavor of this first chapter in the history of American archaeology.

The entire three and a half centuries of the period were pervaded by a general intellectual atmosphere of armchair speculation about the origin of the American Indian. Emerging from this, however, were three trends of thinking which contain within themselves the seeds of the archaeological discipline.

The first of these trends pertained principally to the 16th and 17th centuries. Its focus was Latin America, and it consisted mainly of chronicles by men who accompanied the Spanish Conquistadors and works describing the nature of American Indian cultures by priests and other administrators. The latter studies would be called 'administrative spin-off' in modern parlance.

The second trend began in the 18th, and was particularly strong in the early 19th century. It consisted of accounts by explorers and travellers, mainly in North America, but occasionally in Latin America, who described ruins and mounds in their reports and speculated at great length on the origins of their finds. The object of their travels often was to produce a book of literary merit. The approach, especially in the 19th century, was natural scientific in tone and almost everything that was observed was recorded. It should be stressed that we are concerned here only with those early chroniclers and explorers who had some historical or antiquarian interests. There were a number of writers who provided ethnographic descriptions of American Indian groups from the 16th through the 19th centuries. These ethnographic documents have been and continue to be of great use to the archaeologist for general and specific ethnographic analogies and for showing continuities of various customs.[2] However, we are particularly interested in those writers who not only described the Indians, but who showed an interest in the past history of native American customs and artifacts and speculated on their origins. Many persons, for example, described the life of the Aztecs and the Maya at the time of the Conquest, and these primary sources of data have been widely used by archaeologists. But a few of the writers, such as Bernardino de Sahagun and Diego de Landa, also revealed archaeological interests and asked what we would consider archaeological questions in their works. These latter men and women were forerunners of later 18th and 19th century explorers and archaeologists who also asked questions such as 'whence?' and 'what happened?' in their descriptions of customs of American Indians and archaeological ruins which they encountered.

The third trend was almost ephemeral and actually marked the first stirrings of the later Descriptive-Historical trends which began about 1840. It consisted of the few efforts which had archaeology as their primary concern. The men who went out and excavated or undertook archaeological surveys in the 18th and 19th centuries, such as Jefferson or Atwater, were at best archaeologists by avocation. Nevertheless, they originated a trend which blossomed later on in the 19th century, as a general interest in archaeology was sparked by discoveries throughout the Americas and in Europe.

It is obvious that these trends do not form a tight typology, nor are they intended to. There is a definite overlap among them, not only in time but occasionally in content, too. For example, the 16th-century archaeological expeditions of Diego Garcia de Palacio to the Maya site of Copan, Honduras, and the 19th-century one of Antonia del Rio to Palenque, Mexico, were ordered by governmental directive. In addition, the chroniclers and early forerunners of the discipline of archaeology indulged in speculations as to American Indian origins which were no less imaginative than those of the explorers and writers of belles-lettres. In fact, it is rampant speculation, whether of an enthusiastic or restrained, or of a logical or illogical variety, which acts as the thread linking all the trends and characterizes the entire period.

The dominance of a speculative mode of thought during the period is certainly due to a number of factors. The most important ones probably were a paucity of reliable archaeological data, the lack of European models of archaeological reasoning which the American worker could emulate,[3] the significance of a belles-lettres or literary approach in much of the archaeologically relevant writing, coupled with the virtual non-existence of a tradition of scientific explanation and the deeply rooted acceptance of theological explanations of natural and cultural phenomena. All these factors, plus, on the one hand, a continuing sense of wonder and amazement at the exotic nature of the New World as more and more of it was explored, and, on the other, the immediate need to create an heroic history for the new land (especially in North America),[4] made speculation the dominant element in all discussions of the architectural ruins and material culture of the ancient inhabitants of the New World.

It should be clear that when we speak of speculation, we are talking about non-scientific conjecture.[5] Such conjecture was rampant in this time period because the observers of archaeological phenomena had little or no hard data for comparisons with their observations or in many cases had no information whatsoever upon which to base their speculations. It obviously is quite difficult to produce credible reconstructions without a good foundation of reliable data. However, even in the few cases where primary excavated or surveyed information was available, the workers of the period did not use this data carefully to build or test hypotheses. Rather, the raw data and speculation tended to be compartmentalized. A case in point, which we shall soon return to, is the work of Caleb Atwater, who, after meticulously describing his studies of the mounds of Ohio, proceeded to link the mounds to peoples from 'Hindostan.'[6] One reason for this kind of thinking was the lack of any tradition of scientific reasoning. An archaeological tradition worthy of that name had to await the intellectual migration from Europe of books such as Charles Lyell's *Principles of Geology* in the 1830s. It also was not until the early 19th century that the would-be archaeologist in the Americas had any good European models for his archaeological methods and theories. Until the work of men such as Thomsen, Worsaae, and, later, Boucher de Perthes, there simply were no archaeological studies which could be used by American archaeologists to point their own work in the proper direction.

Without any intellectual tradition in the time span which we have termed the Speculative Period, within which a scientific archaeology might have developed, theological explanations remained the accepted means of reconstructing events of the past. The sword certainly cut both ways, since the strength of theological thought militated against purely scientific modes of thinking. The discovery and recognition of Early Man in the New World, for example, had to await the Darwinian Revolution,[7] just as it did in the Old World.

The Americas: 'Discovery' and Origins of the American Indians

To our mind, the phrase 'discovery of the Americas,' as found in many history books, is most often used in a completely European-ethnocentric manner. The idea that Columbus 'discovered' America would probably have been seen as an unbelievable joke by the many millions of Native Americans who had lived in the New World since their distant ancestors had first arrived in the Americas at least 20,000 years prior to Columbus's expedition.[8] Even in relation to European voyages, it has been clear for many years that the Norsemen visited North America a number of centuries before Columbus. Nevertheless, it was Columbus's and later voyages in the 16th century which had such great intellectual impact on European thought. In this sense, one might say that these exploratory voyages were 'discoveries,' but only in a limited sense relating to the European mind. As has been pointed out by Rowse: 'The Discovery of the New World, it has been said, is much the greatest event in the history of the Old.'[9]

The new explorations had tremendous significance for European philosophical thought in addition to their importance for the

5 Late 17th-century map of the Americas. This is an extract from Sanson's map, with the New World conceived of as the 'Island of Atlantis.' (From Winsor, 1889)

politics and economics of the time. They generated much excitement and stirred the imagination of the intellectuals of the 16th century. Crone has put it quite well:

'The Age of Discovery . . . was not so much a break with the past and a new departure, but rather a quickening of pace, a stimulus to nascent ideas. The New World provided, as it were, a gigantic laboratory in which the speculations of Renaissance man could be tested, modified, and developed.'[10]

The explorations of the very late 15th and the 16th century presented the European philosophers and intellectuals with a number of pressing questions which demanded immediate answers. One of these questions, and the one which is of paramount importance for an understanding of the beginnings of American archaeology, was 'who are the Indians[11] of the New World?'

'The first question which arose with respect to the American Indian concerned his identity or origin. It seems a natural enough question and the only one which at the time could be considered speculatively, that is, without waiting for the tedious accumulation of additional facts.'[12]

The answers to this question were not long in coming and were as varied as they were plentiful. Many, if not most, of the proposed answers appear totally outlandish to the modern archaeologist, but at the time they were taken quite seriously. As Spinden has so cogently remarked: 'It seems that the manifestly impossible has a vastly greater appeal to the imagination than the merely improbable.'[13]

The question of who the Indians were and where they came from was of great importance, because to Europeans, who had been taught that everyone was descended from Adam and Eve and that at the time of the universal flood only Noah and his family survived,[14] the inhabitants of the New World either had to be related to some descendants of Noah or else were not human. Some of the early Spanish explorers and settlers believed that the latter was the case and that the Indians were beasts. But after several key rulings culminating in the historic Papal Bull of Pope Paul III in 1537, and through the efforts of men such as Antonio de Montesinos and Bartolomé de las Casas, it was established that the American Indians were indeed human, that they should be treated as such, and that every effort should be made to propagate the faith among them.[15]

From the moment that knowledge of the 'discoveries' made by the early explorations spread throughout Europe, there were innumerable writers who were willing to speculate on the origins of the Indians. One of the favorite opinions of those men who were theologically inclined was that the Indians were descendants of the Ten Lost Tribes of Israel.[16] Diego Duran, for one, favored this hypothesis.[17] James Adair, an influential 18th century American writer, also believed in it,[18] as did such an eminent 19th century antiquarian as Lord Kingsborough.[19]

Another popular explanation was that the Indians came from the lost world of Atlantis. This hypothesis, which was inspired by Plato's discussion of Atlantis, was suggested as early as 1530 by the poet Fracastoro and in 1535 by Gonzalo Fernandez de Oviedo y Valdes.[20] This explanation, along with its companion, the land of Mu hypothesis, has fallen from its early popularity, but is still revived on occasion by diehard supporters in the 20th century.

5

Several Dutch scholars also entered the debate quite vigorously in the mid-17th century. De Groot supported the idea that the origin of the Indians lay across the Atlantic in Scandinavia, the land of the Norsemen. De Laet and Horn, on the other hand, believed that Scythians from Central Asia and others were responsible for the peopling of the New World.[21]

Many other writers also looked to Asian countries such as China, Korea, or India for the source of the peoples of the New World. Some suggested long boat trips as the means of these migrations. Indeed, the suggestion that the origin of the American Indian lay in Asia was first made in a form which almost has a modern ring. As far back as 1590 Fray José de Acosta, in his *Historia Natural y Moral de las Indias,* suggested that the Americas were peopled from Asia by means of a slow overland migration. Although Acosta did not rule out the possibility of shipwrecks landing people in the New World, he felt that 'small groups of savage hunters' who took an overland route with 'short stretches of navigation' accounted for most of the original population of the Americas. He guessed

6 Cortez treating with the Aztecs. (From Sahagún, 1950–3)

that this migration may have occurred as early as one to 2000 years before the Conquest.[22] Acosta's proposal is especially remarkable in light of the relatively meager geographic knowledge of the time. The existence of a land bridge or a narrow strait between the Old and New Worlds was nothing more than a possibility to the writers of the day.

By the mid 17th century, at least as early as 1637,[23] the presently accepted hypothesis that the first migrant to the New World arrived from Asia via the Bering Strait was being seriously considered. In 1648, Thomas Gage stated that the New World was originally populated by men coming out of Asia through the Bering Strait area. He was also one of the first writers to note the racial resemblances between the American Indians and the Mongoloid peoples of Asia and used this evidence to support his argument.[24] By the time that Cook completed the mapping of the Bering Strait area, Pfefferkorn could say in a book published in 1794, that 'it is almost certain that the first inhabitants of America really came by way of the strait.'[25]

By the end of the 18th century, it could be stated with some surety that the origins of the American Indian lay in Asia and that they did indeed migrate to the New World via the Bering Strait. But this did not put an end to the rampant speculations which had typified the previous three centuries since the 'discovery' of the New World and which continued unabated well into the 19th century. Nor did the growing acceptance of the origin of the American Indian in Asia mean that the archaeologically inclined writers had any notion of when the first migrations actually took place or what was the way of life of the first inhabitants of the Americas; although they did not hold back their varied speculations.[26] It was not until 1845 that a distinguished scholar, Albert Gallatin, could firmly state: 'From whatever place the people of America came, the first important question is the time of their arrival.'[27] As Wilmsen has pointed out, the writers of what we have called the Speculative Period had no concepts of time, space, or culture to handle the idea of what archaeologists now call Early Man.[28] The beginnings of these concepts had to await the birth of the discipline of archaeology in the Classificatory-Descriptive Period.[29]

The Early Chroniclers and Historical Interests

Brief mention should be made here of certain writers whom we might consider as the earliest forerunners of archaeology in the Americas or, better yet, the forerunners of the forerunners. At the time of the Spanish Conquest and shortly thereafter, a number of men, both Spanish and Native American, wrote down descriptive statements about the nature of the native cultures immediately preceding and during the Conquest, as well as narrative descriptions of the Conquest itself. These ethnographic descriptions have provided the archaeologist with a wealth of information about the civilizations of Mesoamerica[30] and the Peruvian area[31] just before they were virtually obliterated by the Conquistadors. Some of the writers also showed a keen interest in the past history of these native civilizations. This kind of interest and curiosity, to our mind, marks the first stirrings of interests which more than three centuries later led to the establishment of American archaeology as a viable academic discipline.

We should further point out that the Native American peoples themselves were not without historical interests. For example, some native documents or codices in Mesoamerica, which consist of chronicles, genealogies, or historical statements, have been preserved in the original or in post-Conquest copies.[32] As Leon-Portilla has stated: 'The Pre-Columbian man truly realized the significance of what we call history.'[33]

The body of 'Historias . . .' and other documents, which includes discussions of the pre-Conquest histories of the peoples of Mesoamerica and the Peruvian area, and varies in length from occasional comments to huge multi-volume books, is relatively large. The reliability and utility of these works are also variable. Yet some of these books, such as those of the Franciscan Fray Bernadino de Sahagun[34] and the Dominican Fray Diego Duran[35] on the Aztecs and Garcilaso de la Vega's *Royal Commentaries of the Incas*,[36] to name just three, definitely display intellectual leanings which we would have to stamp as historical. Since the pre-Conquest past is now the province of the archaeologist, these works are obviously of interest to us. We do not have the space to consider them all; but they should be singled out as the 'pre-historic' base line of the history of the archaeological discipline.

7 Pizarro and the Inca. A drawing from the chronicler Guaman Poma de Ayala

Among the early Spanish and Native American chroniclers, Bishop Diego de Landa and Fray Bartolemé de las Casas deserve special mention. Landa, of all the writers of the 16th and early 17th centuries, shows perhaps the strongest interest in archaeological ruins as well as in reconstructing the history and way of life of a Native American culture – in this case, the ancient Maya. In his *Relación de las Cosas de Yucatán*,[37] he describes ruins such as Chichen Itza and even gives a plan of the main temple at Izamal. He offers a political history of the Maya, discusses the nature of their society, daily life, and technology, and describes many of the material artifacts and religious practices. In addition, he gives a good working description of the ancient Maya hieroglyphic and calendrical systems. One has only to look at the many varied entries under 'archaeology' in Tozzer's syllabus of the *Relación*,[38] to appreciate the kind of archaeological data supplied by Bishop Landa. The Bishop must have been an interesting character, since he was a persecutor and destroyer of Maya documents on the one hand and a preserver of the details of the Maya way of life in his own writings on the other. Nevertheless, as Tozzer has said as regards the content and importance of the *Relación*:

8

'The source material presented by Landa includes practically every phase of the social anthropology of the ancient Mayas, together with the history of the Spanish discovery, the conquest and the ecclesiastical and native history together with the first accurate knowledge of the hieroglyphic writing.'[39]

Fray Bartolemé de las Casas was also a bishop for a short time – of Chiapas in Mexico-Guatemala. He is best known as a champion

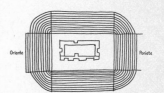

8 A 16th-century drawing of the Castillo at Chichen Itza, Yucatan, Mexico. This is certainly one of the first archaeological plans of an American ruin ever published. (From Landa/Tozzer 1941)

9 (*Opposite*) An important early European view of the Southeastern Indians is provided in the illustrations of Jacques Le Moyne, who accompanied the French settlers to northeastern Florida in the 1560s. This drawing shows a burial ceremony with the grave or small burial mound outlined in arrows and topped by a conchshell drinking vessel. The mourners surround the mound, and in the background is a palisaded village. Pictures such as this were either unknown to or ignored by early writers on the Moundbuilder controversy.

of the rights of the Indians of the New World, and much of his life was spent trying to convince his fellow clergy and the Spanish Crown to treat the Native Americans in a fair and humane manner and to appreciate the value of their civilizations. Two of Las Casas's great works were the lengthy *Apologetica historia de las Indias*[40] and the *Historia de las Indias*.[41] In one of his many penetrating books on Las Casas, Lewis Hanke devotes a full chapter to proving that Las Casas was an anthropologist.[42] Hanke not only proves his case in general, but he also provides evidence which indicates that there is good reason to consider Las Casas as a forerunner of 19th and 20th century American archaeologists.

First of all:

'He looked at all peoples, the ancient Greeks and 16th-century Spaniards as well as the newly discovered New World natives, as human beings in different stages of development from rude beginnings to a higher stage of culture.'[43]

That is to say, Las Casas, even as early as the 16th century, had at least a rudimentary concept of an evolutionary scale of cultural development.

In addition, Las Casas was one of the first, if not the first, to provide a discussion relating environment and culture in the New World. In a tone which we would now consider strongly deterministic, Las Casas spends the first thirty-two chapters of the *Apologetica* describing 'minutely the favorable physical conditions in the New World which make it inevitable that the Indians are men of wise understanding. He shows himself a forerunner of Jean Bodin, usually considered the first European environmentalist.'[44]

Thirdly, as Huddleston has pointed out, Las Casas indicates in his *Historia* that the history of the native inhabitants of the New World might have been quite ancient. Regrettably, Las Casas did not elaborate his brief comments on man's antiquity in the Americas.[45]

Unfortunately, the interests and leads of men like Landa and Las Casas were not really followed up for many years, even centuries.

The Explorers and the Armchair Speculators

For a century and a half to two centuries after the Conquest and the writings of the early chroniclers, there was much new European exploration and settlement throughout the New World and a rapid growth of European colonies in, and political control over, the Americas.

This period, however, produced only sporadic writings, such as those by Du Pratz, which have any relevance to the history of American archaeology and ethnography.[46] New editions, collections, and critical evaluations of the early writers were made throughout the 17th–19th centuries (including *The History of Mexico* by Clavijero, first published in 1780–81,[47] and *The History of America* by Robertson in 1777),[48] and unpublished documents were discovered and finally published. All in all, though, these

10

works were no different in historical spirit from the ones we have already noted.

Beginning in the later part of the 18th century, a new trend emerged, centering much more on North America than on Latin America. Archaeology still had not appeared on the scene as an avocation, let alone a profession, but there was much new exploration, resulting in new data on ruins, mounds, and artifacts. In turn, speculations about these remains began to have a real data base and became slightly, and progressively, more informed.

Much of the new data on the archaeological ruins was a by-product of observations made by explorers who were not specifically interested in collecting archaeological information. Rather, they attempted to record data about, and make observations on, everything they saw in their travels. Their approach can best be labeled as 'natural scientific' and is typified by the work of men such as William Bartram.[49] Interpretations of the mounds varied from sober discussion to bizarre speculation.

A complementary trend, which definitely overlapped the natural scientific-exploratory one, can be termed 'literary.' The ultimate object of many of the explorations was to return home and write a work of literary merit which recounted all of the writer's observations. One did not have to travel to write such a book. There were many armchair 'explorers' who produced books on the history of the Americas or the Indians or whatever. Many of these non-ambulatory writers had friends, such as missionaries or army men, who would correspond with them and describe the nature of the 'West' – which until the beginning of the 19th century still lay east of the Alleghanies. These reports not only

10 (Below) Funeral ceremony of the Natchez Indians, end of 17th century. There is a temple on a mound in the background. The dead man is being carried on a litter, and his several retainers are being strangled preparatory to being buried with him. (From Le Page Du Pratz, 1758)

mentioned mounds but also provided much new data on the living American Indians.

It is from the pens of both the travellers and the chair-bound scholars that the myth of the Moundbuilders arose in North America. Robert Silverberg has traced the beginnings of the myth as far back as 1785,[50] although its real heyday was in the 19th century. In brief, the myth held that the multitude of mounds or ruins, which were constantly being discovered in Ohio and other frontier areas as the colonists pushed to the west, could not have been built by the savages who were then residing in these areas. Instead, they must have been erected by a civilized race which had disappeared a long time ago.

The reasons for the rise of the myth, which was not laid to rest until the end of the 19th century, when Cyrus Thomas reported on the Bureau of Ethnology's Moundbuilder studies,[51] were many. One of the most important was the need for the creation of an heroic past which might resemble that enjoyed by Europe. As Silverberg has said:

'The dream of a lost prehistoric race in the American heartland was profoundly satisfying; and if the vanished ones had been giants, or white men, or Israelites, or Danes, or Toltecs, or great white Jewish Toltec Vikings, so much the better.[52]

A second significant reason was the widely held North American belief that the Indians were savages who were incapable of building the mounds. The Spaniards saw the wonders of Tenochtitlan, capital of the Aztecs, the public works of the Incas, or the other great achievements of the Indians of Middle and South America and were also interested in using the Indians as labor. The English in North America, especially after the French and Indian War, saw the Indians as warlike, degenerate savages who were occupying land which the new settlers wanted for their own use.[53] It was inconceivable to much of the literate public of Eastern North America that the culture of the Indians or their ancestors was civilized enough to have built the mounds. Nevertheless, there were some to whom this notion was not beyond the pale. By the beginning of the 19th century two basic positions had emerged as regards the origins of the mounds: either the Moundbuilders and the Indians (or their direct ancestors) were one and the same people; or the Moundbuilders, whose hypothesized origins were as varied as those first proposed for the peopling of the New World,[54] were an ancient race who had died off or moved away, to be replaced by the later Indians.

No links could be seen between the contemporary Indians and the mounds by most observers of the time. Although observations made by De Soto's exploratory party in the Southeastern United States, reported on in works of Garcilaso de la Vega[55] and the 'Gentleman of Elvas,'[56] definitely showed Indians building and using mounds in that area, these data were forgotten. Instead, various speculative origins for the mounds were proposed, and the debate over these hypotheses became heated. In fact, so little was known about the mounds at the beginning of the controversy that two such eminent men as Benjamin Franklin and Noah

Webster could seriously state in 1787 that the mounds might have been built by De Soto himself.[57]

Toward the end of the 18th century, new and better data on the mounds began to pour in. In turn, the problem of the identity of the builders of the mounds became more clearly defined, emerging as a popular public concern. Observations on the mounds were made by travellers and missionaries such as Kalm, who also found artifacts in New Jersey which had a Quaternary or Recent geological date,[58] Zeisberger,[59] Carver,[60] Barton,[61] Bartram,[62] Madison,[63] Harris,[64] Stoddard[65] and Brackenridge[66] on Louisiana, Haywood on Tennessee,[67] and Rafinesque, who located hundreds of sites in Kentucky.[68]

Benjamin Smith Barton traveled in Ohio and published a book in 1787 which said that the mounds he had observed in the course of his travels had been built by Danes, who then migrated to Mexico and became the 'Toltecs.' In a later book in 1797, and in an article in 1799, he did not pursue this earlier opinion but concentrated more attention upon the living Indians and suggested the ancestors of the Indians might have built some of the mounds.

'I do not suppose that these more polished nations of America have passed away. Some of them, it is probable, are extinguished. But of others, I suppose that it is chiefly the strength and the glory that are no more. Their descendants are still scattered over extensive portions of this continent. . . .'[69]

He believed that the Indians came from Asia, which by the end of the 18th century was the generally accepted opinion. Moreover, he commented that the date of this arrival might have been earlier than the theologically accepted date of 4004 B.C. given by Archbishop Ussher for the creation.[70] This opinion of Barton's was one of the first attempts to give a real time depth to the Pre-Columbian history of the New World.

The natural historian William Bartram was the son of the famous botanist, John Bartram of Philadelphia. He traveled extensively throughout the Southeastern United States with his father, and then by himself, in the 1770s and published an important book on his travels in 1791. This work included descriptions of many mounds, and Bartram reached what Silverberg has called the 'conservative' conclusion that although the ancient mounds had not been built by the contemporary Indians, they had been built by other unspecified Indians. Bartram also was in correspondence with Barton and provided him with much data on the mounds of the Southeast including descriptions of Creek Indian mound-building and use. Unfortunately, these observations of Bartram's did not reach the eye of the general public until 1909, after a series of mishaps which prevented earlier distribution of these data.[71]

As regards some of the other writers, noted above, the Right Reverend James Madison and the Reverend Thaddeus Harris were on opposite sides of the argument concerning the Indian as moundbuilder, with Madison defending the proposition and Harris opposing it. John Haywood, in his 1823 book on Tennessee, maintained that the Cherokee Indians had built at least some of the mounds. The publication by the missionary John Heckewelder of

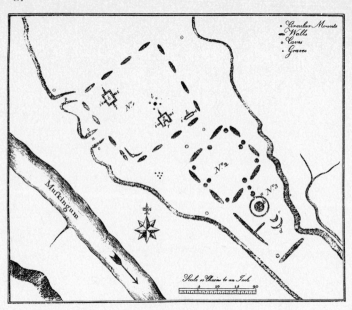

11 Plan of Ohio Valley earthworks by Heart, 1787. (From
American Anthropologist, Vol. 10,
1908)

a work on the Lenni Lenape Indians several years earlier (1819)
had made public Indian legends which said that a group of tall
people with a high culture had lived near the Mississippi River
when the Lenape tried to move through the area. Those supporting
the Indians as moundbuilders said that this group were Cherokees
who later moved south; the 'lost race' or mysterious Moundbuilder school held that the legends provided conclusive evidence
for their side.[72]

H. H. Brackenridge published an article in 1813 on the mound
question and a book, in 1814, on Louisiana. In his article, he made
the important distinction between burial and temple mounds and
stated his view that the former were earlier. This definitely was a
precocious statement and foreshadowed later chronological and
conceptual developments by a number of decades.[73] However,
Brackenridge held the popular view that peoples such as the Toltecs had built the mounds of North America before migrating
south to Mexico. Amos Stoddard, who wrote another book on
Louisiana, included a chapter on antiquities in which he supported
the hypothesis that Welshmen were the great Moundbuilders.

Army men, such as General Parsons, General Putnam, and
Captain Heart, who were stationed in Ohio, also contributed
useful information in the late 18th century through letters and
11 maps.[74] Putnam's map of the earthworks at Marietta, Ohio, has
been called by Shetrone 'the genesis of the science of archaeology
in the Americas.'[75] We would not be so generous. The map was
simply a part of the burgeoning data on the mounds which had
begun to build up in the late 18th century.

The Reverend Cutler also explored the Marietta mounds, which
were at the site of a colonial town, and attempted to date them by
counting the number of rings on the trees which had grown on
top of them.[76] In this effort, we can see one of the earliest attempts
at absolute dating in the New World. Tree-ring dating, of course,

has become immeasurably refined in recent decades and now serves as a useful dating tool in many areas, especially the Southwestern United States.

Some well-known public figures also became involved in the debate on who had built the mounds. Governor De Witt Clinton wrote about the mounds of western New York state and held that they were built by Scandinavian Vikings.[77] Albert Gallatin, Secretary of the Treasury and well-known linguist and ethnologist, linked the Moundbuilders and southward migrating Mexicans, although he perspicaciously stated that agriculture may have diffused in the opposite direction, northward from Mexico to North America.[78] Finally, it should be noted that General William Henry Harrison, who later became President of the United States, described some of the antiquities of the Ohio Valley.[79] He supported the anti-Indian or 'lost race' side of the Moundbuilder debate. Another President with archaeological interests, Thomas Jefferson, did not become involved in the debate, although he

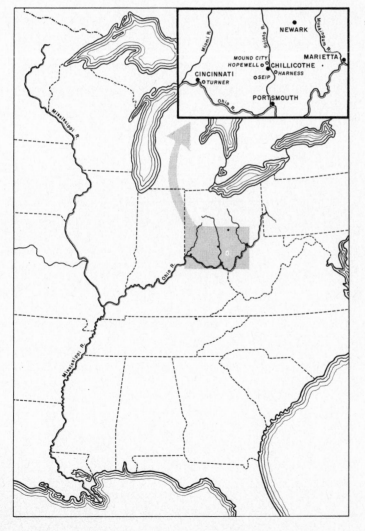

12 Map of the Ohio and Mississippi River Valleys

made important contributions to the development of archaeology. We shall return to him shortly.

As the Moundbuilder debate escalated in participants, hypotheses, and partisanship, the general public were caught up in the arguments and added their numbers to the whole intellectual furore. The evidence for this interest was made clear in 1833, when Josiah Priest's *American Antiquities and Discoveries in the West* sold 22,000 copies in thirty months, a great number for that day, and soon became 'established . . . among laymen as a kind of archaeological classic.'[80] Unfortunately, this book made no archaeological contribution as it championed the most bizarre hypotheses and 'data.' Nevertheless, it did reflect the general feeling of the day, both scholarly and non-scholarly, which was on the side of the 'lost race' of Moundbuilders school of thought.

The 'lost race' idea itself, however, received a blow in 1839, when the famous physical anthropologist S. G. Morton published his *Crania Americana*. Morton had taken measurements of eight skulls from mounds as well as skulls of recently deceased Indians. He concluded that there was just one race represented in his sample, although he further stated that the race consisted of two families, the Toltecan and the Barbarous, which he differentiated purely on cultural and not on physical grounds.[81] Thus although the people who supported a separation of early civilized Moundbuilders from later savage Indians could not claim any more that the Moundbuilders were a different race, the rest of their arguments remained intact for the moment.

Note should also be taken of several men who made solid contributions to the small but growing body of archaeological data which existed by the end of the Speculative Period. Winthrop Sargent collected artifacts, which we can now identify as Hopewellian, and a report on them was published in the 1799 *Transactions of the American Philosophical Society*.[82] N. F. Hyer first described the now famous ruins of Aztalan in Wisconsin in 1837,[83] while one year later R. C. Taylor wrote about the mounds of Wisconsin, with special attention to the fascinating effigy forms.[84] Finally, in 1839 in Missouri, the fossil-hunter Albert Koch uncovered the skeleton of a mastodon, an extinct elephant, in association with some stone artifacts. Koch, who was somewhat of an entrepreneur and showman, displayed the mastodon in a travelling show before selling it. The skeleton then went to the British Museum, while the artifacts ended up in Germany,[85] the association between the artifacts and skeleton not being considered important enough to keep the finds together. The time was not yet ripe for the acceptance of great age for the stone artifacts, and Koch's contemporaries were not willing to accept the significance of the finds or their association. Koch was ridiculed and his discovery forgotten for many years.

All the attention which we have just paid to developments in the United States should not be taken to indicate that there were no archaeological activities in Latin America in the 18th and early 19th centuries, although the 'action' was, by and large, in North America. Still, we should take note of Alexander von Humboldt's travels throughout the Americas. In his writings, which can be considered as perhaps the epitome of the natural science approach discussed earlier, Humboldt described a number of ruins, especially in Peru and Mexico.[86] He also made other contributions to Americanist studies, most notably in cartography. As H.E.D. Pollock has said: '[Humboldt] stands . . . as a landmark in his diligent accumulation of data, in his unbiased presentation of material, and in his attitude toward the remains of antiquity as fragments of history.'[87]

In relation to the prehistoric architecture of Middle America, the work of Walckenaër, de Larenaudière, and Jomard should be noted. They called for the cessation of speculation and the beginning of adequate recording and mapping of archaeological remains.[88] Their plea, which was definitely non-speculative in tone, was at least partially answered within a few years by Stephens and Catherwood. There were other travellers, too, such as Waldeck,[89] Dupaix,[90] and Galindo,[91] who made minor contributions. In South America, Lund began working in the Lagoa Santa Caves of Brazil in the mid 1830s, but his work was not completed and published until the following period.[92]

Earlier on, we commented on the many collections of Conquest and pre-Conquest documents which were made in the Speculative

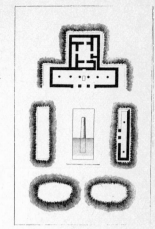

13 Plan of the ruins of Mitla, Oaxaca, Mexico. (From Humboldt, 1814)

14 Drawing of an Oaxacan (Monte Alban style) funerary urn. While correct in some features, it is inaccurate in others. (From Kingsborough, 1831–48)

Period. Perhaps the most important of these collections, commentaries, and histories was Lord Kingsborough's lavish nine-volume *Antiquities of Mexico*, published between 1831 and 1848. Kingsborough gathered together a number of documents and added his own comments on various antiquities in an effort to prove, as we noted above, that the Middle American Indians were the descendants of the Ten Lost Tribes of Israel.[93] Kingsborough's volumes revealed a great enthusiasm for the antiquities of Mexico, an enthusiasm which reflected the growing 19th-century interest in the past of the New World and which helped bring about the birth of archaeology in the Americas. Although *Antiquities of Mexico* is, in most respects, a work of the Speculative Period, its author devoted his whole life to the study of antiquities. This kind of full-time activity, albeit by someone who did not need to practice archaeology for a living, marked the beginning of a trend which was more typical of the following periods.

Thus, by 1840, public and scholarly interest in the antiquities of the New World was very high; yet most of the published accounts of mounds and other archaeological phenomena remained speculative and were often by-products of other endeavors. Debate on the Moundbuilder question was heated but generally uninformed. There were no full-time archaeologists, nor were there many people, among those who followed archaeology as an avocation, who were willing to carry out archaeological fieldwork in order to verify or diagnose their theories and speculations. There were, however, a few important exceptions to this, and these exceptional scholars clearly stand out today as the forerunners of the established discipline of archaeology which was to come into being after 1840.

15 Drawing of a Maya priest figure and accompanying hieroglyphic text. The rendering has many inaccuracies and is greatly inferior to the later work of Catherwood. (From Del Rio and Cabrera, 1822)

The Forerunners of an Established Discipline of Archaeology

Up to this point we have been concerned with the ephemeral beginnings of American archaeology. Various slender threads of archaeological reportage have been picked up and followed. Some of these threads are obviously tied to later trends, while others are only peripherally related. On the whole, though, in a period which lacked all the hallmarks of an established archaeological discipline, including clear goals, professional archaeologists, archaeological courses in colleges, archaeological texts describing accepted methods, concepts, and theories, and detailed culture-historical reconstructions, there was little sign of the kind of work and publication which marked the following Descriptive-Historical Period. Speculation on a narrow data base was the rule. Three exceptions to these statements stand out head and shoulders above their contemporaries; they are, indeed, the true forerunners of American archaeology. The two most important of these forerunners largely eschewed speculation. One of them further realized that archaeology must be attacked by posing problems, undertaking excavations, presenting data, and answering problems in a rigorous manner. In his hands antiquarian interests began to become archaeological ones.

In 1784 Thomas Jefferson, later to become the third President of the United States, decided to discover the nature of the 'barrows' or burial mounds found on his property in Virginia.

'That they were repositories of the dead, has been obvious to all; but on what particular occasion constructed, was a matter of doubt.'[94]

In order to solve this problem, Jefferson took the extraordinary step of carrying out a relatively well-controlled excavation.[95] Jefferson carefully trenched the mound and recognized strata which had no correspondence with each other. He discovered a large quantity of skeletal material and found that the bones had been placed in the mound and then covered and that this process had been repeated many times. The mound had gradually reached its final height of twelve feet through the accumulation of skeletons.[96] As Lehmann-Hartleben states: Jefferson's excavation 'anticipates the fundamental approach and the methods of modern archaeology by about a full century,'[97] and actually more. Sir Mortimer Wheeler, perhaps the most eminent authority on the nature of archaeological excavation, has labeled Jefferson's work 'the first scientific excavation in the history of archaeology.'[98] He further notes that 'it was unique not only in its age but for long afterwards.'[99]

The real significance of Jefferson's digging was threefold. First, the very fact that he excavated at all was important since few individuals throughout the Speculative Period undertook such a step. Second, Jefferson's excavations were sufficiently careful to enable him to observe the nature of the strata in his trench. Third, and probably most important, 'the excavation [was] . . . made, not to find objects, but to resolve an archaeological problem.'[100]

As regards the general Moundbuilder problem, Jefferson would not commit himself. He took the cautious, but for his time, laudable, position that more data was needed to answer the question. Jefferson also became President of the American Philosophical Society which was located in Philadelphia, the intellectual 'capital' of the United States during much of the Speculative Period. The members of the Society took an active interest in the Moundbuilder debate, published many archaeologically relevant papers, and collected archaeological objects. In 1799, as President of the Society, Jefferson sent a circular letter to a number of correspondents in order to obtain data on archaeological remains. The circular began by stating:

'The American Philosophical Society have always considered the antiquity, changes, and present state of their own country as primary objects of their research.'[101]

Among the other things, the circular called on its recipients

'To obtain accurate plans, drawings and descriptions of whatever is interesting, (where the originals cannot be had) and especially of ancient Fortifications, Tumuli, and other Indian works of art: ascertaining the materials composing them, their contents, the purposes for which they were probably designed, etc.'[102]

The discussion of the kinds of information solicited in the circular also included the following:

'With respect to the [above], the committee are desirous that cuts in various directions may be made into many of the Tumuli, to ascertain their contents; while the diameter of the largest tree growing thereon, the number of its annulars and the species of the tree, may tend to give some idea of their antiquity. If the works should be found to be of Masonry; the length, breadth, and height of the walls ought to be carefully measured, the form and nature of the stone described, and the specimens of both the cement and stones sent to the committee.'[103]

In many respects, the directions and general tenor of this paragraph can be seen as the theme of one of the major trends of the succeeding Classificatory-Descriptive Period. Thus, we can see that at least a good part of the orientation of the discipline of archaeology was present as far back as the end of the 18th century, but such works as the circular called for were not carried out until the post-1840 era.

Although Jefferson has often been referred to as the 'father of American archaeology.' We would have to point out that he had no immediate intellectual offspring. Unfortunately, Jefferson's influence as an archaeologist apparently was not important for either his contemporaries or even the next generation.[104] As we hope will become clear, we do not believe that one can point to a single individual as the progenitor of American archaeology but must view the rise of the discipline in terms of the culmination of both specific antiquarian and general intellectual trends in the New World and the Old.

The American Philosophical Society was not all alone in its effort to encourage the collection and publication of archaeological data. In 1812, the publisher Isaiah Thomas founded the American Antiquarian Society in Massachusetts. Its purpose was:

'The collection and presentation of the antiquities of our country, and of curious and valuable productions in art and nature [which] have a tendency to enlarge the sphere of human knowledge, aid in the progress of science, to perpetuate the history of moral and political events, and to improve and instruct posterity.'[105]

The Society was the first of this kind in the Americas and its early members included such famous men as Thomas Hart Benton, Lewis Cass, Henry Clay, DeWitt Clinton, C. C. Pinckney, and Daniel Webster.[106] It was the American counterpart of European antiquarian societies,[107] and its creation was a reflection of a growing public interest in the history of North America and an increase in popular scientific curiosity.[108] The founding of the Society was an important event in the history of American archaeology since it gave the growing but diffuse interest in archaeological concerns a focal point. The Society in and of itself did not change the contemporary antiquarian interests into true archaeological ones, but it did publish one of the most significant studies of the Speculative Period and was associated with several important works during the early Classificatory-Descriptive Period.

In the first volume of the American Antiquarian Society's *Transactions*, dated 1820, there appeared a work by Caleb Atwater

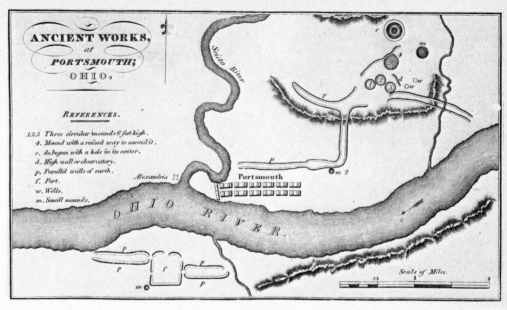

ANCIENT WORKS, *at* PORTSMOUTH; OHIO.

REFERENCES.

1,2,3 Three circular mounds 6 feet high.
4. Mound with a raised way to ascend it.
c. do. begun with a hole in its center.
d. High wall or observatory.
p. Parallel walls of earth.
f. Fort.
w. Wells.
m. Small mounds.

Scioto River

Alexandria

Portsmouth

OHIO RIVER.

Scale of Miles.

16 Map of ancient earthworks at Portsmouth, Ohio. (From Atwater, 1820)

16

entitled 'Description of the Antiquities Discovered in the State of Ohio and other Western States.' Atwater lived in Circleville, Ohio and was the Postmaster there.[109] He explored many of the mounds of his home town and the surrounding region of Ohio and provided the best descriptions and plans of these mounds that had yet been made. Mitra, in his *A History of American Anthropology*, has said that 'the first true archaeologist was . . . Caleb Atwater.'[110] Suffice it to say here that Atwater was ahead of his time in certain respects but very much a part of it in others; next to Jefferson, he was the most important figure of the Speculative Period.

Atwater's book really has two parts, the descriptive, and the speculative. Unfortunately, the latter did not really follow from the former. The purely speculative section, though, is clearly separated from the descriptive one. In his descriptions, Atwater used a relatively simple three-part classification for the observed remains: (a) modern European; (b) modern Indian; (c) Moundbuilder. In his speculative section, Atwater proposed that the mounds had been built by Hindus who migrated from India and who later moved to Mexico. As regards the latter point, Atwater was apparently influenced by Humboldt's writings. He also speculated that the Indians with their simpler culture had arrived in the Americas before the more advanced Moundbuilders and afterwards moved into areas vacated by the latter.[111] Compared to other writers of his day, Atwater was relatively restrained in his speculative hypotheses.[112]

As we now know, Atwater's ideas were incorrect; but there was one other individual in this period who deserves mention here and who was not wrong. This was Dr. James H. McCulloh, Jr. McCulloh, an armchair antiquarian,[113] wrote two books: *Researches in America*, in 1817 (second edition), and *Researches*

Philosophical and Antiquarian Concerning the Aboriginal History of America, in 1829. His principal contribution was his denial that there was an early separate Moundbuilder culture. In the second Appendix of his 1829 work, actually the most important section of this book, he carefully sifted all the previous written evidence and concluded that the Moundbuilders and the Indians were one and the same race and that the Indians were capable of building the mounds. McCulloh also reviewed data on the high civilizations of Latin America and the cultures of the Indians of North America.[114]

Samuel F. Haven, who agreed with McCulloh's views, said of his work in 1856: 'No more perfect monument of industry and patient research connected with this subject has been published.'[115] Cyrus Thomas concurred, calling McCulloh's conclusions 're-markable' for the time.[116] On the other hand, McCulloh's views were unpopular and some people found the book difficult to read. Clark Wissler, writing much later, has stated:

'Had McCulloh possessed a great mind like Gallatin he would have produced the first great classic critique upon the culture origins of the aboriginal civilizations of Mexico and the Andean region instead of producing a poorly organized and ineffectual book. Nevertheless he deserves a place in the history of anthropological thought during the period 1800–1860.'[117]

We would tend to agree with Haven and Thomas and feel that Wissler's criticism demands more than could have been expected of any American antiquarian of McCulloh's time.

An Appraisal, and Signs for the Future

As of 1840, American archaeology as a scholarly entity simply did not exist. There were virtually no full-time practitioners of archaeology and no professionals. There was no field methodology and the conceptual inventory was minimal. The data base was very slim and chronological knowledge, either absolute or relative, was rudimentary at best. It was generally accepted that the New World was peopled from Asia via the Bering Strait, but beyond that there was little agreement, or knowledge for that matter. There were some survey data on the mounds of the Ohio Valley and the Southeastern United States. Some of the major ruins in Mexico, Guatemala, and Peru were recognized and some details of them known. Most of the area of North America was archaeological *terra incognita* as were vast territories of South and Central America.

Nevertheless, there were bright spots on the horizon and certain signposts for future developments were already in existence. The outline for what had to be done in terms of the initial steps of data-gathering in North America had been presented by the American Philosophical Society in its 1799 circular, and a model of how to investigate archaeological problems was present in the excavations of Thomas Jefferson. The framework of an archaeological survey could also be seen in Atwater's Ohio mound studies.

Moreover, by the fall of 1839, John L. Stephens and Frederick Catherwood had already begun their travels in Middle America. Grave Creek Mound in Ohio had been dug and Henry R. School-craft was soon to study it and publish his results. In 1826, James Smithson, an Englishman, left a half million dollar bequest to the young republic of the United States to found an institution 'for the increase and diffusion of knowledge among men.'[118] As a result, the Smithsonian Institution, which was to have such a profound influence on the history of American archaeology, was founded, a few short years after the close of the Speculative Period, in 1846.

By 1840 in the Old World, Lyell had already produced his *Principles of Geology*, and Darwin had made his momentous voyage on the *Beagle*. In addition, the Danes had begun to make important archaeological advances. The lack of European models, to which scholars in the New World could turn, was soon to be rectified.

Finally, travel was becoming easier in the Americas and the United States began to spread westward. With this burgeoning expansion, a new spirit could be seen. As William H. Goetzmann has said:

'The professional explorer and scientist began to take to the field in the 1840's, and with his appearance came a new and significant refinement, not only in the scientific approach to the West, but in all aspects of the search for knowledge. The basis of geographic discovery shifted from the simple notation of landmarks and natural wonders, of settlement sites and overland trails, to the scientific assessment of basic resources, and serious study of primitive cultures different from our own. . . .'[119]

All these events and nascent trends led, in the second half of the 19th century, to the birth of the discipline of American archaeology. But the incipient discipline in 1840 still had a long, long way to go to become a science.

Chapter Three

The Classificatory-Descriptive Period (1840–1914)

'The field investigator [of the Western United States] was spurred on to one of the most rapid and complete inventories ever made on any portion of the globe, and the best scientific minds were so busy recording the mass of data that they had little time to formulate hypotheses about the meaning and utility of it all.' William H. Goetzmann

A Definition of the Period

THE Classificatory-Descriptive Period is distinguished from the preceding Speculative Period by a distinct change in attitude and outlook on the part of many of the major archaeological workers and writers.[1] That is by no means to say that the intellectual trend which characterized the Speculative Period suddenly came to an end in 1840 – the Speculative mode of thought remained a very important element of the Classificatory-Descriptive Period. But the principal focus of the new period was on the description of archaeological materials, especially architecture and monuments, and rudimentary classification of these. Throughout the period, archaeologists struggled to make archaeology into a systematic, scientific discipline. They did not succeed; but they laid the foundations for many of the achievements of the 20th century.

Intellectual developments and the emergence of new ideas in Europe had significant effects on the rise of American archaeology in the middle and late 19th century. Among the developments were the discovery of the great antiquity of man in the Old World, the publication of Darwin's *Origin of Species*, and the rise of the science of geology. Simultaneously, the beginning of professional archaeology in Europe, together with the upsurge of science and scientific thought at the expense of theological dogma, were in their turn reflected on the American continent.

Throughout the Classificatory-Descriptive Period there was a steady increase in the discovery and description of antiquities as the United States expanded westward and as the white man penetrated into other parts of the North and South American continents.[2] In the United States this work was sponsored by the government, by universities, museums, and scientific societies. Archaeology became both an established vocation and a recognized avocation. Towards the end of the period, it began to be taught in universities so that a generation of professionally trained archaeologists became active in the early years of the 20th century. In this connection it is especially worth noting that the alliance of American archaeology and general anthropology began in this period – both academically and in the field. The importance of this union for the conceptual development of American archaeology, and particularly that of the United States, was longlasting, as we shall see later.

In North America the earlier research interests in the mounds and earthworks of the Eastern United States continued, and there was great interest in the question as to who had built the mounds. Were they a 'lost race' of Moundbuilders or simply the ancestors of the Indians? Another focus of attention was the problem of Early Man. Discoveries of Pleistocene inhabitants of the Old World spurred American archaeologists to hunt for comparably early remains on their side of the Atlantic. The period was characterized by a lack of chronological perspective and the development of methods that would lead to such a perspective. On the other hand, typological, classificatory, and geographical distribution studies went forward. In Middle America the trends were somewhat similar although there were some significant differences. These were occasioned by the extraordinary richness of the Pre-Columbian remains, the presence of native writing systems, and the strong influence of European humanistic scholarship. All of these gave the archaeology of this area a different flavor from that of North America. In South America there was relatively less archaeological exploration, but what there was stayed in the Classificatory-Descriptive vein. A singular exception was the development of an area chronology in Peru by the German scholar Max Uhle.

Archaeological Research in North America

The major concern of archaeologists in Eastern North America during the period was the mounds of the Ohio and Mississippi Valleys and surrounding areas. The Moundbuilder controversy raged throughout the 19th century and was not really laid to rest until the publication of Cyrus Thomas's monumental report on the mound explorations of the Bureau of (American) Ethnology in 1894.[3]

The first major contribution of the period was *Ancient Monuments of the Mississippi Valley* by E. G. Squier and E. H. Davis, 17, 18 which appeared in 1848. This work was the best descriptive study published up until then, and its intellectual orientation typified the new trends which emerged during the Classificatory-Descriptive Period.[4] Squier, an Ohio newspaperman who later became a diplomat and travelled widely in Latin America, and Davis, a physician from Chillicothe, Ohio, accurately surveyed a vast number of mounds, excavated in some, and brought together in their book the survey data of other workers. There also was a salvage aspect to their work in that many of the mounds were being destroyed as the pioneers pushed westward.

The overall tone of *Ancient Monuments of the Mississippi Valley* was descriptive, not speculative. As Squier said:

'At the outset, all preconceived notions were abandoned, and the work of research commenced, as if no speculations had been indulged in, nor any thing before been known, respecting the singular remains of antiquity scattered so profusely around us. It was concluded that, either the field should be entirely abandoned to the poet and the romancer, or, if these monuments were capable of reflecting any certain light upon the grand archaeological

17 Ephraim George Squier

18 Edwin Hamilton Davis

questions connected with the primitive history of the American continent, the origin, migration, and early state of the American race, that then they should be carefully and minutely, and above all, systematically investigated.'[5]

It is evident that the descriptive tone of the volume was not only due to the authors' inclinations but to those of the renowned scientist and Secretary of the Smithsonian Institution, Joseph Henry, who edited the Squier and Davis manuscript before publication. As Wilcomb Washburn, working with Henry's correspondence, has noted: 'Henry insisted upon throwing out some of the engravings Squier had prepared which were not "of an original character," and he drew a tight line on the manuscript itself so that "your labours should be given to the world as free as possible from everything of a speculative nature and that your positive addition to the sum of human knowledge should stand in bold relief unmingled with the labours of others."'[6]

The volume was the first publication of the newly founded Smithsonian Institution and appeared in its Contributions to Knowledge series. Moreover, Squier and Davis had the support of the American Ethnological Society which corresponded with them in the field and helped arrange the publication of the monograph. The active involvement of a government body as well as a professional anthropological society in archaeological fieldwork and, especially, publication also indicated a marked change in the trends of archaeological development in the New World.

It should be noted that Squier and Davis used a rudimentary functional classification for the mounds and asked some questions about the probable uses or purposes of such archaeological structures. These questions were formulated as quite explicit hypotheses, and they went further in suggesting lines of investigation that might be pursued to verify or disprove their suppositions. In so doing they anticipated, in a degree, the modern 'hypothesis and test expectation' method.

Even with all the praiseworthy aspects of *Ancient Monuments of the Mississippi Valley*, the speculative mode of thought still retained a significant role in that work. Squier and Davis adhered to the great race of Moundbuilders theory and felt that the American Indians or their ancestors were not capable of erecting the mounds. The subsequent migration of the Moundbuilders to Mexico was considered a likely possibility. They rejected the hypothesis of Whittlesey that there were two peoples in Ohio, one in the north and one in the south.[7] Whittlesey was attempting to differentiate between two Moundbuilding cultures in Ohio, actually a chronological, rather than a geographical, distinction which was made many decades later; but Squier and Davis felt

19 Cross-section drawing of the internal construction, including a burial, of Mound 2 in the Mound City, Ohio group. (From Squier and Davis, 1848)

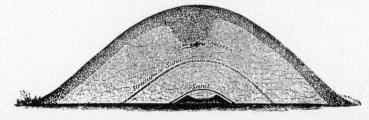

20, 21 The Grave Creek Mound in West Virginia (*above*). An artist's conception in the mid-19th century. A group of 'sepulchral' mounds (*below*). (From Squier and Davis, 1848)

22 Samuel F. Haven. (From
Winsor, 1889)

24

23 Two site maps of mounds
and earthworks. *Left*, the Dunlaps
Works, Ross County, Ohio;
right, the ancient works in Athens
County, Ohio. These maps far
surpassed in care and accuracy any
maps which had preceded them.
(From Squier and Davis, 1848)

that the geographic differences were no greater than are to be
expected between the structures of a sparse frontier population.

Before taking up a diplomatic post in Nicaragua, Squier also
explored the mounds of western New York, and in 1849 the
Smithsonian Institution published this work, too.[8] Squier made
the New York survey because he wished to learn more about the
Moundbuilders and felt that the origins of the Ohio Moundbuilders might be in western New York. He hypothesized that
the remains in both areas would be quite similar. Squier found, to
his surprise, that there was good evidence that the Iroquois
Indians had built many of the mounds in New York. This discovery apparently did not change his opinions about the identity
of the Ohio Moundbuilders, but he was forced to distinguish
between the Ohio and western New York areas and abandon his
hypothesis.

Another contemporary study of the mounds was made by
I. A. Lapham in Wisconsin. Lapham surveyed and explored the
many effigy mounds of that state with the support of the American
Antiquarian Society; the Smithsonian published his findings in
1855.[9]

We have noted that while the majority opinion of the mid 19th
century favored the separate Moundbuilder race theory, there
were some opposing views. These were that the ancestors of the
modern Indians had built the mounds and that the Indians and
the Moundbuilders were one and the same group. Foremost

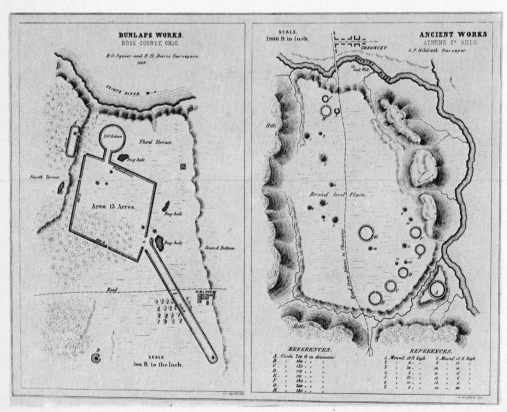

among the scholars holding this latter view were Samuel F. Haven   22
and Henry Rowe Schoolcraft.

In his important review of the state of North American archaeology in 1856, Haven, the Librarian of the American Antiquarian
Society, carefully sifted the available archaeological data and came
to the conclusion that the ancient lost Moundbuilder race hypothesis was untenable.[10] His study, which was commissioned and
published by the Smithsonian Institution,[11] was a model of
reasoned description and discussion in comparison with the speculative works which had dominated the literature until then.
Haven's archaeological outlook typified the new, increasingly
professionalized, descriptive trend which was to dominate the
period by its close.

Henry R. Schoolcraft also opposed the prevailing Moundbuilder hypotheses in his writings, although he had supported
them earlier in his career. After examining the remains from the
Grave Creek Mound in Ohio, Schoolcraft, who was generally
sympathetic toward the Indians, decided that there were cultural
continuities from the Moundbuilders to the contemporary native
inhabitants of the Eastern United States.[12] He further felt that
the mounds need not have been built by peoples with an advanced
civilization, but could have been constructed by peoples at a
'barbarian' level of culture. Unfortunately, Schoolcraft's views
were buried deep in his unindexed (at that time)[13] and rambling
six-volume *Historical and Statistical Information Respecting the*

24 Lapham's map of the ancient
works at Maus' Mill, Wisconsin.
(From Lapham, 1855)

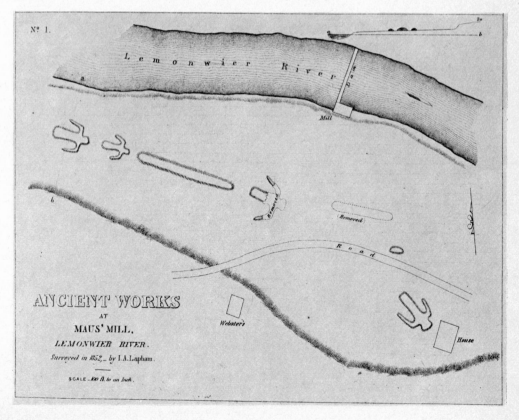

47

History, Condition, and Prospects of the Indian Tribes of the United States, which appeared 1851–57, and few people probably read it at the time (or since, for that matter).

The debate raged through the decades from the 1850s into the late 1890s and was accompanied by continued amateur 'pottings' of mounds. Such excavations and studies were sponsored by individuals or local amateur societies.[14] Many popular books, of highly varying quality, by authors from both sides of the Atlantic such as Pidgeon,[15] Lubbock,[16] Baldwin,[17] Foster,[18] Larkin,[19] Bancroft,[20] and Nadaillac,[21] kept the fires lit and helped to add many an additional wrinkle to the hypotheses as to where the Moundbuilders came from, when they thrived, and where they went. The general public remained caught up in the excitement of the debate. But for many, the interest was more than pure curiosity. The Native Americans of North America were in the process of being exterminated as the United States spread westward, and the more primitive the Indians were thought to be, the easier it apparently was to justify their destruction or displacement. As Silverberg has so cogently pointed out: 'The controversy over the origin of the mounds was not merely an abstract scholarly debate, but had its roots in the great 19th-century campaign of extermination waged against the American Indian.'[22]

In opposition to this popular trend, there was another one which by the end of the period had built up a strong enough foundation to sweep the popular-amateur approach into the background. This new tide, whose first waves we noted earlier, was the increasing professionalization of archaeology. It was certainly related to the huge growth of science in the United States and the rapid rise and expansion of universities.[23] The heyday of local scientific societies quickly drew to a close at the beginning of the 20th century as amateur enthusiasts were replaced by local college and university scholars and researchers. This trend was as true for archaeology as it was for other disciplines.[24]

In addition, a number of archaeological journals and professional societies were born during this period. Such journals as the *American Antiquarian* (founded in 1878 by the Reverend Stephen D. Peet)[25] and the *American Anthropologist* (founded in 1888) were particularly important. The American Association for the Advancement of Science (Anthropology Section), the Anthropological Society of Washington (later the American Anthropological Association), and the Archaeological Institute of America (now mainly interested in Old World archaeology) were among the more important societies. The last, in fact, asked Lewis Henry Morgan, one of the most eminent American anthropologists of his day, to prepare a plan in 1879 for archaeological exploration and research in the American field.[26]

25 Cyrus Thomas

Two institutions in particular had immeasurable impact on the dawning age of professional archaeology in the 19th century. They were the Smithsonian Institution (founded in 1846) and the Peabody Museum of Harvard University (founded in 1866). The former, especially, laid the foundation for and dominated the Classificatory-Descriptive Period of American archaeology. In the persons of men such as Powell, Thomas, and Holmes, the

26 Mound in South Memphis, Tennessee, in Fort Pickering. From an original pencil sketch in the manuscript of Cyrus Thomas's mound surveys

Smithsonian Institution and two of its arms, the Bureau of Ethnology (founded in 1879 with Powell as its head and renamed the Bureau of American Ethnology in 1894) and the National Museum (also founded in 1879), provided some of the most influential scholars of the period. As A. Irving Hallowell has forcefully stated in relation to the former: 'It was under the auspices of the Bureau of American Ethnology, in short, that, through a series of widely gauged programs, the empirical foundations of archaeology in the United States were established on a broad geographical scale.'[27]

Cyrus Thomas of the Bureau of Ethnology was responsible for demolishing the lost Moundbuilder race hypothesis in 1894. Thomas, an entomologist from Illinois, was picked by Major John Wesley Powell (the great explorer and first man to descend the Grand Canyon rapids of the Colorado River in a boat), who was the Director of both the Bureau of Ethnology and the United States Geological Survey,[28] to head a Division of Mound Exploration in 1882, after the United States Congress, much to Powell's chagrin – he wanted to concentrate on ethnological and linguistic pursuits – insisted that the Bureau of Ethnology spend $5,000 a year on mound studies.[29]

Thomas was a believer at first in the separate Moundbuilder race hypothesis, but after he began working in the field, he changed his mind and soon became a champion of the opposing view. This latter view was also strongly held by Powell, as can be seen by reading any of his introductions to the *Annual Reports* of the Bureau of Ethnology in the later 1880s and early 1890s. Other workers in the Bureau, such as Henshaw,[30] also attacked the 'lost race' hypothesis in no uncertain terms. Thus, Powell's Bureau of Ethnology became the leading advocate of the idea that the ancestors of the Indians built the mounds, a view which is now accepted as fact and which carried the day well before the end of the Classificatory-Descriptive Period. Unfortunately, this triumph may have had some ironic results in helping to retard certain developments in the archaeology of the Eastern United States and in North American archaeology in general as we shall see later;

25

27

27 (*Opposite*) Major John Wesley
Powell consulting with an Indian
on the Kaibab Plateau, near the
Grand Canyon of the Colorado
River in northern Arizona. This
picture was taken by Hilliers on
the Powell Expedition of 1871–5

while, at the same time, it did nothing to change the prevailing
popular attitudes against the American Indian.

Upon receiving his appointment and assignment from Powell,
Thomas quickly realized that he would have to undertake an
extensive program of survey and excavation in order to salvage
many mounds which were being rapidly ravaged and to maximize
his labor force throughout all four seasons of the year. The data
which his able assistants uncovered and which Thomas studied
convinced him that the connections between the mounds and the
Indians were clear. Furthermore, he felt that different tribal
groups had built different mounds.[31] Although he attributed too
many of the mounds to a post-European time of construction, and
was not alert to the possibilities of cultural sequence or development, Thomas's basic views were in other respects modern in
tone.[32]

Thomas's conclusions were published in the monumental 12th
Annual Report of the Bureau of Ethnology which appeared in 1894.
Utilizing culture area units, this work presented all the Bureau's
data on the mound explorations and effectively brought a long
era of speculation to an end, at least among the growing group of
professionals in the field. In fact, the Report has recently been said
by one archaeologist to mark 'the birth of modern American
archaeology.'[33]

Thomas, who was interested in such subjects as Maya hieroglyphics in addition to the mounds, also wrote a general text in
1898 summarizing North American archaeology.[34] Of all the
archaeologists at that time, he was probably most qualified for
the task.

Another major contributor to the solution of the Moundbuilder question was Frederic Ward Putnam, Curator of the Peabody Museum from 1875 to 1909 and Peabody Professor of
American Archaeology and Ethnology from 1887 to 1909. Putnam was one of the leading figures of the Classificatory-Descriptive Period, both as an excavator, or excavator sponsor, and as an
administrator or founding father of museums and departments of
anthropology.

Before discussing Putnam's role in the growth of American
archaeology, we should take note of the earlier history of the
institution with which he was associated for so many years. The
Peabody Museum of Harvard University was founded in 1866
through the efforts of O. C. Marsh, a nephew of George Peabody.
Marsh had been influenced by Lyell, who had advised him to take
up archaeology in the Americas. Marsh participated in excavations in Ohio and was the prime mover behind Peabody's gift to
Harvard.[35] The first Curator of the Peabody Museum was Jeffries
Wyman, a famous natural scientist of the day. Wyman excavated
shell-mounds on the Atlantic Coast and then, more importantly,
on the banks of the St. Johns River, Florida.[36]

Wyman's shell-mound excavations reflected the influences of
similar work in Europe. The immediate catalyst was the publication by the Smithsonian Institution of an English translation of an
article by Morlot on the shell middens of Denmark as well as the
Swiss lake dwellings.[37] This publication also stimulated the work

32

30

28

SECTION OF SHELL-HEAP
Six inches of modern soil
(Later stage) Fine thin pottery beautifully ornamented. Neatly made implements of bone, shell, etc. Axes, arrow and spear heads of stone; also stone-beads and objects of stone used in games Three feet
Two feet of soil containing a few fragments of pottery
(Middle stage) Better pottery, rudely ornamented. Primitive implements of bone and shell Four feet
(Earlier stage) Rude, heavy pottery, destitute of ornament Three feet

28 Shell-mound at Old Enterprise, Florida. (From Wyman 1875)

29 A stylized stratigraphic diagram from S.T. Walker's shell-mound excavations in Florida. (From Walker 1883)

30 (*Opposite*) The Peabody Museum of Harvard in Putnam's time (1893)

31 The Middle American exhibits at the Columbian Exposition of 1892 in Chicago, Illinois

32 Archaeologists photographed at the Chillicothe Group, Ohio. Putnam is at the right with Metz next to him

of J.J. Jones in the shell-heaps of Nova Scotia.[38] Wyman's work helped prove conclusively that the shell-heaps were man-made and that they pre-dated the time of the historic Indians.[39] Wyman was also able to recognize some stratigraphy in them and showed that the heaps of the St. John's River region were different from those of other regions.

One other significant shell-midden excavation of the time was by S.T. Walker at Cedar Keys, Florida.[40] Walker recognized strata in the midden and defined several periods on the basis of changing pottery styles. Walker, however, treated the cultural strata like geological ones and generalized a sequence for a whole region. Unfortunately, the work of Wyman and Walker had little effect on the archaeology of Florida and failed to provide an impetus for the building of cultural chronologies.

It was after Wyman's death in 1874 that Frederic W. Putnam became the Curator of the Peabody Museum.[41] Putnam's original professional interests were in zoology, but turned to archaeology and general anthropology after his new appointment. Putnam has been called by some the 'father of American archaeology.'[42] Although we would not go that far, we would agree that he was a major force in its development. Perhaps it might be best to label Putnam, if one must attach labels to great figures, as the 'professionalizer of American archaeology.' Besides bringing the Peabody Museum to a position as one of the leading anthropological institutions in the United States, Putnam was in charge of the Anthropology Building and Exhibit at the 1892 Exposition in Chicago; he helped found the Field Museum of Natural History in Chicago, the Department of Anthropology at the University of California (Berkeley), and the Anthropology Department of the American Museum of Natural History.[43] He also was the Secretary of the American Association for the Advancement of Science for twenty-five years.

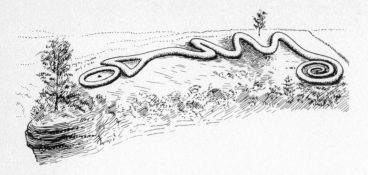

33 Artist's drawing of the Great
Serpent Mound of Ohio. (After
Putnam 1890)

34 A burial exposed in Putnam's
Madisonville, Ohio, excavations

35 (*Opposite*) Putnam in his 1890
mound excavations in the Little
Miami Valley, Ohio

36 Drawings of Trenton Gravel
'paleoliths'. (From Haynes 1889)

Putnam's archaeological interests lay in two areas: the mounds
of the Ohio Valley and the study of Early Man. In relation to the
former, he and his associates excavated at Madisonville, the
Turner mounds, and at the Great Serpent Mound, among
others.[44] He even obtained the Serpent Mound for the Peabody
Museum in order to save it from destruction; the Museum later
turned the mound over to the state of Ohio. Putnam also dug in
Tennessee and analyzed and published the prehistoric collections from California obtained by the Wheeler Geographical
Expedition. His excavations were models of good technique for
the time, and he trained many students in the basics of scientific
surveying and mapping, digging, cross-section drawing, and the
careful plotting and recording of finds.[45] He also recognized
stratigraphy in the mounds of the Ohio Valley, but he did not go
on from there to form local or regional culture sequences.

Putnam's second great interest was in proving the great antiquity of man in the New World. That is to say, he believed, and

wished to prove conclusively, that man was present many thousands of years ago and that he arrived before the end of the Pleistocene Ice Age. To this end, he sponsored various archaeological projects including the work of C. C. Abbott in the Trenton Gravels of New Jersey. Abbott discovered tools made out of argillite which 'looked' early and some of which appeared in strata which he believed dated to Glacial times.[46] At the time, there was some support for the views of Abbott and Putnam, although it was later shown that the layers were of much more recent date.[47]

The Trenton Gravels finds were just one facet of a major debate which was waged toward the latter part of the Classificatory-Descriptive Period and well into the Classificatory-Historical. Many other discoveries were brought forward as proof of Early Man in the Americas, and this view, which was also supported by men such as Henry Haynes,[48] held the day for much of the 19th century.

The desire to prove the great antiquity of man in the New World had been stimulated by discoveries in the Old in which a Pleistocene and Paleolithic date had been demonstrated for Boucher de Perthes's discoveries in France. These discoveries, together with the triumph of Darwinian evolution and its implications, overrode the limiting theological views concerning the age of man.[49] The publication of such popular books as Lubbock's *Prehistoric Times*, which went through many editions, further fanned the flames of interest in the subject in the Americas. It was believed by many that men had first reached the New World

37 An Ohio mound excavation in 1889. A trenching operation under the direction of C.L. Metz

in Glacial times, and a few even believed that the date might be pre-Pleistocene.[50] Unfortunately for the successful demonstration of man's early presence in these continents, Quaternary geology was very imperfectly understood in the Americas in the 19th century. It was not known just when the Pleistocene had ended nor to what date such extinct animals as the mastodon had survived. Nor was there a refinement of geological-archaeological excavation techniques that would have been of help in resolving the question of man's association with the Pleistocene.

Even today, in the Americas, the whole situation concerning Early Man is disputed on many fronts. His Pleistocene presence is clearly demonstrable, but just how early he arrived in the New World is still a source of debate. The circumstances are not comparable to the Old World where remains of the genus *Homo* may be dated in hundreds of thousands of years and where the stone artifacts made by these men are found in relatively great numbers in numerous deep Pleistocene deposits. It comes as no surprise, then, that archaeologists in the 19th century rushed precipitously into an archaeological situation which required methodological care and rigorous standards of proof. Every new find which appeared to have some antiquity on the basis of rude-looking tools or putatively ancient geological associations was proclaimed as a conclusive proof of the antiquity of man in the New World.

But, as virtually all of the supposed finds of Glacial age (either artifactual or human) turned out to be unacceptable, the pendulum of opinion began to swing in the other direction. The two men most responsible for this change were William Henry Holmes and Aleš Hrdlička.

38 Carved tablet from a Hopewellian mound. These small objects possibly were used as textile or body stamps. Such finds as these curious little tablets still helped maintain a popular faith in the mysterious Moundbuilders as opposed to the Indians. Such beliefs long outdistanced the rising scientific excavations of Putnam, Thomas and their contemporaries

Holmes was first trained as an artist, but after travelling in the Western United States with the United States Geological Survey, his interests soon turned to geology and then to archaeology. He worked in the United States National Museum and the Bureau of American Ethnology for much of his career and succeeded Powell as chief of the Bureau in 1902. As we shall see later, he also did a brief stint of fieldwork in Mexico. Holmes was particularly interested in prehistoric ceramics and stone technology, and his classificatory work helped set the stage for typological developments in the following period.[51] In relation to stone technology, his studies of the so-called 'paleoliths', which were claimed by others to be artifacts from Glacial times, showed that these 'implements' were actually rejects of much later native craftsmen.[52] This work convinced him that man did not reach the New World until after the Pleistocene, and he became a strong defender of this point of view.

Hrdlička also had a major effect on American archaeology, although his role has often been misinterpreted.[53] A physical anthropologist, he was brought to the United States National Museum in 1903. He became Curator of the Division of Physical Anthropology in 1910.[54] Hrdlička was particularly interested in Early Man finds and studied almost all the alleged Early Man sites and associated skeletal material that were discovered in the early part of the 20th century. He was relentless in his criticisms of the

39 William Henry Holmes

40 Holmes was the great classifier of Eastern North American pottery. Among other things, he identified and segregated the fiber-tempered wares of Florida. Many years later, these wares were demonstrated to be the earliest pottery of America north of Mexico. (From Holmes 1903)

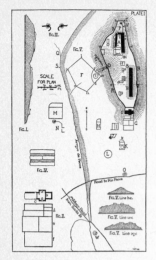

41 Bandelier's plan of the ruins of Pecos, New Mexico. (From Bandelier 1881)

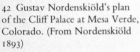

42 Gustav Nordenskiöld's plan of the Cliff Palace at Mesa Verde, Colorado. (From Nordenskiöld 1893)

supposed early datings of these finds and the often sloppy techniques involved in their excavation. He did not 'certify' as acceptable any of the Early Man discoveries of the time, although he still believed that evidence would be uncovered which would show that man first came to the New World more than 10,000 years ago.[55] As time went on, Hrdlička came to be somewhat dogmatic in his rejection of new finds,[56] and, as Frank H.H. Roberts has stated, an atmosphere of fear pervaded the Early Man scene, with many workers afraid to face Hrdlička's scathing attacks.

'The question of early man in America became virtually taboo, and no anthropologist, or for that matter geologist or paleontologist, desirous of a successful career would tempt the fate of ostracism by intimating that he had discovered indications of a respectable antiquity for the Indian.'[57]

Nevertheless, as Clewlow has perceptively pointed out, Hrdlička's work must be evaluated in terms of its historical context.[58] Instead of looking at Hrdlička as a negative force, his criticisms of various archaeologists should be seen as an attempt to bring some degree of rigor and an established mode of validation into archaeological fieldwork and interpretation. That is to say, he may have helped to hold back Early Man studies in a substantive sense, but he advanced the cause of American archaeology as a whole by attempting to make its methodology more scientific. Thus, Hrdlička was helping to lay the foundation which made possible the transition from the Classificatory-Descriptive to the Classificatory-Historical Period. Whether the price which had to be paid was equal to this advance is, of course, another question.

The net result of all the Early Man claims and the disproofs by Holmes, Hrdlička, and others was that by the end of the period,

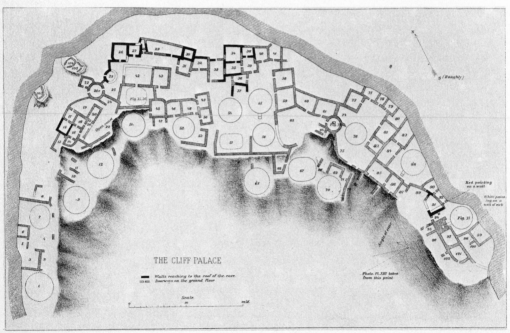

THE CLIFF PALACE

there was little time depth to American prehistory. The concate-
nation of circumstances which led to this situation had a major
impact on the development of American archaeology. We will
further discuss this impact below in our review of Classificatory-
Descriptive Period concepts and, again, in the following chapter.

As we have mentioned, archaeology, or at least an interest in
antiquities spread geographically during the Classificatory-
Descriptive Period. As white explorers and later new populations
moved into areas hitherto the preserve of the American Indian,
such as the Southwestern United States, there was an explosion
of *descriptive* archaeological knowledge. In other areas, too, such
as the Southeastern and Northeastern United States and even
Alaska, the growing group of professional archaeologists carried
out valuable new work.

Much of the early archaeological work in the Western areas of
the United States was done by members of expeditions or took the
form of surveys by the Federal Government.[59] It often consisted
simply of descriptions of ruins, especially in the Southwest,
although as the period moved on there was more and more excavation. In the Southwest, the first descriptions of archaeological
remains were by William H. Emory, 'who almost singlehandedly
. . . began the study of Southwestern archaeology,'[60] J. H. Simp-
son, the Kerns, and other members of topographic surveys
organized by the United States Army. Later investigators included men from the Bureau of Ethnology and members of
private expeditions such as James Stevenson, husband of the
ethnographer Mathilda Coxe Stevenson and associate of Major
Powell, the Mindeleffs, the Wetherills, A. Bandelier, F.H.
Cushing, J. W. Fewkes, B. Cummings,[61] G. Nordenskiöld, and
E. L. Hewett, who all braved less than ideal working conditions
to advance the descriptive state of archaeological knowledge.
Frank Hamilton Cushing, the leader of the privately sponsored
Hemenway Expedition, helped pioneer the direct-historical

43 Photograph of Spruce Tree
House, Mesa Verde, Colorado,
taken at the turn of the century

41
42

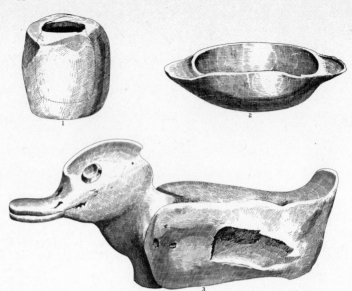

44 Pottery found by C. B. Moore in the sand burial mounds of the St. John's River, Florida. 1 Duval's, 2,3 Tick Island. Earthenware. (From Moore 1894)

45 Pottery from the Maine shell-heaps. These vessels were identified as 'Algonquian' by Willoughby. It is possible that this ethnic and linguistic identification is correct; however, it is now known that pottery such as this dates to the Early Woodland Period of the first millennium B.C. (From Willoughby 1909)

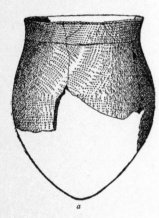

a

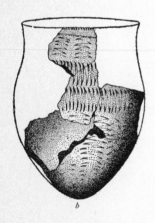

b

approach in the Southwest and combined both ethnography and archaeology in his work,[62] while scholars like Bandelier, Hewett, and Hough showed a precocious interest in Southwestern chronology and made some fairly accurate guesses about sequences there.[63] In other words, Nels C. Nelson and A. V. Kidder, both pioneers of the following Classificatory-Historical Period, did not make their striking archaeological advances in a vacuum.

In the Southeastern United States, Clarence B. Moore visited and explored a number of key sites in his private houseboat. Many of the sites were located, naturally, on or near the various rivers of the area. Moore published a number of descriptive reports with voluminous illustrations concerning this work.[64] Earlier on, C. C. Jones had studied the antiquities of Georgia. Gates P. Thruston had worked in Tennessee in the late 19th century and, somewhat later, H. I. Smith excavated the Fox Farm site in Kentucky. Others working on the eastern sea-coast and in the Ohio Valley included Gerard Fowke, who also excavated in the Southeast, Willoughby who worked in several regions, including Maine and Ohio, and various men, such as Volk, Cresson, and Metz, who excavated under the auspices or sponsorship of Putnam.

W. K. Moorehead studied some of the mounds of Ohio, including Fort Ancient and the Hopewell Mound group, and, later on, he published his studies on the state of Maine and on the great site of Cahokia in Illinois.[65] He also wrote in two volumes *The Stone Age of North America*,[66] and was Director, for many years, of the Department of American Archaeology of the Phillips Academy, Massachusetts.

Finally, in our more than rapid survey of some of the scholars who added to our descriptive knowledge of Eastern North American prehistory in the Classificatory-Descriptive Period, we should

47 note the works of William C. Mills on the mounds of the Ohio Valley. Mills, Curator for the later part of his life of the Museum of the Ohio Archaeological and Historical Society, can be seen as a

significant transitional figure between the myth-demolishing Cyrus Thomas in the Classificatory-Descriptive Period and the cultural-typologizing W.C. McKern in the Classificatory-Historical Period.

After excavating various mound groups in Ohio, Mills could separate a Fort Ancient from a Hopewell culture,[67] but chronology was still a matter of guesswork. In other words, at the beginning of the 20th century, an attempt was being made to see cultural variety within what had been thought of as 'mound culture.' Moreover, these newly defined 'cultures' were not classified solely on the basis of geography (or 'space'), as was the case in Thomas's work,[68] but by cultural similarities. Mills was not the first to do this – Thruston, for one, had defined a Stone Grave culture (or 'race' as he called it) in Tennessee[69] – but he based his cultural definitions on careful excavation and analysis. He was unable, however, to align these cultures on the basis of stratigraphy in order to construct a regional sequence. This is not to say that Mills was unaware of time;[70] he simply lacked an archaeological basis to discuss it scientifically.

46 *In situ* copper and imitation deer antler headdress. This find was made in a burial mound of the Hopewell Group. Freshwater pearl beads, copper breastplates, and other ornaments were found in association. (From Moorehead 1892)

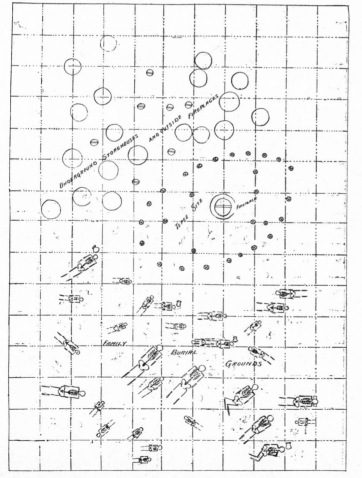

47 Gridded field plan of burials, house ring (as indicated by post-molds and fireplace), and other fire areas and storage pits. Mills's work in this case involved greater reporting and recording accuracy of excavated features than had heretofore characterized Ohio Valley archaeology. (From Mills 1906)

In the Far West and Alaska, archaeologists such as H.I. Smith, Max Uhle, and N.C. Nelson, as well as the eminent naturalist W.H. Dall, all made significant contributions. Dall and Uhle are especially important because of their attempts to apply stratigraphic methods in order to build chronologies. Dall was a conchologist and natural scientist who participated in several expeditions to Alaska. During one of these, he had the opportunity to excavate a series of shell-heaps on the Aleutian Islands. He published his results in an article entitled 'On Succession in the Shell-Heaps of the Aleutian Islands' which appeared in Volume I of Major Powell's *Contributions to North American Ethnography* in 1877.

Dall trenched several shell-mounds and was able to recognize strata in them. Moreover, he was also able to formulate a three-period chronological scheme for the mounds based on the stratigraphy. As Dall states: '[The ditch] gave us a clear idea of the formation and constitution of the shell-heaps; enabled me to distinguish between the different strata and their contents; to make the observations repeatedly; to fully confirm them by experience in many localities; and thus to lay the foundation for the generalizations suggested in this paper.'[71] He goes on further to conclude:

'That a gradual progression from the low Innuit stage to the present Aleut condition, without serious interruption, is plainly indicated by the succession of the materials of, and utensils in, the shell-heaps of the islands. . . .
That the stratification of the shell-heaps shows a tolerably uniform division into three stages, characterized by the food which formed their stapel of subsistence and by the weapons for obtaining, and utensils for preparing this food, as found in the separate strata; these stages being –
I The Littoral Period, represented by the *Echinus* Layer.
II The Fishing Period, represented by the Fishbone Layer.
III The Hunting Period, represented by the Mammalian Layer.
That these strata correspond approximately to actual stages in the development of the population which formed them; so that their contents may appropriately, within limits, be taken as indicative of the condition of that population at the times when the respective strata were being deposited.'[72]

In addition, Dall recognized the probable influence of the environment on the differential development of culture on the islands, although in typically unfortunate 19th century termino-

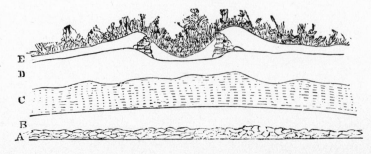

48 Dall's cross-section of a shell-heap excavation in the Aleutian Islands, Alaska. A original hardpan, B echinus layer, C fishbone layer, D mammalian layer, E modern deposits and vegetable mold.

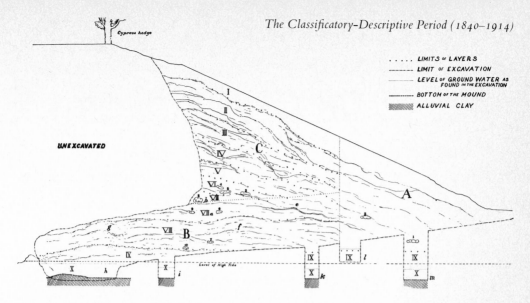

Cypress hedge

UNEXCAVATED

I
II
III
IV
V
VI
VII
VIIa
VIII B
IX
X

C
A
e
f
g
l
k
m
h
i

Level of High Tide

· · · · · LIMITS of LAYERS
‒ ‒ ‒ ‒ LIMIT of EXCAVATION
———— LEVEL of GROUND WATER as FOUND in the EXCAVATION
- - - - - - BOTTOM of the MOUND
▨▨▨▨ ALLUVIAL CLAY

49 Uhle's cross-section drawing of strata in the Emeryville (California) Shell-mound. (From Uhle 1907)

logy he talks of 'lower' and 'higher' stages of culture. Perhaps Dall's geological knowledge and background as a naturalist enabled him to view the archaeological data in a more skillful manner than many of his contemporaries.[73]

It is unfortunate that Dall's excavations were not followed up in new localities and that his article and three-period scheme, along with the methodology used to formulate it, seem to have had no impact at all on other archaeologists of the time. Both the remoteness of the Aleutians and lack of follow-up excavations may have helped to obscure Dall's advances.

Max Uhle, fresh from his excavations in Peru, made a significant breakthrough in his excavations at Emeryville Shell-mound in the San Francisco Bay area of California.[74] Uhle, a German, had been trained in his native land before coming to the United States. He excavated in Peru for both the University of Pennsylvania and the University of California. These important digs will be discussed later in the South American section. At Emeryville, Uhle clearly excavated parts of the mound 'stratum by stratum.'[75] He discusses the age of the mound and the cultural stages represented by the ten principal strata. He even includes a table which shows the number of implements in the mound, stratum by stratum,[76] and clearly indicates that 'It is evident that the character of the objects in the upper strata is entirely different from that of the implements which are found in the lower beds.'[77] Uhle also recognized continuity from stratum to stratum. Uhle compares the Emeryville Shell-mound with others on the West Coast, East Coast, and even in Denmark. He argues that it was occupied for more than a thousand years, and that cultural change is definitely evident in the changing contents of successive layers. Uhle's work was followed by that of Nels C. Nelson, a student of A. L. Kroeber, at the Ellis Landing Shell-mound and others of the San Francisco Bay region.[78] Nelson, however, did not advance Uhle's work any further and, in fact, Nelson in contrast to his later innovative work in the Southwest tended to be much more cautious in his interpretations than Uhle.[79]

49

Unfortunately, Uhle's work did not have the impact that it deserved. Certain aspects of his Emeryville report might leave something to be desired, but Uhle still utilized and saw the significance of culture change through stratigraphic succession. However, A. L. Kroeber, who was in charge of the Department of Anthropology at the University of California and was the Administrator of the Hearst funds which supported the work of Uhle and other archaeologists, did not approve of Uhle's conclusions. It is ironic that Kroeber, who within a decade became a champion of the historical use of archaeological data, was unable to accept Uhle's findings. In his contribution to the Putnam Anniversary Volume in 1909, Kroeber blasted Uhle's conclusions although he did not mention Uhle by name. 'The one published account of a systematic though partial exploration of a shell-heap of San Francisco Bay,' he states, 'upholds the view of a distinct progression and development of civilization having taken place during the growth of the deposit. An independent examination of the material on which this opinion is reared, tends to negate rather than to confirm it.'[80] Kroeber was unable to accept evidence of micro-change or small-scale cultural process in the archaeological record. As Rowe has so perspicaciously noted: 'Kroeber at this time [1909] visualized cultural change in terms of major shifts in technology and subsistence, any changes of less moment were insignificant. He could not comprehend Uhle's interest in all changes, however minute.'[81] Within a decade after Uhle's California excavations, archaeologists in Southwestern North America and Mexico did master the description of cultural micro-change and laid the foundation for the Classificatory-Historical Period; however, explanation of these changes was not to be seriously attempted in the Americas until after 1960.

Archaeological Research in Middle America

The development of archaeology in Middle America (or Mesoamerica) paralleled that of North America in general trends, although its tempo and concerns were quite different from those of North America. Middle American archaeology had also been influenced by Europe, but more by individual Europeans than by general intellectual or archaeological developments there, in contrast to North America. The differences between the two areas was obviously related to the relative richness and grandeur of the Middle American remains as well as the presence of a great native literature and indigenous writing systems. These latter attracted the interests of European and North American scholars who devoted much energy to their study and decipherment. The differences in outlook and consequences of the Spanish Conquest versus the English and French colonization, noted in the previous chapter, are also relevant in terms of the development of differences in the two areas.

The beginning of the Classificatory-Descriptive Period in Middle America was marked by the two explorations in Yucatan and Central America by John L. Stephens, a lawyer,[82] jointly with Frederick Catherwood, an architect and artist, and the

publication of their *Incidents of Travel in Central America, Chiapas, and Yucatan* in 1841 and *Incidents of Travel in Yucatan* in 1843.[83] Stephens had previously travelled extensively in the Old World and had published three accounts of his explorations.[84] The work of Stephens and Catherwood literally opened up the field of Mayan archaeology in particular and Mesoamerican archaeology in general. As has been said:

'The explorations alone of these men would mark them as important figures in Maya archaeology, but the straightforward uncolored description of Stephens, and the accurate drawings of Catherwood, assisted by the use of daguerreotype and camera lucida, left a work of immense value, Stephens' sound opinion, moreover, as to the indigenous origin of the ruins and their lack of tremendous age was of great importance at a time when there was so much loose thought on the subject.'[85]

The two *Incidents of Travel . . .* were widely read and stimulated new explorations and writings. Moreover, like *Ancient Monuments of the Mississippi Valley* by Squier and Davis, the volumes of Stephens and Catherwood became models for new work.

These two explorers were followed by a diverse and colorful group of men including Charnay, a Frenchman who made the first photographs of Maya ruins;[86] Le Plongeon, who made some early excavations and was one of the most fantastic characters in American archaeology;[87] Alfred P. Maudslay, an Englishman who explored and mapped many sites including Yaxchilan and Copan and published the huge *Biologia Centrali Americana*, which includes four volumes of archaeology;[88] Teobert Maler who worked for the Peabody Museum and mapped, photographed, and carefully described a number of Maya ruins;[89] Adolph Bastian and S. Habel, two Germans who wrote about the sculptures of Santa Lucia Cotzumalhuapa in the Guatemalan

50 Drawing of a palace at Yaxchilan. This site was designated as 'Lorillard City' by Charnay. (From Charnay 1887)

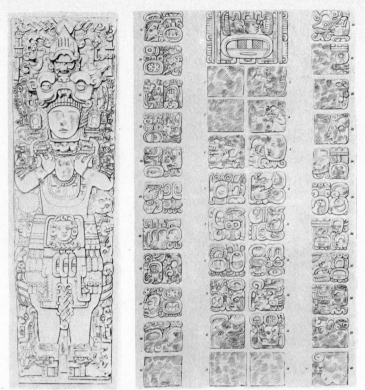

51 (*Right*) Drawing of Copan, Honduras Stela 2. (From Maudslay 1889–1902)

52 (*Far right*) An Initial Series and hieroglyphic text from the back and sides of Stela 2, Copan, Honduras. Drawings such as this were invaluable to the interpreters of Maya glyphs, such as J. T. Goodman. (From Maudslay, 1889–1902)

Highlands;[90] Karl Sapper, a geographer and ethnographer who classified ruins into architectural types and related these to ethnographic and linguistic areas;[91] Thomas Gann, a doctor who surveyed and excavated in Honduras and British Honduras;[92] and E.H. Thompson, the American Consul in Yucatan who dredged the great Sacred Cenote at Chichen Itza and explored other ruins.[93]

56

The Maya area was the center of most of the activity, but work was also done in Central Mexico. Leopoldo Batres worked at the great site of Teotihuacan,[94] Zelia Nuttall published studies on a wide variety of Mexican archaeological topics; W. H. Holmes, whom we discussed earlier, also made an important contribution to Mesoamerican archaeology. In *Archaeological Studies among the Ancient Cities of Mexico*, Holmes classified ceramic vessels and various kinds of ceremonial architecture and attempted careful archaeological comparisons.[95]

55

The combined work of these men and women helped to form the descriptive background of Middle American, and especially Mayan, archaeology and paved the way for the advances of the following Classificatory-Historical Period.

The first important large-scale excavations in Middle America were undertaken at the major Classic Maya center of Copan, Honduras by the Peabody Museum of Harvard University. The work was conducted by M. H. Saville, John Owens, who died in the field, and G. B. Gordon; and the results were published as part of a new series of Memoirs of the Peabody Museum.[96] These reports were almost totally descriptive in content and tone. New

54

53 (*Opposite*) An example of Maler's fabulous photography. Stela 11 at Seibal, Peten, Guatemala

54 (*Left*) Photograph of a Copan stela taken during the Peabody Museum's excavations of the 1890s. Compare with Catherwood's drawing of Copan stela 2 (Ill. 1)

55 (*Above*) W.H. Holmes's drawing of the ruins of Teotihuacan in the Valley of Mexico. The artist's view looks from back of the Pyramid of the Moon down the 'Street of the Dead'. The famed Pyramid of the Sun (B) lies on the left as does the enclosure (E) designated as the Ciudadela. This sketch is an example of Holmes's masterly draftsmanship. It is amazingly accurate even though done impressionistically. (From Holmes 1895–7)

56 (*Right*) E.H. Thompson using a palace room at Labna, Yucatan, Mexico as an office *ca.* 1890

57 The Maya ruins of Palenque,
Chiapas, Mexico. Photograph
taken early in the 20th century

58 Sculptured head of the 'Maize
God' from Copan, Honduras

59 Temple I at the Maya Lowland site of Tikal, Guatemala. Photograph taken at
the time of Tozzer's explorations there (*ca.* 1911)

59   steps forward were taken with the work of Alfred M. Tozzer[97] and R. E. Merwin in the Maya Lowlands and Edgar L. Hewett and Sylvanus G. Morley at Quirigua. In descriptive treatments, their works were virtually modern in the accuracy of recording and completeness of presentation. They also attempted some chronology, but this was through relating their excavated buildings and tombs to hieroglyphic inscriptions and Maya calendrical dates recorded on associated monuments.[98]

It is in the realm of hieroglyphic inscriptions and native literature that a second important theme emerges in our survey of Mesoamerican archaeology during the Classificatory-Descriptive Period. This field of study was dominated by Europeans including the Abbé Brasseur de Bourbourg, Ernst W. Förstemann, Edward Seler, and Léon de Rosny, although Americans such as Cyrus Thomas, D. G. Brinton, Joseph T. Goodman, and Charles P.

60   Bowditch also made important contributions. The interests of most of these men were definitely humanistic in nature and none of them, with the exception of Thomas, was actually a practicing field archaeologist. Their studies, however, did aid Mesoamerican archaeologists in several significant aspects.

The work of Förstemann, who has been called 'the father of

61   Maya hieroglyphic research,[99] on the Dresden Codex (an original Maya book) led him to the decipherment of much of the numerical and calendrical data in it.[100] It thus became possible for archaeologists to date inscribed monuments in the Maya area. The work of Brasseur de Bourbourg on Landa's *Relación de las Cosas de Yucatán*[101] and native Maya documents from Yucatan and the Guatemalan Highlands,[102] respectively, provided much useful data which the archaeologist could use for numerous analogies with Maya civilization of more ancient times and gave them a great appreciation of the development and richness of that civilization just prior to the Spanish Conquest.

The wealth of data on the Maya, as well as the other great civilizations of Mesoamerica, was later to prove a boon to archaeologists as they began to investigate scientifically processual problems such as the rise of settled village life and civilization and the development of cities and the state. The rich data, however, had a somewhat negative impact as well. For many decades throughout the Classificatory-Descriptive and Classificatory-Historical Periods, the relatively vast quantities of data about the élite aspects of Maya civilization, especially the religious, and the obvious magnificence of élite architecture and art arrested the archaeologists' attention and kept his efforts within an artificially narrow scope. Historical reconstruction of the Mesoamerican past became the historical reconstruction of the élite past. This narrow purview was not to be shattered until late in the Classificatory-Historical Period.

Finally, in more general terms, note should be taken of Prescott's monumental account of the conquest of Mexico by the Spanish.[103] In this connection, the doubts of Lewis Henry Morgan and Bandelier as to the culturally advanced nature of the Aztec state should also be pointed out.[104] The question was one of both interpretation and classification. Morgan and Bandelier reasoned from prior evolutionary assumptions and tended to belittle the accomplishments of the Aztecs, believing that there was no true native American civilization. Although it is now quite apparent that Morgan and Bandelier were wrong, their raising of these questions about the cultural level and the nature of Aztec socio-political organization foreshadowed concerns of a later period when archaeologists turned to questions of cultural development.

In 1914, at the very end of the period, Thomas A. Joyce, a British archaeologist, was able to draw together all the available archaeological data on Mesoamerican archaeology in a general work entitled *Mexican Archaeology*.[105] He attempted to set up a chronology for the area based on the dates on carved Maya monuments and the sequences offered by native legends and traditions. One year earlier, however, an even more important study was produced by H. J. Spinden.[106] *A Study of Maya Art* was definitely a precocious work, which still provides many stimulating hypotheses about Maya culture. Most significantly, Spinden attempted to order Maya art chronologically with the evolutionary development of stylistic traits as the framework for this chronological sequence. By 1914, a new age in Mesoamerican archaeology was definitely dawning.

60 Charles P. Bowditch, from a portrait by Ignace Gaugengigl. Bowditch, an accomplished scholar in Maya astronomy and mathematics, was the principal patron of Harvard's Peabody Museum in its early Maya archaeological program

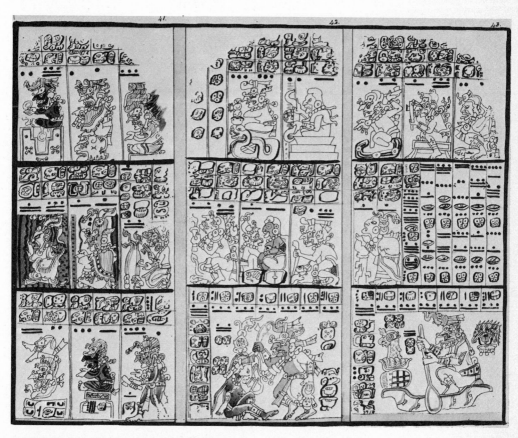

61 Pages from the Dresden Codex, which was the document used by Förstemann in much of his decipherment work. (From Kingsborough 1831–9)

Conventional archaeology of the Classificatory-Descriptive Period was carried out in a number of places in South America. Much of it approached the tradition of Stephens and Catherwood: that is, traveller's accounts, well illustrated and generally accurate in factual reporting. Peru, that area of the continent with the most spectacular ruins, attracted the most interest, and such books on the archaeology (and living native peoples) of Peru began to appear in the 1850s and continued on into the 20th century. Among some of the best known are those by Tschudi,[107] Castelnau,[108] Wiener,[109] Middendorf,[110] and Squier,[111] the last being the Squier of Mississippi Valley fame. Perhaps the leading Peruvianist of the time, in the sense of high quality of scholarship, was Sir Clements Markham.[112] Excavation accounts, too, were published in the period, including those of Reiss and Stübel[113] and Bandelier.[114] But the outstanding figure for the Classificatory-Descriptive Period in Peru, and in South America as a whole, was Max Uhle. Uhle was more of an archaeologist, in the present-day 'dirt-archaeological' sense of that word, than any of the others. His substantive contributions were great, and, from a methodological standpoint, he should be regarded as an important transitional figure between the Classificatory-Descriptive and the Classificatory-Historical Periods.

63, 64

62

Uhle[115] was born and trained in Germany, beginning in philology but switching soon after receiving his academic degree to archaeology and ethnography. While a curator in the Dresden Museum he met Alphons Stübel, who, with Wilhelm Reiss, had just excavated the Ancon cemetery on the Peruvian coast. Stübel collaborated with the young Uhle on a study of notes and photographs which the former had made at Tiahuanaco. Together, they brought out *Die Ruinenstaette von Tiahuanaco* in 1892.[116] That same year Uhle began field research in South America and continued there, intermittently, for over thirty years. His most brilliant work was in Peru-Bolivia in the 1890s and the first decade of the 20th century. Later, he was to work in Chile and Ecuador.

65, 66

67–69

His museum work in Germany had given Uhle a commanding knowledge of Inca and Tiahuanaco pottery and sculptural styles, and this served him well in his major field excavation in Peru, that at the great site of Pachacamac, just south of Lima, on the Peruvian coast. It was here that he set the first important stake in a Peruvian area chronology. Knowing the Inca materials from the site to be just anterior to the Spanish Conquest, and knowing Tiahuanaco and Tiahuanaco-like styles to be fully Pre-Columbian, he reasoned that a third distinct style of pottery, which showed no Tiahuanacoid influence but was sometimes associated with Incaic pieces, had an intermediate chronological position. In other words, Uhle was applying both stylistic and associational seriation on a similiary principle. He was familiar with stratigraphic principles, and some grave and structural superpositions at Pachacamac further verified this sequence; yet most of Uhle's Peruvian digging was a search for graves and a careful recording of grave lot associations so that he never put stratigraphy to the test there in refuse excavations.

62 Max Uhle

63 The Inca ruins of Ollantaytambo, Peru. (From Squier, 1877)

64 The 'Gateway of the Sun' at Tiahuanaco, Bolivia. (From Squier, 1877)

65 Excavating in the cemetery of Ancon, Coastal Peru. (From Reiss and Stübel, 1880–7)

66 Drawings of pottery from the Ancon cemetery. These specimens are represented with good accuracy and can be identified easily as to styles as these are defined today (Inca, Chimu, etc.). (From Reiss and Stübel, 1880–7)

67 (Opposite) The 'Gateway of the Sun', Tiahuanaco. This photograph was taken by Stübel in the late 19th century. Compare it with Squier's drawing (Ill. 64). (From Stübel and Uhle, 1892)

68 Diagrammatical drawing of the 'Gateway of the Sun', Tiahuanaco. Prepared as a key to the iconographic descriptions of the text. (From Stübel and Uhle, 1892)

76

69 The central figure from the 'Gateway of the Sun', Tiahuanaco. Photography of this excellent quality characterized some of the archaeological work of the latter part of the Classificatory-Descriptive Period. (From Stübel and Uhle, 1892)

70, 71

It was, however, in an interim between the Peruvian expeditions that he did the stratigraphic digging in the California shell-mounds. The Pachacamac explorations were published in 1903, in Philadelphia, by the University of Pennsylvania, and the report remains one of the monuments of American archaeology.[117] Uhle went on from the Pachacamac findings to propound a Peruvian area-wide chronological scheme. Other coastal excavations indicated that earlier advanced styles antedated Tiahuanaco-stylistic influence. He thus had a four-period sequence:[118] (1) early regional styles; (2) Tiahuanaco-influenced styles; (3) late regional styles; and (4) Inca-influenced styles. The efficacy of the chronology was demonstrated at a number of places along the Peruvian coast, including the Rimac, Ancon, Chancay, and Moche Valleys.[119] It utilized the principle of 'horizon styles' – in this case Tiahuanaco and Inca – and it has withstood the test of seventy years of subsequent research, being modified only by the discovery of earlier archaeological cultures and horizons.[120]

In 1912 Uhle left Peru to work in Chile and, later, in Ecuador. While he contributed significantly to the developing discipline of archaeology in both countries, his overall success was somewhat less. In Chile, Incaic and Tiahuanacoid relationships were pointed out, and Uhle recognized the north Chilean coastal preceramic cultures.[121] He dubbed the latter 'Paleolithic,' but, as Rowe has explained, he was claiming no great age for them, only 'exercising the comparative method of the cultural evolutionists.'[122] In Ecuador there was more of a descriptive archaeological base than there had been in Chile. This went back to the systematic

work of Fedérico González Suárez, beginning in 1878,[123] and also included explorations, excavations, and publications by the North Americans, G. A. Dorsey[124] and M. H. Saville[125] (both protégés of Putnam), and the French anthropologist, Paul Rivet.[126] What the situation needed was sound chronological ordering. The task, however, was more difficult than in Peru; for one thing, there were no easily recognizable horizon markers. Incaic influence could be identified in parts of the country, but the attempt to extend the Tiahuanaco horizon so far north met with failure. By this time, too, Uhle's interests in work of confined regional scope seemed to be lagging. His later Ecuadorian writings show an increased tendency to follow out extreme diffusionist theories, with the Middle American Maya, the *fons et origo* of New World higher cultures, about which he knew nothing at first hand.[127] Uhle

70, 71 The ruins of Pachacamac, Peru (*above*); Uhle's cross-section drawing of architectural and grave stratigraphy at Pachacamac (*below*). (From Uhle, 1903)

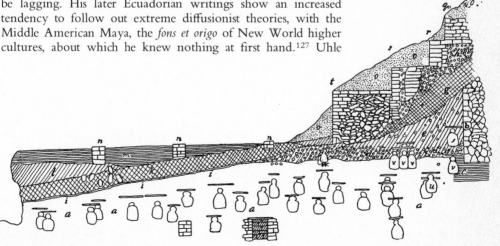

79

remained in Ecuador until 1933, and after this he continued writing and library and museum research up to the time of his death in 1944; however, it is a fair judgment to say that his truly influential work was over long before this and that, indeed, it had been done in Peru before 1912.

In retrospect, Uhle appears at the very top of any list of the outstanding archaeologists of the Classificatory-Descriptive Period; and, in fact, he helped transform American archaeology of that period and bring about a new era. He was ahead of any of his contemporaries in a realization of the importance of chronology. This is summed up perfectly in his statement:

'In Americanist studies, the first thing that had to be done was to introduce the idea of time, to get people to admit that the types could change.'[128]

This shows a sophisticated awareness of cultural micro-change of the sort that Flinders Petrie was then propounding, and Uhle had been influenced by Petrie.[129] In fact, Uhle's archaeological sophistication must be attributed, in very large part, to his European background, training, and continued contacts. He was not hampered by the parochial view of many of the Americans, both North and South, who tended to conceive of New World archaeology of a kind of undifferentiated time plane of the American Indians and their forbears. Uhle was able to apply seriational and limited methods to resolve problems of chronology. He was clearly at his best when operating with the specifics of a relatively limited cultural-geographical area, such as Peru; and, in our opinion, his cultural evolutionary theoretical orientation stood him in good stead here.[130] It convinced him that 'the types could change' through time. When he projected these theories farther afield he was on shaky ground; neither the information nor the proper comparative approach was at hand. An excess of uncritical diffusionism also marred his later work.

Nowhere else in South America was there anyone of Uhle's stature as an archaeologist. Perhaps if Baron Erland von Nordenskiöld had gone in more for archaeology, rather than restricting his principal efforts to ethnography, he would have made comparable contributions to prehistory. Nordenskiöld's one serious archaeological field attempt, the excavation of dwelling and burial mounds in the Bolivian lowlands, resulted in important stratigraphic observations on one mound and the definitions of an earlier and a later culture. This was published in 1913, at the very close of the Classificatory-Descriptive Period.[131] Another case of stratigraphy or superposition was recorded a few years earlier by the Argentine archaeologist, J. B. Ambrosetti, who, excavating at Pampa Grande, in the northwestern part of that country, defined a grave sequence.[132] Argentine archaeologists were quite active in the late 19th and early 20th centuries, working from museums and universities. As in the United States, the methods were classificatory and distributional, and archaeological remains were studied in concert with ethnography and ethnohistory. Ambrosetti[133] was the best of the group, in many ways comparable – in his broad knowledge and careful reporting – to W. H. Holmes in

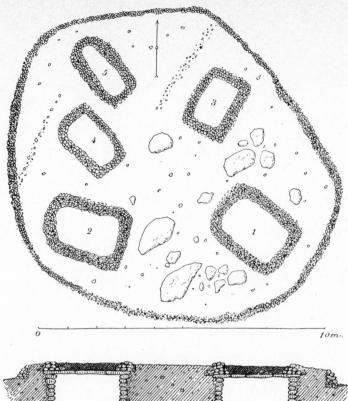

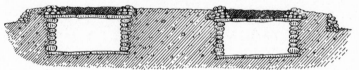

72 Plan and cross-section drawing of burial enclosure in Costa Rica. (From Hartman, 1901)

North America. An Argentine colleague, S. Debenedetti,[134] deserves mention, as do the Swedish explorer-archaeologists, Eric Boman[135] and Count von Rosen.[136] For the Argentine lowlands, L.M. Torres[137] made a valuable contribution on Paraná delta archaeology, and F.F. Outes[138] established himself as the leading authority on the archaeology of the Pampas-Patagonia. This was also the time of Ameghino's claims for very early artifacts from the Argentine littoral, claims which Hrdlička and others effectively demolished.[139]

Elsewhere in South America archaeology of the period was descriptive, occasionally classificatory, and sometimes there were attempts to relate archaeological remains to historic Indian groups. The latter exercise was often quite uncritical, with relation to the proof of prehistoric-to-historic continuities assumed. William Bollaert[140] wrote on Colombia, and Vicente Restrepo[141] brought out his well-known monograph on Chibchan ethnohistory (and archaeology). Marcano[142] and Karl von den Steinen[143] reported on excavations in Venezuela. J.W. Fewkes[144] was a principal worker in the West Indies, and Thomas A. Joyce[145] devoted a part of a book to the archaeology of that area. This same book of Joyce's also included Central America, where Squier,[146] Holmes,[147] MacCurdy,[148] and Hartman[149] all worked. C.V. Hartman's archaeological researches in Costa Rica are worthy of special note.

72

73 Marajó ceramics, from
Marajó Island, Brazil. (From
Hartt, 1885)

73

A European-trained scholar, he was appreciative of grave lot segregation and grave superposition. All in all, he was a careful fieldworker, and his well-illustrated and presented publications were outstanding for their time. Of all the South Americanists (if we include Costa Rica in this geographic assemblage), he was the best archaeologist except for Uhle. In Brazil there were excavations on the Amazon and in Brazilian Guiana by Derby,[150] Hartt,[151] Farabee,[152] Steere,[153] and Goeldi[154] and, farther south, Hermann von Ihering dug in the coastal sambaquis.[155] Inland, in Minas Gerais, argument continued over the Lagoa Santa crania.[156] Finally, we should mention Thomas Joyce's other book, on South American archaeology as a whole.[157] It appeared in 1912 and, like his *Mexican Archaeology* of 1914, was the first of its kind to attempt to give an archaeologic-ethnohistoric story of the whole continent. Based wholly upon library and museum research, it is a remarkable and admirable summary of the state of archaeological knowledge for South America at the close of the Classificatory-Descriptive Period.

The rise of systematic archaeology, the beginnings of scientific geology, and Darwinian evolutionism – all European developments of the mid 19th century – were the stimuli that gave rise to the formal discipline of archaeology in America. The old mold of sheerly speculative thought about the antiquities of the past was broken. Carefully recorded description and classification of the phenomena of the past had begun, and typologies were developed; geographical distributions of the data were plotted; archaeological field techniques were greatly improved; a vastly greater amount of field exploration was carried out than ever before; and all of this was accompanied by a steadily growing professionalization of the discipline in an academic alliance with anthropology as a whole. Such was the positive picture. On the negative side, there was a failure to develop control of the chronological dimension of the data, especially through stratigraphy. The period also witnessed a decline, toward its end, in the evolutionary theory that had stimulated and informed its inception.

To turn to the positive aspects first, pioneer work on classification of stone artifacts in the Descriptive-Classificatory Period was carried out in North America by Charles Rau of the Smithsonian Institution.[158] Thomas Wilson,[159] Curator of the United States National Museum, also made contributions of this nature, as did Gerard Fowke.[160] Wilson's interests appear to have flowed naturally from his official position. The United States Congress was eager to make the Museum the primary repository for important and representative collections of native antiquities from all parts of the nation, and the Museum's curators had to devise schemes for the classification, exhibition, and storage of the collections. While this was a step in the right direction, it also led to a tendency to consider the specimens in isolated cross-cultural classes. That is, all stone axes, from all over the United States, were grouped together rather than being considered within a framework of culture complexes or units.[161] The culture-complex concept had not yet emerged with any clarity in American archaeology. Nevertheless in spite of its limitations, artifact classification of the 19th century was 'on the side of the angels' in that it pointed the way toward systematic treatment and objective examination.

Classificatory advances were also made in the treatment of earthworks of the Eastern United States, as may be seen by comparing the Squier and Davis 1848 report with that of Thomas's survey published in 1894. Such progress followed faithfully the directive of Joseph Henry's *Annual Report of the Smithsonian Institution for 1874*:

'It is considered important to collect all possible information as to the location and character of ancient earthworks, which exist in various parts of the United States, with a view to classify them and determine their distribution in relation to special topographical features of the country as well as to different regions.'[162]

W.H. Holmes performed the outstanding typological and classificatory work of the period on the pottery of the Eastern United States.[163] Holmes worked with the available literature and with hundreds of pottery collections which, for the most part, bore only general geographical provenience. His monograph, published in 1903, was a major substantive contribution for it laid the groundwork of archaeological knowledge for ceramics for a large part of North America. In it he went beyond previous studies, since for the first time in the New World field great attention was paid to minor stylistic differences in ceramic designs and forms and in the materials and inferred methods of their manufacture. These several criteria, taken in conjunction, enabled Holmes to identify several well-defined pottery regions within the Eastern United States. American archaeologists had long been cognizant of geographical-cultural variation. At first they had simply recognized that the archaeological remains of a certain arbitrarily defined region – as, for example, in *The Antiquities of Tennessee*[164] – were different from those of another such region similarly selected. Holmes put this into systematic comparative perspective and in doing so, he participated in, and contributed to, the 'culture area' formulations of Mason[165] and Wissler.[166]

75

Good typological control of the archaeological data did lead to other conceptual advances in some instances. These were, however, relatively little developed by most scholars and would not become standard parts of archaeological thinking until the next period. For example, the integrative concept of a specific 'culture' was used frequently and effectively by Max Uhle, in Peru. Mills also employed it in Ohio.[167] Yet the concept remained vaguely defined in most of its substantive applications and not defined at all as an abstract methodological device. The broader integrative concept of 'horizon style' was used very successfully by Uhle who established the first American area chronology by this means. In this, as in many other things, Uhle was well ahead of his time; but he appears to have taken the 'horizon' concept for granted, never applying this name to it nor trying to define it as a concept. The still more inclusive concept of culture stage, which combines both historical and evolutionary dimensions, was evoked by some writers of the Classificatory-Descriptive Period; but this followed along, more or less, with the European-derived 'Savagery-Barbarism-Civilization' concepts of the day and was little more than an affirmation of faith in the doctrine of 'psychic unity.' The assumed developmental levels of culture were not tested against the real American data. Indeed, there was no way to do this without adequate chronologies, of which almost none existed.

There was some interest in use of functional explanations of the archaeological data. Squier and Davis[168] employed a simple functional classification to the mounds and earthworks they investigated and classified, inferring function in a very general analogical way – burial places, building platforms, fortifications, etc. There was considerable speculation about the way artifacts functioned, and even a measure of experimentation to test some of these speculations or hypotheses.[169] More significantly, a very few archaeologists, notably Cushing among the Zuñi, tried to arrive at functional explanations of prehistoric artifact forms by comparing them with those of their presumed tribal descendants among living Indians.[170] Archaeologists of the period also showed some

74 Modern pueblo pottery-making as depicted by Cushing. (From Cushing, 1886)

MAP OF
NORTH AMERICA

interest in the possible influences of natural environment on cultural development. This was usually with relation to site locations and resource utilization; or, in some instances, environment was seen as the real determinant of culture. In neither case, however, was there any systematic consideration of environment in archaeological studies that even vaguely resembled that of modern ecology.

As we have noted, the sheer quantity of archaeological work in North, Middle, and South America increased throughout the Classificatory-Descriptive Period. Museums, both in Europe and in the Americas, sponsored fieldwork to obtain specimens for display, and there was a growing interest in archaeological work

75 'Cultural Characterization Areas' based on archaeological data. I North Atlantic; II Georgia–Florida; III Middle, Lower Mississippi Valley; IV Upper Mississippi–Great Lakes; V Great Plains–Rocky Mountains; VI The arid region; VII California; VIII Columbia–Fraser; IX Northwest Coast; X Arctic Shoreland; XI Great Northern Interior; XII Northern Mexico; XIII Middle Mexico; XIV Southern Mexico; XV Maya Province; XVI Central America. (From Holmes, 1914)

on the part of governments in the United States and in Latin America. This led to the founding of new museums and participation in international expositions (such as the 1892 Columbian Exposition in Chicago) and scientific congresses (such as the biennial Congress of Americanists which began in 1875).

The general increase in archaeological interest and activity and the professionalization of the subject were intimately bound up with the academic development of archaeology, especially in the United States. Brinton founded a department for the teaching of archaeology and anthropology at Pennsylvania, and Putnam did the same at Harvard.

From the very beginning, American archaeology was in close alliance with the rest of anthropology. Actually, the links were first firmly forged in the Smithsonian Institution by J. W. Powell who, as Chief of the Bureau of Ethnology, also instigated the mound and earthwork archaeological survey of Cyrus Thomas who was in his employ. The obvious importance of a related archaeological-ethnological attack upon the problems of the American Indian and his origins was an upshot of Thomas's mound survey and the demonstration that the earthworks had, indeed, been constructed by the forbears of the Indians. The physical anthropological study of skeletal material from the mounds was also found to be relevant to the solution of such problems, and this third major branch of anthropology was brought into the American alliance. All of this stands in notable contrast to the situation in the Old World where the three disciplines tended to develop separately. Many of the differences between New World archaeology and Old World archaeology can be traced to this time and to this turn of events in the Americas.

American archaeology has, undoubtedly, benefited greatly from this association within the house of anthropology. Through it archaeologists have been made more aware of the structural variation of simpler cultures. It has also helped power a unified attack upon problems of culture history by the way of a 'direct-historical approach' from the ethnographic present into the archaeological past and has provided the archaeologist with a rich reservoir of information for ethnographic analogies pertinent for prehistoric situations. But, we think, there has also been a debit side to the alliance. The distrust of evolutionary thinking and the marked historical particularism of American anthropology forced the American archaeologist into a niche with a very limited horizon. The strength of archaeology is its perspective in which it examines culture change and development through time. These were definitely not the objectives of the American anthropological-ethnological establishment as it emerged into the 20th century.[171] As a result, archaeology enjoyed little esteem and soon became the intellectual 'poor boy' in the field of anthropology.

The rejection of cultural evolutionism in American anthropology began with Franz Boas and his students. Various reasons have been cited for this,[172] and we will not try to go into them here. It is, however, fair to note that by the late 19th century many of the claims of the evolutionists had become absurd. The most obvious instances of culture contact and diffusion were ignored;

cultural similarity was explained by 'psychic unity' operating within the severe constraints of uniform culture stages. Boas demanded a return to factual evidence and to what was to be called 'historical particularism.' It was a salutary reaction, but like many such it was carried too far. One might have thought that American archaeology would have withstood this reaction, would have profited from an insistence upon firm evidence and then gone on with its essentially diachronic task. But it did not, and this we believe was owing to three factors. First, there was a lack of any well-documented long-term culture sequence in the New World. The Early Man claims of the Classificatory-Descriptive Period had not stood up to critical scrutiny. Thus, at the beginning of the 20th century there was no good evidence that the American aborigines had been in this hemisphere for any appreciable length of time. Second, there was no good support for significant or major culture change within the archaeological evidence that pertained to the Indians and their ancestors. And third, and closely related, there was no concept of micro-change in culture and its importance. Uhle was the notable exception, as we have seen; but his influence, or the influence of the ideas which he represented, was not to spread to the rest of the Americas until the beginning of the Classificatory-Historical Period. Culture change still had to be viewed in broad outline. The models were those of the Old World jump from Paleolithic to Neolithic or the social theorist's stage scheme of 'Savagery-Barbarism-Civilization.' American archaeologists of the time could not adduce evidence for such dramatic macro-change on the New World scene, and so they felt they were in no position to rebut the historical particularists.

These factors reveal the weaknesses of American archaeology as being as much responsible for the outcome of events as Boasian anti-evolutionism, if not more so. Without the stratigraphic method, the American archaeologist of the turn of the century was in no position to determine culture sequences and to develop any concept of small-scale cultural change through time; conversely, until such a concept could be appreciated he would be slow to conduct stratigraphic excavations with this as a goal. All of this tended to be reinforced by an anti-evolutionary intellectual climate where a search for such change was hardly an important research target. In another score of years American archaeologists would break out of this self-defeating circle. Ironically, Boas would be one of those instrumental in helping them do it.[173] For the time being, though, the loss of the evolutionary mode of thought also meant the loss of general problem orientation in American archaeology. Problems, such as they were, remained specifically historical. More general questions of development, function, and process were left alone. After the 'stratigraphic revolution' of the Classificatory-Historical Period American archaeology began to build a solid culture-historical foundation. On this foundation it has since constructed, largely from its own resources, a new conceptual framework; and today there is a new alliance with anthropology. But this takes us far ahead of our story. Our immediate concerns now are the developments of the Classificatory-Historical Period.

Chapter Four

The Classificatory-Historical Period:
The Concern with Chronology (1914–40)

'Chronology is at the root of the matter, being the nerve electrifying the dead body of history.' Berthold Laufer

A Definition of the Period

THE central theme of the Classificatory-Historical Period in American archaeology was the concern for chronology. The name of the period, 'historical,' carries this implication, at least insofar as the minimum of history is a time-ordering of events. We will consider the period in two parts; an earlier, extending from 1914 until 1940, which will be the subject of this chapter, and a later, from 1940 until 1960, which will be dealt with in Chapter Five. While the search for chronology prevailed in both the earlier and later parts of the period it was especially dominant in the earlier; after 1940 other problems began to compete for attention.

Stratigraphic excavation was the primary method in the drive for chronological control of the data. It was introduced to American archaeology in about 1914, and in the next two decades spread to most parts of the New World. The principle of seriation was allied to stratigraphy, and, also serving chronological ends, it developed alongside, and in conjunction with, stratigraphic studies. Typology and classification, which had their systematic beginnings in the previous Classificatory-Descriptive Period, now became geared to stratigraphic and seriational procedures. Whereas earlier classifications of artifacts had been merely for the purposes of describing the material, they were now seen as devices to aid the plotting of culture forms in time and space. Besides artifact classifications, American archaeologists also began culture classifications. These, too, were strongly influenced by chronological considerations.

Beyond the immediacy of stratigraphic, seriational, and classificatory methods, the ultimate objectives of American archaeology in the Classificatory-Historical Period were culture-historical syntheses of New World regions and areas. Some of these began to appear before 1940. For the most part, they tended to be mere skeletons of history – pottery type or artifact sequences and distributions. Some archaeologists did attempt to clothe these skeletons in more substantial cultural contexts. The old close relationship between American archaeology and ethnology led easily to the use of ethnographic analogies in interpretations of use and function in prehistoric cultures; and the interest in the relationships between culture and the natural environment that had its beginnings in the culture area concepts of the ethnologists provided a base for cultural-ecological study. But prior to 1940 these trends were barely in the making; only later did they come into prominence.

Lastly, the early part of the Classificatory-Historical Period was characterized by continued improvements of field methods and excavation. These refinements were, indeed, a necessary part of the stratigraphic method which so dominated the period. They were also a part of the recognition of the importance of a careful recovery of materials and features.

The 'Stratigraphic Revolution'

The stratigraphic method had been developed in European geology and adapted to European and Mediterranean archaeology. It was known in the Americas at least as early as the 1860s, and we have told how Dall, Uhle, and others carried out occasional stratigraphic excavations. These operations included observations as to the superimposition of the strata and, at least in a gross way, a recording of their artifactual and feature contents. But the method did not become widely popular, nor was it much used by those few who showed an awareness of it.

The reasons for the delay in the acceptance of the stratigraphic method in American archaeology have been discussed in the preceding chapter. We believe that they lay in the general rejection of evolutionary thinking on the part of American archaeologists, the failure of the first Early Man studies, and a general lack of interest in cultural micro-change.[1] Cultural evolution appears to have been conceived of as a series of major, dramatic shifts. When these did not materialize in the American archaeological record, few archeologists gave attention to the problems of minor, gradual changes through time. Added to these reasons there may have been others of a less philosophical, more immediately practical, nature. Many American sites, especially those of Eastern North America, did not lend themselves readily to stratigraphic digging. Refuse deposits were thin and without easily discernible physical strata. Artificial burial tumuli and other earthworks were not ideal for stratigraphic purposes. Their constructions were often complex; they contained redeposited materials; and their excavation demanded sophisticated digging and interpretative techniques which had not yet been developed. The same disadvantages applied to the great mounds and pyramids of Mesoamerica and Peru. Deep refuse deposits did exist in some places, and, eventually, these would be disclosed; but for a time they went unnoticed. Thus, as we come up to the years just before World War I, little stratigraphic digging of consequence had been carried out in the Americas, and archaeological chronology was in its infancy.

The 'stratigraphic revolution' began at about the same time in two areas – Mesoamerica and the North American Southwest. The two archaeologists responsible for the innovation were Manuel Gamio and N. C. Nelson. Both were young scholars who had been trained in the rising new discipline of anthropology. Gamio had been a student of Franz Boas's, at Columbia University; and Nelson had worked under Kroeber (a former Boasian disciple) at Berkeley. Significantly, Boas played a part in Gamio's stratigraphic work. In 1911 Boas had become one of the directors of a short-lived organization known as the 'International School of

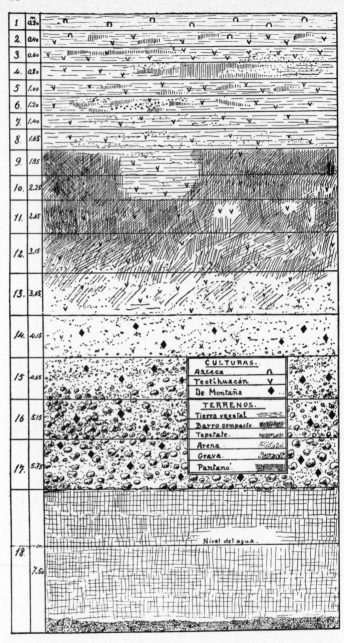

76 Cross-section diagram of Gamio's excavations at Atzcapotzalco, Valley of Mexico. Numbers of levels and metric depths at left. Soil strata indicated. The inverted 'U' symbol stands for presence of Aztec pottery; the 'V' for Teotihuacan; and the solid diamond for 'Archaic' pottery. (From Gamio, 1913)

American Ethnology and Archaeology', with offices in Mexico City. He, together with A.M. Tozzer and G.C. Engerrand, encouraged Gamio to conduct stratigraphic excavations in the Valley of Mexico in order to clarify and objectively demonstrate the sequence of Mexican Pre-Columbian cultures.[2] As far back as the 1880s W.H. Holmes[3] had observed that Aztec and earlier potsherds and artifacts were to be found in deep strata in the Valley of Mexico, but Holmes made no detailed stratigraphic examination of this situation. In 1911, Gamio, along with the German scholar

Eduard Seler, called Boas's attention to the archaeological zone of Atzcapotzalco where pottery fragments were found in great quantity on the surface and in barranca collections. Some of these pertained to the Aztec civilization, others to Teotihuacan, and still others to a third, unknown complex. While it was generally taken for granted that pottery of the Teotihuacan style preceded that of the Aztec, the position of the third, unidentified style was in doubt. Boas, in response, suggested stratigraphic digging to resolve this problem of sequence.

Gamio began his stratigraphic work by sinking a 7·00 meter deep test pit into the Atzcapotzalco refuse. Ceramics and other artifacts were removed from arbitrarily chosen levels of the pit. These varied from as little as 20 cm. in thickness to as much as 60 cm. Cultural materials were found to a depth of 5·75 meters below the surface. Although the digging and provenience lots were by arbitrary depth, considerable attention was paid to the depositional nature of the debris and soil and to its physical strata. 76 Aztec pottery was found rather superficially in the humus and dust of the two uppermost arbitrary levels; below this was Teotihuacan pottery, occurring in decomposed volcanic tufa down to a depth of about 4·15 meters; and from this latter depth down to 5·75 meters sherds of the unnamed ceramic group (tentatively referred to as the 'Tipo de los Cerros') were found in river sands and gravels which overlay sterile clay. This unnamed ceramic group was, indeed, soon to be called the 'Archaic' pottery of the Valley of Mexico. Subsequently, it would be referred to as 'Preclassic' or 'Formative' by a later generation of archaeologists. Gamio and his colleagues recognized it as similar to materials from Zacatenco and elsewhere, establishing an 'Archaic' pottery horizon for the valley. The Atzcapotzalco stratigraphic evidence also supported the interpretations of a gradual transition from this 'Archaic' horizon into that of the Teotihuacan culture. This interpretation of gradual cultural change appeared to be demonstrated by a mixture of both pottery styles in levels of intermediate depth as well as by the transitional nature of certain ceramic and figurine forms in these levels. No pottery counts were made, although a crude sort of quantification was attempted by weighing the potsherds from the various levels of the test pit. From this Gamio drew some conclusions about relative chronological durations of the respective occupations and the densities of these occupations – a procedure of rather dubious value. The true significance of Gamio's work lay in the fact that he had established the basic archaeological sequence for central Mexico. Seler and other scholars had long worked in the region but had seen things from a descriptive, typological, and iconographic point of view. While highly aware of ethnohistory, their perspective on the whole Pre-Columbian past was blurred and foreshortened. With Gamio's single pit, Middle American archaeologists began to appreciate time depth and, better yet, to realize that something could be done about it.[4]

Nelson's stratigraphy dates from three years after Gamio's but his use and refinements of the method go much further.[5] His background is pertinent in helping us trace the spread of ideas in

Thickness of Section	Corrugated Ware (1)	Biscuit Ware (2)	Type I, Two, and Three Color Painted Ware	Type II, Two Color Glazed Ware			Type III, Three Color Glazed Ware
			Black-on-White Painted Ware (3)	Red Ware, Black or Brown Glaze (4)	Yellow Ware, Black or Brown Glaze (5)	Gray Ware, Black or Brown Glaze (6)	Gray, Yellow, Pink and Reddish Wares, Combination Glaze-and-Paint Design (7)
1st. ft.	57	10	2	24	23	34	5
2d "	116	17	2	64	90	76	6
3d "	27	2	10	68	18	48	3
4th "	28	4	6	52	20	21	
5th "	60	15	2	128	55	85	
6th "	75	21	8	192	53	52	1 ?
7th "	53	10	40	91	20	15	
8th "	56	2	118	45	1	5	
9th "	93	1 ?	107	3			
10th "	84	1 ?	69				
= 8 in.	(126)		(103)				

77 Nelson's pottery type counts by level from the excavations in the Galisteo Basin, New Mexico. (From Nelson, 1916)

archaeological methods. In 1913, in an off-season during the period in which he was working in the Southwest, he visited Europe and the French and Spanish caves where Obermeier and Breuil were conducting stratigraphic excavations. In fact, he aided in the digging of the Castillo Cave in Spain. By his own account, this experience made a strong impression on him. He had already had some experience with stratigraphic digging, in the California shell-mounds, under Kroeber's general direction and under the influence of Max Uhle.[6] Uhle, it will be recalled from our comments in the previous chapter, had attempted to excavate the San Francisco Bay shell-mounds stratigraphically and had put forward a culture sequence of their occupation. Kroeber had remained unconvinced of the value of the sequence in defining significant culture change, and this appears to have had a dampening effect on Nelson's work or, at least, his interpretations.[7] But the European experience of a few years later must have turned his mind in this direction again. He returned to the United States and the Southwest between 1913 and 1915 determined to give the stratigraphic method another try. Some results were published as early as 1914. But it was not until 1916 that he made his stratigraphic findings known in an important journal article.[8]

To see Nelson's Southwestern work in proper perspective, it is necessary to go back a bit. When he began the surveys and excavations for the American Museum of Natural History in the Galisteo Basin of New Mexico there was a substantial amount known about Rio Grande region archaeology. He had been preceded by Bandelier[9] and Hewett,[10] and there was a general concensus of opinion 'that the Rio Grande Pueblos underwent certain cultural transformations in prehistoric times.'[11] Several pottery styles had been identified. These were known to be associated, respectively, with different kinds of Pueblo ruins. One of these styles was clearly associated with early European materials, and a fairly good guess could be made about the chronological order of the others. But, as Nelson said, tangible proof of this chronology was still wanting.[12]

Nelson obtained this proof of chronology by stratigraphic excavations at a number of sites in the region, among them: San Pedro Viejo, Pueblo San Cristobal, and San Marcos. At several sites superpositions of one pottery type over another were found, but a full sequence placing all of the known pottery styles of the region eluded him at first. In some of the sites Nelson noted that the superpositions were of styles in which the later was probably separated from the earlier by a hiatus – a hiatus in which, he reasoned, one or two of the chronologically unplaced styles of the region would probably fit. It was at Pueblo San Cristobal that Nelson finally found the deep refuse accumulation that gave him the stratigraphic order of all of the Galisteo Basin styles. The debris deposit was ten feet deep, and it was exposed in a creek bank where it had been cut by the stream. Near the Pueblo, but not in it, it had been used as a place of burial. This fact was duly recorded by Nelson who comments on the possible dangers of intrusions and disturbances that might confuse true stratification; however, he selected a spot where there were no visible disturbances or distortions in the near-horizontal bedding planes of the refuse. His photograph shows this bedding to be extremely thin and fine, with no clear cut physical strata of any thickness. Perhaps because of this, he excavated by arbitrary levels, one foot in thickness. The size of the excavation was a three by six foot block.

Potsherds from each of Nelson's arbitrary levels were kept separately, and these sherds were classified and counted, by level. No percentages were computed, but the numerical results were presented in a small table. Commenting on the vertical distributions of the sherd styles in this table, Nelson observed that corrugated and 'Biscuit' wares showed no significant top-to-bottom changes. In contrast, black-on-white types had their maximum occurrence at the bottom of the test and gradually diminished upward. So the Black-on-white style had 'died out' during the occupancy of San Cristobal, or at least during the use of this particular rubbish dump. Early Glaze wares had their inception deep in the refuse, had reached a maximum of popularity in middle levels, and had then diminished at the top. A Paint-Glaze combination style occurred only in the uppermost levels, and Nelson observes that if the refuse had continued higher this style, too, would have increased in volume. Obviously, he was thinking very much in terms of the unimodal life curves of pottery styles and types that are, today, the stock-in-trade of the archaeologist.

While the title of Nelson's 1916 article and the initial pages devoted to the stratigraphic presentation show that the author was aware of its innovative character, he says nothing whatsoever about the employment of a 'new' method or technique. This is also true of Gamio's article and Boas's contemporary comments about it. Thus, one might think that American archaeologists of *ca.* 1914 took the stratigraphic method for granted. But the published records of the time just do not bear this out. There is no

77

record that Gamio had ever done any digging or observing that was comparable to the pit at Atzcapotzalco prior to that time. Nelson had had his California shell-mound experience, but this did not involve frequency counts per level in the manner of the Galisteo analyses. We cannot but conclude that Gamio and Nelson had made a 'breakthrough' in archaeological method, at least for the New World, despite the fact that neither claimed any credit for originality or revolutionary discovery.[13]

Nelson's work led immediately to regional chronology building. In the same article he tells us how he used this chronology of pottery styles in dating other sites from unit surface collections or from excavated collections from individual Pueblo rooms. In this he did not compute percentages or even tabulate frequencies but only noted occurrences or absences of chronologically diagnostic types. For the region, Nelson interpreted the steady, gradual stylistic change – as revealed in the San Cristobal stratigraphy and as suggested in the surface and room collection – as indicating a continuity of populations at the sites. Southwestern archaeology was on its way with a field method and with hypotheses about cultural sequence successions generated from this method.

The first Southwestern archaeologist to make use of the stratigraphic method on a large scale was A. V. Kidder. A contemporary of Nelson's, Kidder had been trained under Tozzer at Harvard and also had taken a course in field methods with the noted Egyptologist, G. A. Reisner, one of the most 'modern' archaeological excavators of the early 20th century. Kidder began his work in the Southwest at about the same time as Nelson, and the latter, in two footnotes to his 1916 paper, records that Kidder's investigations on the Pajarito Plateau[14] and at Pecos had confirmed his Galisteo pottery sequence. Kidder's dig at Pecos was to be the largest undertaking of its kind up to that time in the Southwest, indeed in America north of Mexico, and it still stands as a major site operation.[15] The Pecos site, in the Upper Pecos Valley of New Mexico, is actually composed of two ruins, Forked Lightning and Pecos Pueblo proper. As it turned out, Forked Lightning was the earlier settlement, dating back to Pueblo III times (*ca.* A.D. 1000), and after its abandonment the villagers apparently moved across the arroyo to a more defensible position. This move is believed

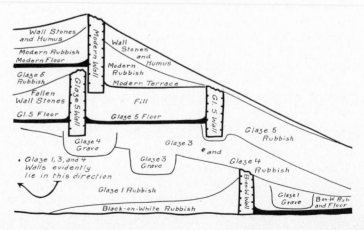

78 Cross-section diagram of refuse stratigraphy and building walls and floors, Pecos Ruin, New Mexico. The presence of ceramic styles in the refuse is indicated by 'Black-on-white', 'Glaze 5', etc. (From Kidder, 1924, by permission Yale University Press, New Haven)

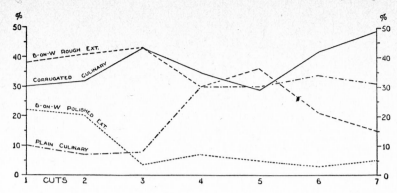

	Number of Sherds							Approximate Percentages						
Cut Number...	1	2	3	4	5	6	7	1	2	3	4	5	6	7
B.-on-w. polished ext. ...	63	65	20	28	9	10	12	22	20	6	7	5	3	5
B.-on-w. rough ext.	108	137	143	126	70	64	39	38	41	43	30	36	21	15
Plain culinary	30	23	27	129	59	106	78	10	7	8	30	30	34	31
Corrugated culinary....	82	104	141	144	58	129	127	30	32	43	33	29	42	49
Totals............	283	329	331	427	196	309	256	100	100	100	100	100	100	100

to have occurred at about A.D. 1200. Pecos Pueblo was then occupied through the Pueblo IV period (A.D. 1300–1700) and on into the early 19th century.

79 Table and graph showing sherds and percentage changes, per type, by level (or 'cut'). Forked Lightning. (From Kidder, 1931)

The refuse at these sites had been deposited adjacent to the living structures, and it had also been built over in successive room additions to the Pueblo construction. In some places, where debris had been thrown over old escarpments, it had accumulated to a depth of 20 feet. Kidder described the nature of this refuse, the probable history of its deposition, and his methods of excavation in great detail.[16] For the pure rubbish heaps at the edges of the site, initial trenches were first cut into these great piles in order to obtain deep profile exposures. Only selected sherds were saved and noted from these initial trenches; but, with these deep profile exposures as guides, more thorough and careful excavation then proceeded by natural or physical strata, and potsherds were assigned proveniences according to such strata units. The profiles were carefully examined for signs of intrusion or disturbance, and places where these were observed were eliminated as locations for stratigraphic tests. In some instances columns or blocks of refuse were isolated on two, three, or four sides to allow for a more rigorous examination for intrusions. In these instances pegs and strings were used to mark off physical strata on all sides of the block for the convenience of the excavators.

78

The potsherds from these controlled Pecos proveniences were classified and tabulated, and in the final report these tabulations were offered both as numbers of sherds per type per provenience unit and as corresponding percentages. These results were also expressed in linear graphs drawn for percentages of types per unit

79

or level. In general, the Forked Lightning-Pecos ceramic history was much the same as that which Nelson had found in the Tano refuse heaps of the Galisteo Basin – a decline of Black-on-white wares through time with an increase of Glaze wares – and, in fact, Nelson's results were of aid to Kidder in the excavations at Pecos. No single test of Kidder's gave quite the whole chronological story, but the percentage frequency figures for the Forked Lightning strata-pit were easily fitted onto the figures for the lower levels of the Pecos Pueblo excavations; and the well-tested ceramic chronology derived from all of these excavations and analyses was then applied to the dating of between-floor and between-wall deposits in the more complex stratigraphic situations.

From the Pecos excavations Kidder went on to extend and integrate his stratigraphic method into a regional strategy of cultural-chronological research. In his own words, this strategy or plan of attack consisted of five steps:

'1 Preliminary survey of remains in the region under consideration.
2 Selection of criteria for ranking those remains in chronological order.
3 Comparative study of the manifestations of the criteria to arrive at a tentative chronological ranking of the sites containing them.
4 Search for and excavation of sites in which materials may be found in stratigraphic relationship in order to check up on the tentative ranking and also to obtain a large number of specimens for morphological and genetic studies.
5 A more thorough resurvey of the area in the light of the fuller knowledge now at hand in order definitely to rank all sites and, if necessary, to select for excavation new sites which may be expected to elucidate problems raised during the course of the research.'[17]

In other words: (1) reconnaissance; (2) selection of criteria; (3) seriation for probable sequence; (4) stratigraphic digging; and (5) more detailed regional survey and dating of sites.

Before Kidder had concluded his work at Pecos the stratigraphic method was being employed by others in the Southwest. Erich Schmidt made tests of this nature on the Lower Gila in 1925, publishing pottery type frequency count and percentages, along with graphic representation of the results.[18] He was followed in this tradition by other Southwestern archaeologists, including Gladwin,[19] Haury,[20] Roberts,[21] and Martin.[22]

Outside of the Southwest, G. C. Vaillant, who had been a student assistant of Kidder's at Pecos, published his first detailed stratigraphic work on the Valley of Mexico in 1930,[23] refining and extending back further in time the knowledge of the 'Archaic' or Preclassic cultures which Gamio had revealed in the bottom of his Atzcapotzalco test. In 1932 W. C. Bennett[24] carried out similar tests at Tiahuanaco, Bolivia, a site known for its stylistic relationships to one of the horizon markers in Uhle's early chronological scheme for the Peru-Bolivian area. H. B. Collins, Jr.[25] developed an Alaskan Arctic chronology in Eskimo archaeology through combined uses of stratigraphy and seriation. And in the latter part of the 1930s detailed stratigraphic procedures became the

80

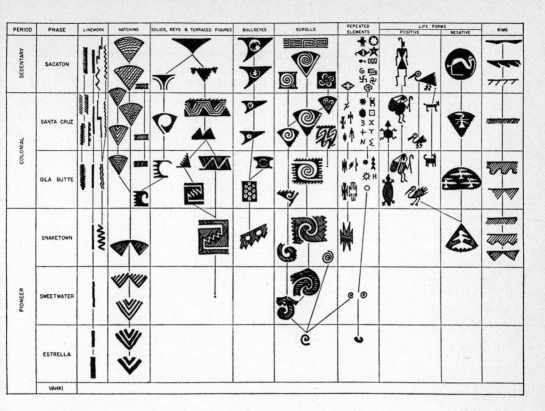

The table headers: PERIOD | PHASE | LINEWORK | HATCHING | SOLIDS, KEYS & TERRACED FIGURES | BULLSEYES | SCROLLS | REPEATED ELEMENTS | LIFE FORMS (POSITIVE | NEGATIVE) | RIMS

Periods and phases:
- SEDENTARY: SACATON
- COLONIAL: SANTA CRUZ, GILA BUTTE
- PIONEER: SNAKETOWN, SWEETWATER, ESTRELLA, VAHKI

80 Pottery type designs and their changes through time as seen in the Snaketown (Hohokam sub-area) sequence. (From Gladwin *et al.*, 1937)

vogue in the Eastern United States, particularly in the Southeast under the leadership of Ford,[26] Webb,[27] and others.[28]

One interesting aspect of this American development of the stratigraphic method was the strong emphasis on 'metrical,' as opposed to 'natural' stratigraphy. As we have seen, this metrical digging began with Gamio and Nelson. In commenting upon the latter's work in the Galisteo Basin, R. B. Woodbury, an Americanist, states that Nelson added a refinement to the long-familiar principle of superposition by excavating in arbitrary and uniform metrical levels rather than depending upon visibly separable strata.[29] On the other hand, the merits of metrical stratigraphy are questioned by many Old World archaeologists. Among these, Sir Mortimer Wheeler[30] argues that visible or 'natural' strata are the only safe guides in excavating the events of the sequent past. Kidder appears to have been one of the few, or perhaps the only, American stratigrapher of the 1920s and 1930s who favored the natural as opposed to the metrical method. He states this very explicitly:

'In dividing the column (of refuse) into layers (preparatory to excavation) care was taken to follow a natural division, such as a layer of ash or charcoal, a hard-packed living surface, etc., rather than an arbitrary line. The resultant layers were not always of equal volume, nor did they have necessarily a uniform trend, but they did represent the actual structure of the column. . . .'[31]

But his Americanist colleagues seem to have believed, or at least to have operated, otherwise. Schmidt, Haury, Vaillant, Bennett, Collins, and the Eastern North American archaeologists all dug by metrical units. In so doing, in almost every case there was an awareness of the importance of physical strata as a part of the record of the past, and physical soil zones were correlated with arbitrary digging levels or provenience blocks on profile diagrams and in text discussion; however, the physical zone, stratum, or lense was rarely utilized as the provenience unit in artifact or pottery analyses.

The reasons for this difference between the American stratigraphic digging methods and the more frequent use of the natural or physical soil zone unit of digging in the Old World are, like the reasons for the delay in the acceptance of the method as a whole in the Americas, uncertain and open to speculation. To be sure, reasons have been given by some diggers. Haury[32] explains his preference for the arbitrary block-unit digging in the Snaketown refuse heaps by pointing out that this method gave him a more satisfactory vertical and horizontal control of the excavated materials that if he were to attempt to dig by following the numerous small and complexly bedded strata and lenses of the refuse. In this connection he mentions that these natural or physical strata were too small and represented spans of time too brief to be of individual significance in determining the periods or phases of the refuse growth. Vaillant[33] argues that the physical complexities of the Zacatenco site, in which refuse and semi-destroyed architectural features were found over a hill slope, made physical strata digging impossible or inadvisable; and most of the other Americanists, when they comment upon it at all, explain their preference for metrical stratigraphy in terms of the peculiarities of the formation of the deposits in question. We would also suggest that the widespread use of metrical stratigraphy in the Americas, and especially in the United States, reflects the lack of physically visible strata in many relatively shallow sites.[34] Finally, we would also say that while we agree with Old World colleagues as to the limitations and hazards of metrical stratigraphy we do not see it as all bad. It is true that it can never be substituted for natural stratigraphy; but it can be used for further refinements within a framework of natural stratigraphy, and it can serve well in calibrating culture change in physical situations where it is the only kind of stratigraphy that can be employed.[35]

Seriation

Seriation, in its simplest definition, is the arrangement of phenomena or data into series by some consistent principle of ordering. In archaeology, however, seriation is almost always concerned with time-ordering of the data. Other kinds of ordering, those reflecting geographical or functional variation in culture, are certainly possible, but seriations of this nature are relatively rare in archaeology.

Seriation is effected by taking into account the characteristics of the archaeological materials themselves and the differences among these characteristics. In this sense, the method is more uniquely archaeological than stratigraphy, the other prime method of determining relative chronology, for while stratigraphy derives from the geological principle of superposition, seriation might be said to have its theoretical framework entirely in cultural history.[36]

Archaeological seriation has proceeded by observing two basic principles. One of these has been to assume that some kind of inevitable order guides culture change through time. Usually this has been an evolutionary conception of simple-to-complex development, and such seriation has, accordingly, been referred to as 'evolutionary seriation.' The second principle of seriation is by similarity, and, hence, is called 'similiary seriation.'[37] This means that the data units – the archaeological objects, groups of objects, or features of objects – are arranged in a series in accordance with their similarities, one to another; like is placed closest to like. The assumption behind this is that cultural change is gradual – at least within the same cultural tradition. The first and most notable example of evolutionary seriation in archaeology was Thomsen's ordering of the collections in the Danish National Museum on the assumption that the local culture had developed through a sequence of Stone, Bronze, and Iron Ages.[38] In this case subsequent archaeological research has validated this seriation many times over; however, other evolutionary seriations have sometimes been disproven by stratigraphic or absolute dating checks so that the evolutionary principle of seriation cannot be considered as routinely valid archaeological procedure. On the other hand, the results arrived at by similiary seriation, when the method has been properly applied, have been uniformly reliable, being frequently confirmed by stratigraphy and various means of absolute dating. As a result, the similiary seriational principle is a widely accepted means of arriving at chronology – both in America and elsewhere – and, in fact, the word 'seriation', as now used, virtually always refers to similiary seriation. It should be noted, however, that evolutionary and similiary principles have often been applied jointly. In American archaeology a classic example would be Spinden's *A Study of Maya Art*, to which we have referred in the previous chapter. This work, published in 1913, utilized both evolutionary reasoning and similiary ordering of art forms to seriate chronologically Maya monuments and sculptures.

In tracing the rise and development of similiary seriation in the Americas, we should first record that it had become an accepted principle in European archaeology by the latter half of the 19th century. Worsaae's grave lot study of the 1840s utilized unit collections for comparison with each other and embodied the seriational idea.[39] John Evans and others applied the similiary seriational principle to British data shortly after this. By the end of the century the concept was well developed, especially as practiced and explained by Sir Flinders Petrie in Egypt.[40] Petrie, we know, influenced Uhle, and this suggests one line of contact whereby the seriational principle may have spread to the New World. Of course, it is also possible, or even likely, that Uhle already was aware of the earlier European grave lot seriational studies before he was familiar with Petrie's work. Another possible source for the spread of similiary seriation to the New World might have been Franz Boas. The 'father of American anthropology' was German born and trained; he was probably acquainted with European studies of a seriational nature; and we know that he had made a kind of informal seriation of potsherd refuse from surface collections in the Valley of Mexico shortly before Gamio's stratigraphic excavations in the same region. In fact, the study of these collections, and the implications which they held for chronology, were among the reasons that prompted Boas to urge Gamio to carry out his stratigraphic tests. In any event, it may well be significant that A. L. Kroeber, who was the first to demonstrate the effectiveness of similiary seriation for chronological ordering in the Southwestern United States, was both a student and colleague of Boas as well as a close associate of Uhle.

Kroeber's paper on seriation, entitled 'Zuñi Potsherds,' was written in 1915, immediately upon the conclusion of the fieldwork upon which it was based, and published in the following year.[41] Together with the monograph by Leslie Spier, which appeared in 1917, and which we shall discuss later, it proved to be the viable beginnings for the propagation of the seriational method in New World archaeology, Kroeber describes his field operations as rather casual ones. He began collecting potsherds from the surfaces of Southwestern ruins as a kind of pastime on afternoon walks in the vicinity of Zuñi Pueblo where he was primarily engaged in ethnological studies. In the course of these walks he encountered eighteen abandoned site locations within a half-hour's hiking distance of the inhabited Zuñi Pueblo. At first, even before collecting specimens, Kroeber noted that some of these sites showed surface potsherds of a Black-on-red style, while only White-slipped or Black-on-white types were found on others. Eventually, he began systematic collection of sherds from the surfaces of all of the sites. Concurrently with this, he read summaries of Zuñi history; and then he saw that those sites which were known to have been inhabited by the Zuñi peoples in the 17th century all showed predominantly Red and Black-on-red wares. In contrast, those sites with mostly White or Black-on-white pottery were not recorded as having been inhabited in this early historic period. This established the Red and Black-on-red pottery complex at the 'upper,' or historic end of a postulated chronological series and the White and Black-on-white pottery complex at the 'lower,' or most remotely prehistoric, end of the series. Other sites displaying mixtures of Black-on-red and Black-on-white types were seriated, according to the relative proportions of these complexes, to intermediate chronological positions in this time scale. Such a procedure led to the establishment of six subperiods, each marking off a distinct segment of ceramic stylistic change (and time) on the seriated scale. The sequence was further confirmed by the steady decrease of a single pottery ware, corrugated, throughout the time scale from the earliest to the latest subperiods.

Although Kroeber started out this investigation by what is sometimes called 'occurrence seriation.'[42] in which only the presence or absence of the seriated units (the pottery complexes) were noted, he shifted his approach to 'frequency seriation' in the course of the study, utilizing percentages of potsherds of the different types within the complexes to carry the refinements of the seriation in the six subperiods; and his presentations of the data include tables listing sites and the percentages of the diagnostic pottery types found in each site collection. This frequency approach led him to conclude that the cultural history of the Zuñi region, insofar as it was represented by the eighteen sites in question, did not 'represent two different migrations, nationalities, or waves of culture' (as exemplified by the Black-on-red and Black-on-white pottery complexes), 'but rather a steady and continuous development on the soil' – as for example, was implied in the gradual replacement of one group (or type) by another and the continuity throughout of the corrugated ware.[43] Kroeber concluded by saying that his sequence needed stratigraphy to substantiate it and that future studies of this kind should first be carried out on a similar small regional basis before attempting multi-regional comparisons and erecting more sweeping chronologies. In all of this, it is interesting to note that not once did Kroeber use the term 'seriation.'

A longer and more detailed study of Zuñi region chronology followed immediately upon Kroeber's work. This was by Leslie Spier, and was published in 1917.[44] Spier, of course, was familiar with what Kroeber had done and also had spent three weeks in the field with Nelson in the summer of 1916. He devoted thirty pages of his report to a location and description of the ruins which he included in his survey, along with a good site map. He referred to Kroeber's work as 'associational seriation' based on 'concurrent variations in associated constituents in the samples.' This appears to be the first use of the term 'seriation' in American archaeology. He also noted Nelson's stratigraphy and declared it his purpose to test both methods, cross-checking them against one another. One way in which he did this was to excavate stratigraphic pits in some of the same sites from which Kroeber had made surface collections. The results confirmed the surface collection seriations.

Of his own surface collection seriations Spier tells us:

'The first subgroup (of pottery collections) contains thirty-five samples from as many ruins. The wares are corrugated, black-on-white, black-on-red, and black-and-white-on-red. These samples may be arbitrarily ranked according to their percentages of corrugated ware from highest to lowest. The test of such a seriation as an historical series will lie in the observed seriation of the accompanying wares; for, when a group of three or more distinct, but mutually dependent, values are ranked according to some postulated sequence for one, and the other values are found to present serially concurrent variations, it may be concluded that the result is not fortuitous.'[45]

This is one of the best and most concise definitions of archaeological seriation in the literature. Spier supported his presentations of the data with tables and frequency graphs. He extended Kroeber's sequence substantially further back into the past with a second subgroup of pottery collections from other sites. In this second subgroup there was, again, concurrent variation between corrugated ware and painted types, but Spier was aware that the concurrences and painted types were not the same as those for the first subgroup of sites. What this meant was that in the second subgroup of sites he had the earlier half of the corrugated ware frequency curve, the half in which this ware was on the increase. The full, and extended, seriational sequence thus showed a complete 'life' curve for corrugated pottery, beginning with its inception at slightly more than 0 per cent of the sherd sample, increasing to as much as 50 per cent in mid-sequence, and dropping from this 'popularity' peak to 0 per cent again at the historic period end of the sequence. In this 'life span' the corrugated ware was first associated with Black-on-white pottery types and, then, with Black-on-red types. Spier concluded his report with a statement in defense of seriation:

'We have no reason to doubt that the samples of potsherds collected from successive levels of ash heaps present us with valid chronological indices. Why then cavil at the use of similar samples from the surfaces of ash heaps?'[46]

Following Spier's work, seriation became standard archaeological procedure in the North American Southwest. It was utilized especially in site survey in connection with surface pottery collections and the relative dating of these. Nor was the similiary seriational principle altogether confined to pottery. Nelson applied it to Southwestern masonry types,[47] and F. H. H. Roberts seriated Southwestern architectural forms in a time sequence running from single-room pit-houses to multi-room above-ground pueblos.[48] In this last, Roberts was guided by architectural-pottery associations as well as by sequent similarity in building forms; however, this was in keeping with the general build-up of chronological knowledge within the Southwestern area. As more became known it grew progressively easier to fit newly discovered data into a framework of existing information, with the results of stratigraphy and seriation cross-checking each other.

Whereas the Southwestern archaeologists were operating with potsherd collections, and percentage frequencies of pottery types within these unit collections, a variant seriational procedure was being employed in Peru. This was a stylistic similiary seriation in which individual pottery vessels were assigned to style groups, and then traits or features on the vessels were tabulated and plotted from group to group. This particular kind of similiary seriation had been done by Petrie in Egypt; and Uhle, perhaps through his knowledge of Petrie's writings, had made use of it in Peru. Uhle, though, published little in this vein that was explicit. It remained for Kroeber, together with some of his students, to make the Peruvian seriations explicit. This was done in a series of papers in the 1920s in which Kroeber shifted from the potsherd frequency seriation he had pioneered in the Southwest to a grave lot and stylistic approach that could be adapted to the Uhle collections. These collections came from a great many Peruvian cemeteries, and, fortunately, Uhle had carefully tabulated the specimens and determined their provenience by the grave lot associations in which he had found them. The collections from the Ica Valley of the south Peruvian coast may be taken as an example of Kroeber's seriational treatment. W. D. Strong, then a graduate student at Berkeley, was the junior author.[49] The entire pottery vessel collection, numbering over 600 specimens, was classified by Kroeber and Strong into seven distinct styles. The grave lot associations of these vessels offered clear clues to the chronological separateness of the styles. As the authors say: 'In no case do the contents of one grave include objects of more than one style.'[50] The main burden of the seriation, however, was not in the grave lot units but in the nature of the styles themselves. Treating each of the seven styles as a unit, all the vessels assigned to a given style were then tabulated for traits of vessel form, uses of color or modelling treatment, and decorative design elements. From these tabulations a similiary seriation was effected whereby the seven styles were arranged in what was believed to be a chronological order. As one of the styles was recognizable as Inca, this gave an upper chronological end to the series; immediately preceding this was the Late Ica II style, so placed because it shared certain vessel form and decorative traits with the Inca style: Late Ica I preceded this on the basis of its similarities to Late Ica II; and the series was carried from here backward in time through the remaining four styles which were also assumed to have been culture phases.

Further Uhle collections from other Peruvian valleys were similarly studied by Kroeber and his associates. An interesting innovation in one instance was Strong's use of statistical coefficients of correlation in a seriational arrangement of styles.[51] The materials in this case came from the Ancon Necropolis, and the statistical treatment verified the more usual observational analysis of pottery traits as well as the excavation notes of Uhle who had detected some grave superpositions that served to indicate chronological ordering.

Stylistic similiary seriations in the manner of Uhle, Kroeber, and Strong were to be continued in Peru by John H. Rowe and his students, but these studies were not made until the 1950s and 1960s. The more immediate exploitation of the similiary seriational method followed the Southwestern surface sherd collection and type frequency model, and the archaeologist most responsible was James A. Ford, working in the Southeastern United States.

At the beginning of the 1930s Ford had worked with Henry B. Collins, Jr. in Alaskan archaeology. There, relative chronology had been worked out by a combination of stratigraphy, and the association of prehistoric Eskimo villages with a series of old beach lines (the older ones farther inland, the younger ones progressively closer to the modern shore).[52] This provided a chronological yardstick by which to arrange bone and ivory implements and ornaments in sequence and to study the gradual change in the forms and decorations of these artifacts through time. Although Collins's procedures were not initially seriational they became secondarily so, and Ford was especially impressed with the gradualism of culture change as registered in the materials and with the rise and fall in popularity of types and styles.[53]

Ford carried this in mind when he returned to his home in the Southeastern United States and obtained a post as an Archaeological Research Associate with the Louisiana State Geological Survey. He did some stratigraphic digging in the middle 1930s, but his most important work of the period was a monograph on prehistoric village-site potsherd collections which appeared in 1936.[54] In the introductory pages to this work Ford sounded the call for chronological information for the Southeastern area. He pointed out that archaeological sites of the area tend to be thin, lessening the possibilities for stratigraphy. To overcome this he recommended a method of site survey and surface collecting and an approach to chronology which begins with the documented European historic horizon and works backward from there in time. He also concerned himself with a number of methodological questions. In arguing that change in ceramic styles will be gradual, and, generally, uniform over the area of his survey, he noted that the area selected – the adjacent portions of Louisiana and Mississippi – is reasonably small and that within it the ceramic art must have been kept within fairly definite stylistic bounds. In other words, he attempted to define a ceramic or a cultural tradition and to recognize the necessity for such traditional boundaries as a prerequisite for similar seriation, concerns which we do not meet with in the literature on American archaeological seriation until several decades later.[55] He showed an awareness to some of the limitations of dealing with surface collections of potsherds alone, admitting that some deposits of pottery at a site might lie completely buried and, therefore, not be represented in surface collections. For the relatively thin Southeastern Indian Village sites he dismissed this, however, as being an unusual circumstance not frequently met with. In further concerning himself with the representativeness of random pottery surface collections, Ford made as many as three separate collections at some sites. Tabulating the difference between type percentages from one collection to another he arrived at an average variation which, subsequently, he observed is consistently smaller as the collections are larger. In sum, he makes a convincing case for his method.

In his substantive results Ford defined seven ceramic complexes. Each complex is represented by the collections from a certain number of sites. Four such complexes can be designated as historic and, through geographical location of sites, documentation of historic site locations, and associations of glass beads and other early European trade items, these four complexes are identified, respectively, with the Caddo, Tunica, Natchez, and Choctaw tribes that occupied the Lower Mississippi Valley country in the 16th and 17th centuries. Three other complexes – Coles Creek, Deasonville, and Marksville – are regarded as fully prehistoric. Their chronological relationships in regard to the historic complexes and to each other are then arrived at by what is, in effect, 'occurrence' similiary seriation. That is, some of the historic period complexes share some few types with the Coles Creek complex. Coles Creek and Deasonville are reckoned to be at least in part contemporaneous through the evidences of trade between the two; however, there is no typological overlap between Deasonville and the historic horizon complexes. Thus, Deasonville is presumed to have come to an end as a cultural or ceramic complex before Coles Creek died out. Lastly, there is some typological overlap and similiary continuity between certain pottery design motifs running from Marksville, through Coles Creek, to Natchez. Here the reasoning is of the order of that employed by Kroeber and others in Peruvian stylistic seriations.

Two years later Ford published an article on the applicability of a seriational method in the Southeast.[56] Whereas in the earlier monograph he appears to have been groping his way toward such a method, it has now come clear in his mind. It remains, nevertheless, a rather sketchy outline. He seems to be speaking of 'occurrence' rather than 'frequency' seriation although in the monograph he had made the statement that frequency, or quantitative, analysis of pottery types per collection was of major importance. Although Ford cites no specific bibliographic references in this second article, he lists titles including a later, retrospective work of Spier's on Southwestern stratigraphy (and seriation)[57] and Kroeber's famous paper, 'On the Principle of Order in Civilization as Exemplified by Changes of Fashion.'[58] The latter is concerned with the configurations of gradual and rhythmic trends or curves of change – as illustrated by women's dress lengths – rather than with seriation proper; however, Kroeber's concepts undoubtedly reinforced Ford's thinking. In all this early work of Ford's one has the impression that his methodology was largely self-discovered. Only later, as he became more sophisticated and better read in anthropology, did Ford begin to appreciate what he had achieved in the context of the anthropological and archaeological literature. A good many years later he brought out his more evolved frequency seriations.[59]

If we confine ourselves strictly to the earlier part of the Classificatory-Historical Period, the most elaborate and refined similiary seriational procedures in American archaeology were those of Irving Rouse, published in 1939 in his monograph, *Prehistory in Haiti, A Study in Method*.[60] As the title implies, the intent of the book was essentially methodological; more strictly substantive treatments of the Haitian archaeological data were presented separately.[61] In formulating a 'time scale' for these West Indian cultures Rouse was forced to rely primarily upon seriation, deep stratified sites being lacking. Like Ford, he dealt entirely with ceramics. These were collections of sherds taken from a series of site excavations on the island. The sherds were grouped into twelve 'types,' Rouse's 'type' being more or less the equivalent of Ford's 'complex.' On a more detailed level of typological examination were fifty-one 'modes.' These modes pertained to vessel-form features (flat-topped rims), surface decorative elements (naturalistic ornamentation), or materials or conditions of manufacture (temper, firing, etc.). As such, the modes overlapped, to a degree, between types and provided a means of chronologically seriating the types. To demonstrate this seriation Rouse selected eight modes which appeared to differ most in frequencies of occurrence from site to site. Percentages of occurrence were computed and graphed for these modes, and the site collections were placed serially by percentage trends. Time direction to the seriation was given through the aid of very short stratigraphic sequences from some of the sites. In these seriations Rouse worked on the assumption that all of his ceramic data belonged to a single cultural-ceramic tradition, and he recognized that without this assumption seriation would have been impossible. The assumption was, indeed, borne out by the very clear continuity of many modes between his earlier Meillac and his later Carrier ceramic types. He was also specific about two other assumptions, one that frequencies of modes varied independently and the other that each mode described a normal, or cyclical, frequency curve through time. Rouse felt that both of these assumptions were validated, respectively, by the fact that the graphed curves for changes in modal frequency were all somewhat different and by the further fact that all such curves were unimodal.

Rouse's seriations were finer-grained than Ford's, particularly in their use of the mode entity; but, perhaps more significant than this, Rouse was more conscientiously explicit in describing and explaining all of his seriational operations in great detail. No other work in American archaeology up to that time – not even Spier's 1917 study – had shown such a selfconscious awareness of archaeological assumptions and procedures as *Prehistory in Haiti, A Study in Method*.

Typology and Artifact (Pottery) Classification

Typology and classification lie at the very core of archaeology; and our names, 'Classificatory-Descriptive' and 'Classificatory-Historical,' point up the difference in typological-classificatory procedures and goals for these two periods. Classification of the earlier period was, indeed, 'descriptive' taxonomy. The diagnostic attributes or modes which were selected for definition of artifact types were chosen for what they indicated about the intrinsic nature of these artifacts. Beyond this, the goals of the typology were not stated. It was enough that the data of prehistory were being treated systematically, perhaps for a purpose no more philosophically profound than the arrangement of items in a museum case. Toward the end of the Classificatory-Descriptive Period the dimension of geography did creep into classificatory studies. Although the initial operations were descriptive, students like Holmes observed that certain pottery and artifact types did have certain geographical distributional correlates. But this was as far as it went.

With the introduction of chronology into the data in the Classificatory-Historical Period archaeologists were forced into more finely detailed and formally defined typologies in order to properly plot their data on the time chart. As Rouse has said, such types were clearly 'historical,' as opposed to being merely 'descriptive.'[62] Such historical taxonomy dominated the period, and, especially, its earlier part. Not until after 1940, when concerns of context and function began to share the archaeological stage with chronology, did other kinds of artifact classifications appear.[63]

But to go back to the beginning of the Classificatory-Historical Period, we see some studies which might be described as 'transitional' between purely descriptive classification and classification designed to aid in chronology building. S.K. Lothrop's two-volume monograph, *Pottery of Costa Rica and Nicaragua*, would be an example.[64] Written in 1920–21, and published in 1926 after some revisions, it was based on a museum examination of some 3500 to 4000 pottery vessels. These were specimens which had come from graves, all excavated by amateurs and without provenience data except of a general geographic sort. Realizing these deficiencies in the data, Lothrop knew he was limited primarily to descriptive treatment; however, he could do some gross geographical distribution studies, and, hopefully, he might make comparative studies with reference to adjoining areas (such as Mesoamerica) which would give clues to chronology. Indeed, he was able to do this after a fashion by noting the presence of certain Maya 'Old Empire' (or Classic) elements on some of his Costa Rican-Nicaraguan polychrome pottery of the Nicoya style, and he also saw central Mexican (Toltec and Aztec) relationships to other Nicoya pieces.[65] Still, developing a chronology in this manner was a risky business, and Lothrop left the matter with the final observation that although considerable time depth must be represented in the Costa Rica-Nicaragua collections, any regional chronology would have to be developed through fieldwork on and in the ground.[66] In retrospect, it seems likely that similiary seriation might have been a help in working out chronology for Lothrop; however, he makes no mention of the possibility.

Lothrop's actual classification procedures are discussed in less than two pages.[67] He established ware groups: Polychromes, 'Intermediates' (two colors), and Monochromes. Within a group – the Polychromes, for example – he had named wares (Nicoya Polychrome), each defined by decorative motifs and techniques, and sometimes he divided these wares into sub-wares. But Lothrop's attention really focused on the individual specimen rather than the class or type. There are no statistical or numerical treatments of the data, either as whole vessels or as attributes of vessels.

It remained for the archaeologists in the Southwestern United States to take the lead, again, this time in devising types geared for chronology. As such, these pottery types were the logical outgrowths of stratigraphic and seriational methods on potsherds. The potsherd, by its very nature, became a kind of tab, a statistical unit highly adapted for counting and manipulation; and, as a result, chronological advances in the Southwest were rapid. On the other hand, the whole methodology had a feedback that was not altogether happy. The potsherd grew steadily farther away from the whole pot, from the larger cultural context, and from the men who made the pottery. A reaction was to set in against this some years later, but, for the time, such potsherd archaeology represented the vanguard in American studies.

One of the earliest, ablest, and most indefatigable exponents of such Southwestern pottery classifications was H. S. Gladwin, working from a private foundation archaeological survey base in southern Arizona. Together with Winifred Gladwin, he began a series of publications in 1928 which outlined a procedure for site description and designation, potsherd collection, and pottery classification and nomenclature.[68] This was followed, through the 1930s, by other publications which described and illustrated pottery types in handbook fashion.[69] Not a man for undue methodological or theoretical reflection, Gladwin went directly to the substantive matter at hand, the description of the types. As a consequence, there is much that is implicit and little that is explicit in his operations. Nevertheless, it is clear that he regarded pottery styles as sensitive indicators of culture change and viewed the potsherds as keys to spatial-temporal variation in culture. Along with his Southwestern colleagues,[70] he saw the necessity of keeping the pottery type as a unit that could be easily manipulated. Thus, in type naming:

'It was also decided to omit, as far as possible, designations which introduce factors of time or comparison, since their use injects elements which later might require correction.'[71]

Biological taxonomy served as a guide in establishing a binomial system of pottery type designation. Thus, the color combination or surface treatment of the pottery became the 'genus' name (e.g. Black-on-white) with a geographical locality as the 'specific' name (e.g. Tularosa). Type descriptions were published in a set format, with name, vessel shape, designs, type site, geographical distribution, known cultural affiliations, and chronological data.[72] The 'biological' taxonomy, with its possible implications, was disturbing to some archaeologists, and a distinguished physical anthropologist of the time made the caustic observation that 'potsherds don't breed.' Nevertheless, the procedure had great usefulness and flourished. The essential thing was that the pottery types were the commonly agreed-upon units which the archaeologists could examine in space and time with relative ease, and it is unlikely that any but the most unsophisticated conceived of pottery manufacture and development as constrained by the analogue of biological parenthood. To be sure, lines of development leading from one pottery type to another were plotted on the culture time charts,[73] but these were recognized as the best available convention for diagramming the spread of cultural ideas through space and time. The limitations of the procedure and the model were not in their 'genetic' implications but in the abstraction from context and overall barrenness. In spite of this, a structure of type, space, and time was erected in the Southwest which has remained unequaled in its detail and refinement in any other archaeological area of the Americas.

As in the case of stratigraphy and seriation, 'historical' typology moved to the Eastern United States from the Southwest in the 1930s, and the archaeologist deserving most of the credit for this was, again, J. A. Ford. Previously, what had been 'descriptive' types in the area were beginning to be recognized as being chronologically indicative. Such categories as 'Hopewellian pottery,' 'Woodland pottery,' 'Mississippian pottery' were a part of archaeological discourse in the 1920s and 1930s. Ford's real contribution, over and above this, was to present pottery typology as a part of the 'package' of stratigraphy-seriation-typology which made possible regional chronologies first in the Southeast and then in the Ohio Valley-Upper Mississippi area. In his seriational and survey monograph of 1936 Ford first made the case for the pottery type as the measuring device of cultural variation in space and time;[74] but it was in a conference report on Southeastern pottery

classification and nomenclature that he set down his most unequivocal statements on this theme.[75]

'The inadequacy of the procedure of dividing pottery into "types"
merely for the purposes of describing the material is recognized.
This is merely a means of presenting raw data. Types should be
classes of material which promise to be useful as tools in interpreting
culture history.'[76]

And, continuing to drive home the case for the definition of types
as 'historical' tools, he goes on to say that pottery types must be
defined as combinations of all discoverable features – paste, temper,
methods of manufacture, decoration, etc. – and

'By this [sic] criteria two sets of material which are similar in nearly
all features, but which are divided by peculiar forms of one feature
(shell contrasted with grit tempering, for example) may be separated into two types if there promises to be some historical justifi-
cation for the procedure.'[77]

In other words, no formal splitting of types unless this demon-
strably correlates with spatial or temporal difference.[78] The necessity of selecting a set of mutually exclusive features to serve as the
primary framework of the pottery classification was emphasized,
and as the classification was usually to be applied to sherds, such
features would most advantageously be those pertaining to surface
finish and decoration. The resultant nomenclature was binomial
and much like that of the Southwest. For example, 'Complicated
Stamped,' a surface treatment, was the type 'genus' while the
geographical site name, 'Swift Creek,' was the specific designant
in the type 'Swift Creek Complicated Stamped.' The first Southeastern area pottery type descriptions of the sort were published in
the *News Letter of the Southeastern Archaeological Conference in
1939.*[79]

Elsewhere in the New World such 'historical' typology was
much less formal. In Middle America, in the 1930s, Vaillant gave
descriptive names to 'wares' and 'types.' Some of them remained
as little more than 'descriptive' types; others, which he dubbed
'marker types,' were truly 'historical' in that they carried his
sequence story in the stratigraphy.[80] Bennett's typology at Tiahuanaco was similar, and some of his categories were meaningful
chronologically.[81] Both Vaillant and Bennett tended to look upon
the pottery complex or the 'pottery period' as a whole. That is,
certain forms and features characterized a period, in contrast to
another period. This way of conceiving the data was also expressed
in R. E. Smith's Uaxactun work, in the Maya Lowlands.[82] There
the physical nature of the site, with refuse deposits sealed off and
separated from other deposits by plaster floors and stone architectural features, led to a ready utilization of architectural or
building periods as a chronology. Pottery complexes were then
associated with these periods. As a result, there was less attention
to the life-span of the individual type, and frequencies of occurrence were much less important in chronology formulation than in
the Southwest or Southeast.

It remains only to mention that in his 1939 monograph Irving
Rouse introduced the 'analytical' type into American archaeology.

Here, the emphasis was on attributes or modes, rather than on the artifacts themselves, and it was an archaeological attempt to analyze the procedures and intent of aboriginal manufacture. Although typology still had chronology as an objective – and Rouse, as we have already noted was much concerned with seriation – there were now the new goals of context and function.

Culture Classification Schemes

The other main classificatory interest of the early Classificatory-Historical Period was in culture classification. This had no real forerunners in the preceding period. Apparently, some spatial-temporal control over the data was a necessary prerequisite to culture-classificatory thinking. Certainly, it is consistent with this that the first culture classification scheme appeared in the South-west. This was the 'Pecos Classification,' which derived, especially, out of the early work of Kidder.

In 1927 a meeting of the leading archaeologists then working in the Southwestern area was called at Pecos, New Mexico. The objective of this 'Pecos Conference' was to formulate a general classificatory scheme that would facilitate communication among archaeologists working on related problems.[83] Chronology was foremost in the minds of those present. They wanted a chronological classification of Southwestern cultures that would be generally applicable for the area as a whole. Kidder had already made a beginning along these lines in his first synthesis of the area published three years before,[84] and his concepts and terminology largely prevailed at the conference.

The earliest peoples of the Southwest of which archaeologists then had record were the preceramic 'Basketmakers' of the 'four corners' country of the adjacent portions of Arizona, New Mexico, Utah, and Colorado. Thus, the chronology of the Pecos Classification began with the Basketmakers. Believing that they had not yet found the earliest beginnings of this tradition, the conference group designated their earliest period 'Basketmaker II,' leaving room at the bottom, so to speak, for an undiscovered 'Basketmaker I.' Basketmaker II peoples lived in pit-houses and practiced agriculture. So did their descendants of Basketmaker III, but the later period was further characterized by the appearance of pottery. Subsequent changes in architecture, community arrangement, pottery styles, and other artifacts were marked off as the diagnostics of the succeeding Pueblo I–V Periods, the last two periods bridging, respectively, from Pre-Columbian to the early historic horizons and from historic to modern Indian pueblo villages. The Pecos Classification has stood the test of later archaeological research. Some modifications have been suggested,[85] and tree-ring dates have given it a greater precision. The accuracy in dating, however, raised theoretical problems, for it became apparent that the Pecos 'periods' were perhaps better described as 'stages.' For instance, some Southwestern regions were seen to have achieved a Pueblo III or a Pueblo IV 'condition,' as this was marked by architectural styles, before other regions; and H. S. Gladwin, among others, made the criticism that the Pecos Classification was a yardstick of cultural development rather than a scale of time.[86] This problem of time lag, from region to region, and also the fact that the Pecos Classification was better adapted to the northern or Basketmaker-Pueblo (Anasazi) portions of the Southwest than to the southern Hohokam and southeastern Mogollon territories, led Gladwin to propose another kind of culture classification.

Gladwin's culture classification was a direct outgrowth of his site survey and pottery classification approaches. In 1934, with Winifred Gladwin, he published *A Method for the Designation of Cultures and Their Variations*.[87] The title of this short paper is revealing. Gladwin saw the problem as essentially one of nomenclature. As in his classifications of pottery, there seems little concern about the implications which his genetic-chronologic scheme might carry. Using the analogy of a tree, the basic and most fundamental grouping in his culture classification was designated the 'root'. These roots were the major cultural divisions of the Southwest as these were conceived of at that time: the 'Basketmaker' (later to be called 'Anasazi'), the 'Hohokam,' and the 'Caddoan' (later designated 'Mogollon').[88] Roots were then seen as subdividing into 'stems'. These were assigned regional names, such as San Juan or Playas (of the Basketmaker Root). Stems were similarly split into still more reduced cultural units called 'branches,' and these branches were also designated by geographic terms – Chaco or Kayenta, for example. The final subdivision was that of the branch into a 'phase.' These, too, were given geographical names – Jeddito, Puerco, etc. The phase was the actual working archaeological unit. Phases were defined by comparing site or component remains with other site or component remains and establishing such a unit on the basis of a very high degree of culture trait similarity.

Although the Gladwin classification was primarily one of cultures, grouped by their relative degrees of culture trait similarity, space and time were given consideration. The root, stem, and branch formulations all involve geographical territory as well as culture forms. The temporal dimension was given implicit recognition by the genetic model of the scheme: that is, roots, by their very nature, preceded stems, and stems preceded branches. Of course, the further implications of this were a kind of monogenesis of Southwestern cultures: as the archaeologist worked backward in time, or down the 'tree,' he would be discovering fewer and fewer cultural ancestors. Such a monogenesis, while a possibility, was by no means demonstrated for the Southwest. In other words, the scheme had built into it one of the kinds of things it should be designed to test. Actually, as it worked out, these more 'basic' levels of the classification caused little practical difficulty. Sites were dug or surveyed; they or the components within them were classified into the working units, the phases; and these phases were arranged in explicit regional chronologies by stratigraphy and seriation. Modifications of the Gladwin scheme are used today in the Southwest, although in these current uses the rigid genetic structure has been largely dropped, leaving the phases and the regional sequences as the main operational features. While such regional sequences gave the archaeologist closer chronological control over his data than the reference frame of the Pecos Classification, the Gladwin scheme lacked the area-wide generalizing usefulness of the Pecos chronology.

If we refer to the Pecos Classification as 'chronologic,' and to the Gladwin scheme as 'genetic-chronologic,' then a third culture-classificatory arrangement is probably best designated as 'genetic-taxonomic.' This is the 'Midwestern Taxonomic Method' which was widely in vogue in the Middle Western and Eastern United States in the 1930s and 1940s. Its principal proponent was W. C. McKern, and it is sometimes referred to as the 'McKern Classification;' however, the system was first outlined by a conference group of Midwestern United States archaeologists in 1932 and subsequently revised by conference in 1935.[89] It was, thus, in formulation at more or less the same time that Gladwin's scheme was in the making.[90] The Midwestern Taxonomic Method deliberately eschewed the dimensions of space and time in the mechanics of its classification; nevertheless, we think that it would be fair to say that it would not have been devised except in a general climate of archaeological opinion where great stress was being laid on chronology. The difficulty was that in the Midwest and Eastern United States archaeological chronology seemed precluded by the apparent lack of deep refuse sites suitable for stratigraphy. The research of subsequent decades would show that this was not altogether true; however, as of 1930 few such sites had been discovered. In addition to this problem of no stratigraphy, there was another condition that prepared the way for the Midwestern Taxonomic Method. This was the presence of a great number of archaeological collections, available in museums or in private hands. These had been gathered over the years from site surfaces and from excavations. Most of the work had been done by amateurs, and in many cases there was little provenience information other than site or regional location. Still, such materials were a resource for the prehistory of the area, and a way would have to be found to deal with them. What was needed was a scheme that would give some order to these data. The Midwestern Taxonomic Method was a response to these circumstances and needs.

The Midwestern system operated solely with the cultural forms themselves, that is, with typology. Classification began with the unit of the culture complex as this complex could be recovered from the artifacts and features of an archaeological site. Such a unit was called a 'component.' In most instances the component was a site *in toto*, although in those few cases where stratification did obtain the component might be a level within a site. Such components were then grouped into 'foci,' the first and 'lowest' classificatory step on the genetic-taxonomic ladder. Components composing a focus were those which shared a very high percentage of trait similarities. Foci, in turn, were classified into 'aspects,' the next higher bracket in the system. Here there was still a substantial trait sharing. The next genetic-taxonomic level was the 'phase.' At this level traits held in common diminished in number from those of the aspect level. Phases were then classed into 'patterns' on very broad cultural criteria. For instance, in the Eastern United States it was generally conceded that among the prehistoric pottery-making cultures there were only two patterns, the Woodland and the Mississippian. The cultural characteristics of the former were semi-sedentary territorial adjustment, cord-marked or other surface-roughened pottery of sub-conoidal form, and stemmed or notched chipped stone points. In contrast, the broad Mississippian diagnostics were sedentary living, incised or modelled pottery of varying vessel shapes, and small triangular projectile points. Finally, the 'highest' classificatory bracket in the Midwestern system was the 'base,' a level on which distinctions were to be made between horticultural-pottery patterns and those lacking farming and ceramics.

Neither McKern nor the other proponents of the Midwestern scheme were turning their backs permanently on space and time, the two indispensable dimensions of culture history. In fact, the basic assumption of the system was that formal similarity reflected shared cultural origins and culture history. Thus, history was implicit in the method, if covert. McKern and his colleagues felt that once the classification had become reasonably complete it, and the archaeological cultures which composed it, could then be placed in spatial-temporal perspective by studies directed to these ends. In opposition to this view were those archaeologists working in the Southeastern United States where a promising beginning had been made with stratigraphy and seriation. These researchers were impatient with a strictly taxonomic method which, in their opinion, merely slowed down the march toward the ultimate goals of culture history. Viewed with hindsight, this argument was resolved in a way that might have been anticipated. As more became known about Eastern archaeology, especially from the standpoint of chronology, the debate over the merits and limitations of the Midwestern method began to recede. Gradually, taxonomic categories were given chronological dimension. 81

While the Pecos, Gladwin, and Midwestern Classifications all developed within the context of working field archaeology, one other culture-classification scheme comes from theoretical ethnology. This is the system of the Austrian *Kulturkreislehre* school'[91] It has had only limited application in American archaeology, and our reference to it will be brief. Its theoretical assumptions are those of worldwide culture spread, either through migration of peoples, diffusion, or both. Certain definable culture complexes, or *kreise*, have, thus, been spread. In the course of this, the complexes have frequently been modified by trait loss, addition, or alteration. A time-lag factor has operated in these spreads so that a complex will not describe an horizon of the same absolute dates in all parts of the world where it is found; nevertheless, the original relative time positions which culture complexes had in their hearth of origin often will be maintained in remote areas to which they have spread. As early as the 1930s, José Imbelloni, in Argentina, was a proponent of the approach in New World physical anthropology and, to some extent, in archaeology.[92] Later, O. F. A. Menghin, the European prehistorian working in Argentina, treated American archaeological data from this point of view.[93] But, except for some students of Menghin's and Imbelloni's, the *Kulturkreislehre* method has not had wide appeal for Americanists –

either as a scheme for local New World culture classification or as a means of demonstrating interhemispheric diffusions. The majority of American archaeologists while much concerned with diffusion and migration as processes are unwilling to see them 'built into' a classification scheme.

The Direct Historical Approach

At several places we have mentioned the close alliance of American archaeology and ethnology. One of the most important ways in which this association has been expressed is in what has come to be called the 'Direct Historical Approach' to archaeology. Very simply stated, the Direct Historical Approach means working back into prehistoric time from the documented historic horizon. In archaeology it involves sites where Native American Indian groups are known to have lived in early historic times so that the excavation of these sites reveals artifact complexes that can be associated with identifiable tribes or ethnic groups. The archaeologist may then find other sites in the region whose artifact complexes show stylistic overlap with the historically identified complexes but whose origins or beginnings go back to prehistoric times.

The term 'Direct Historical Approach' seems to have been first used in a formal designatory way by W. R. Wedel, in 1938;[94] however, the basic principle behind it is almost as old as archaeology. It was used by the Spanish explorers in Middle America and Peru in the 16th century when they identified certain living Indian groups with earlier monuments; Cyrus Thomas and F. H. Cushing employed the approach, albeit in a limited way, in their respective mound and Southwestern Puebloan studies; and it is the principle that linked Kroeber's prehistoric potsherd seriations to the historic and modern Zuñi sites. The Direct Historical Approach was also followed by A. C. Parker, in New York State, as early as 1916, when he investigated Indian village sites and related them to historic period Iroquoian tribes.[95] Later, W. A. Ritchie continued Parker's work in developing the prehistoric sequences for the region which were antecedent to the historic Iroquoian and Algonquian cultures.[96] Collins pioneered the approach in the Southeast, and Ford followed his lead.[97] But it was W. D. Strong who gave the greatest impetus to the Direct Historical Approach with his important monograph, *An Introduction to Nebraska Archaeology*, in 1935.[98]

Strong, assisted by W. R. Wedel, began with a rich background of historic site documentation that had been assembled by ethnologists and amateur archaeologists.[99] They excavated historic Pawnee sites and the closely related protohistoric period sites of the same tribe. From these they went on to dig the fully prehistoric sites of the region. This, and subsequent research,[100] laid the firm groundwork for Plains archaeology with its prehistoric Upper Republican, protohistoric, and historic Pawnee culture sequence in Nebraska. The chronologic and ethnohistoric aspects of the work were further enhanced and dramatized by the striking cultural changes that Strong was able to demonstrate in the develop-

Basic culture	Phase	Aspect	Focus	Component
Mississippi	Upper Mississippi	Nebraska	Omaha	Rock Bluffs, Gates Saunders, Walker Gilmore II.
			St. Helena	Butte, St. Helena, etc.
	Central Plains	Upper Republican	Lost Creek	Lost Creek, Prairie Dog Creek, etc.
			Sweetwater	Sweetwater, Munson Creek, etc.
			Medicine Creek	Medicine Creek
			North Platte	Signal Butte, III, etc.
		Lower Loup (Protohist. Pawnee?)	Beaver Creek	Burkett, Schuyler, etc.
		Lower Platte (Historic Pawnee)	Columbus	Horse Creek, Fullerton, Linwood, etc.
			Republican	Hill, etc.
	Woodland	Iowa "Algonkian"	Sterns Creek	Walker Gilmore I
Great Plains	Early Hunting	Signal Butte II(?)	Signal Butte	Signal Butte II
		Signal Butte I	Signal Butte	Signal Butte I
		Folsom	Northern Colorado	Lindenmeier (Colo.)

81 Strong's classification of Plains cultures in accordance with the Midwestern Taxonomic system. Strong, however, has arranged the classification in a chronological ordering – a procedure not a part of the Midwestern system. (From Strong, 1935)

ment of this tradition of Plains cultures. Riverine horticulturists were seen transformed to horse nomads in the span of the late prehistoric-to-historic centuries.[101] The potential of the approach for cultural interpretation and the examination of culture change was obvious. Strong's 'Nebraska Archaeology' became a model for this kind of archaeology as the method was then carried to other American areas in the late 1930s and after.

The Direct Historical Approach is, quite properly, termed an 'approach,' not a classification. Classificatory or taxonomic procedures are in no way essential to it. At one time J. H. Steward posed it in opposition to the Midwestern Taxonomic system as an alternative, and better, way of doing archaeology.[102] But there is no real conflict between the two on methodological grounds. The Midwestern scheme is taxonomic and comparative; the Direct Historical Approach is a method for investigating specific culture histories.[103]

81

Area Synthesis: The Goal

Stratigraphic and seriational methods, pottery and artifact typology, culture unit classification, and the Direct Historical Approach were all means employed during the early Classificatory-Historical Period in American archaeology for the eventual 'reconstruction of culture history.' The term 'reconstruction of culture history' may be interpreted to mean a good many different things, and the connotations placed upon it by archaeologists in the 1970s are not quite the same as those of thirty years ago; but to most New World archaeologists of 1940 the goal of such 'reconstruction,' or certainly

82, 83 Pre-Columbian Peruvian pottery. *Above*, a Recuay style vessel with negative-painted decoration. *Opposite*, a Moche style effigy vessel. Both specimens date from what Uhle designated as his 'Early Period' (now referred to by archaeologists as 'Early Intermediate Period')

82, 83

a very respectable 'half-way house,' was the 'area synthesis.' Such a 'synthesis' was usually little more than an ordering of the archaeological remains of a given area in a spatial-temporal framework. The essence of this ordering was the archaeological 'chronology chart,' a diagram arranged with chronological periods in a vertical column and geographical subdivisions across the top so that the various culture units (phases, foci) could be placed in their appropriate boxes. By 1940 a number of such American area charts could be drawn with reasonable confidence. In the North American Southwest the time column could be calibrated in absolute years, thanks to dendrochronology; and for parts of Middle America absolute chronology was provided by the Pre-Columbian Maya calendar. Elsewhere relative chronology still prevailed. Besides the Southwest and Middle America, large-scale area syntheses had been attempted in Peru, the Eastern United States, Alaska, and the West Indies. In addition to these areas – all of which correspond more or less to the culture areas of the ethnographer – there were others in which archaeological chronologies had been begun on limited regional bases but had not yet been extended in area-wide fashion.

We have already observed (Chapter Three) that the first American area archaeological synthesis actually preceded the Classificatory-Historical Period. This was the achievement of Max Uhle who pieced together a Peruvian area chronology – from stylistic seriation, the horizon-marking effectiveness of the Tiahuanacoid and Inca styles, and occasional data of cultural superposition – as early as 1900. For a while little was done with the Uhle synthesis. He was followed in Peru by J. C. Tello and P. A. Means. These were both able scholars, but they were as much interested in ethnohistory and Inca ethnology as in archaeology; and neither presented his archaeological conclusions with adequate supporting evidence. Tello's 'reconstruction' of the Peruvian past paid little attention to the Uhle chronological scheme. Instead, he saw the rise of Peruvian civilization entirely from the point of view of the highlands as the *fons et origo* of all significant cultural development and spread.[104] Means was more influenced by Uhle. For instance, he utilized the concept of a Tiahuanaco horizon;[105] however, he was not a field archaeologist, and he did nothing to verify or disprove the Uhle chronological structure.

The leading proponent and chief conceptualizer of the Uhle synthesis was Kroeber. As already noted, he made detailed seriation studies on the Uhle collections in the 1920s and also carried out field explorations in Peru in the same decade. In 1927 he published an important article, 'Coast and Highland in Prehistoric Peru.'[106] In this he summarized Uhle's work and his own investigations, commented upon the Tello and Means schemes, and went on to outline what he considered to be the major problems of Peruvian archaeology. He conceived of these mainly as the clarification of chronological relationships. Subsequently, following the excavations of W. C. Bennett[107] and Rafael Larco Hoyle[108] in the 1930s, Kroeber visited Peru once more, traveling over the country, reviewing sites and collections, and conferring with a

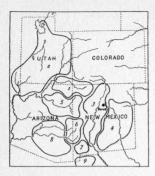

84 Southwestern cultural 'areas' (or regions) following Kidder's 1924 synthesis. 1 San Juan; 2 Northern Peripheral; 3 Rio Grande; 4 Eastern Peripheral; 5 Little Colorado; 6 Upper Gila; 7 Mimbres; 8 Lower Gila; 9 Chihuahua Basin. (From Kidder, 1924)

number of young colleagues who were then digging in the country. The result of this visit was the short monograph, *Peruvian Archaeology in 1942*.[109] In it he accepted Larco Hoyle's and Tello's early dating of the Chavin culture and placed Chavin as another major horizon style in the Peruvian area synthesis. In addition to the substantive chronological summary, the Kroeber 1942 synthesis is also noteworthy for its first clear definition of this concept of the 'horizon style.'

As might be expected, the North American Southwest was not far behind Peru in chronological synthesis. In 1924 Kidder published *An Introduction to the Study of Southwestern Archaeology*.[110] In this, he mapped out nine subdivisions of the Southwestern area,[111] and then treated the archaeology of each in accordance with a chronological scheme of: (1) Basket Maker; (2) Post-Basket Maker; (3) Pre-Pueblo; and (4) Pueblo. These generally correspond to the periods of the Pecos Classification which was to be devised in the 1927 Conference, a few years later. Basket Maker was to become Basketmaker II, the pre-pottery but horticultural beginnings of the Southwestern sequence as it was then known; Post-Basket Maker was changed to Basketmaker III, the 'modified' Basketmaker culture which possessed pottery; Pre-Pueblo, with its small above-ground structures and relatively simple pottery, was more or less synonymous with Pueblo I in the later Pecos Classification; and fully developed Pueblo corresponded to the periods of Pueblo II, III, and IV. Kidder prefaced his detailing of the archaeology with a short chapter on the modern pueblos. This described something of their life ways and history, and it also offered suggestions as to just how the various Puebloan groups may have descended from the earlier prehistoric cultures. Most of Kidder's archaeological information came from the northern regions and from the Rio Grande. For other parts of the Southwest, such as the southern deserts, little more could be offered in 1924 than a description of 'Red-on-buff' pottery and some of the adobe architecture.

In spite of its limitations, Kidder's *Introduction* marked the 'coming of age' of the Southwest as an archaeological area. New work could be fitted into a spatial-temporal structure, and such a structure pointed the way to problems. Great advances were made in the 1930s. One of these was methodological and interdisciplinary. A. E. Douglass, the astronomer, had long been studying Southwestern tree-ring growth patterns as an aid in research on sun-spot cycles. Beginning with living trees, he also extended his search for materials into archaeological Pueblo ruins which had preserved wooden timbers. By 1929 he had built up two long tree-ring sequences. One ran back from the present, through the historic, and into the late prehistoric Pueblo periods; the other was a floating chronology, which pertained to some as yet unassigned segment of the prehistoric past. In the summer of 1929 timbers were found in certain prehistoric ruins in eastern Arizona that allowed Douglass to 'close the gap' between his two tree-ring chronologies. The result was a means of accurate year-to-year dating which could be applied to those Southwestern ruins located in the northern regions of the area where the proper trees and tree growth circumstances permitted. A beam specimen, of either preserved wood or charcoal, was simply compared against the 'master chart' tree-ring chronology and placed at that point where its patterns of ring growth (large or normal year rings contrasted with small or drought year rings) indicated a match.[112] By the middle 1930s Southwestern chronology for the north and north-eastern regions could be quoted in absolute time. Thus, it became known that Basketmaker II antedated A.D. 500; Basketmaker III fell between 500 and 700; Pueblo I between 700 and 900; Pueblo II between 900 and 1100; Pueblo III lasted from 1100 to 1300; and Pueblo IV from 1300 to 1600.[113] One of the things this exact dating did was to make the archaeologists aware of the time-lag factor in cultural diffusion and spread, and this pointed up the fact that the 'periods' of the Pecos Classification were really 'stages' of cultural development rather than absolute time periods. With chronology held as an 'extra-cultural' constant, the archaeo-logist could now ponder things like rates of cultural spread and culture change where previously he had only culture change, itself, as a measure of time.

The other advances were in sheer substantive knowledge. Gladwin and his cohorts opened up the southern Arizona Hoho-kam cultural division of the Southwest through the systematic chronological-distributional work that has been noted in our discussions of stratigraphy, seriation, and classification. Haury and Martin did the same for the Mogollon country. Hohokam was seen to have ties to Mexican cultures; and Mogollon could be linked to both Hohokam and to Anasazi (the new name for the Basketmaker-Pueblo cultural continuum). In general, the area was proving to be more culturally diverse than had been thought.

New area syntheses of the 1930s attempted to take this cultural diversity into account. Roberts did this in two summary articles,[114] and Gladwin offered another overview in the concluding mono-graph on the Snaketown excavations.[115] When J. C. McGregor brought out his book-length *Southwestern Archaeology* in 1941 he had to make accommodation for still more regional diversity as well as for chronological expansion. It was now clear that a hunting-collecting 'Cochise culture' had preceded the Basket-makers and the other early Southwestern farmers by several thousand years.[116] McGregor even suggested a new South-western-wide area chronology,[117] with a period terminology that was intended to capture the salient characteristics of each period; however, he did not use the scheme in his actual data presentation but reverted, instead, to the more conventional subareal chronologies of Anasazi, Hohokam, Mogollon, and Patayan.

In Middle America there had been some chronological ordering in the Maya Lowlands prior to 1914. This had been made possible by the translations of Maya calendrical inscriptions and the corre-lations of these calendrical dates with those of the Christian calendar. Although there was some debate as to just how these correlations should be made, the result was a 'floating chronology' almost 600 years in length which fell somewhere in the first millennium A.D.[118] Unfortunately, this important means of

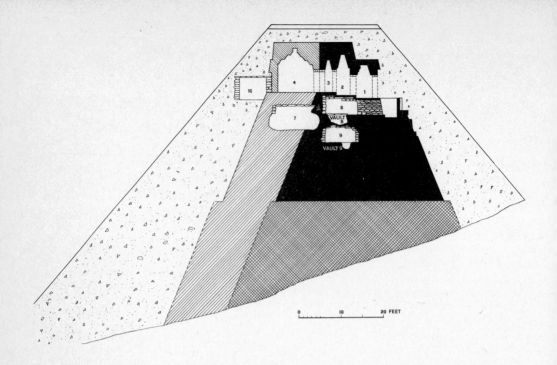

85 Cross-section drawing of pyramid, Holmul, Guatemala. This Maya Lowland building was excavated by Merwin in 1912, and it is important in Maya archaeology because of its architectural stratigraphy (which was not made known until 1932). The outer casing of the pyramid dates as Late Classic; that portion of the interior structure with the corbelled-vault rooms dates as Early Classic; the earliest building phase, without vaulted buildings and with tombs 8 and 9, dates as very late Preclassic. The pottery from these tombs was the first from the Maya Lowlands to be identified as similar to Spinden's 'Archaic' pottery from the Valley of Mexico. (From Merwin and Vaillant, 1932)

dating was limited to the Maya Lowlands, where such inscriptions were found. Elsewhere in Middle America there was little in the way of chronology. There was, of course, the Valley of Mexico, where a gross relative chronology had been begun by Gamio, but this was the only exception. Spinden's handbook on Mexico, the best synthesis for the Mesoamerican area in the 1920s, suffered from this lack of regional chronological information.[119] Although an admirable summary, and one which went beyond sheer description in his concept of an 'Archaic' culture, the attempts to order the various Mesoamerican cultures chronologically were far wide of the mark. Forced to operate wholly by conjecture, he surmised, for instance, that Classic Maya civilization had preceded that of Teotihuacan and Monte Alban – something that has not withstood the tests of further research.

In fact, even as early as the late 1920s, G. C. Vaillant was beginning to question Spinden's chronological ordering. Vaillant's own experience in the Valley of Mexico, his work with Maya pottery, the Carnegie Institution's recent diggings in the Maya Lowlands[120] and Highlands,[121] and Alfonso Caso's explorations at Monte Alban in Oaxaca[122] all combined to suggest significantly different interpretations from those offered by Spinden. Vaillant had actually begun such a synthesis in 1927 in an unpublished Ph.D. dissertation.[123] He went further along these lines in a 1935 article;[124] and, in 1941, he gave his ideas detailed expression in his book, *Aztecs of Mexico*.[125] In this book he offered an area-wide period terminology. He reserved the bottom-most bracket on the time chart for undiscovered Paleo-Indian cultures. For the next period, advancing in time, he changed Spinden's name of 'Archaic' to that of 'Middle Cultures,' in recognition of the very likely possibility that they were not the earliest on the Mesoamerican scene. Vaillant then applied the names 'Full Inde-

86

pendent Civilizations' and 'Late Independent Civilizations' to what are, today, the Early and Late Classic Periods. For the Post-classic Vaillant used the name 'Mixteca-Puebla Period.' after the dominant culture of that time. A spatial-temporal organization of the data was beginning to take shape. With the perspective of thirty years, we see that the most significant changes have been in the downward chronological extension of the 'Middle' (or Preclassic) cultures, the realization of the importance of Olmec among these, and in the identification of Tula, rather than Teoti-huacan, with the Toltecs. Of course, radiocarbon dating, which was not available to Vaillant, had deepened the time scale for the 'Middle' (or Preclassic) cultures well below the 1941 estimate of 200 B.C.

In the Eastern United States a purely taxonomic synthesis, in the manner of the Midwestern Taxonomic Method, had been pub-lished by Thorne Deuel in 1935.[126] There had also been some regional syntheses which dealt with chronology, such as those of Parker and Ritchie in New York,[127] Strong's in Nebraska,[128] and Setzler's in the northern Mississippi Valley.[129] But the first major temporal-spatial organization of the prehistory cultures of the entire East was Ford and Willey's in 1941.[130] They devised an area chronology, somewhat after the fashion of the Pecos Classification, but instead of employing the period concept they conceived of stages or periods of 'sloping horizons.' Virtually nothing was known of 'Early Man' in the East at this date (al-though there was important information from the western Plains) so this stage was omitted from the Ford–Willey synthesis. They began with the 'Archaic,' a term then used in some regions

86 'Archaic' or 'Middle Culture' figurines from Central Mexico. (These are more commonly re-ferred to now as Preclassic or Formative Period.) Heights (from left to right): 10.3 cm., 13.2 cm., 11.5 cm. (From Vail-lant and Vaillant, 1934)

 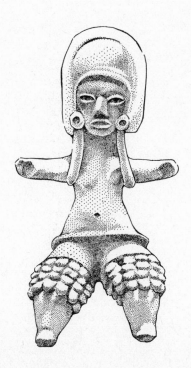 

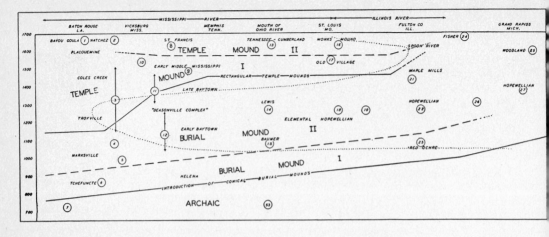

87 Chronology chart from Ford and Willey's Synthesis of Eastern North American archaeology. Successive stages are indicated with time-lag slope following authors' interpretations of the direction of diffusion of traits. Culture phase names are shown, and the small numbers in circles refer to individual sites. (From Ford and Willey, 1941)

of the Eastern United States to refer to preceramic, presumably non-farming cultures.[131] On the extensive chronology charts Ford and Willey gave no indications as to the origin point or direction of movement of Archaic cultures; but for the first of their pottery-making stages, which they called 'Burial Mound I' (Early Woodland and Adena cultures), the direction of cultural diffusion (and perhaps population migration) was plotted as from south-to-north. Similarly, the innovative influences and/or peoples on the succeeding 'Burial Mound II' (Middle Woodland and Hopewellian cultures), 'Temple Mound I' (Early Mississippian), and 'Temple Mound II' (Late Mississippian) stages were all thought of as coming from somewhere in the south (ultimately from Mesoamerica) and then spreading up the Mississippi Valley and its tributaries. The scheme was more all-embracing and ambitious than the Pecos chronology. It not only covered more territory and more cultural variation, but it took on the task of describing the diffusional dynamics for the area. This last was speculative, and it is now clear that the picture Ford and Willey sketched was much too simple a one. The East was not an empty area, or a low-level culture zone, which was then filled by successive movements of people or diffusions of ideas from Mesoamerica. Archaic culture has since been demonstrated to have great time depth, regional variation, and richness; and we know that subsequent developments in the East must have owed as much to this heritage as they did to exotic intrusions. Also, the guess-dating estimates which Ford and Willey applied to their chronology have been shown, by radiocarbon, to have been ridiculously late, especially for the earlier stages of their scheme. Nevertheless, the chronological-developmental order of the synthesis proved correct as did most of the specific culture unit assignments associated with it. A few years later J. B. Griffin was to publish another general chronological scheme for the East, using the Archaic-Woodland-Mississippian terminology for his periods and being much more cautious about the directions of cultural diffusion.[132] Together, these two syntheses provided the larger chronological framework for archaeological discourse about the East for the ensuing decades.

In the Arctic a number of archaeological excavations[133] oriented to problems of chronology laid a basis for area synthesis. Several syntheses or partial syntheses appeared prior to 1940,[134] but Collins's[135] summary of that data was, perhaps, the most successful and may be taken as a summary of what was known at the end of the early part of our Classificatory-Historical Period. In it he postulated an original Eskimo culture being brought across the Bering Strait from Asia at some unknown time in the past. From this beginning he conceived of a splitting-off of a Dorset culture of the East, a Kachemak Bay I development of southern Alaska, an Aleutian Islands branch, and an Old Bering Sea culture. The Birnirk, Punuk, and Thule cultures later developed out of the Old Bering Sea culture. Thule first spread eastward and then, on a very late prehistoric horizon, spread back to the West to give a uniformity to all modern Eskimo cultures of the Far North. Collins's dating estimates on most of this have turned out to be not far out. The basic Eskimo culture has been pushed back to the third millennium B.C. in the form of Denbigh, and there now are clues to much earlier Eskimoid or Denbigh-like cultures as far east as Greenland. Still older lithic cultures have also been discovered in the Arctic. But the picture as seen by Collins in 1940 gave a secure nucleus around which further chronological-distributional findings could be formed.

In the West Indies Rouse's Haitian investigations provided a core of chronological information around which he constructed a general sequence for most of the Greater Antilles by a series of comparisons.[136] In California the excavations in the Sacramento Valley began chronology for this area.[137] For the rest of North America in the 1914-40 period archaeological chronology was still in the future. This was also true for most of South America. In spite of the considerable systematic work that had been carried out by the Argentines and Chileans there was still little or no chronological ordering for these countries.[138] An exception was in far southern South America where J. B. Bird had revealed a long sequence going back to an 'Early Man' horizon and continuing forward in time to the historic period.[139] This Strait of Magellan sequence was to be most important to American archaeology for it showed that man had reached the southern extremity of this hemisphere at a relatively early time. How early was not known then, but subsequent radiocarbon dates for Bird's earliest period have placed it in the 9000-8000 B.C. range.

Inter-Areal Considerations

Although area synthesis was the overall goal in the early Classificatory-Historical Period, some attention was also paid to inter-areal relationships. These could hardly be called 'syntheses.' At best, they were attempts at cultural correlations, usually with an eye toward chronology. Many of them focused attention on occasional long-distance similarities in odd pottery forms or designs which suggested some sort of prehistoric culture contacts.[140] Some brought linguistic affiliations and possible movements of people into the argument to bolster similarities in the archaeological record.[141] Some viewed the data quite critically and made every effort to plot diffusion or trade within believable chronological limits.[142] Lack of absolute chronological control was a major stumbling-block in examining or testing these hypotheses for contact.[143] It was obvious that there had been currents of influence running from Middle America north to the Southwestern United States as well as to the Mississippi Valley, but the questions of when, what, and how eluded the archaeologists.[144]

Actually, the most interesting and fruitful of all of these attempts to correlate or in some way integrate the data of two or more American areas was Spinden's 'Archaic Hypothesis.' First enunciated in 1917,[145] and further elaborated in his handbook of 1928, the 'Archaic Hypothesis' had both chronological and developmental implications. Spinden had been inspired by the results of Gamio's Valley of Mexico excavations which had revealed a simpler culture underneath the remains of the more elaborate Teotihuacan civilization. This culture had competently made pottery, hand-made pottery figurines, and was further characterized by deep village refuse and evidences of farming. Spinden noted that similar pottery and figurines were found in

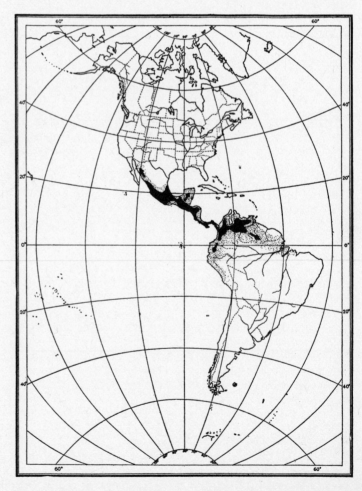

88 The distribution of 'Archaic' culture in the Americas as conceived by Spinden. (From Spinden, 1917)

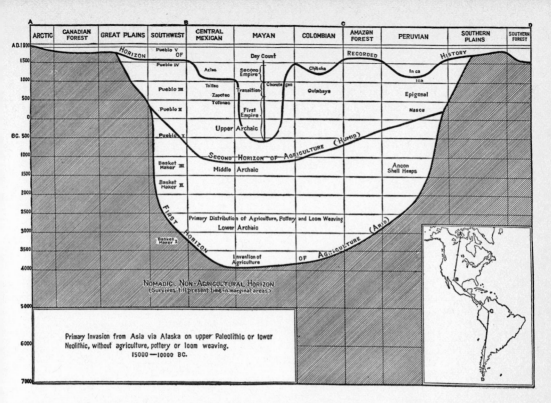

other parts of Mesoamerica, and this suggested to him that the later civilizations of Mesoamerica – Teotihuacan, Maya, Zapotec, and so forth – were the regionally specialized developments arising from a common American village farming base which he called the 'Archaic.' Further considerations led him to see signs of the 'Archaic' in the American Southwest, in Peru, and Argentina. In other words, this 'Archaic' was a kind of American Neolithic. Having its origins in the Valley of Mexico, it had spread outward to other parts of the hemisphere from this center and was, in this sense, an historically interrelated phenomenon. But its significance was also as an evolutionary stage in the rise of New World civilization. Vaillant, among others, took issue with Spinden.[146] As cultures contemporaneous with the Valley of Mexico 'Archaic' began to be revealed in other parts of Mesoamerica, it became obvious that many of these had quite complex or sophisticated traits that were not found in the supposed 'Mother Culture' of the Valley of Mexico 'Archaic.' Gradually, it became clear that Spinden's Valley of Mexico 'Archaic' was a relatively late phase in the development of the 'Archaic,' or Preclassic, and that the story of these early, presumably basic, farming cultures was infinitely more complex than he had imagined. In spite of this, Spinden had been on the right track. Certainly it was on this general time level of the 'Archaic,' or Preclassic, farmers that many fundamental ideas of New World cultures, including agriculture and pottery-making, were transmitted from one to another. Further, such a basic farming condition was also a developmental prerequisite to later cultural elaborations and civilizations.

In concluding our brief comments on inter-areal relationships, this seems an appropriate place to make even briefer ones on the

89 Spinden's conception of the development of Pre-Columbian civilizations. The establishment of 'Archaic' culture defines the base or 'floor' of the white loop. Incidentally, it is interesting to note that Spinden dated the primary invasion of the Americas from Asia, via the Bering Strait, at *ca.* 15,000–10,000 B.C. This was probably a sheer guess on his part, but it indicates that not all Americanist thinking on this matter was following Hrdlička's shortened chronology. The Figgins Folsom discoveries, which validated man's late Pleistocene presence in the Americas, were published in 1927. Spinden was probably not aware of them when he prepared the manuscript for his 1928 *Handbook* from which this diagram is taken. (Spinden, 1928)

concern with inter-hemispheric contacts. By this we do not refer to the ancient Bering Strait crossings of Paleolithic men from Asia to the Americas but, rather, the possibilities of contacts between later Old World cultures and those of the New. As noted, this was a major theme of archaeology in the Speculative Period, and these concerns persisted into later periods where they were treated both speculatively and objectively. Only the latter treatment needs mention here. We have already remarked on the *Kulturkreislehre* classifactory approach and have indicated how it was geared to inter-hemispheric migration-diffusion studies between the Old and New Worlds. Another less programmatic but equally systematic approach was that of Erland von Nordenskiöld. He compiled lists of similar traits from Asia and the New World.[147] Many of these were of definite Pre-Columbian provenience. Some may have been accidental convergences; others possibly could have been brought by early immigrants on a Paleolithic-Paleo-Indian level; but others, such as the technique of 'lost-wax' casting of metals, were of a complexity that suggested later contacts. Nordenskiöld was cautious in his presentations, pushing no particular claims. For the most part, the temper of American archaeologists of the time on this issue was 'wait-and-see.'[148]

Advances on the Early Man Front

We left 'Early Man' studies in the Classificatory-Descriptive Period in a state of doubt and confusion. Various finds had been put forward as being of great age – some on the basis of rather general similarity to European Paleolithic implements and some because of apparent association with Pleistocene fauna or geological strata – but none of these finds could be validated as being truly ancient. The 'breakthrough' came in 1926 when J.D. Figgins discovered chipped stone projectile points and extinct bison remains in a geological context of undisputed Late Pleistocene age at Folsom, New Mexico.[149] The stratum in which the artifacts and bones were found was a deeply buried clay layer

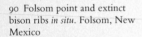
90 Folsom point and extinct bison ribs *in situ*. Folsom, New Mexico

which represented a former water hole, apparently a site where the ancient hunters killed the large herbivores when they came there to drink. The projectile points of the Folsom site were of highly distinctive form, lanceolates with incurved bases and flutings of the sides. After the Folsom discovery, similar points were found under similar Pleistocene conditions, and with extinct faunal associations, in the Clovis-Portales region of New Mexico[150] and at Lindenmeier, Colorado.[151]

Thus, by 1940 the case for 'Early Man' in the Americas had become established. The 'Hrdlička position' of man's relatively late entrance on the New World scene, which had dominated the thinking of the earlier decades, had fallen. Age estimates were still geological guesses, generally ranging from 15,000 to 10,000 years. Since then, radiocarbon dates have shortened this somewhat for Clovis-Folsom although not by very much. Distinctions in typology and differential ages of the various early complexes were then only vaguely discerned. Writing in 1940, Roberts made no formal separation between the Folsom and Clovis points.[152] Another point, the 'Yuma,' which had fine flaking but no fluting, was thought, perhaps, to be somewhat later than Folsom. Other early artifact complexes were also known by 1940, including those of Sandia Cave (New Mexico), Gypsum Cave (Nevada), Signal Butte (Nebraska), Clear Fork (Texas), Mojave and Pinto Basin (California), and Cochise (southern Arizona).[153] The antiquity of these was implied by typology, geological or faunal associations, cultural stratigraphy, or combinations of these. In the next three decades some would be validated, some rejected, and others continued in a limbo of debate. Patterns in affiliation, distribution, and chronological placement would emerge; but as of 1940 it was still too early for this.

91, 92 Excavations at Lindenmeier (Colorado) in 1937, and fluted Folsom points and knives from the Lindenmeier site

93 A partially excavated Maya temple. The building is the famous 'E-VII-Sub', a Late Preclassic stucco-faced pyramid at Uaxactun, Guatemala. The Carnegie Institution archaeologists who excavated it in the late 1920s (Ricketson and Ricketson, 1937) removed the overlying fill of the badly damaged later pyramids which had been built over it, to reveal the earlier building. This kind of architectural digging, by peeling or cleaning hard-surfaced structures, was typical of Middle American archaeology of the period and still is

94 Field map of a mound excavation in Illinois showing the five-foot grid and burial and other features. Such a plan was available at the close of mound-slicing operations. (From Cole and Deuel, 1937)

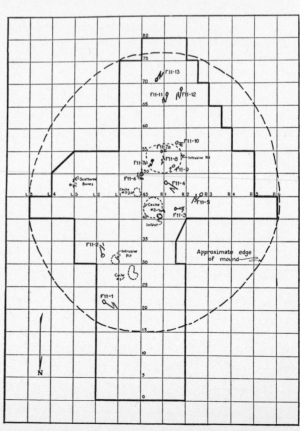

95, 96 Mound excavation in the Southeastern United States. Beginning the profiling or slicing of a mound (*top*). Technique of drawing soil profiles of a mound with portable string and frame grid (*bottom*). (cf. Webb and De Jarnette, 1942)

Field Methods and Techniques

The improvement of field methods and techniques continued unabated into the Classificatory-Historical Period. The necessities of stratigraphy furthered this, for one thing, but the more spectacular field innovations in the 1914–40 period were in the excavation of features. In Middle America and, to some extent, in the Southwest, what might be thought of as feature digging or architectural digging devolved from the nature of the remains themselves. The stone-covered pyramids or plaster-gravel floors of Middle American sites made themselves known to the uncovering spade in an unambiguous fashion.[154] They were easy to follow. Southwestern pueblo walls and floors were similar.

93

97 Excavation of a Pre-Columbian house structure in Tennessee, possibly a temple or chief's house. It was situated on the top of a flat-topped mound. The construction technique of small poles set in slit-like trenches has been disclosed by the peeling or scraping excavation technique in which differences in soil texture and color have been very closely followed. A fire basin can also be seen near the center of the building

But in the Eastern United States it was more difficult. Earthen mounds and houses which had been made of wood or thatch left much less in the way of definite outlines. The archaeologist had to proceed more cautiously if he wanted to obtain a proper feature record. At first, this was done by arbitrary control points: surveyed grids, benchmarks, and the like, from which features were measured and plotted as the excavation proceeded. Burial mounds were sectioned by five-foot slices, and cross-sectional mound profiles were drawn at these intervals.[155] In some instances this probably provided an adequate record, but in others it soon became obvious that much in the way of former surface features – either from sub-mound levels or from various buried mound surfaces – was either being lost or was being made extraordinarily difficult to recover by a subsequent piecing together of a series of small vertical-slice records. Clearly, a peeling technique, like that long used in the Old World Middle East, or, to a degree, in Middle America or the Southwest, was called for; and this was soon widely employed in the North American East.[156] Clay house floors, temple floors, or special building floors were carefully scraped, with diggers following lines of soil color and texture. Old post holes were revealed, sometimes filled with charred burned posts, sometimes marked only by a dark smudge of earth where the wood had decayed (a 'post-mold'). Entries, fire-basins, and other features were disclosed. These not only gave a better record for the field notebook, but it made possible photographs that offered the viewer or reader a much better idea of the feature in question than even the most painstaking descriptions. There was nothing very profound or brilliant about any of this except that the point was being made that it was to the archaeologist's advantage to uncover the disjointed fragments of the lost past in such a way that they could be as fully re-articulated into their original condition as possible. At this lowly and mechanical level these were the first steps on the way to the recovery of context, function, and, hopefully, an understanding of culture process.

94
95
96
97
98

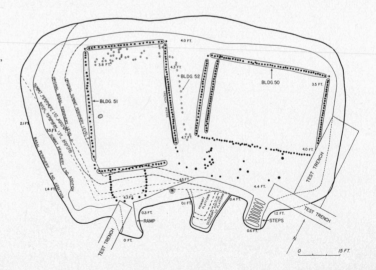

98 Map of structure plans, as indicated by post-molds and other features, on mound platform. (From Lewis and Kneberg, 1946)

Chapter Five

The Classificatory-Historical Period:
The Concern with Context and Function (1940–60)

'Archaeology . . . is always limited in the results it can produce. It is doomed always to be the lesser part of anthropology.' E. *Adamson Hoebel*

A Definition of the Period

The somewhat depressing quotation above, taken from the writings of a leading American ethnologist of the time, is a fair statement of how anthropology as a whole regarded archaeology in the Classificatory-Historical Period. Ethnology and social anthropology were considered to be the places where the main bastions of theory and wisdom were located. Archaeology was definitely peripheral. Any attempt on the part of the archaeologist to contribute to the larger problems of cultural understanding was met with an astonishment like that in the classic case of the 'talking dog'; it was not what the dog said that was so amazing but the fact that he could do it at all. Most archaeologists accepted their marginal position and second-class status with becoming humility; only a few were restive. While the latter were willing to admit that 'archaeology is always limited in the results it can produce,' they were also inclined to inquire if ethnology did not also have its limitations. Might not an archaeological study of the cultural succession of material objects over a long and otherwise unrecorded span of time reveal to us things of importance that even the most omniscient of living informants could not disclose to an ethnologist? Why, indeed, should archaeology be 'doomed always to be the lesser part of anthropology'? Perhaps it had a potential as yet unrealized. Such, in any event, were the seditious thoughts in the minds of some archaeologists who were also encouraged by a few sympathetic ethnologists to ask such questions. These thoughts and questions were to lead to a critical re-examination of the aims and procedures of archaeology and the instigation of some new experimental trends that were to characterize the latter half of the Classificatory-Historical Period.

These new experimental trends concerned context and function – and hinted at process. They did not replace the prevailing preoccupation of the Classificatory-Historical Period which remained firmly set in chronological ordering. The dissatisfactions, stirrings, and experiments did not cohere into a 'revolution' – that was to come later – but they were portents of the future. The decades from 1940 to 1960, we think, are appropriately contained within the definitions of the Classificatory-Historical Period, but it was also a time of ferment and transition.

The new contextual-functional approaches are considered under three headings in our discussions. The first of these headings or categories takes as its theme the proposition that artifacts are to be understood as the material relics of social and cultural behavior. While earlier attempts had been made to ascribe use or function to archaeological artifacts, the difference in the 1940–60 period was in the close attention paid to context in arriving at functional inferences.

A second contextual-functional approach is that of settlement patterns. It was felt that the way man had arranged himself upon the landscape, with relation to its natural features and with relation to other men, held important clues for the archaeologist in his understanding of socio-economic adaptations and socio-political organizations.

The third approach, relating to the other two is that of the relationships between culture and natural environment. That is, it involved man and his resource base. While sometimes referred to as 'cultural ecology' in the 1940–60 period, it was generally something less than the ecosystem approach of more recent years.

In the search for context and function, these methodologies were abetted and further stimulated by scientific aids from other disciplines. Geological findings become steadily more important to archaeology; botany and biology were keys in furthering culture-natural environment studies and in tracing out the histories of domestication; material analyses of all kinds, in chemistry, metallurgy, and physics, allowed for greater insights into the processes of artifact manufacture as well as for identifications of sources of raw commodities. Above all, radiocarbon dating provided absolute dates for archaeologists, and this had important repercussions in freeing them from their overwhelming concern with chronology and the means for obtaining it and allowing them to turn their attention to other aspects of culture history and development.

As we have noted, these new trends and interdisciplinary borrowings in no way stifled the conventional archaeological tasks of constructing spatial-temporal syntheses for New World regions and areas. After World War II archaeological investigations in the Americas became many times more what they had been in the pre-war era, and the great majority of these investigations were directed to the goal of chronology building. Old sequences were corrected or refined, and new ones were established in regions heretofore unexplored. The concepts of 'horizons' and 'traditions' were formulated and widely used. These were historical constructs concerned primarily with the occurrences of styles or technical features in space and time and in the establishment of diffusional or genetic connections between such forms. At the same time they had other properties in that they attempted to reconstruct or elucidate the circumstances of these relationships and, in this way, might be said to have linked strict historical with functional objectives.

The latter half of the Classificatory-Historical Period also saw the formulation of archaeological syntheses which went beyond the historical and functional and added to these the dimension of cultural evolutionary process. Such syntheses, with their cross-cultural or comparative orientation, were harbingers of the search for process and explanation which became so important after 1960.

The First Dissatisfactions

The first signs of dissatisfaction with the limited goals of chronological ordering in American archaeology appeared in the late 1930s. The earliest, in point of time, was William Duncan Strong's essay, 'Anthropological Theory and Archaeological Fact,' published in 1936.[1] In it he challenged archaeologists and ethnologists to work in concert in order to understand cultural development and change. The year before, Strong had given eloquent testimony to the pertinence of ethnology in his 'direct-historical approach' to Nebraska archaeology. He advocated that archaeologists look to ethnology for theoretical leads as well as strictly factual ones.

Paul Martin also sought the theoretical collaboration of archaeologists and ethnologists. In his summaries and conclusions to two Southwestern archaeological site reports in 1938 and 1939, he went beyond the suggestions of Strong by using Redfield's concept of 'folk culture' to explain variation in the size, form, and contents of prehistoric Pueblo ruins.[2]

Neither Strong's nor Martin's 'dissatisfactions' were put forward as such. Rather than pointing out the error of old ways, they were indicating new paths that night be explored. Instead it was left to the ethnologists to sharply criticize the archaeologists. One of those to do so was Julian H. Steward, who teamed with the archaeologist F. M. Setzler in bringing out an article called 'Function and Configuration in Archaeology.'[3] By that time Steward had published a major ethnological monograph on the native tribes of the North American Great Basin[4] and had also carried out and published archaeological research in the same area.[5] Therefore he was familiar at first hand with both of these aspects of anthropology. In their essay, Steward and Setzler took the position that most American archaeologists were so immersed in minutiae that they never came to grips with the larger objectives of archaeology. In their opinion, these objectives should be the same for the archaeologist as for the ethnologist: an understanding of culture change as well as a geographical-chronological plotting of its manifestations. Archaeologists should try to see their particular cultures in general, as well as detailed, perspective. For example, they should ask questions about the subsistence base as well as about the form of arrowheads or the designs on pottery. They should seek information on the sizes of the human populations through examinations of subsistence potentials and settlement pattern studies. In this last connection it is of interest that in the preceding year Steward had published an article – now a classic – with the title of 'Ecological Aspects of Southwestern Society,' in which he had drawn together archaeological and ethnological settlement data in demonstrating a thesis on cultural-environmental interaction in the North American Southwest.[6] All in all, the tone of the Steward-Setzler article, while not severely polemical, was definitely critical of the way archaeology was being practiced in the Americas.

A much more caustic statement on the then current condition of American archaeology was one made by Clyde Kluckhohn, 'The Conceptual Structure in Middle American Studies.'[7] published in the 1940 Festschrift volume, *The Maya and Their Neighbors*, in honor of the 'Dean' of Maya studies, Alfred M. Tozzer.[8] Most of the articles in the volume were by Mesoamerican archeological specialists, and most were solidly in the traditions of the early Classificatory-Historical Period. Kluckhohn, although an ethnologist-social anthropologist, had done some archaeological work.[9] At that time he probably would have agreed with the statement that archaeology was 'the lesser part of anthropology,' but he would also have insisted that it need not be. This, in fact, was what his article was about. He asks some of the same questions that Steward and Setzler had put: What are the objectives of archaeology? To what ends are data gathered and presented? He felt that most Middle American archaeologists, scholarly and expert as they were, had a tendency to wallow in detail for and of itself alone. In addition to this, the field seemed pervaded with a fear of 'theory.' In fact, in the American archaeological lexicon of the 1930s – for Middle America as well as elsewhere – the word 'theory' was a pejorative synonym for 'speculation.' In Kluckhohn's words:

'Ask an archaeologist to set forth and justify his conceptual scheme. It is an induction from my experience that the betting odds are enormous against this having even occurred to him as a problem.'[10]

In brief, Middle American archaeology – and American archaeology as a whole – operated without explicit theoretical or conceptual formulations. This meant that theory was often implicit and unexamined. Assumptions about such things as cultural stability, the mechanics of diffusion, monogenesis or polygenesis, and the relationships of race, language, and culture went untested although they were passed along as common coin. Kluckholn felt that Middle American archaeology, or any archaeology, had two choices in conceptual direction. One of these would be 'historic' in the sense of following out and re-creating unique events in their particularity. The other alternative would be 'scientific,' or comparative, namely a consideration of the data with an eye toward examining trends and uniformities in cultural development and process.

He contended that Middle American archaeologists had never faced up to this choice. He saw most of the scholars in the field up to that time as being essentially involved in historical particulars. He cited Vaillant and Kidder as having had interests which verged on the 'scientific' although, in his opinion, neither of them had followed through with systematic research nor expositions of conceptual means. Kluckhohn, himself, voiced a preference for the 'scientific' course. While he admitted that there was an argument that the two approaches might be looked upon as sequent phases of planned research, he leaned toward the belief that data collected for 'historical' purposes would seldom be serviceable for 'scientific' ones.

The early complaints about the state of archaeology shared two basic themes. One of these concerned the need for archaeologists to translate their findings – the material remains with which they dealt – into cultural behavior. The other theme was that the archaeologist should be alert to culture process. In the latter part of the Classificatory-Historical Period it was to be the first of these themes that claimed attention. The second, the consideration of culture process, was to wait.

The translation of artifacts (as this term may be used in the broadest sense) into social and cultural behavior proceeded through attempts to re-create the contexts of the past and to elucidate the functions of the material remains of those contexts. By 'context' we mean here the full associational setting of any archaeological object or feature: its position on or in the ground and its positional relationships to other objects and features. With these data the archaeologist orders his materials, relating them to 'assemblages' or 'complexes' which ostensibly have cultural significance, and he may also relate these materials to natural environmental settings. Our definition of function is of the broadest sort. We mean both use and function as these terms have been defined by cultural anthropologists.[11] This subsumes the way artifacts and features were made and used by a vanished people and the meanings that they once had for these people.

Context and function may be viewed either synchronically or diachronically. Both views are necessary. However, in the latter part of the Classificatory-Historical Period the emphasis was on the synchronic view. In part, this was a reaction against the strong diachronic emphasis on pottery sequence chronicles that still dominated archaeology; in part, it was a reluctance to view cultural development in an evolutionary manner. It was only after 1960, when the goal of cultural process became an important one in American archaeology, and evolutionary thinking had re-emerged, that there was a shift to a diachronic consideration of context and function.

The first systematic attempts to view American archaeological data from a functional point of view occurred in the late 1930s and early 1940s. Obviously, the functional implications of archaeological artifacts are as old as man's antiquarian interests. The recognition of a man-made stone object as an axe carries with it connotations of behavior, and we have mentioned 'functional' classifications of this sort in the Classificatory-Descriptive Period; but programmatic efforts to look at all of the excavated materials from an archaeological site in this manner were a relatively late innovation. Among the first to do so were F. C. Cole and Thorne Deuel in their *Rediscovering Illinois*, published in 1937.[12] In this monograph the authors followed the procedure of listing all of the discovered archaeological traits of any site component (a single occupation site or a level within a multiple occupation site) under functional categories, such as 'Architecture and House Life,' 'Agriculture and Food-getting,' or 'Military and Hunting Complex.' Traits were so classified depending upon their form, appearance, and the contexts in which they were found. While the innovation seems a slight one, it had the advantage of keeping the investigators thinking in terms of these 'activities,' rather than simply in terms of the objects themselves.

While Cole and Deuel offered no rationale for this kind of presentation, simply taking it for granted that artifacts imply behavior, Martin, to whom we have already referred as one of those to first question conventional archaeological procedures, did provide such a rationale in his 1938 monograph. Martin began by observing that culture cannot be considered as the physical objects (artifacts) themselves, nor can it be the generalized resemblances existing among sets of such objects (types). Instead, he felt it referred to patterns of social behavior which were based upon a body of meanings held by a society and transmitted by tradition. Assuming this, he then goes on to ask if typological variation in artifacts can be assumed to indicate a corresponding variation in culture. His reply, based on observations from ethnological instances, is positive. In his words:

'This conviction is obviously based on the proposition that in a primitive society, for every variation in style of artifacts there is, within limits, a corresponding variation in the meanings which they have to their makers. If the proposition is true, it further follows that, subject to the same limits, the degree of variation in artifacts through time is indicative of a corresponding degree of variation in that part of the culture to which they pertain.'[13]

Irving Rouse, writing at about the same time as Martin, had a similar conception of culture and the artifact. His 1939 monograph, *Prehistory in Haiti, A Study in Method* (cited in Chapter Four) had been one of the first attempts to devise a typology that would be sensitive to functional as well as chronological factors. In it Rouse states:

'. . . culture cannot be inherent in the artifacts. It must be something in the relationships between the artifact and the aborigines who made and used them. It is a pattern of significance which the artifacts have, not the artifacts themselves.'[14]

However, Rouse seemed to differ with Martin, and with some other archaeologists, in that he saw artifacts as reflecting the behavior involved in their manufacture but not the behavior involved in their use. His view of the artifact – as of 1939 – was as more or less of an isolate, with an emphasis on the form and material rather than on the context of its associations.

It was John W. Bennett who realized the functionalist implications of Martin's and Rouse's writings. In 1943 he published an article, 'Recent Developments in the Functional Interpretation of Archaeological Data,'[15] in which he reviewed some of the same writings we have discussed here and formally proposed the concept and term 'functional archaeology.' In addition, he referred to archaeological uses of the concept of 'acculturation,' by T. M. N. Lewis and Madeline Kneberg in Tennessee[16] and by D. L. Keur in the Southwestern United States.[17] He also mentioned W. R. Wedel's work in culture and environment interaction studies in the Great Plains,[18] seeing the importance of this line of research and its obvious functional dimension. A year later Bennett, himself, published on this same general theme in a paper, 'The Interaction of Culture and Environment in the Smaller Societies,'[19] in which he employed both archaeological and modern sociological data to make a case for environmental pressures on cultural forms.

Bennett was also much interested in the use of the social anthropological concept of a 'religious cult' to explain the function and use of certain copper and shell artifacts found throughout the Southeastern United States on a Late Pre-Columbian time level. These artifacts, from their nature and appearance and from the contexts in which they were found, were most readily interpreted as ritual paraphernalia, quite probably the symbols of status and power. That almost identical pieces were found in sites as distant from each other as Etowah, Georgia and Spiro, Oklahoma, in sites of otherwise quite different regional cultures, and almost always in large mound or ceremonial sites, had suggested to A.J. Waring, Jr. and Preston Holder[20] that they were dealing with the material remains of a widespread, inter-regional and intercultural 'cult.' As Bennett said, the Waring-Holder analysis:

'. . . embraces ethnological data, general sociological concepts of religious organization, and other functional criteria.'[21]

It demonstrated that both 'micro-context' (paraphernalia found in obviously important graves) and 'macro-context' (presence of similar paraphernalia or objects in comparable site contexts in major sites throughout the Southeast) could be used together to arrive at highly logical functional interpretations. Twenty years later archaeologists would not have been satisfied to stop here and would have attempted to go on from this interpretation to devise 'tests' for it; but in the early 1940s it was a significant step forward.

Another macro-contextual study of about this time was Ralph Linton's 'North American Cooking Pots.'[22] This was an 'armchair' article but one based on long experience with the data in question from both archaeological and ethnological points of view. In brief, his thesis was that the 'Woodland' elongated and pointed-bottomed pot with a roughened exterior surface was a vessel primarily adapted to the slow boiling of meats and that its functional relationships were with peoples whose primary subsistence was that of hunting. This was supported by ethnological observations, by archaeological observations and inferences about subsistence practices, and by the complementary negative evidence that peoples who were basically agriculturists made and used quite different pottery. The study is a nice example of a combination of formal artifactual properties and broad-scale contextual setting as a means for functional elucidation.

Bennett also wrote a kind of macro-contextual study, 'Middle American Influences on Cultures of the Southeastern United States.'[23] This was a topic that had been approached in more conventional diffusionist ways by other authors,[24] essentially by trait comparisons. Bennett's approach was also comparative, but he tried to narrow down the range of expectations in diffused traits by considering the functional implications of the trait, the context from which it was derived, and the context into which it could have been introduced and accepted. The last qualification was the key. He hypothesized that certain Mesoamerican features would have been readily accepted into the lower threshold cultures of the Southeastern United States while others would have been rejected no matter how many times they would have been made available. Bennett's attempt was an early and trial one; unfortunately, it has not been followed up by those interested in Meso-american-Southeastern connections.

Two macro-contextual and functional studies appeared in Peruvian archaeology in the 1940s. In one of these, 'Interpretations of Andean Archaeology,'[25] Wendell C. Bennett posed some interesting questions about traditional persistences of artifactual and technical traits and their probable linkages with different kinds of socio-political orders. Again, this idea was never carried further, either by the original author or others. The other article, 'A Functional Analysis of "Horizon Styles" in Peruvian Archaeology,'[26] by Gordon R. Willey, was directly stimulated by the John W. Bennett writings and published in 1948. Willey endeavored to identify the socio-political or religious characteristics of Chavin, Tiahuanaco, and Incaic stylistic horizons by examining the cultural contexts (nature of artifacts, settlements and overall patterns of distributions) of these horizons. The 'horizon' concept, as we shall show later, was basically an historical device; however, it was also possible to look at it from a functional point of view.

By 1948 functional concerns were, thus, a minor but noticeable element in American archaeology. This foreknowledge did something, although not much, to prepare the way for Walter W. Taylor's *A Study of Archaeology*,[27] which appeared in that year. This was the first monographic critique of American archaeology, and it embodied a programmatic outline of archaeology for the future that was contextual and functional. Taylor had been working on these ideas for his doctoral dissertation as early as the late 1930s and early 1940s. Significantly, he wrote his dissertation at Harvard where Kluckhohn, who was then writing his own critique of Middle American archaeology, influenced his thinking. Taylor submitted the thesis in 1943 and revised it for publication after World War II.

Taylor began by noting the same ambiguity in the aims of American archaeology that Kluckhohn had stressed; namely the indecisiveness as to whether 'historical' or 'scientific' (anthropological) goals are to be pursued. He defined history or historiography as:

'. . . projected contemporary thought about past actuality, integrated and synthesized into contexts in terms of cultural man and sequential time.'[28]

In contrast, cultural anthropology:

'. . . is the comparative study of the statics and dynamics of culture, its formal, functional, and developmental aspects.'[29]

According to Taylor, archaeology became historiography when it went beyond antiquarianism (the securing of isolated and unrelated artifacts and data of the past) and mere chronicle (the arrangement of these objects and data in chronological sequences) to integrate the data of the past into a cultural context. Such a context refers to all of the affinities among the data as these may be expressed in spatial associations or in quantitative or qualitative values. After such a reconstruction of context, the archaeologist may then go on to comparative studies about the nature and workings of culture in the formal, functional, and developmental aspects mentioned above.

Taylor, thus, saw historiography and cultural anthropology as two sequent phases of a research procedure, in contradistinction to Kluckhohn who had advocated one approach or the other. Taylor also saw the reconstruction of cultural context as a part of historiography or the historic operation. A functional interpretation of this reconstruction (or model) would then be the anthropological study which would follow. Although other archaeological writers of the time are not clear or explicit on this point, there seems to have been a general tendency (as one can judge from the statements of Strong, Steward, Martin, and others) to lump together everything that went beyond typology and bare sequence or chronicle into the newer 'functional archaeology.' Thus, such 'functional archaeology' embraced the reconstruction of contexts, inferences as to use and function, and attempts to say something about process. These are obviously interrelated but, nevertheless, analytically separable concerns. As we have said, the decades of 1940–60 saw the focus of attention on the first two objectives, and Taylor's monograph had this emphasis.

Taylor devoted much of the book to a fine-grained critique of the writings of the prominent archaeologists of the Classificatory-Historical Period. Kidder, who had been a leader in the stratigraphic 'revolution' and was the foremost Americanist of the time, was especially singled out for attack as representative of conventional archaeology. According to Taylor:

'When Kidder writes theory he often talks historiography and anthropology. When he directs field work and published reports he talks comparative chronicle.'[30]

In his more detailed argument, Taylor held that no picture of past life had been reconstructed from any of Kidder's excavations, nor did he use his data to analyze or discuss functional matters. His nearest approach to either had been in his studies of the pottery from the Pecos, New Mexico ruin, but even here the main objective was that of identifying cultural influences from other regions of the Southwest rather than looking at the significance of the pottery in the total culture of the Pecos site. Taylor notes that Kidder is aware of such possibilities and that he raises questions about the relationships between pottery decorative motifs and other Puebloan art but that he had done nothing to follow up these questions. He concludes:

'If such problems had been attacked with regard to the nature and interrelations of pottery within Pecos itself, Kidder would have been "doing" historiography, at least of the ceramic complex. If he had then proceeded to compare his findings with similar findings from other sites or areas with the intent of abstracting the regularities between the two sets of [ceramic] data, he would have been "doing" cultural anthropology. As the matter now stands, he has done neither.'[31]

Kidder's Maya studies, and the program of the Carnegie Institution in the Maya field, are also attacked, especially for their failures to seek out or even be concerned with the data of settlement pattern and the implications of these. For instance, after thirty years of research, Taylor complained, there was still no real information or informed opinion on the degree to which the Lowland Maya centers were or were not urban phenomena; there were virtually no archaeological data on ordinary Maya dwellings; little or nothing was available on ancient Maya food habits. Pottery, as in the Southwest, has been employed in the reconstruction of chronicle or bare sequence, not in the reconstruction of use and function.

In Taylor's opinion, most of the archaeologists then practicing in the United States or anywhere in the Americas were as much at fault as Kidder. This included such men as Thompson,[32] in Maya studies, Haury[33] and Roberts,[34] in the Southwest, and W. S. Webb[35] and J. B. Griffin,[36] in the Eastern United States – to name only a few of those Taylor took issue with.

As might be expected, Taylor's praises were reserved for those few functional attempts from the 1940s that we have reviewed: Martin, Wedel, J. W. Bennett, Lewis and Kneberg, Waring and Holder.[37] He also noted that some archaeologists, including Kidder, wrote occasional statements which revealed both an interest in, and insight into, contextual and functional archaeology but that these writings were usually quite slight and often brought out in journals other than the standard professional ones, as though the authors were mildly ashamed of such excursions into popularization. This, we think, was an apt observation, for at that time such forays away from recognized and approved procedures were considered 'unsound,' and the archaeologist who went too far in this direction was suspect.

In concluding, Taylor was at pains to lay out what he considered to be an improved approach for American archaeology, one designated in his terms as the 'Conjunctive Approach.' By this he meant the drawing together, or the conjunction, of all possible lines of investigation on a specified archaeological problem. To chronicle and intersite relationships would be added close contextual intra-site study, with attention given to both the artifacts and features in themselves and to their relationships with all other artifacts and features. Such relationships would be sought not only in spatial or physical associational dimensions but in possible functional and systematic ties. For example, the archaeologist in his pottery study might look at the changing relationships between the numbers of jars to those of bowls. A drop in the numbers and percentages of large jars might indicate a decline in the need for water storage and thus, in turn, prompt the investigator to turn to other types of evidence to see if there had been a climatic change with possible increases of precipitation. Or, if warfare is suggested by fortified sites, the archaeologist should be alert to the possibilities of increases in the numbers of projectile points or other artifacts suitable for weapons. Nor should the archaeologist ignore cultural patterns for which no apparent functional correlates can be found. Taylor cites, as an example, the complete lack of symmetry in Coahuila Cave basketry designs and contrasts this with the concept of 'regularized decorative wholes' which dominates the designs of the San Juan basketry several hundred miles to the north of Coahuila. These decorative differences cannot be explained by either the basketry materials or the weaving techniques, which are the same in both regions. It is a fundamental difference in cultural patterning not readily understood. What does it relate to functionally? Maybe we will never find out, but it is the kind of datum to be borne in mind by the investigator.

Speculation, Taylor stoutly maintained, was not only justified in archaeology but required. It was the very life of the discipline, for if archaeology was to investigate the non-material aspects of culture through its material ones it must have recourse to hypothesis:

'With the proper and sensible proviso that conclusions are based on "the facts at hand" and are subject to revision in the light of fuller and better data, it is a premise of the conjunctive approach that interpretations are both justified and required, when once the empirical grounds have been made explicit. Why has revision been such a bugbear to archaeologists? Other disciplines are constantly reworking their hypotheses and formulating new ones upon which to proceed with further research. When these are found to demand modification and change they are altered. Why should archaeology assume the pretentious burden of infallibility?'[38]

Not surprisingly, Taylor's monograph was not happily received by the archaeological 'establishment.' Some members of that group were inclined to shrug it off angrily as nonsense; others, who had chafed under the narrow restrictions of conventional archaeology, may have had secret resentment at not having had Taylor's courage; still others, including some of those most pointedly attacked, felt that they had been reprimanded for failing to do what they had *not* set out to do. That is, Taylor's goals were recognized as admirable but believed to be beyond the 'data strength' of American archaeology at that time. Spatial-temporal and taxonomic systematics had to be carried farther before contextual and functional archaeology could have any real chance of success. Or so ran one argument.[39]

In spite of the immediate negative reaction from a large part of the archaeological profession, Taylor's words were not forgotten. A decade and a half later some of them were echoed in the 'new' archaeology of the Explanatory Period. More immediately, they helped keep alive the interest in context and function for some archaeologists in the 1950s.

One important aspect of the concern with context and function that drew attention after 1950 was in artifact typology. Between 1914 and 1940 artifact typology (and especially pottery typology) was geared almost wholly to problems of chronology. Ford and others referred to typologies in terms of their 'usefulness' in this

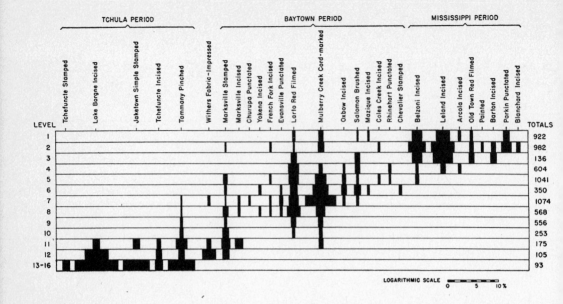

99 A percentage frequency chart from a Lower Mississippi Valley archaeological excavation in which pottery types are graphed by level and in which the graphs approximate unimodal curves (the curves would so appear with the smoothing of the graphs). This is a typical chart following J.A. Ford's procedures. (After Ford, Phillips, and Haag, 1955)

regard.[40] If types were not 'useful' in effecting chronological separations in the material they were considered essentially worthless – little more than sterile exercises in description. Such a view was, of course, in keeping with the narrowly limited definition of archaeology as being concerned with chronological ordering and little else. From this position, it was logical to conceive of the type as being something 'imposed' upon the data by the classifier. However, if one wished to broaden the goals of archaeology to include function and context, as well as chronology, then the artifact had other things to tell us. With this outlook the 'imposed' type, the concept of the archaeologist, would be of little service. Instead, the archaeologist should be looking for the types, or mental templates, that were once carried in the minds of the original makers and users of the artifacts. As we have seen, this approach to typology appeared in the late 1930s, with Martin's insistence upon the artifact as a registration of past cultural behavior and Rouse's similar premises. Taylor, in his launching of the 'conjunctive approach,' devoted a chapter of his book to typology and classification and took a comparable position. He reasoned, that for the proper re-creation of cultural context, the typologist should make every effort to 'discover' or recapture the types as these once existed in the vanished culture. In this way, the lines of a debate on typology were drawn between those predisposed to see the artifact type as something 'imposed' upon the data and those who saw it as something to be 'discovered' within the data.

In this debate Ford championed the type as an 'imposed' or 'designed' construct of the archaeologist; A.C. Spaulding led the attack on behalf of those who saw it as 'discovered.' The controversy started with Ford's publication, in 1952, of a short monograph with the title 'Measurements of Some Prehistoric Design Developments in the Southeastern States,'[41] It concerned Lower

Mississippi Valley ceramics and comparisons drawn between these and similar styles in northwest Florida and northeast Texas. Relative chronologies existed in all of the regions involved, for the most part based on individual site stratigraphies with percentages of types per level computed in unimodal frequency curves. Such frequencies were compared from site to site and region to region. By his term and concept of 'measurement' Ford was referring to relatively gradual changes, accretions, and losses in pottery design motifs and elements and the correlation of these with relative time and with geographic space. That is, form (the designs), time, and space were the variables, and observations on their covariance were called 'measurements.' In his 'Introduction' to the monograph Ford took exception to Taylor's insistence on the importance of the reconstructed context and a determination of function, saying:

99, 100

'If a clear and complete reconstruction of all possible details of man's unrecorded history in all parts of the world is the primary goal of modern archaeology, then we have merely refined the ancient curio and fact-collecting activities of our predecessors and still can only beg that our studies be tolerated for esthetic purposes.'[42]

100 Stylized presentation of unimodal curves representing pottery type frequencies with illustrations of vessels of each type also on the chart. This particular chart attempts to correlate ceramic sequences from Northeast Texas, Louisiana, and Florida. (After Ford, 1952)

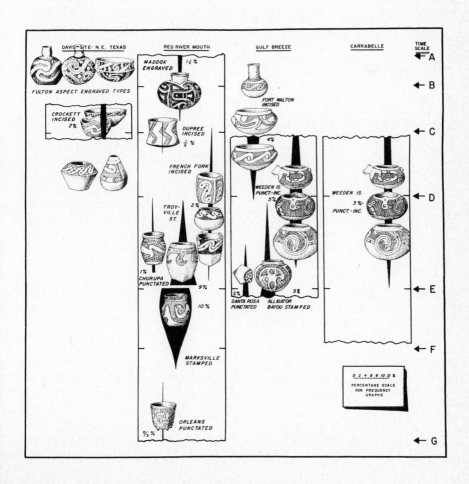

It was his feeling that archaeology should march more rapidly from its concern with chronology to become a 'science of culture' and:

'. . . to provide basic data for a close examination of general principles, of causes, speed, inevitability and quantitative aspects of culture change over long periods of time.'[43]

Such basic data, in his opinion, were offered by the 'Measurements' monograph.

Spaulding's highly critical review took issue with much of this.[44] To him the tone of the monograph, particularly the use of the word 'measurements,' gave a specious scientific precision to the operation. Although in this work Ford had not pressed his opinion that types were imposed or created by the archaeologist – in effect, arbitrary units sliced out of the reality of the continuum of evolutionary change – there was just enough of this philosophy in it to provoke a highly negative reaction from Spaulding. The latter had a very different concept of the type, and this he set down in an article which was published in the same year as his review of Ford. In 'Statistical Techniques for the Discovery of Artifact Types,'[45] Spaulding proposed that culture did not evolve as an even, constant 'flow'; instead, it was characterized by 'clusterings' or 'irregularities,' by sudden spurts and relatively static periods. These 'clusterings,' in Spaulding's view, could be discovered by statistical analyses – analyses that would show just how various traits or trait modes had been truly associated. Such 'clusterings' were 'discovered' types, and because of their reality they would tell the archaeologist a great deal more about human behavior and culture change than those types which purported to be arbitrary segments sliced out of the continuum of a uniform cultural evolution.

The Ford-Spaulding debate was joined along these lines with several exchanges in the professional journals.[46] It centred on the nature of the type and of culture change. What was also being argued – although this did not surface as such – was the basic purpose, or purposes, of the typology and the classification. If these purposes were those of chronological ordering, and no more, Ford's 'imposed' or 'designed' types were sufficient. Certainly, they had been subjected to considerable empirical testing in this regard and had not been found wanting. But, if in addition to chronological control, the archaeological objectives also included an appreciation of cultural context and function it would appear that Spaulding's statistically 'discovered' types were more appropriate. Beyond these considerations lay the question of which kind of type was more suited to the elucidation of culture change or process. Ford, as we have pointed out, wanted to go swiftly from chronological ordering or chronicle to process. In the final pages of his 'Measurements' monograph he gives us the distillate of these processual findings.

The authors of this history question whether or not Ford has, in any effective way, come to grips with process. Has he told us anything about the 'general principles' or the 'causes, speed, inevitability, and quantitative aspects of culture change,' as these were listed in his 'Introduction'? Of 'general principles,' perhaps. Cultural forms evolve from like cultural forms; change tends to proceed by gradual modifications – at least in the pottery types which Ford had under examination. But it is highly doubtful if we have come any closer to an understanding of the other aspects of change. The concluding statement to the monograph is, rather, a description of the formal, observable aspects of stylistic change in pottery. Except for possible diffusional influences, we have no inkling of 'cause.' It is our considered opinion that the archaeologist will best place himself for the study of process by a preliminary consideration of context and function – and, as follows from this, by a typology that is best geared to serve these ends. The leap from chronological ordering to process is too great a one to be negotiated successfully. The 'workings,' the functionings of culture have to be understood as a preliminary to casual explanations. Again, these comments carry us ahead of our story, and we shall come back to them in the next Chapter.

The majority of American archaeologists, or at least those that were immediately concerned with pottery typology, tended to side with Spaulding in the Ford-Spaulding debate. At least most of them became explicit in maintaining that types were, indeed, cultural realities and that they could be discovered by statistical or other proper analytical approaches.[47] As the 1950s moved into the 1960s, the issues of the Ford-Spaulding debate receded and were replaced by a new argument which was joined by those who preferred a 'taxonomic' or 'type-variety' classification[48] versus those who favored an 'analytical' or 'modal' approach.[49] Both of these 'schools' conceived of types as models that once existed in the minds of the makers and users of the objects concerned, and, as such, both kinds of types were suited to contextual and functional problems in addition to their chronological purpose. The question now became which approach was more effectively designed to study cultural change. The debate continues and probably will continue for some time; but it is fair to say that a choice depends very largely on the kind of change and degree of change which the archaeologist is attempting to delineate.

To leave typology and return to the wider aspects of the 'artifact as behavior,' we can observe continued interest in and concern with context and function throughout the 1950s. Some of this was expressed in writings which showed the archaeologist's increasing selfconsciousness concerning objectives, theories, and methods of his discipline.[50] The book, *Method and Theory in American Archaeology*, by Gordon R. Willey and Philip Phillips, is perhaps the best-known example of such writings. Originally issued as two journal articles, in 1953 and 1955, it came out in final revised form (some revisions being in response to critics) in 1958.[51] Its first part is devoted to methodological and procedural matters, incorporating the general trend of the thinking of the times.[52] The authors conceive of archaeological research on three operational levels: (1) observation (fieldwork); (2) description (culture-historical integration); and (3) explanation (processual interpretation). They define 'culture-historical integration' as:
'. . . almost everything the archaeologist does in the way of organi-

zing his primary data: typology, taxonomy, formulation of archaeological 'units,' investigation of their relationships in the contexts of function and natural environment, and determination of their internal dimensions and external relationships in space and time.'[53]

As defined thus, culture-historical integration very clearly includes both spatial-temporal ordering and context and function. Willey and Phillips then go on to say that while archaeologists have sometimes used explanatory concepts such as acculturation, diffusion, and stimulus diffusion, they have largely been concerned with specific and limited cultural situations, with no attempt to draw generalizations. In their words:

'So little work has been done in American archaeology on the explanatory level that it is difficult to find a name for it. The term "functional interpretation," which has gained a certain amount of currency in American studies . . . is not entirely satisfactory . . . [and] we have substituted here the broader "processual interpretation". . . .'[54]

According to this view, historical integration (which subsumes context and functional interpretation) should precede the search for process.

In the 1950s, however, the distinction between contextual-functional and processual interpretations was not always clearly made nor understood. Although in the 1958 quotation cited above, Willey and Phillips did separate the two, their earlier 1953 article did not.[55] In another article published in the same year Willey addressed himself quite directly to the matter of process in attempting to understand culture contact phenomena. This article, entitled, 'A Pattern of Diffusion-Acculturation,'[56] used a comparative approach in analyzing the circumstances surrounding the apparent implantation of foreign colonies in the territory of another culture. From this analysis Willey thought he saw a similar sequence of events or cause-and-effect relationships: (1) a period of different cultures existing side-by-side; (2) an interval of dominance by the foreign invader; and (3) a final fusion or synthesis of the two cultures in which certain traits of the invading culture (elements of politico-religious symbolism) persisted. This same theme was expanded and refined in a 1955 seminar, 'An Archaeological Classification of Culture Contact Situations,' held under the auspices of the Society for American Archaeology.[57] The principal result of the seminar was, as the title implies, a classification which described different types of contact between two distinct cultures. One category of these (which included Willey's 'cultural colonization' model of the earlier article) was designated as 'Site-unit Intrusion,' the other, 'Trait-unit Intrusion.' The seminar group avoided claims of explanation or 'cause,' either in the specific examples chosen to illustrate their several types of culture contact or in comparative generalization; however, the possibility of cause-and-effect generalizations being drawn was implicit in the whole seminar venture and in the final sentence of their report:

'In culture contact situations, we can, for example, look for factors influencing the results of contact under different circumstances, taking advantage of the fact that we can observe the before, during, and after with equal perspective.'[58]

Another seminar in the same 1955 series, 'An Archaeological Approach to the Study of Cultural Stability,'[59] was more ambitious in its consideration of process and cause than the one on culture contacts. In this seminar emphasis was on *in situ* culture change, or lack of change, through time; and the participants sought to define and classify types of culture change by conceiving of these as 'tradition segments.'[60] Criteria of the definitions were in the diachronic configurations of the 'segments' rather than their particular culture contents. For example, configurations were seen as 'direct' (essentially unchanging cultural continuity) or 'elaborating' (increasing complexity of the tradition through trait addition) – among other types. While the steps leading to such a classification involved a consideration of cultural contexts and function, just as in the type definitions of the culture contact situations of the other seminar, the main interest was centred on the framing of hypotheses about causal factors or processes involved in the shaping of the 'tradition segments.' These factors included such things as environment, demography, diffusion from other cultural traditions, and the cultural heritage of the tradition under consideration. The causal reasoning of the seminar was inferred from what was generally known in anthropology and culture history at large (e.g. large or increasing populations would tend to result in 'elaborating' tradition segments).

This interest in process within the framework of culture stability-instability examination was one of the main themes of a regional archaeological monograph by Robert Wauchope, who had been one of the members of the 'Cultural Stability' seminar. The monograph, to a very large extent, is a site excavation and survey descriptive presentation on northern Georgia;[61] however, it includes a twenty-page section on 'Cultural Processes.' While not published until 1966, the monograph was in preparation in the late 1950s and reflects the thinking of the period.[62] At the same time, Wauchope was going well ahead of most of his contemporaries of the late 1950s in attempting to quantify culture change (largely in pottery types) on a 1–100 scale, and in appraising such things as 'Technical versus Esthetic Change' and 'Peasant versus Urban Change.' In commenting on 'Technical versus Esthetic Change,' he noted that the Georgia data do not support an often-stated anthropological assumption that technology changes more readily than art. For the 'Peasant versus Urban' model, insofar as it could be applied to the Georgia data, he felt these data tended to substantiate greater and more rapid rates of ceramic change at the urban, or urban-like, pole. He comments, from this Georgia viewpoint, on broad developmental trends in culture growth that have been suggested by other archaeologists and anthropologists.[63] Some of these trends, 'regularities,' or 'laws' find possible confirmation in the Georgia data, others do not. Throughout the tone is cautious, the mood clearly experimental. How far can archaeological data and methods go toward checking anthropological assumptions concerning cultural development (these mostly drawn from evolutionary theory) and how far can they pioneer in these directions on their own? These are the questions asked. However, on the whole, no answers are given.

Other archaeologists who were thinking and writing along these lines in the 1950s include J. B. Griffin, L. S. Cressman, and J. B. Caldwell.[64] Like Wauchope, Willey and Phillips, and the seminar participants, they all saw the approach to process to lie in cross-cultural comparisons, and in this they all tended to move from the specific to the ever-widening generalization.

Although the 1940 to 1960 decades had been ones of an increasing realization of the importance of context and function, there was a tendency on the part of the archaeologists writing at that time to slight these aspects of prehistory when they transferred their attention to 'trends,' 'regularities,' 'laws.' There was, perhaps, a too ready search for universals, however much this was accompanied by cautious back-tracking, and too little attention to an examination of the actual mechanics of process as these might be observed in contextual-functional settings. Wauchope and Caldwell (the latter in his *Trend and Tradition in the Prehistory of the Eastern United States*)[65] were, perhaps, better in this regard than the others, and, to some extent, their work foreshadows the archaeological views of process that were to appear in the 1960s.

Up to this point, we have talked of context and function under the rubric of the 'artifact as behavior,' construing this in the broadest sort of way. There are, however, two significant contextual-functional approaches from the late Classificatory-Historical Period, which also helped to focus attention on process, and which deserve some separate comment here. These are the 'settlement pattern' and the 'culture and environment' approaches. We will take them up in that order.

Settlement Patterns

Prior to the 1940s archaeologists paid little attention to settlement patterns in the Americas. They prepared site maps and sometimes were concerned about site locations with reference to terrain features, but that was about as far as it went. There had been no studies in which the emphasis had been placed on the disposition of ruins, one to another, over sizable regions; nor had much attention been given to the arrangement of features, with reference to each other, within a site. In 1946, however, Steward encouraged Willey to make settlement survey and analysis his part of the combined Virú Valley investigations.[66] The Virú Valley fieldwork went forward during most of 1946, and in 1953 Willey brought out his *Prehistoric Settlement Patterns in the Virú Valley*, Peru the first monograph-length treatment of regional settlement patterns.[67]

Detailed maps were prepared of all sections of the valley; aerial photographs were used extensively in mapping; on-the-ground investigations checked mapping; and observations were made on building and architectural features. The dating of sites was worked out through excavations by other members of the Virú Valley

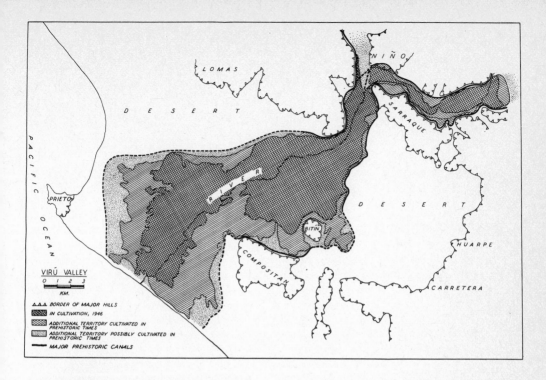

Virú Valley had been chosen originally because it was moderately
well known archaeologically and lay in the Peruvian North Coastal
zone for which a preliminary ceramic sequence was already available. The Virú Valley diggings and surveys corrected and refined
this sequence, and Willey's settlement study would have been
impossible without it; however, the central objective of the
settlement investigation was context and function. How did the
different communities of the Virú Valley interrelate and function
on the successive time planes, or culture periods, of the Virú Valley
sequence?

101 Map of the Virú Valley
showing areas in cultivation in
modern times in contrast to those
under irrigation and cultivation
in prehistoric times. The plotting
of canals and garden sections was
one of the principal aspects of
the Virú settlement pattern survey. (After Willey, 1953b)

Willey defined settlement patterns as:

'. . . the way in which man disposed himself over the landscape
on which he lived. It refers to dwellings, to their arrangement,
and to the nature and disposition of other buildings pertaining to
community life. These settlements reflect the natural environment, the level of technology on which the builders operated,
and various institutions of social interaction and control which
the culture maintained. Because settlement patterns are, to a large
extent, directly shaped by widely held cultural needs, they offer a
strategic starting point for the functional interpretation of
archaeological cultures.'[68]

In the last sentence Willey revealed a certain ambiguity between
function and process, for 'widely held cultural needs' implies
a basis for ready cross-cultural comparisons; the study, though,
is essentially one of *in situ* context and function.

Most of the Virú Valley settlement monograph is substantive
presentation. The author acknowledges the 'experimental' nature
of the work, but such comments are confined to little more than a
page. Archaeological sites and features are presented by cultural

phases or periods. A rather gross functional classification of sites further orders the presentation. There are 'dwelling sites,' divided into those which showed exposed architectural foundation arrangements and those which were simply refuse hillocks; 'Pyramid mounds,' of apparent ceremonial or public function; 'pyramid-dwelling-construction complexes' or sites which seemed to combine public-ceremonial and dwelling functions; 'cemeteries'; and 'fortifications.' The period presentation is followed by a chapter which considers the development or evolution of the various functional classes of sites. That is, 'dwelling-sites' or 'politico-religious structures' (pyramids, etc.) are traced through the some 1500 years or more of the Pre-Columbian occupancy of the Virú Valley. A section on 'community patterns' follows in which the author attempts to show how different kinds of sites were integrated into overall patterns of living at the different time periods. A chapter on 'Settlements and Society' is the most boldly theoretical, with inferences drawn from settlement to population sizes and to socio-political organization; however, even here Willey was exceedingly cautious and does not advance the numbers and kinds of hypotheses that he might have. A final chapter is a more conventional archaeological one – at least for the early 1950s – which compares the Virú Valley settlement types with those of other regions of Peru insofar as this was possible with the limited data then at hand.

The reaction to the Virú Valley work was, in general, favorable, if mildly so. The completely non-polemical tone aroused no hard feelings; the massive substantive presentation was eminently respectable, even if a reader might be wary of the short 'theoretical' forays. It was not immediately followed up in Peru although it was to be within a decade.[69] Willey shifted his interests to the Maya area in the 1950s, and, in 1954, began a settlement pattern investigation – combined with more standard archaeological operations – in the Belize Valley.[70] Archaeologists of other New World areas showed an interest in the approach by participating in a symposium on the settlement pattern theme in 1954, the results of which appeared in 1956.[71] Willey, who edited the volume, provided only a very brief 'introduction' and failed, thereby, to give the book the theoretical setting and *raison d'être* that it needed. Some of the contributors limited themselves to rather cautious descriptions of sites and site distributions; others addressed themselves somewhat more to context and function; and two papers – one by W. T. Sanders on central Mexico and another on the Lowland Amazon by B. J. Meggers and Clifford Evans – went daringly beyond this to talk about process and cause.

Another joint effort, essentially on a settlement pattern theme, was also published in 1956. This was the result of another of the 1955 'Seminars in Archaeology' and was entitled, 'Functional and Evolutionary Implications of Community Patterning.'[72] The seminar group established a series of community types, for both sedentary and nomadic peoples and then inquired into the functional and evolutionary aspects of these types. The approach was broadly comparative, being both world-wide in scope and concerned with ethnographical as well as archaeological data. As the title implies, the results were seen as both functional and evolutionary, thus moving beyond function to process. This was clearly the most 'advanced' (in the sense of being theoretically oriented) use so far made of settlement data.

While the above-mentioned seminar report was framed in the rather broad evolutionary terms and reasoning that, whether acceptable or unacceptable, were familiar to anthropologists and archaeologists, another theoretical treatise on settlement patterns was more controversial. This was K. C. Chang's 'Study of the Neolithic Social Grouping: Examples from the New World,' which was published in 1958.[73] The title is not altogether revealing as Chang drew upon extensive Old World ethnographical information in establishing correlations between social-organizational and settlement types on a Neolithic level. He then took these correlations and applied them to archaeological settlement data in the New World – in Mesoamerica, Peru, and the North American Southwest. Chang concluded by suggesting:

'. . . that it should be the archaeologist's first duty to delimit local social groups such as households, communities, and aggregates, rather than to identify archaeological regions and areas by time-spacing material traits, since cultural traits are meaningless unless described in their social context.'[74]

This was a bold call for the pre-eminence of the social dimension in archaeological study – a pushing forward of the settlement pattern approach as the first order of archaeological business. Some archaeologists demurred;[75] and we are not inclined to follow Chang all the way on this procedural argument;[76] still, it is all too clear in retrospect that American archaeology was for a long time hampered by its failure to come to grips with the social settings of the cultures which were being studied and to realize that an awareness of settlement patterns is a first step in this direction.[77]

Culture and Environment

In the latter part of the Classificatory-Historical Period an attempt was also made to place archaeological cultures in their appropriate natural environmental settings. This was, in part, a reaction to the strong anti-environmentalist tone of American anthropology which, under Boasian leadership, had proscribed environment as a possible explanatory factor in the development of culture. This is not to say that environment was completely overlooked by archaeologists; it was usually described but thought of as having, at best, a permissive or passive role in conditioning culture. This philosophy is especially clear in A. L. Kroeber's 'Cultural and Natural Areas of Native North America.'[78] Occasionally, some archaeologists would regard environment in a more active or causative sense as a catastrophic agent. For instance, a major drought, an earthquake, or even man-made environmental imbalances were conceived of as destroying a culture, as in the case of the fall of Classic Maya civilization.[79] But in all of these cases a holistic view of culture and environment in an interacting, systemic relationship was lacking. Culture and environment were regarded as two separate entities. The holistic approach, which is the true ecological approach, was not to be a part of American archaeology until the succeeding Explanatory Period.[80] What did develop in the latter part of the Classificatory-Historical Period, and which went beyond the very simple descriptive treatments of the environment that had been current, was the attitude that the environmental setting of any culture should be studied as thoroughly as possible in order to reconstruct an appropriate prehistoric environmental context which, in turn, would allow for functional interpretations.

In these late Classificatory-Historical Period developments in environmental archaeology in America it is only fair to note that such concerns had a much earlier inception in European prehistory, and American archaeologists undoubtedly were influenced by these pioneer Old World studies. For instance, in Scandinavia an interest in environmental reconstruction can be traced well back into the 19th century, and in Great Britain Sir Cyril Fox, O. G. S. Crawford, and Grahame Clark had long been working along these lines. The Europeans had been stimulated in all of this by German and British geographers, and we would also surmise that the lack of a strongly intrenched anti-environmentalist school of thought, as in America, allowed for earlier European considerations of the environmental factor.[81]

With relation to the matter of the reconstruction of past environments for contextual-functional interpretations, June Helm has said that by the end of the 1950s 'the ecologically con-textual study had become an established model in American archaeology.'[82] Although not agreeing with her use of the word 'ecology' in this particular context, we would agree that the functional emphases of the period did include, as would seem logical, considerations of environmental setting. Such considerations took the form of attempts to reconstruct environments and diets of ancient cultures and relied heavily upon data and techniques from the natural sciences. The cultures involved in these studies were most often hunting and gathering ones which tended to leave meagre artifactual remains.[83]

Typical of these important early attempts at environmental reconstruction was the work of Waldo R. Wedel on the Great Plains of the United States. Wedel attempted to put native sub-sistence activities in the context of environment, especially the former climatic environments, of the Plains.[84] Another example was the study of Emil W. Haury and his associates at Ventana Cave, in Arizona. Haury utilized the knowledge and skills of geologists and other natural scientists in a major job of prehistoric environmental reconstruction.[85] A similar bringing together of archaeological, geological, paleobotanical, faunal, and pollen studies was carried out by Frederick Johnson at the Boylston Street Fishweir site in Massachusetts.[86] Still other instances of archaeological-environmental studies of the period are to be seen in the writings of J. D. Jennings, W. G. Haag, and G. I. Quimby.[87] Also worthy of special mention are a series of investigations on the California shell-mounds pioneered by E. W. Gifford,[88] and later continued by R. F. Heizer, S. F. Cook, and other colleagues.[89] They reconstructed the diet of the ancient shell-mound dwellers, and, with some ingenious formulae based on weight and quantities of midden debris, arrived at site population estimates. But in all of these studies, as we have said, the goal was that of the descriptive creation of an environmental context, with little or no concern with environment as a systemic causative factor in cultural development.

The conception of environment as a determinative force in the rise and growth of cultures went well beyond the contextual-functional environmental reconstructions and moved American archaeological interests in the direction of cultural evolution. The environmentalist perspective must be considered as an important trend of the late Classificatory-Historical Period. In this connection, it is of interest to remember that environmental determinism and cultural evolution had been jointly submerged in American anthropological thinking at about the turn of the century. Now, in the mid 20th century, we see them re-emerging together. The major focus of this re-emergence was in the study of the complex cultures of the New World, those usually referred to as the 'civilizations' of Mexico and Peru.

The principal figure in the environmental-evolutionary trend was Julian H. Steward. We have already commented upon this ethnologist-social anthropologist's influences on American archaeology, particularly with reference to settlement pattern research; his contributions in the realms of what he was to call 'cultural ecology' and 'multilinear evolution' were to be even greater.[90] Basically, Steward called for the archaeologist to compare specific cultural sequences in specific environmental settings in order to look for developmental regularities. He hypothesized that particular aspects of the environment would influence what he called the 'core' elements of a culture. These 'core' elements were essentially technological ones. In other words, different kinds of environments would influence the nature of technological adaptations which, in turn, would influence and condition other aspects of culture. For the first time in many decades, an American anthropologist was saying that environment could determine cultural adaptation.

Although Steward's over-emphasis on the role of the 'core' in cultural development and his lack of an holistic or true ecological view of culture and environment can be criticized,[91] he had a major and salutary influence on American archaeological theory. His 1949 article, 'Cultural Causality and Law: A Trial Formulation of the Development of Early Civilizations,' was a bold attempt to put his theoretical ideas into practice;[92] and his 1955 collection of essays, *Theory of Culture Change,* was especially influential.[93] Following the lead of the Sinologist Karl Wittfogel,[94] he also stimulated research on the role of irrigation in the rise of civilization. In South American studies his 'Circum-Caribbean' hypothesis not only engendered lively debate but produced constructive rebuttals.[95]

There were also other important figures in the environmental and evolutionary trend in the late Classificatory-Historical Period. Pedro Armillas, a Spaniard who emigrated to Mexico, brought a materialist point of view to bear on the problems of the rise of urban civilization in the Valley of Mexico, quite

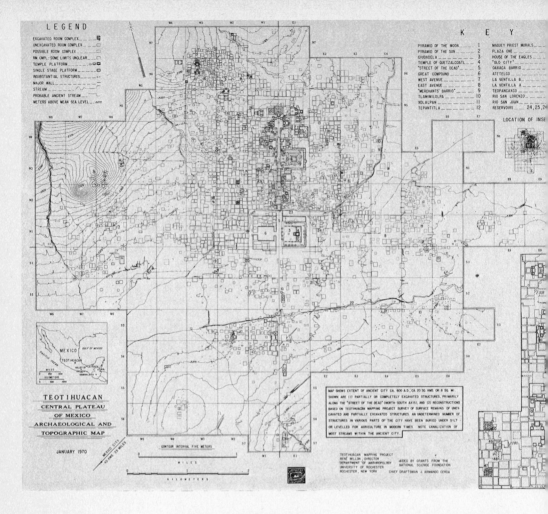

102 Plan of the great Pre-Columbian city of Teotihuacan, Valley of Mexico, with inset at right showing detail of center of the city. This much reduced version serves to illustrate the immense care taken by René Millon and associates in mapping the urban zone at Teotihuacan as one step in their study of the processes of urbanism at this important site. From such detailed settlement pattern studies, the archaeologists have estimated that at its zenith Teotihuacan had a population of over 100,000

independently of Steward. He, too, was especially interested in the role of irrigation and helped to inculcate a similar interest in a number of Mesoamerican archaeologists including W. T. Sanders.[96] Angel Palerm and Eric Wolf, the latter a student of Steward's, also concentrated their efforts on investigating the correlations between differing Mesoamerican environments, agricultural techniques, and the development of civilization.[97] A slightly modified version of Wittfogel's 'hydraulic hypothesis' became a working premise for many of these workers and later helped to give rise to a number of fascinating ecological studies in the 1960s.

While Steward's influence, direct and indirect, was strongly felt in the 1950s, that of another American ethnologist-social anthropologist, Leslie A. White, was delayed until the 1960s. Even though his *Science of Culture* was published in 1949, American archaeologists did not follow up his theories to any great extent until the following decade.[98] One student of his, however, Betty J. Meggers, was an exception to this. She produced several important theoretical papers in the 1950s, all of marked evolutionary orientation.[99] Her article, 'Environmental Limitation on the Development of Culture,' argued for the deterministic

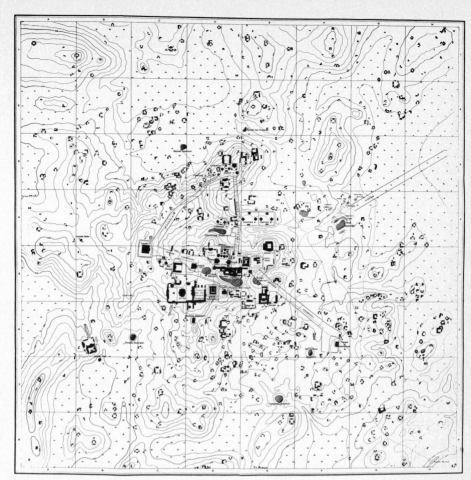

nature of environmental influences, discussing and categorizing various types of environment which would be conducive, in varying degrees, to the rise of civilization or which would preclude this condition. This 1954 article was heavily criticized at the time it was written,[100] but while it may have been in error in specific examples, it also offered some important insights.[101] Moreover, much of her fieldwork, in collaboration with Clifford Evans, was designed to test evolutionary and environmentalist hypotheses.[102]

To conclude, concern with the role of environment *vis-à-vis* culture began to rise during the latter part of the Classificatory-Historical Period. An understanding of ancient environments was a readily recognizable need, fully consistent with other contextual-functional emphases in American archaeological studies. Over and beyond this, a consideration of environments was seen as essential to an understanding of the development of culture by those few archaeologists who had begun to quest for the 'whys' of culture change. As Frederik Barth, a social anthropologist, said, after noting that the invention of radiocarbon dating would obviate the necessity for the American archaeologist to concentrate all his energies on matters of chronology:

103 A settlement pattern map of the major ceremonial center and outlying ruins at Tikal, Guatemala. The area shown measures 4 × 4 km. (After Carr and Hazard, 1961)

'It can no longer be the archaeologist's ultimate ambition to make chronological charts of cultures. . . . . The only way the archaeologist can contribute to the general field of anthropology is by asking questions of *why*, for which a general framework is needed. One simple and directly applicable approach is that of ecologic analysis of cultural adaptations, treating problems of relationship of the ecologic area, the structure of the human group, and its cultural characteristics.'[103]

But Barth's call would not be answered on any scale for more than a decade. Only a beginning had been made in the 1950s in the fight for the reintroduction of environmental concerns to archaeology and anthropology.

As late as 1958, it could be stated:

'Archaeologists too often leave their ecology in the ground, due to interest in artifacts and ignorance of techniques for observing and interpreting ecological evidence.'[104]

But 'ignorance of techniques' was not the primary reason. The American archaeologist all too often lacked a clear understanding of the goals of his research and did not always know at the time he excavated what kinds of data would be needed to understand the nature of the cultural development at a particular site or in a particular region. It would only be with the clarification of the goals of archaeology in the Explanatory Period that the fragmented *environmental* concerns of the 1940s and 1950s would become the holistic *ecological* concerns of the 1960s. The prime element in this clarification of archaeological goals would be the reintroduction of the concept of cultural evolution. This reintroduction would not become sophisticated and effective until after 1960. We have, however, referred to some of the initial attempts to apply evolutionary theory in connection with cultural-environmental relationships, and later in this chapter we will return to other trial formulations of evolutionary concepts in the 1950s. For the moment, though, let us consider other matters as we move forward with the course of our history in the late Classificatory-Historical Period.

Scientific Aids from Other Disciplines

One of the most significant developments of the latter part of the Classificatory-Historical Period was the American archaeologists' increasing awareness of new inventions or possible applications of various scientific techniques.[105] To the popular mind, which tends to view scientific change phenomenologically, this new awareness of scientific techniques is often considered 'revolutionary.'[106] That is to say, it is often felt that with the advent of the 1950s, American archaeology suddenly added a scientific 'pack' to its regular equipment and became a radically changed discipline. This, however, was not quite what happened. While new dating techniques, and particularly radiocarbon dating, did have an immediate impact on American archaeology, techniques from other disciplines have only just begun to affect archaeology in the New World; and while the archaeologist began to use a host of new scientific aids, he was not prepared conceptually to use them in holistic combinations or in ways which would affect significantly the kinds of data he was unearthing. Certainly, the necessity for an interdisciplinary approach was recognized in the Americas by the 1940s, and various scientific studies often formed descriptively impressive but generally neglected appendices to site reports. There were even some brilliant uses of scientific techniques in reconstructing the culture histories and cultural contexts of individual sites, but these had the effect of 'supplements' to already existing methodologies and seemed to do little to develop new ones.

As might be anticipated, the most widely used scientific aids were those that could be employed in chronology building. These led to both relative and absolute dating refinements. Of all of these, the most revolutionary was W. F. Libby's radiocarbon or carbon 14 method. It was devised in the late 1940s; and radiocarbon tests were made available to archaeologists in all parts of the New World during the 1950s. The method operates on the principle that the radio-active carbon of the atmosphere is, and was, absorbed by all living organisms. This absorption ceases at their death, and decay, with loss of radiocarbon, then begins at a steady and predictable rate. By testing the remains of such organisms found archaeologically – such as pieces of charred wood or bone – for their residual amounts of radiocarbon, they could be dated on an absolute scale. If such remains were found in firm association with other cultural materials, and had not been re-used, then the cultural remains in question could be dated absolutely.[107]

Radiocarbon dating had a great impact on many areas of American archaeology. For example, it showed once and for all that man had reached the North American continent more than 10,000 years ago.[108] It also helped archaeologists to fill the 'Archaic' gap between the migratory Early Man groups and the later sedentary cultures in several parts of North America.[109] In the Great Basin, radiocarbon dating enabled J. D. Jennings to erect a 10,000-year-long sequence for the migratory bands of that harsh area and to hypothesize the existence of a long-lasting Desert culture.[110] In Middle America, the enigmatic Olmec culture was shown to antedate the Classic Maya civilization by many centuries,[111] and its great significance as regards the development of civilization in Middle America and in general was finally realized. The list could go on and on, but suffice it to say that radiocarbon dating had a major influence on the ordering and lengthening or shortening of numerous cultural sequences throughout the Americas.

Radiocarbon dating also helped to set the stage for the following Explanatory Period in several interrelated ways. First, it helped establish full cultural sequences so that the archaeologist could look at the evolution of culture in a more precise manner than before. Second, it gave an absolute time range to the various sequences so that rates of evolution in differing or similar environments, cultural conditions, and so on could be studied. Third, it helped the archaeologist to compare cultures at a single time period and therefore enabled him to look at and hypothesize about a variety of factors which caused differences or similarities among these cultural systems.

Although many archaeologists today have become somewhat sceptical of the exactness of radiocarbon dating and impatient with the *caveats* of the radiocarbon laboratories, due to a host of new discoveries which have modified some of Libby's original hypotheses and assumptions,[112] the contribution of this technique has been great in terms of the development of archaeology in general and in terms of New World culture history in particular.

While radiocarbon dating was the most important chronological aid in the 1940–60 era, other absolute and relative dating procedures were pursued. Among these, dendrochronology, to which we have had reference in the preceding chapter, was carried to new refinements, resulting in Southwestern North American culture sequences being the most finely calibrated in the New World.[113] Other chemical and physical methods and techniques used in dating include paleo- or archeomagnetism, obsidian hydration, and fluorine analyses of bone.[114] Geological dating, essentially of a relative nature, also enjoyed many advances in the late Classificatory-Historical Period. Through the efforts of Kirk Bryan, Ernest Antevs, and others, associations of cultural materials with geological strata and glacial deposits and relations to climatic sequences were all used to give approximate dates or to help in the interpretation of the stratigraphy of a number of archaeological sites, especially Early Man ones. The sites which were dated by these two scientists included such important ones as Lindenmeier (Colorado), Ventana Cave (Arizona), Leonard Rockshelter (Nevada), and Bat Cave (New Mexico).[115] Some geological dating was also accomplished, as Heizer has pointed out, through glacial varve sequences (although this technique was more successful in Europe), through changes in shore-line levels, and rates of stream-channel meandering, dune migration, or travertine deposition.[116] Fisk's work on the changing channels of the Mississippi River was especially useful to archaeologists working at sites bordering this long river.[117]

Dating was not the only subject for which American archaeologists looked for help although it was the most important one. In their contextual concerns, as we have already noted, they turned to geological, zoological, and botanical sciences for aid in climatic and dietary reconstructions. Attention was also paid to technical studies of artifacts, through the use of such techniques as spectroscopic analysis. With relation to pottery, Anna O. Shepard's work is an outstanding example,[118] while the same can be said for the geologically oriented analyses of such scientists as Howel Williams.[119] However, when compared in sophistication and in quantity to the analyses of these kinds in the 1960s, this early work along these lines was small indeed.[120]

Aerial photography and electronic detecting are two other techniques which deserve mention. The former was used to good advantage in Peru as early as 1931 by the Shippee-Johnson Expedition[121] and in the later 1940s in the Virú Valley,[122] as well as in the Southwest.[123] But again, aerial photography did not come into its own in relation to site survey and discovery until

104

104, 105 Aerial photography as an aid in detailed mapping as well as in site location and discovery. *Above*, the Chimu city of Chan Chan of the Northern Coast of Peru, where aerial photography is currently playing a crucial role in the detailed mapping by M. E. Moseley. *Left*, Low-altitude photograph of an archaeological excavation in the Pueblo-type ruins of Casas Grandes, Chihuahua, Mexico

106 (*right*) Radiocarbon laboratory with view of combustion train from the conversion of sample to pure carbon dioxide

the 1960s. The same can be said for detecting devices. One only has to contrast the early and very limited use of mine detectors by C. W. Meighan at Drake's Bay, California[124] with the more recent sophisticated employment of a variety of such devices, to see the difference.[125]

In addition, as noted earlier in our discussion of artifact types, there was a growing interest in statistics in the Classificatory-Historical Period. The earlier-mentioned works of Brainerd, Robinson, and Spaulding are good examples of this interest.[126] But it was not until the following Explanatory Period that American archaeologists began to take advantage of the new computer advances which had already begun to affect other disciplines.

Thus, the late Classificatory-Historical Period saw a gradual increase in the attention paid to developments in other disciplines that could offer aids to archaeological research: physics, chemistry, the natural and biological sciences, and mathematics. In a somewhat helter-skelter fashion more and more American archaeologists became aware of the advantages of these aids and began to experiment with them on their own or to consult appropriate experts. Our very brief discussion here has touched upon these various aids only lightly; but their importance is, we think, obvious. By the 1960s an acceptance of them became general practice; and, moreover, a conceptual structure was erected after that date which enabled the archaeologist to integrate and to point these aids toward particular research goals.

The Continued Concern with Chronology and Space-Time Synthesis

So far in this chapter we have devoted our attention to innovations in archaeological goals and procedures; however, as we have stated, the preponderance of archaeological research carried on during the 1940–60 period was of the traditional kind, oriented toward the building of chronological sequences and the development of regional and areal syntheses. We cannot hope to summarize or even comment upon more than a sampling of the results of this work here. The best we can do is to touch upon some of the highlights. In so doing we will extend our coverage forward to include the decade of the 1960s. This takes us into the Explanatory Period, with its significant changes in theoretical outlook and methodology which we will deal with in the next Chapter; however, much of the work of the 1960s, with its continued emphasis on the schematics of space-time synthesis, does not differ in kind from that of the preceding period.

Before turning to substantive results, it is worth noting, again, that there was a great burgeoning of archaeological interest and activity following World War II. This was especially true for the United States, but it also occurred in most other American countries. Archaeology became much more a part of the public consciousness; this resulted in governmental support; and this increased support, in turn, fed back into the growth of archaeology. A good example of this was 'salvage archaeology.' This was inaugurated in the United States in 1945 as a measure to rescue archaeological information from thousands of prehistoric sites

that were to be flooded in governmental hydrological developments of the nation's river valleys. Through the intervention of a
committee of professional archaeologists, and with the sympathetic help of some legislators, the Federal Congress was persuaded
to set aside funds for such 'salvage' research. Beginning with a
modest budget and limited program, salvage archaeology expanded rapidly into all parts of the United States, and it continues
into the 1970s.[127] A second governmental venture (or series of
ventures) was in the planning, preparation, and publication of a
set of *Handbooks* of the American Indians. This followed in the
tradition of the first *Handbook of American Indians North of Mexico*,
which was brought out early in the 20th century by the Smithsonian Institution.[128] This was an ethnographic and ethnological
compendium with very little archaeological data; but in the 1940s
the Smithsonian, under its Bureau of American Ethnology and the
editorship of Julian H. Steward, published the much more extensive *Handbook of South American Indians*, which contained substantial archaeological sections.[129] In the 1950s government
financing also made possible the preparation of the multi-volume
Handbook of Middle American Indians, which incorporated even
more extensive archaeological syntheses and which began publication in the 1960s.[130] This, in turn, is being followed by plans and
preparation for a giant ethnological-archaeological *Handbook of
North American Indians*, once again undertaken by the Smithsonian Institution.[131] All of these *Handbooks* have served, or will
serve, as archaeological 'stock-takings,' stimuli and bases of
departure for further research. In the United States a third governmental boost to archaeology has been the financial support for
field research channeled through the Social Sciences Division of
the National Science Foundation. Beginning in the 1950s, this
organization has put millions of dollars at the disposal of private
institutions for research in all parts of the world and, particularly,
in the Americas.

To this governmental support within and from the United
States can be added various privately endowed ·archaeological
operations and governmental and private research programs by
the Canadian and Latin American governments and private institutions and individuals in these countries.[132] There has also been a
renewal of work by Danish archaeologists in the American Arctic
and by European and Japanese archaeologists in Middle and South
America.

All of this has contributed enormously to our substantive knowledge of the New World's past. On the Early Man level we now
have hundreds of important sites where previously the reliable
discoveries numbered less than a dozen. Radiocarbon dates have
also given some firm chronological structure to an area of investigation that previously had had only the most general sort of
estimates. By the mid 1960s it had become apparent than an early
fluted projectile point horizon could be documented for the North
American High Plains and parts of the Southwest at *ca.* 9500–8000
B.C. Two periods appeared distinguishable within this horizon, an
earlier Clovis and a later Folsom. Clovis, or Clovis-like points had
a much more widespread North American distribution, being

found at various places in the eastern half of the continent. Datings on these eastern finds were not as secure, either through geological contexts or radiocarbon determinations, as those of the West; but the general interpretation was that early hunters of the terminal Pleistocene had spread over most of North America with a Clovis-like technology and that later point forms had evolved from the Clovis into a number of separate regional point styles, including Folsom, Plainview, Midland, Yuma, Eden, etc., in the West, and such types as Suwannee and Dalton in the East. This evolution could be dated to the Early Post-Pleistocene, lasting until about 7000 B.C., plus-or-minus 500 years.[133]

A major Early Man debate was carried on over the possibilities of a 'pre-projectile point' or 'pre-bifacial-flaking' horizon or occupancy of the New World, some authorities arguing for the reality of such a relatively crude technological era in the Americas and others insisting that man first came to the Western Hemisphere from Asia only at about 10,000 B.C. and with a heritage that allowed him to rapidly develop the Clovis-type hunting gear.[134] By 1971, however, the picture had changed significantly. A 'Paleo-Indian' or 'Big-Game Hunting' horizon (the names applied to the Clovis and related point technologies) had been established for the Far West, as well as the rest of North America,[135] and related materials from South America were recognized as marking an approximately contemporaneous horizon for that continent. Moreover, finds from both Mexico and Peru, of the order of 20,000 to 18,000 B.C., left little doubt but that man had come to the New World well in advance of the 10,000 B.C. date line and that these earliest immigrants had been possessed of a simple flint technology that lacked bifacially flaked projectile points.[136]

The era from about 7000 B.C. until about 2000 B.C., generally referred to as the time of the 'Meso-Indian' or 'Archaic' cultures, became increasingly well documented after 1950. Subsistence economies varied from land game-hunters, to fishers, shellfish-gatherers, and seed-collectors. In many regions this was a time of notable population increases and relatively stable, if still semi-sedentary, patterns of life. Some technological continuities can be traced from earlier times. Projectile point forms, for instance, show gradual modifications from the early hunting modes of the terminal Pleistocene and Early Post-Pleistocene into the Meso-Indian or Archaic types; however, there can be no doubt but that major changes in life style had occurred. This is reflected in various tool types adapted to new food-getting techniques. Ground stone artifacts, which had been absent or extremely rare in the earliest American cultures, had become common. These changes of the 7000–2000 B.C. period, it transpired, came about in various ways, but characterized all parts of the Americas from which there were available archaeological data.[137]

On later time levels chronological control, through more stratigraphic work and through radiocarbon dating, provided the underpinning for areal syntheses, and systematic chronological investigation was pushed into areas and regions which had been only sketchily known before World War II. In South America, the well-established Peruvian area chronology was extended back in

107 Monumental stone sculpture from San Agustin in southern Colombia. Height about 90 cm. Only after World War II did archaeologists begin to learn enough about this fabulous site to date such monuments in a relative chronology

time through coastal shellfishers and minimal horticulturists to earlier hunters and gatherers. In the well-preserved refuse of deep midden sites the transition from plant-collecting and shellfish-gathering, to incipient cultivation, and on into established farming, was traced in both the food remains themselves and in the artifactual complexes associated with them.[138] The settlement pattern studies on the coast, already referred to, led on to an interest in the rise of Pre-Columbian urbanism in the area.[139] Considerable attention was also paid to the 'horizon style' concept and to the way in which this had been applied in Peruvian studies. More refined analyses of the Tiahuanaco horizon, which Uhle had conceived of so many years before, gave greater insight into the actual origins of this powerful style and the mechanisms of its spread to other parts of Peru.[140] In the same way, the earlier Chavin horizon was more closely scrutinized through new excavations at Chavin de Huantar and elsewhere;[141] and Peruvian archaeologists were made aware of a whole early period of pottery development, chronologically intermediate between the Chavin horizon (*ca.* 900 B.C.) and the late preceramic cultures (terminating at *ca.* 1800 B.C.).[142] In keeping with the relatively advanced state of Peruvian culture sequence control, it is also to be noted that no less than four general books of area synthesis were published on Peru between 1949 and 1967.[143]

108 Pottery figurine of the Chone type from the Ecuadorian coast. (After Estrada, 1957)

Other South American areas, while considerably behind Peru in the amount of archaeological research carried out in the spatial-temporal organization of the data, came along swiftly in the decades between 1940 and 1970. Important stratigraphic work was carried out in Ecuador by Clifford Evans, Betty J. Meggers, and Emilio Estrada in the 1950s and 1960s, and Meggers brought out a general synthesis of the area in 1966.[144] Archaeological sequences in that country revealed a long history of pottery-using cultures, with ceramics beginning even earlier here (*ca.* 3000–2500 B.C.) than in Peru or Mesoamerica. In Colombia, Gerardo Reichel-Dolmatoff, a French-trained archaeologist with a European background, took the lead in stratigraphic archaeology in that country, and he, too, climaxed his efforts with a general book.[145] To generalize, the archaeological cultures of Ecuador and Colombia, as well as those of Lower Central America,[146] exhibited marked regional differentiation, with a bewildering variety of ceramic styles. For the most part, they lacked the impressive public works or great buildings of Peru or Mesoamerica; the trend toward urban patterns of life was not as far advanced; nor were there good archaeological evidences (or ethnohistoric data) that would suggest phenomena of the order of the Inca or the Aztec states or empires. At the same time, many regions of this 'Intermediate Area' (so named for its geographical position between Peru and Mesoamerica) showed archaeological signs of dense populations, and, throughout, a high level of craft development (especially in pottery and metallurgy).

Archaeological synthesis had been begun in the Caribbean area in the late 1930s, with Rouse's West Indian studies, and in subsequent years he expanded and refined it.[147] From the West Indies he moved to the mainland where, in conjunction with J. M.

105

Cruxent, he extended his overall Caribbean chronological scheme to embrace the several archaeological regions of Venezuela.[148] Farther south in Tropical Lowland South America were Meggers and Evans who began by establishing a long ceramic sequence at the delta of that great river.[149] A few years afterwards D. W. Lathrap initiated a program of excavation and survey in the Upper Amazon Basin which provided crucial information for linking Amazonian ceramic styles with those of Peru and Ecuador.[150] Another scholar in Amazonian archaeology in the 1960s period was the German-Brazilian, P. P. Hilbert, who did a number of stratigraphic excavations in the Middle Amazon.[151] Systematic knowledge in the East Brazilian Highlands and along the Atlantic Coast was pushed forward rapidly in the 1960s by a cooperative program of Brazilian and North American archaeologists organized and guided by Meggers and Evans.[152] Here, along the coast, the cultures of the Brazilian *sambaquis*, or shell-mounds, were found to date back to the third and fourth millennia B.C. and to exhibit an 'Archaic' way of life and a conservatism comparable to that of some of the 'Meso-Indian' or 'Archaic' shell-mound cultures of the North American Atlantic and Pacific littorals. This 'Archaic' type of existence was succeeded some time in the first millennium A.D. by cultures of an Amazonian tropical agricultural pattern, presumably carried into eastern Brazil by expanding Tupian tribes.[153]

In Northwestern Argentina, A. R. Gonzalez began intensive and detailed stratigraphic studies at various cave sites in the San Luis and Cordoba Provinces and also took the lead in the chronological organization of what was generally thought of as the Argentine 'Diaguita region.'[154] Gonzalez was also the first to attempt a chronological integration of Northwest Argentine and North Chilean archaeological sequences based upon scientific ceramic trait comparisons.[155] Farther south in Argentina the Austrian prehistorian, O. F. A. Menghin was active in Early Man studies in the 1950s.[156] He has been followed by a number of younger Argentine scholars who have continued these interests.[157] But later, ceramic cultures of the Parana-Paraguay River system, of the Pampas, and Patagonia have received little attention, and chronological ordering here has advanced little beyond the stage reached in the 1940s. In far southern South America, J. B. Bird's earlier work of the 1930s was followed up by the French archaeologists, J. M. Emperaire, Annette Laming-Emperaire, and Henri Reichlen, who confirmed and refined Bird's findings and also provided new information and chronological data on the early peoples of the Chilean Archipelago.[158]

In Mesoamerica, the 1940s, 1950s, and 1960s have brought the archaeology of that area to a point where a variety of contextual-functional and processual problems can be attacked from a firm data base. One of the most important 'discoveries' has been the realization that the great Olmec art style, with its major sites in southern Veracruz and Tabasco, represents a stratum of civilization anterior to any other in the area. This had been suspected by M. W. Stirling as early as 1940, but for a decade or more there was no clear proof. Eventually, radiocarbon dating and stratigraphic

109

studies demonstrated the antiquity of these early Gulf Coast cultures and the art style which extends throughout much of southern Mesoamerica and which dates to a range of 1200–800 B.C.[159] Other 'discoveries' in Mesoamerican archaeology were similar in that they did not so much involve the actual finding of new materials as seeing materials and data in new perspectives. One good example of this is in the advances made in hieroglyphic studies. In 1950, J. E. S. Thompson, the leading Maya glyphic scholar, brought out his notable *Maya Hieroglyphic Writing: an introduction*, a systematic compilation of our knowledge of Maya writing to that date.[159a] In the early 1960s Tatiana Proskouriakoff made important contributions in new partial decipherments which threw light on ancient Maya political structure and royal lineages.[159b] In addition to Maya writing, considerable advances had been made on early Zapotecan hieroglyphics and calendrics by the Mexican authority, Alfonso Caso.[159c] The spectacular urban dimensions and functions of the site of Teotihuacan would be another kind of 'discovery'. The site had been known to archaeologists for many years, but it was not until the 1950s and 1960s that its true physical nature and its former widespread influences in commerce and politics on the Mesoamerican-wide scene were realized and appreciated.[160] Another 'discovery' would be the clarification of the relationships between the Classic Lowland

102, 111

109 A stone sculpture in the Olmec style, representing a man holding an infant were-jaguar. Height 55 cm.

Maya civilization and other Mesoamerican cultures during the
Late Classic Period (A.D. 600–900).[161] Some 'discoveries' did,
indeed, involve new materials, such as those of MacNeish in
Tamaulipas and in southern Puebla where, in both instances, the
archaeologists found long preceramic sequences associated with
the slow transition of plant-gathering to plant cultivation.[162] Parts
of Mesoamerica still lack adequate exploration and chronological
systematization – Guerrero and west Mexico would be examples –
but, on the whole, the area is one of the best known, albeit the most
complex, of the New World. The conception of it as a culture area
was tacitly accepted as early as the late 19th century, and the
Spinden and Vaillant area syntheses of 1928 and 1941 helped to
establish this conception still more. In 1943 Paul Kirchhoff addressed himself directly to this question of Mesoamerica as a culture area or culture sphere, with the implications that such an
entity was, in effect, a culture-area-with-time-depth and not the
'flat,' synchronic culture area of the ethnographer.[163] This was
followed by a number of area syntheses. Some of these were essentially historical and descriptive;[164] others combined both historical
and evolutionary perspectives.[165]

In North America, the Southwestern United States, in which
archaeological systematics were most developed prior to 1940,
continued to be a center of intensive research. One obvious problem was that of southern relationships of the cultures of the area,
and a number of archaeologists, including C. C. Di Peso, have
concerned themselves with this.[166] Questions of migrations or
diffusions between Mesoamerica and the Hohokam and Mogollon
regions are still debated although the evidence that is coming in
suggests that both processes were at work at different times and
places. Another problem has been that of the antecedents of the

112 A reconstruction drawing of
the Classic Maya ballcourt (*ca.*
A.D. 600–800) at Copan, Honduras. This drawing is the work
of T. Proskouriakoff, a member
of the Department of Archaeology of the Carnegie Institution
of Washington, an organization
that undertook much important
work in the Maya area from
1914 to 1958

110 (*Above left*) The great La
Venta pyramid. Upon clearing
by archaeologists, this mound
was revealed to have a conical
fluted form, a most unusual shape
for a Mesoamerican structure.
Made of earth, it is the largest
mound of the Olmec ceremonial
center of La Venta, Mexico. La
Venta is believed to have flourished *ca.* 1200–800 B.C.

111 (*Below left*) Aerial photograph of the huge urban site of
Teotihuacan

113 Excavated and partially restored pyramid of the Maya site of Tikal, Guatemala. Compare this photograph with Ill. 59, which was taken more than a half-century earlier

114 Cross-sectional diagram of the main plaza, temples, and other structures at Tikal, Guatemala. This diagram shows the complexities of large architectural excavations. (After William R. Coe, 1965)

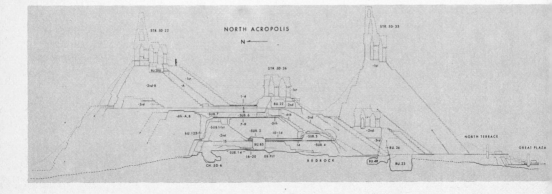

Puebloan and Desert farmers; but now the chronological gap between Early Man and these pottery-agricultural cultures was filled by 'Meso-Indian' or 'Archaic'-type discoveries.[167] As might be anticipated in view of the relatively advanced state of Southwestern distributional and dating studies, the area has been one of the main centers for contextual-functional and processual inquiries. We have already referred to some of these and will come to them again in the next chapter.[168]

Eastern archaeology had farther to go than the Southwest to come abreast in space-time ordering. As of 1971 it might be said to still lag a bit, but great progress has been made. As in the Southwest, and elsewhere in the New World, the 'Meso-Indian' or 'Archaic' era has been brought into focus.[169] The origins of many elements in the Adena-Hopewellian cultures are still somewhat mysterious – including the beginnings and importance of agriculture in the East – but a much more sophisticated appreciation of the nature of Hopewellian 'culture' has replaced the earlier taxonomic conception of it.[170] A great many regional monographs have been published,[171] in addition to the hundreds of site reports, although there have been no book-length syntheses of the East as a whole.[172] As in the Southwest, a good many studies of recent years have been concerned with context, function, and process. These studies usually have rested on fairly adequate regional or site data bases although for much of the East fundamental spatial-chronological information is still sparse. A very large amount of fieldwork has been carried out in the river valleys of the Plains, most of it in connection with the salvage programs, and this has made possible such a general book as Wedel's on the Plains area.[173]

Archaeology in the Far West of the United States and Canada enjoyed a great boom in the 1940–70 decades. Previously, there had been little or no sequence information from these areas. This includes California, the Great Basin, and the Northwest Coast and Plateau.[174] The cultures of these areas did not come within the American agricultural orbit but followed modes of subsistence comparable to those of the 'Meso-Indian' or 'Archaic' cultures down to historic times. The chronological groundwork that has now been done in these areas has provided archaeologists with frames of reference for studying the generally gradual changes in these cultures, especially in relation to the natural environmental settings.

In the North, Subarctic archaeology had its beginnings in these recent decades, and the data from there have posed a number of interesting problems as to origins and directions of influence. Arctic (and at one remove Asiatic) influences are seen intermixed with those from North American 'Archaic' cultures.[175] In the Arctic proper, the good beginning made by Collins in Eskimo chronology has been continued by Larsen and Rainey and by Giddings and Anderson.[176] Cultures immediately antecedent to 'classic' Eskimo ivory-using ones have been linked to a widespread 'Arctic Small Tool tradition,' embracing complexes all the way from the Cape Denbigh in the West to Sarqaq in Greenland. This tradition, with its emphasis on flint microblades, is clearly of

115 Detailed natural stratigraphy in Danger Cave, Utah

Asiatic Mesolithic derivation. A still earlier horizon, the 'Paleo-Arctic,' also has Asiatic affinities, but they are less well defined.

Inter-areal syntheses, some of them of continental or hemispheric scope, began to appear in considerable numbers in the latter part of the Classificatory-Historical Period and on into the 1960s. Some of these were primarily chronological and descriptive. The Martin, Quimby, and Collier book on the archaeology of America north of Mexico, *Indians Before Columbus*, published in 1947, was of this nature. It offered a factual and chronologically ordered account of archaeological findings (with some attempts at contextual-functional presentations) in a series of regional and areal sequences. Little or no attempt was made to break down area compartmentalization, either by plotting lines of diffusion or by viewing the data in accordance with broad developmental patterns of stages.[177] Salvador Canals Frau's two books, *Prehistoria de América* and *Las Civilizaciones Prehistoricas de América*, which appeared in Argentina in 1950 and 1955, were hemispheric in scope.[178] While utilizing some broad diffusional categories, of a highly speculative and not very convincing sort, they did not differ greatly (except in their lack of precise control of the data) from the Martin-Quimby-Collier effort. The huge compendium, *Manual de Arqueología Americana*, by the Spanish Americanist José Alcina Franch, which was prepared in 1958, although not published until 1965, is again, compartmentalized and catalogue-like, a compilation rather than a synthesis.[179]

Radiocarbon dates, which began to pour in during the 1950s, enabled the archaeologists to cross-date culture sequences from one area to another. This aided in both diffusional and developmental perspectives[180] and resulted in New World syntheses that

were somewhat more truly that. Such syntheses were expressed in both historical and developmental (evolutionary) terms, often with a blending of the two. The developmental or culture-stage principle was utilized by Willey and Phillips in their 1955 article and 1958 book.[181] This outlook owed much to Julian Steward's earlier articles on South American cultural evolution or development.[182] It was employed by Steward and Faron in a combined archaeological-ethnographical summary volume on South America,[183] and has been used by Sanders and Merino in a concise 1970 volume on the New World as a whole.[184] We shall return to the developmental stage classifications of New World cultures later, in a more theoretical context.

A more strictly historical outlook is seen in the volume by H. M. Wormington, on *Ancient Man in North America*, which is concerned only with Pleistocene and Early Post-Pleistocene cultures,[185] in George Kubler's *The Art and Architecture of Ancient America. The Mexican, Maya, and Andean Peoples*,[186] which examines the New World civilizations from an art history point of view, and in the archaeological articles in a book by R. F. Spencer and J. D. Jennings, *The Native Americans*.[187]

Two other books are collections of articles by various regional specialists. One of these, *Aboriginal Cultural Development in Latin America: An Interpretative Review*, edited by Meggers and Evans, and published in 1963, deals with Middle and South American archaeology as of that date;[188] the other, *Prehistoric Man in the New World*, edited by Jennings and Norbeck and dating to 1964, runs from the Bering Strait to Cape Horn in its coverage.[189] Both are fundamentally descriptive-historic, although summary articles by Meggers and Bernal, respectively, essay some stage concepts. Such

116 Irrigation canal excavation at the Hohokam site of Snaketown in southern Arizona. This site, the source of most of the archaeological knowledge of the Hohokam culture, was excavated by Gladwin and Haury in the 1930s. Sections of the site have been re-excavated by Haury in the early 1960s

collections have the advantage of bringing the most up-to-date specialized knowledge available to the treatment of particular areas, but they have the counterbalancing weakness of the lack of a unified point of view in interpretation and presentation that a single author can give to a general work.

Two of the most recent single-author syntheses are those of Jennings, *Prehistory of North America*,[190] which appeared in 1968 and which covers America north of Mexico in a combined developmental stage-historical organization, and of Willey, *An Introduction to American Archaeology*,[191] a two-volume treatment of the entire New World, published in 1966–71, which follows an historico-genetic scheme. Such works are designed primarily as college textbooks and general references; but they also serve the purpose of formalizing the discipline, and are one more sign of American archaeology's coming of age.

The only major American work of synthesis of recent years which could be considered in the vein of doctrinaire diffusionism is James Ford's *A Comparison of Formative Cultures in the Americas*,[192] brought out in 1969, in which he attempts to explain the first appearances of ceramics and a number of other Neolithic-level traits in North America as a result of their diffusion from an original hearth in northwestern South America. The scheme is an involved one, incorporating what Ford calls an initial 'Colonial Formative' diffusion and a later 'Theocratic Formative' wave (characterized by ceremonial center constructions). In many ways it is comparable to Spinden's 'Archaic hypothesis', although Ford worked with much more chronologically controlled data.

While the tradition of American culture history as an essentially self-controlled one, without important contacts or relationships to the Old World, continued to dominate the thinking of most archaeologists, some new points of view about this appeared in the late Classificatory-Historical Period and then into the 1960s. Of course, Old World-New World relationships on a Paleolithic-New World Early Man level had always been a respectable line of inquiry although very little had been done about it. Even as of 1971 not much is known on the subject which still remains largely speculative; however, with Russian discoveries in Siberia being made available in English translations, a number of clues for connections have emerged.[193] The significance and interpretation of these have varied, but the consensus of Americanist opinion as we go into the 1970s is that Levallois-Mousteroid techniques, by whatever slow and circuitous diffusion, were transferred from Asia to the Americas and may well have provided the bi-facial-flaked blade technology which, eventually, gave rise to the early American Clovis and related industries.[194] Somewhat better documented, and similarly respectable, has been the case for Asiatic Mesolithic traits spreading or being carried to the New World across a Bering land bridge in later millennia to form the bases for arctic and Subarctic techniculture prior to the appearance of the more typical Eskimo complexes. These last, too, are generally seen as incorporating Asiatic traits.[195]

More dubious and debatable have been the claims for Trans-Pacific relationships between Asia and America in relatively Late

117

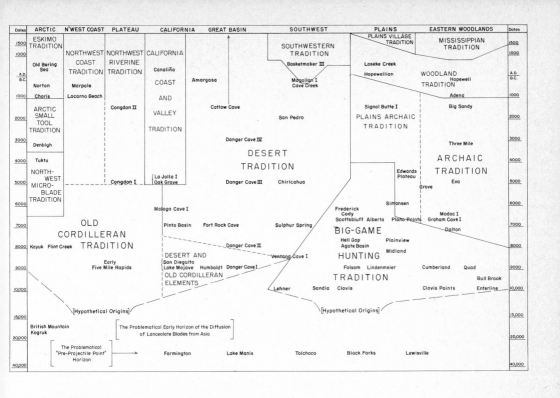

117 Area and chronology chart showing the development of major cultural traditions in North America. (After Willey, 1966, Vol. I, *An Introduction to American Archaeology*, by permission of Prentice-Hall, Inc., Englewood Cliffs, New Jersey)

118 Ecuadorian Valdivia and Japanese Jomon pottery. *a–d, g* are Japanese sherds; *e–f, h–i* are Ecuadorian sherds

Pre-Columbian times. The Austrian ethnologist-archaeologist, Robert von Heine-Geldern, had long been the spokesman for the importance of such diffusions in the rise of the New World Mesoamerican and Peruvian civilizations, and he continued to argue his case in the 1950s and 1960s.[196] Generally, American archaeologists were not convinced, citing difficulties in finding the proper Asiatic antecedents with the proper dating and arguing for the more likely possibility of independent development and evolution.[197] Nevertheless, there is a haunting similarity about such things as Shang and Chao bronzes of China and the more or less contemporaneous Chavin stone sculptures and ceramics of Peru – just to name a single example – and although the trend of American archaeology in the late 1960s and early 1970s is away from long-range diffusionistic explanations, and more convinced of *in situ* evolutionary forces in culture development, it is still fair to say that these questions have not been finally resolved.

One of the most compelling arguments for Trans-Pacific contact was put forward in the late 1950s and into the 1960s by the late Ecuadorian archaeologist, Emilio Estrada, in collaboration with Meggers and Evans. All three had worked in coastal Ecuadorian archaeology where the Valdivia ceramic complex, dating to *ca.* 3000–2500 B.C., was discovered by them as the earliest pottery of the area.[198] This Valdivian pottery is of relatively simple vessel forms, although competently made, and it features incised and other surface-plastic decorative motifs. Its resemblances to pottery of about the same age from the Japanese Jomon shell middens is startling, and the three archaeologists hypothesize that Jomon fishermen, carried out into the Pacific currents, eventually landed in coastal Ecuador where they introduced the trait of pottery-making to other fishers and shellfishers who were on a more or less comparable technological level to themselves. Probably, the majority of American archaeologists have not been convinced;[199] some have;[200] and others still assume a 'wait-and-see' attitude.[201]

Historical and Developmental Concepts

The main methodological innovations of the late Classificatory-Historical Period were, as we have said, in the realm of contextual and functional interpretations. Some historical concepts were also developed during this time and deserve special mention. They are most fittingly referred to here because they were concepts which were invented and employed in connection with the culture area and chronological syntheses – which we have just reviewed – and also because they all have processual dimensions and, appropriately, serve as transitions in theory and method between the late Classificatory-Historical Period and the Explanatory Period. These concepts are the horizon style, the cultural tradition (in its various guises), and the culture stage. The first two are fundamentally historical in their properties, that is, they relate primarily to cultural description and spatial-temporal locations; however, both are also secondarily concerned with process in that certain kinds of human behavior must be invoked to explain their existence. The third, the culture stage, has primary referents in both history

118

(chronology) and process (cultural evolution). Such stage appraisals led, naturally, to cross-cultural comparisons. We have already noted some of these in connection with cultural-environmental relationships, but the comparisons were wider in scope than this.

Although we are treating these concepts here, apart from our above discussions of context and function, it should be recognized that horizon styles, cultural traditions, and culture stages were very much a part of the widening interests in the nature of the prehistoric record and of the archaeologists' attempts to enrich that record and to understand it.

The horizon style concept was formalized by Kroeber in 1944. He defined the horizon style as:

'... one showing definably distinct features some of which extend over a large area, so that its relations with other, more local styles serve to place these in relative time, according as the relations are of priority, consocation, or subsequence.'[202]

The three major Peruvian horizon styles, which were recognized at that time, and which subsequent research has further confirmed, were the Chavin, Tiahuanaco (Tiahuanaco-Huari), and the Inca. Kroeber also suggested two other horizon styles, the Negative-painted and the White-on-red;[203] but, as these are characterized by technical (kinds of painting) rather than stylistic or icono-graphic features, the name 'horizon markers' might be more appropriate in their case. Functionally, the dissemination of a highly complicated iconography and the spread of a simple ceramic painting technique must have had quite disparate implica-tions.[204] The horizon style and horizon marker concepts are now standard features of American archaeological procedure although the way in which they are applied and their utility has occasioned some discussion.[205]

The concept of the tradition was introduced into Peruvian archaeology by Willey in 1945 as a kind of counterpoise to Kroeber's horizon style. Whereas the latter emphasized the dis-semination or diffusion of a complex of traits or elements (a style) over a relatively large geographical area in a short span of time, the former emphasized the persistence of certain cultural traits or elements in the same area over a relatively long span of time. In his article Willey dealt with a particular class of tradition, the pottery tradition, and, defined it as follows:

'A pottery tradition comprises a line, or a number of lines, of pottery development through time within the confines of a certain technique or decorative constant. In successive time periods through which the history of ceramic development can be traced, certain styles arose within the tradition. Transmission of some of these styles during particular periods resulted in the formation of a horizon style; other styles in the continuum of the tradition re-mained strictly localized.'[206]

The tradition, then, as the word implies, had reference to 'tradi-tional' or time-persistent ways of doing things – in the particular instances discussed for Peru, of making pottery. It was an historico-genetic concept and, as such, related in its fundamental approach to culture-classification schemes like Gladwin's which had been proposed for Southwestern North America during the earlier half of the Classificatory-Historical Period.[207] Goggin broadened the tradition concept in applying it to whole cultures in Florida.[208]

The tradition concept was also related to that of the culture area or the culture-area-with-time-depth. Kirchhoff did not apply the term 'tradition' to his Mesoamerican area definition, but he might well have done so.[209] W. C. Bennett did in his definition of a Peruvian culture-area-with-time-depth, or in what he called the Peruvian 'Co-Tradition.'[210] Martin and Rinaldo followed Bennett's lead, both in concept and terminology, in defining such a co-tradition for the Southwestern United States.[211] This latter usage occasioned a reply by Rouse who questioned their application and definition of the co-tradition concept.[212] According to Rouse, the co-tradition was intended by Bennett to be more than just a culture-area-time-depth. It was, rather, a culture area in which all of the lines of cultural development could be traced back to one single line – a monogenetic conception.[213] However, it is probably fair to say that this rather special definition of the co-tradition concept is not one employed by most American archaeologists who still tend to think of it as the more loosely structured 'culture-area-with-time-depth.'

As to the term tradition itself, there has been no clear concurrence of opinion on just how it should be defined. Some archaeologists prefer to use it in the more restricted sense of Willey's Peruvian pottery traditions; others would see it as something considerably more inclusive.[214] Still other archaeologists have come up with similar, although not entirely identical, historical concepts. J. R. Caldwell's Hopewellian 'interaction sphere' is one of these.[215] In this he refers to a series of regional cultures linked by a common participation in some elements of culture (mortuary ritual and paraphernalia) but not in others. As such, the interaction sphere, a highly useful way of looking at the obvious results of trade and other forms of intercommunication and common cultural bonds, partakes of some of the properties of both a tradition (in the broader sense of the definition) and an horizon style.[216]

The culture stage concept, as we know, has an early history in archaeological and anthropological studies, going back to the early Danish Stone, Bronze, and Iron Age formulations and to the more anthropologically oriented evolutionary scheme of Savagery, Barbarism, and Civilization.[217] This kind of classification was reintroduced into American archaeology by Julian Steward. His experience in editing *The Handbook of South American Indians*, with its vast array of archaeological and ethnological cultures and the necessity for organizing these into some kind of a meaningful overall pattern, was undoubtedly a conditioning factor in Steward's thinking, although one must also take into account his earlier culture-and-environmental and evolutionary studies in the North American Great Basin.[218] Steward's views on culture stages and cultural evolution are expressed in his *Handbook*[219] articles as well as in the organization of the *Handbook* itself in which his major culture 'types,' which to a large extent could be blocked out as culture 'super-areas' of that continent, were, in effect, stages.[220] Steward went from these to his better-known article, 'Cultural

Causality and Law: A Trial Formulation of the Development of Early Civilizations,'[221] to which we have already referred in our discussion of environmental factors in cultural development and evolution. Still another article of Steward's, 'A Functional-Developmental Classification of American High Cultures,'[222] forecasts the more detailed Willey-Phillips stage scheme of a few years later.[223]

The Willey-Phillips 'Historical-Developmental Interpretation' of New World prehistory, appearing first as an article in 1955 and, in 1958, as a part of the book *Method and Theory in American Archaeology*, was clearly influenced by Steward and also by an outline which had been propounded very briefly by A. D. Krieger at a 1952 symposium.[224] Beyond this, it should be recognized that prototypes for such a scheme had for a long time been a part of the more or less routine archaeological area syntheses in the Americas. The Southwestern 'Pecos Classification' had periods which were also stages because the criteria for these did not appear at the same time in all parts of the area.[225] The Ford-Willey chronology for the Eastern United States recognized that the major 'periods' of the area were best described as stages.[226] A number of the Peruvian area chronologies, devised shortly after the Virú Valley program, are also stage schemes, for the criteria by which the 'periods' were established (esthetic florescence, imperialism, conquest, etc.) were not fully synchronous for all parts of the Peruvian area.[227] The same is also true of the Armillas chronology for Mesoamerica.[228] Thus, there were numerous area models for Willey and Phillips to use; they simply projected the model for the whole New World. Their scheme, as it finally appeared, comprised five major New World stages.[229] In chronological and developmental order, these were: (1) Lithic (Paleo-Indian and other Early Man beginnings in the Americas); (2) Archaic (Post-Pleistocene hunting-collecting adaptations); (3) Formative (the village agricultural threshold and/or sedentary life); (4) Classic (beginnings of urban development); and (5) Postclassic (the imperialistic states). While Lithic cultures were defined as being entirely extinct, it was argued that many existing or historic New World societies (those of Northern and Far Western North America and of southern South America) had remained on an Archaic stage level. Similarly, most agricultural or horticultural peoples of the New World were conceived of as having tarried on a Formative level. Only in Mesoamerica and Peru were the Classic and Postclassic stages admitted to have existed.

The Willey-Phillips interpretation met with considerable interest for it raised, again, the idea of cultural evolution which for so long had lain dormant in American archaeology. Much of the comment was critical, for to some archaeologists such developmental or evolutionary schema were rejected on principle.[230] Others, while in general theoretical agreement, felt that the Willey-Phillips criteria for the proposed stages were not wisely selected.[231] Still others suggested modifications or variant schemes.[232] But, most importantly, evolutionary thinking had been rejuvenated, and this ferment of ideas was to form the transition from the late Classificatory-Historical Period into the Explanatory Period.

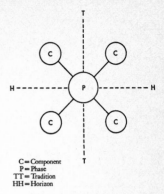

C = Component
P = Phase
TT = Tradition
HH = Horizon

119 Diagram showing the relationships between horizons and traditions and culture components and phases. (After Willey and Phillips, 1958, by permission of the University of Chicago Press)

Chapter Six

The Explanatory Period (1960–   )

> 'Nobody ever got to a single truth without talking nonsense fourteen
> times first.' Fyodor Dostoyevsky

An Introduction to the Period

Any attempt to view these last ten years of American archaeology
in historical perspective is most difficult. The events are too recent;
the time is still upon us. Nevertheless, we must make this decade a
part of our history. Not to do so would be to fail in one of our most
important objectives: to see the developments of the immediate
present in relation to those of the past. That we devote an entire
chapter to do so will seem disproportionate to some, an excessive
preoccupation with the current and fashionable. Others may feel
that events of these last few years should compose the real body of
the book, with all that led up to them a mere introduction re-
counting the follies and fumbles of a pre-modern era. We have
taken a middle road. It is a time of change. What is new is being
said by many voices. No doubt some of it is wise, some foolish, and
much contradictory. We view it, however, with optimism.

Our presentation of the period begins with the thesis suggested
at the close of the preceding chapter – that the re-emergence of
evolutionary concepts in the late 1950s, after long years of dis-
favor, prepared the base for the 'new archaeology' of the 1960s.
We will examine this 'new' archaeology in the light of its links
with the past and in its innovations. This will lead us on to a
consideration of systems theory in archaeology, to the concept of
the ecosystem, and to a word about statistics and the role of the
computer. After this we will turn to a brief review of deductive
reasoning, the positivist philosophy of science, and the vogue these
have enjoyed in the archaeology of the 1960s. A very rapid survey
of some recent archaeological researches in the 'new archaeological'
vein follows, and we will close with an overall appraisal of the
period and the prospects for the future of American archaeology.

The Re-emergence of Cultural Evolution

In the mid 1950s, when Willey and Phillips published their scheme
for New World prehistory, cultural evolutionism was still largely
proscribed in American anthropological circles.[1] For a long time
Leslie White had been its only protagonist.[2] Steward, as we have
seen, joined the issue in the late 1940s and 1950s with a brand of
evolutionary theory that seemed somewhat more immediately
pertinent to the problems of archaeology. Willey and Phillips were
familiar with numerous culture sequences in the New World, and
they could also see beyond the particulars of these sequences to
realize that the story carried in them was the story of the rise of

civilization. At the same time, they were also aware of the many areal and regional peculiarities of American Pre-Columbian history and its complex cross-currents of diffusion. They shied away from anything that seemed to them to be deterministic or that would readily *explain* the series of stages by which they viewed the New World past:

'The method is comparative, and the resulting definitions are abstractions which *describe* culture change through time in native America. The stages are not formulations which *explain* culture change.' (Original italics.)[3]

They were, therefore, hesitant to use the word 'evolution' because of what seemed to them to be its deterministic and causal implications. They felt that explanation must lie in a complex interplay of diffusion, cultural-environmental interaction, demographic change, 'homotaxis in a true evolutionary sense,' and psychological factors.[4] Throughout, they showed a disinclination to separate evolution from history. In one sense, Willey and Phillips were obviously right: process was not to be plucked easily from the matrices of history. At the same time, their refusal to recognize their approach as an evolutionary one – even if no more than a preliminary step in the arrangement of the data – was a hesitancy in keeping with the anti-evolutionary attitudes of the times.[5]

Much more direct evolutionary statements than those of Willey and Phillips were also made by a few other American archaeologists in the 1950s. Perhaps significantly, these were people who had been more influenced by White than by Steward. Betty J. Meggers was one of these. We have already referred to her 1954 paper on natural environment as a limiting factor in culture growth, in which she combined a cultural-environmental approach with evolutionism. In 1955, in an article entitled 'The Coming of Age of American Archaeology,' she defended evolutionary theory against the criticisms of the historical particularists by arguing that:

'Its validity stems from the fact that observable conditions can be more easily understood and more simply explained if the law is assumed.'[6]

Observing that the main trends in social anthropology between 1930 and 1955 had been in the direction of psychological explanations of cultural phenomena, she pointed out that archaeologists, particularly in their area schemes of developmental stages, had been moving toward evolutionary explanations. Referring to the social anthropologist Hoebel's statement about archaeology being the 'lesser part of anthropology' (see p. 131, this book), Meggers goes on to add:

'The strides that have been made [in archaeology] in recent years indicate that far from being a handicap, there is considerable advantage in being forced to deal with culture artificially separated from human beings.'[7]

In other words, a concept of cultural evolution came easy for the archaeologist, given the very nature of his data; in contrast, the social anthropologist, Leslie White, had to arrive at it by a much more difficult course.

In a more substantive vein, Meggers made a signal contribution as a participant and editor of the symposium group that produced the paper on 'Community Patterning,'[8] already referred to in the previous chapter in our discussions of settlement pattern studies. In this work, the basic evolutionary assumptions of progress through improved subsistence and the greater survival value of sedentary as opposed to nomadic life were made at the outset – definite explanatory and causal statements which go beyond anything offered by Willey and Phillips. These assumptions were then examined cross-culturally to arrive at a stage scheme of settlement or community patterning applicable to the Americas and beyond.

At the close of the 1950s and into the 1960s a number of writings appeared on evolutionary theory or on applications of it to specific substantive problems. J. A. Ford, G. I. Quimby, and W. G. Haag – all former students of White's – were among the authors. Ford's field researches had long been guided by evolutionary precepts; these now became even more explicit.[9] Quimby used Naskapi and Eskimo data – both archaeological and ethnological – in combining White's evolutionary perspective with environmental determinism in attempting to explain the nature of Northeastern North American cultures.[10] Haag, in a critical review article, 'The Status of Evolutionary Theory in American Archaeology,' offered a definition of evolution for archaeologists:

'Evolution is change in form and function through time of material culture and any bodily acts, ideas, and sentiments that may be inferred therefrom.'[11]

He went on to say that it had long been a part of American archaeology, but essentially on a subconscious level.

Willey, in an article published in 1960, moved somewhat farther toward an evolutionary outlook by stating that the processes of cultural evolution are selective ones and that through these the species (man, society, and culture) promotes its survival and fulfilment. He cautioned, however, that the courses by which this comes about are not 'programmed by any laws of inevitability' and further observed that while technico-environmental adaptations seem easy to plot on an historical-evolutionary scale those of the ideological realm (art) are not.[12]

Old World archaeological and evolutionary influences began to make themselves felt in American archaeology, also, at about this time. Robert J. Braidwood, although, like Willey, somewhat hesitant to conceive of cultural evolution as a process outside of specific historical contexts, had viewed Near Eastern prehistory in an evolutionary light.[13] He, as most other Near Eastern archaeologists, had been influenced by the archaeological and evolutionary writings of V. Gordon Childe.[14] In 1959, he traced the history of evolutionary theory in archaeology in a summary article, focusing attention mainly upon the Old World, but with some reference to the New, and showing how Darwinian concepts as applied to culture had changed from the early De Mortillet usages to those of Childe and others.[15]

A former student of Braidwood's, Robert McC. Adams brought Old World and Americanist ideas about cultural evolution even closer together by carrying out research in Mesopotamia and Middle America and directing his attention in both areas to the quantum advance from temple-centered societies to those of the urban states. In his 'The Evolutionary Process in Early Civilizations,' Adams was critical of Steward and Wittfogel, arguing that causal relationships cannot be established by stage definitions and cross-cultural comparisons alone.[16] He challenged single-explanation hypotheses, such as Steward's belief that over-population led to warfare or Wittfogel's[17] insistence that the administrative requirements of large-scale irrigation produced the despotic state. The only way to avoid self-contained causal theories, in Adams's view, was to recognize the complexity and interdependence of events leading up to major stage transformations and to present these in the greatest possible range of historical detail. In this, he recognized no inherent opposition between cultural-historical integration and evolutionism. Adams is calling for two things, one of which we have referred to before. This is the necessity for contextual-functional analysis as an intermediate step between chronological ordering and processual understanding. The other, which is implicit but not explicit in Adams's writings, is systemic analysis – the only way in which the 'complexity and interdependence of events,' in Adams's terms, may be viewed in their proper relationships to one another.

Adams's major work along these lines – and one in which he followed up his call for full historical and contextual detail – is his brilliant, *The Evolution of Urban Society. Early Mesopotamia and Prehispanic Mexico.*[18] In it he traces with great care the parallel evolution of two societies, one in the Old World and one in the New, from kin-based farming villages to stratified, politically organized states. While Adams rejected any single-principle explanation of cultural evolution, Steward, in reviewing his work, felt that:

'. . . the author has documented the incipiency of crop improvement, better utilization of microenvironments, and increased specialization and interdependency of local population segments as the new processes or trends that led to state institutions.'[19]

Certainly, by 1966, the date of the publication of Adams's book, it was the outstanding example of the cross-cultural comparative approach to an understanding of cultural evolution, the only such attempt in which there had been a micro-analysis of the archaeological (and ethnohistorical) data bearing upon the cases at hand.

By the late 1960s a change had taken place in American archaeology. There had been a tacit acceptance of cultural evolution. Any representative sampling of recent American archaeological literature, with its strong reliance on the ideas of White and Steward and the younger cultural evolutionists among the social anthropologists, such as Sahlins, Service, and Fried, bears this out. For example, in the first three issues of the journal *American Antiquity* that were published in 1971 there is a total of sixteen references (in thirteen articles) to the theoretical works of these five men. A decade earlier, the four issues of the 1960–61 volume contained only two references to Steward (twenty-eight articles) and none to any of the other four authors. This swift and quiet change is one of the most interesting phenomena of the Explanatory Period.

As we have seen, the theory of cultural evolution was generally anathema as late as the 1950s. The factors bringing about the change are not altogether understood, but they were probably multiple. The general trend toward a more scientific approach in all of the social sciences (and even some of the humanities) was undoubtedly one of them. Another was probably the change in political climate in the United States. In the 1940s and 1950s it was not uncommon for the spectre of Marxism to be raised by the anti-evolutionists in the heat of argument.[20] The 1960s have seen a somewhat more realistic appreciation of the relationships between evolutionary theory and political dogma. On the more strictly academic side, some credit must be extended to those social anthropological thinkers, such as Leslie White[21] and Julian Steward, as we have indicated.

In spite of all these factors, we are inclined to feel that the most basic reason for the change was generated within archaeology itself. If archaeology, by its very nature, is concerned with chronology, and if chronology is the dynamic dimension of evolution, then it should come as no surprise that evolutionary theory should at last establish itself in archaeology. Remember that the Classificatory-Historical Period was a story of the successes of chronological ordering. Toward the close of that period, while American social anthropology was still largely ruled by the anti-evolutionists and functionalists, evolution came quietly into archaeology through comparative considerations of the long, precise chronological sequences of culture change that had been developed in the years between 1914 and the late 1950s. Without this well-documented chronological ordering we doubt very much that the theoretical exhortations of White or Steward would have moved American archaeologists. But the hard and indisputable facts of chronology, particularly when revealed by the methods of stratigraphy, were too much for the literal-minded archaeologists to ignore. They were convinced that culture did, indeed, change through time and that this change was not altogether random. That such a condition for the acceptance of evolutionary theory was self-generated within archaeology seems borne out by the fact that this same acceptance has not yet been won in social anthropology. Thus, as recently as 1968, Marvin Harris felt it necessary to carry the fight against anti-evolutionism and anti-materialism in social anthropology and ethnology in a highly polemical manner.[22] Perhaps it could be argued that White and Steward have had more influence in archaeology than in their own disciplinary domain.

We do not wish to overstate the case. There is still some opposition to evolutionary theory in American archaeology. More importantly, there is considerable difference of opinion as to just how evolution works. What are its prime causes and its processes? We have seen how these questions troubled many of the archaeologists who were concerned with cultural evolution in the 1950s and 1960s, and the same questions are still with us.

Although the revival of evolutionary theory in the late 1950s prepared the way for the advances of the Explanatory Period, this revival, in and of itself, did not constitute the beginnings of that period. Its inception is placed a few years later, for the Explanatory Period is most meaningfully characterized by what has been called the 'new archaeology.' This name does not tell us much, other than that it differed from the archaeology that preceded it; it does not in itself indicate in what way it differed, and so it is still incumbent upon us to attempt a definition of the 'new archaeology' – and of the Explanatory Period.

Our definition will be seen in clearer perspective if we first describe certain attitudes that provided a background for the rise of the 'new archaeology.' To begin with, it was a product of anthropological archaeology, of young archaeologists who, as graduate students, had been, in part, trained by social anthropologists as well as archaeologists. Their central concern was the elucidation of cultural process. While there had been, as we have seen, a certain amount of talk about the necessity for archaeologists to come to grips with cultural process in the late Classificatory-Historical Period, this had remained – like the proverbial concern about the weather – just talk. No one had done much about it. The 'new archaeologists' felt that the time had come for a serious attack on questions of process. Second, the 'new archaeology' was (and is) pervaded with a great optimism about the possibilities of success in processual explanation and in arriving at 'laws of cultural dynamics.'[23] A third attitude held that archaeology, in its revelation and explanation of cultural process, could be made relevant not only to the rest of anthropology but to the problems of the modern world as well.

In the light of the above, let us turn more specifically to a definition of the 'new archaeology' in its approaches. The first of these was (and is) a predominantly evolutionary point of view. We have just discussed this from an historical perspective, and we emphasize its importance to the 'new archaeology' and to the Explanatory Period. In fact, we do not feel that they would have been possible without a cultural evolutionary bias. The second approach is that derived from general systems theory, in effect, a systemic view of culture and society, with its interacting parts or subsystems. The third approach which is most characteristic of the 'new archaeology' is its stance of deductive or logico-deductive reasoning.

Other aspects of the 'new archaeology' are extensions or expressions of these three basic approaches to ways of viewing the data of prehistory. The evolutionary position of most 'new archaeologists' – while not always overtly formulated – assumes the technico-economic realm of culture to be the primarily determinative one in change, with the social and ideational realms changing in secondary relation to it. This marks a distinct difference from that of the historical-developmental stage approach of Willey and Phillips where no attempt was made to pinpoint causality.

The employment of systems theory has led to ecological considerations and the adoption of the concept of the ecosystem. It is here that the circumstance of studying relatively simple cultures has been of particular value to the 'new archaeologist,' however, it should be added that the 'new archaeologists' – or at least some of them – reject any limitations on the type of information the past may yield up, arguing that all systemic interrelationships, of whatever sort, will leave some kind of a trace, directly or indirectly, in the material record. The 'new archaeology' has close ties with the physical and natural sciences, in a variety of materials identifications and analyses, and it is also here, within the compass of this systemic view of culture, that statistics and the computer can play such an important role.

The 'new archaeologist' tests hypotheses about the past through deductive, as opposed to inductive, reasoning. While these hypotheses may be suggested by ethnographic or ethnohistoric data, they are considered to be in no way dependent upon such data. Thus, it is not the source of the hypothesis that is important but the way it can be formulated to allow for its deductive proof or disproof in the archaeological record.

If this brief statement may serve as a minimal definition for the American 'new archaeology' – and if this 'new archaeology' marks the threshold of our Explanatory Period – just when and where did the synthesis take place? To what extent were the important elements of the 'new archaeology' present before the date of 1960, our dividing line between the Classificatory-Historical and Explanatory Periods? In reviewing a collection of essays,[24] edited by S. R. and L. R. Binford and published in 1968 as a representative expression of the 'new archaeology,' Walter W. Taylor, Jr. has challenged the contention of 'newness.'

'. . . a full discussion of a very similar overall approach to our discipline has been in print since 1948 (W. W. Taylor, *A Study of Archaeology*). The systemic view of culture has been a basic premise of American anthropology, including archaeology, certainly since Malinowski, if not since Boas, and as for Binford's other tenets, I can point to passages in *A Study of Archaeology* covering each of them, even that of testing hypotheses. . . . What the Binfords have produced in this book is not an exposition of the theory and practice of a new perspective but an explicit restatement of an old one, with some new and modern additions, together with some very pertinent, cogent, stimulating examples of current archaeological research resulting from it.'[25]

But Binford feels quite differently about it, observing:

'Despite a recent statement that one should not speak of a "new archaeology" since this alienates it from the old . . . we feel that archaeology in the 1960's is at a major point of evolutionary change. Evolution always builds on what went before, but it always involves basic structural changes.'[26]

Who is correct? This is not simply a dispute over intellectual credit, but a question about the way ideas are formed, synthesized, and propagated. A re-reading of Taylor's *A Study of Archaeology*, to which we have referred at considerable length in the previous chapter, will verify his contention that some of Binford's 'tenets' were, indeed, present in what he advocated. One of the fundamentals of Taylor's 'conjunctive' approach was full contextual recovery of the data of prehistory which is surely related to the 'new archaeologist's' insistence on a complete recovery of all of the variability in the archaeological record. Taylor's claim to hypothesis testing, through deductive reasoning, 'is also borne out in several places in his text. Nor can it be denied, as Taylor insists, that a systemic view of culture had been held by the anthropological functionalists since the 1920s.

What, then, are the differences between Taylor's position of 1948 and that of the 'new archaeologists' of the 1960s? We would argue that they are in three features which characterize the latter but not the former: (1) a cultural evolutionary point of view; (2) a systemic model of culture which incorporates this evolutionary point of view; and (3) a battery of new methods, techniques, and aids that were not available in 1948.

An examination of Taylor's book reveals that it does not embody a cultural evolutionary outlook. In this, it is probable that Taylor was influenced by Kluckhohn whose opinions in the 1940s were very much those of the traditional anti-evolutionist position of the main body of American social anthropology.

As to a systemic view of culture, it is our opinion that unless such a view is informed by an evolutionary outlook it is severely limited as a means of observing and understanding culture change. While the functionalist position conceives of culture and society systemically it does so either in the manner of what systems theorists would refer to as a 'mechanical equilibrium model' which, like a clock, has no internal sources of change; or it does so by means of a model in which all 'feedback' is negatively reinforcing, thereby maintaining the *status quo*. Such models are not ideal for socio-cultural study. More pertinent for this purpose are 'complex adaptive models' which allow for positive and negative 'feedback' and which are self-informing and adaptive.[27] Such models, when viewed in diachronic perspective, reveal an evolutionary trajectory of culture change. The 'new archaeologist' has been concerned essentially with such models and with their evolutionary potential, and in this we would see a significant difference between Taylor's 1948 systemic perspective and that of the 1960s. In making this observation, it is only fair to point out that in 1948, systems theory had made little or no impact on the social sciences. The 'new archaeological' advance along these lines owes much to similar advances in ecology, geography, and sociology.

This passage of time, from 1948 to the 1960s, has also made it possible for archaeologists to draw upon new methods, techniques, and aids from the sciences. The computer, for example, is beginning to revolutionize the systemic approach in archaeology. Sheer quantitative control has resulted in qualitative differences in what archaeology can and cannot accomplish, and materials analyses of all kinds have opened up new investigative leads that were not conceived of in 1948. From a philosophical point of view, these things are, of course, less important in distinguishing between the 'conjunctive' archaeology of the late 1940s and the

'new archaeology' of the 1960s. The essential ideological differences, as we see them, lie in the more recent applications of cultural
evolutionary theory and systems theory and in the synthesis of
these that has been made in the 'new archaeology.'

Without much question, the archaeologist responsible for this
synthesis, which made the 'new archaeology' possible and which
marks the threshold of the Explanatory Period, is Lewis R. Binford. The term 'new archaeology' was first used, in its modern
sense, by Joseph R. Caldwell in a 1959 article.[28] This admirable
paper contains many of the elements we have been discussing,
but it does not draw these together and lay down the methodological guide-lines in the way that Binford was able to do in his
1962 essay, 'Archaeology as Anthropology.' In this, and in a series
of important papers in the 1960s,[29] Binford was able to absorb
the rising tide of evolutionary and environmentalist thinking of
the late Classificatory-Historical Period, along with the more
vocal dissatisfactions about the traditional descriptive-chronological goals of American archaeology, and to synthesize these
with a systems outlook and logico-deductive reasoning. He combined all of this with polemic force in pointing to the inadequacies
of existing archaeological theory and method, and he formulated a
coherent program for archaeological research with goals which
were to be attractive to the coming generation of research students.[30] For all of this he deserves great credit in any history of
American archaeological thought.

We have made the point more than once in this book, that we
wish to visualize current developments in American archaeology
in their relationship to those that have gone before. The accompanying diagram [Ill. 120], complicated though it may appear at
first glance, is a highly simplified charting of lines of intellectual
influence in the growth of American archaeological concepts over
the past thirty years. Only the latter part of the Classificatory-
Historical Period – from about 1940 to 1960 – and the Explanatory Period are included in the diagram. The previous lines of
development, leading up to 1940, are, we believe, self-evident
from what we have had to say in the preceding chapters.

At the bottom of our diagram, the 'Dominant Trends of the
Classificatory-Historical Period' would be those represented by
such men as A. V. Kidder. This is, in effect, the 'main line' of the
American archaeological discipline as of *ca.* 1940, which was given
important codification and direction by Rouse's 1939 methodological treatise. On this same general time level are the social
anthropologists who were to significantly influence the American
archaeology of the next few decades: Kluckhohn, White, Kroeber, and Steward. Kluckhohn's influence is seen in Walter
Taylor's *A Study of Archaeology*, a denunciation of the limited
objectives of chronological ordering and a call for contextual and
functional interpretation. In this line of development we can also
see the secondary influence of Radcliffe-Brown and Malinowski,
via the academic house of American anthropology. Reading from
left to right, we see Leslie White's influence extending to Betty
Meggers. Hers was the clearest formulation of the cultural evolutionary position in American archaeology in the 1950s. Moving

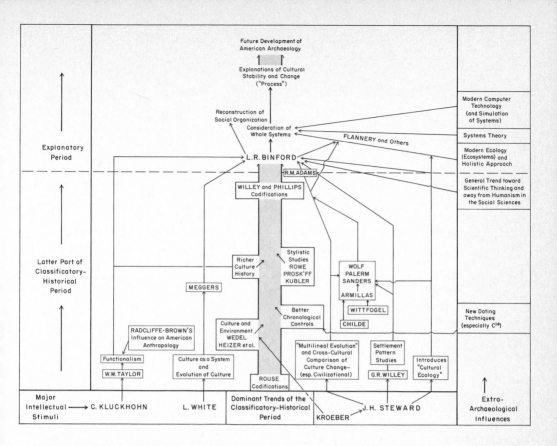

still farther across the chart is Kroeber's culture historicism (and muted evolutionism) and environmental concerns as these influence Steward, and, farther along in time, Heizer and Wedel. From Steward, three lines may be traced. One of these is evolutionary, concerned with multilinear evolution and cross-cultural comparisons as a means of looking at cultural 'regularities' or laws. Another is the settlement pattern approach, taken up by Willey in the Virú Valley study. Still a third is Steward's 'cultural ecology' which informed both of the other lines and which also was an important stimulus in preparing archaeologists to accept more modern ecological approaches.

Later important influences on American archaeology in the late Classificatory-Historical Period were those fed into it by V. Gordon Childe and Karl Wittfogel, being expressed, especially, by the archaeologists Pedro Armillas and William Sanders and the ethnologists Angel Palerm and Eric Wolf, all involved in Mesoamerican research. Such influences merged easily with the multilineal evolutionary and 'cultural ecology' approaches of Steward.

Meanwhile, within the 'main line' of archaeological studies, new dating techniques, especially radiocarbon, gave archaeologists better chronological controls over their material. Traditional archaeology was also further reinforced by precise and sophisticated stylistic studies, as in Peru and Mesoamerica, by John H. Rowe, Tatiana Proskouriakoff, and George Kubler. All of these scholars brought in ideas from the field of art history, beginning,

120 Schematic chart showing the history of theoretical and methodological developments in American archaeology during the latter part of the Classificatory-Historical Period (1940–60) and the Explanatory Period (1960–)

thereby, some consolidation of the interests and outlooks of American anthropological archaeologists with those of the fine arts school.

Contextual culture history was greatly enriched during this time. While Taylor's frontal attack on the archaeological establishment had been formally resisted, his message began to come through, in varying degrees, in the writings of many of his colleagues.

Our chart and summary do not include a host of others who have been discussed in the preceding chapter and who carried forward, within the 'main line' of traditional archaeology, descriptive and chronological work which reflected, in steadily increasing degrees, the influences we have been enumerating. Towards the close of the late Classificatory-Historical Period, the Willey-Phillips book served to codify and to make explicit many of the current practices of American archaeology and also to indicate the still serious lack, to that time, of what might be called processual studies.

At about the same time, but extending over into the early 1960s, the fine-grained cross-cultural comparative studies of Robert McC. Adams drew together, both critically and positively, the line of development represented by the multilinear evolutionary studies of Steward, Armillas, Sanders, *et al.* and the settlement pattern approach that had been pioneered by Willey.

All of this brings us to the threshold of the Explanatory Period where, it is our contention, we have a synthesis of these many lines of the development of American archaeology – the contextual-functional approach of Taylor, Leslie White's cultural evolutionism via Betty Meggers, the multilineal evolutionism and 'cultural ecology' of Steward and others, and the settlement pattern interests – in the writings of Lewis Binford. Also entering into this courageous synthesis were important extra-archaeological influences, those of modern ecology, of systems theory, of computer technology, and of the general trends toward a more 'scientific' approach to the problems of man, society, and culture. It is our feeling that the future of American archaeology will be built, at least in its central orientations, on this synthesis. We already see some of its directions, and these will be referred to below. The modern ecological or ecosystem approach holds great promise, as exemplified by the works of Kent V. Flannery. Important steps have been taken in an attempt to reconstruct extinct social systems within the bounds of reasonable verification. A consideration of cultures as whole systems, we believe, will lead archaeology to its best opportunities for explanations of cultural stability and change.

It needs no saying that it is extraordinarily difficult to appreciate the nature and meaning of change when we are in the midst of it. There are those who see the developments of the last ten years in American archaeology as effecting a break with the past so profound that there is a complete alienation between the 'new archaeology' and all that has gone before. To these persons the 'new' is completely *sui generis* with no derivations from the past. Others are unwilling to see the 'new archaeology' as such a drastic revolution. Obviously, neither ourselves nor anyone else can settle this debate at the moment. As another social scientist has said:

'The concept of "revolution" is difficult to transfer from its origins in politics to other fields of social science. Its essence is unexpected speed of change and this requires a judgement of speed in the context of a longer perspective of historical change, the choice of which is likely to be debatable in the extreme.'[31]

We have conceived of the change as profound but with visible antecedents in the past that make it something short of miraculous. But while it is interesting to speculate over whether what has happened is of the magnitude of a 'Darwinian revolution' or not, this is not really very important at the present juncture. We may leave it to historians of the future and pass on to some further considerations of our Explanatory Period.

Systems Theory and the Ecosystem Concept

We have defined the 'new archaeology' by what we consider to be its three basic approaches and characteristics: cultural evolutionary theory, systems theory, and logico-deductive reasoning. The re-emergence of evolutionary theory in American archaeology has already been discussed. Let us take a look at systems theory in archaeology.

In the first place, we must recognize that the revival of evolutionary thinking and the introduction of a general systems model in archaeology are systemically related; and these, in turn, are also systemically related to the development of environmental concerns into ecological ones and to the growing use of computers in archaeological research. Utilization and development of each of these approaches have had ramifications for the others. The current state of American archaeology cannot be understood without consideration of the growing acceptance of these innovations in the context of a burgeoning intellectual trend towards more 'scientific' research.

The initial push towards a systems viewpoint in American archaeology can be traced to Binford's path-breaking 1962 article, 'Archaeology as Anthropology,' which we have mentioned above.[32] Following Leslie White, Binford directed archaeologists' attention to the subsystems of culture, particularly the major cultural subsystems: the technological, social, and ideological. He stated that the artifactual assemblages relevant to these subsystems must be identified and their functional contexts elucidated. By doing this, the archaeologist would then be able to study the changing structural relationships between these assemblages and their subsystemic correlates. In this manner, the archaeologist could move toward the goal of understanding the evolution of cultural systems.

It is interesting to note, however, that although Binford clearly had a systemic conception of culture, he lacked, at least in 1962, a systemic, holistic view of cultural systems in relation to their environments. He cites with approval Steward's methodology of 'cultural ecology' and points out that it 'certainly is a valuable means of increasing our understanding of cultural processes.'[33] But if Binford was not to champion immediately both a systemic view of culture *and* a systemic view of culture-and-environment, he soon stimulated others to combine the two viewpoints.

As we stated in the preceding chapter, in relation to environmental studies, the key conceptual change which marks the Explanatory Period has been from a linear model (i.e. environment influences culture) to a holistic or systemic one (human populations seen as parts of ecosystems.)[34] Early movements towards a holistic view of the man-environment interaction can be seen in William T. Sanders's concept of the 'symbiotic region' as applied to prehistoric Central Mexico and the search for the origins of New World agriculture by Richard S. MacNeish, first in Tamaulipas, Mexico, and then, most importantly, in the Tehuacan Valley of Mexico.[35] But on the whole, although much of the ecological research of the 1960s was a quantum step above the early work of the Classificatory-Historical Period, in both theoretical and methodological sophistication and use of modern ecological concepts, the *overall* conception of most archaeological projects still lacked a holistic view. A good example would be the research into the prehistoric ecology of the Upper Great Lakes region of North America which has produced the excellent full-scale monographs by Yarnell on the flora and by Cleland on the fauna of the region, in addition to good excavation reports, including one by McPherron which is in the 'new archaeological' tradition.[36] However, the very fact that separate faunal, floral, and archaeological monographs have been produced is indicative of the failure to integrate these research efforts and their results into a comprehensive whole.

Even though the beginnings of the conceptual shift in environmental studies can be seen in the 1950s, it can be argued that the shift has affected the thinking of a significant number of American archaeologists only within the past few years. In fact, no archaeologist has yet produced an American monograph which is consistently holistic in its approach to man and the environment. It is to be hoped, however, that the current research of Flannery and his associates in the Valley of Oaxaca, Mexico, will do just this.[37] Certainly, Flannery should be singled out as the leader in establishing the ecosystem as a basic model for viewing the adaptive changes between man and his environment. His work represents the logical advance beyond the theoretical foundation laid by Binford.[38]

While the ecosystem concept has only recently become known on the American archaeological scene, it has a much more respectable antiquity in ecological studies. It was first used as far back as 1935 by Tansley,[39] and its place in ecological research was secured with the publication of the first edition of Eugene Odum's classic *Fundamentals of Ecology* in 1953.[40] It is important to note, though, that Marston Bates's article 'Human Ecology,' which appeared in the same year as part of the encyclopedic *Anthropology Today*, and presumably was widely read at the time, did not discuss the ecosystem concept.[41]

Basically, the ecosystem can be defined as the interactions, involving energy and matter, between one living population (such as man) or all living populations (an ecological 'community') of an area and the non-living environment.[42] By adopting the ecosystem model into his research, the American archaeologist provides a framework for his investigations with clearly defined units and boundaries, unifies his models with those of other scientists, and permits the quantification of his materials. To our mind, the advantages of the ecosystem strategy are many, and the future possibilities for studying the processes involved in the evolution of ecosystems (with the focus on human populations) are unbounded.[43]

A further conceptual advantage beyond viewing culture internally as a system and externally as a part of a larger ecosystem has been the realization by archaeologists of the compatibility of these viewpoints and that of general systems thinking in the sciences. Building on ideas first advanced by such brilliant thinkers as Bertalanffy, Weiner, and others, a general system outlook, complete with a growing body of theory, has emerged during the past two decades.[44] The applicability of these theories to the new archaeological scene of the Explanatory Period was quickly realized. Again, one of the leaders of this new advance was Flannery. His 1968 article, 'Archaeological Systems Theory and Early Mesoamerica,' is an especially clear landmark statement.[45] The most detailed discussion of the utilization of systems thinking in archaeological research, however, has come not from an American but from a British archaeologist, David Clarke. His *Analytical Archaeology* is easily the most ambitious effort in this frontier area and the best introduction to systems in archaeology available to students. It should stimulate the rethinking of basic archaeological concepts in relation to their applicability to systems research in both the New and Old Worlds. It is another testament of the growing international communication among archaeological scholars that especially characterizes the 1960s.[46]

The viability of a general systems approach to archaeological problems and its growing acceptance is illustrated by the fact that in 1969 Frank Hole and Robert F. Heizer felt compelled to rewrite their leading textbook, *An Introduction to Prehistoric Archaeology*, which had first been published just three years previously, in order to include a section of general systems theory.[47] At the same time, this text illustrates one of the major problems facing American archaeology today: the disjunction between theory, method, and practice. As is to be expected, advances in the former have far outstripped the latter two. Thus, approximately nine-tenths of *An Introduction to Prehistoric Archaeology* discusses the methods and results of an 'old' archaeology which are difficult to correlate with the new theoretical slant of the text as seen in the opening and closing chapters.

But this same point could be scored against the entire field of American archaeology. While there are many new and exciting ideas floating around, there is little indication as yet as to how these can be applied or tested in order to produce significant results about culture process. Although some heed has been paid to

121 Advances in ecologial theory are reflected in, and abetted, by, advances in field techniques. One such technique is the flotation of organic particles from midden debris in order to recover plant and food remains

logical procedures and the planning of fieldwork, little attention
has been given to the utility of the current conceptual inventory
of American archaeology. For example, can archaeologists
continue to use the existing concepts from Willey and Phillips's
'descriptive' or 'culture-historical integrative' level of operation
as a base for research on the 'explanatory' level? Or should such
concepts be either by-passed or reformulated?

An initial pioneering effort in this direction has been made by
Binford in his 1965 article, 'Archaeological Systematics and the
Study of Cultural Process.'[48] He suggests possible processual
definitions for the concepts of 'tradition' (as distinct from Willey
and Phillips's 'tradition'), 'interaction sphere,' and 'adaptive
area.' Unfortunately, there has been little follow-up to Binford's
suggestions, except perhaps in relation to 'interaction sphere.'[49]
Obviously, what we need is more thinking along the lines suggested by Binford.

It may be that in the Explanatory Period the time for theoretical
polemics and minute-scale testing is over and that we should turn
our efforts to the utilization of newly formed concepts through
large-scale field-testing of specific processual hypotheses. It is
further to be hoped, of course, that the theoretical-methodo-
logical-practical disjunction will be closed before long with the
publication of promising research now in progress and with the
instigation of new and carefully planned projects.

Statistics and the Computer

One reason to be optimistic about the successful on-the-ground
follow-through of the new systemic concepts is the fact that
archaeologists now have available to them a sophisticated technological tool which may help to bring their plans to fruition. This
tool is the computer.

It can be argued that without the increasing application of
various statistical techniques and the use of computer programs,
many archaeological ideas would remain pipe-dreams, while
others would not even have been conceived. For full discussions of
recent advances in the use of statistics and the computer in archaeological research, the reader is referred to the excellent reviews of
the subject by George Cowgill and Donald Tugby.[50] Of particular note in terms of recent advances are the means for data
storage and retrieval now available and the statistical tools for
chronological ordering, artifact classification, the unbiased sampling of sites, and multivariate analyses of past cultural patterns.[51]
With the ready availability of computer facilities at many universities, these latter kinds of studies can easily be carried out. Significantly, in terms of the development of American archaeology,
they make possible the kinds of analyses which Binford called for
in 1962 in his discussion of artifact assemblages and the systemic
inferences which should be made about their patterning in
archaeological sites.[52]

One additional advance in computer utilization stands out
above the rest. It is the growing use of computer simulations as
regards systems analyses and their possible application to archaeo-

logical research.[53] In the future, it should be possible for archaeologists to feed data about small selected subsystems, which they
have studied intensively, along with other relevant archaeological
information, into the computer, enabling them to produce a
simulation, or a series of alternate simulations, of the entire system.
Archaeologists can then go back and test the predictions of the
simulations against other subsystems. They can also hold constant various factors and develop new simulations which will
show what the systemic effects of different changes would be.
Predictions and tests concerning the nature of systemic change
through time can then be made. Thus, even with data on whole
systems incomplete, archaeologists should be able to test hypotheses about the evolution of such whole systems.[54]

It is important to realize, nevertheless, that use of the computer,
like the various scientific techniques discussed in the preceding
chapter, cannot in and of itself 'revolutionize' American archaeology. As William A. Longacre has said: 'statistical techniques are
not magical.'[55] Statistical techniques and computer programs are
simply tools which can be used profitably by archaeologists. The
results of studies that utilize these tools will be as good as the
archaeological research strategy in which the tools play a role and
as good as the archaeologist's knowledge about the parameters of,
and the assumptions behind, the applicability of the tools.[56]
However, archaeologists who write off computer analyses, out of
dislike, distrust, ingnorance, or perhaps fear of mathematical
manipulation, will be cutting themselves off from an integral
part of modern archaeological methodology.

Deductive Reasoning and the Positivist Philosophy of Science

We have considered cultural-evolutionary theory and systems
analysis; the remaining pillar of the 'new archaeological' wisdom
is logico-deductive reasoning. More specifically, it might be
referred to as 'scientific explanation' via the logico-deductive
testing of hypotheses. It looms large in the 'new archaeology.'
Indeed, in reading some of the 'new archaeological' literature it
assumes a much larger role than either cultural evolution or
systems theory.[57] Of all the topics of the Explanatory Period and
the 'new archaeology' this one has been accompanied by an un-
conscionable amount of 'preachiness.' Whereas cultural evolution
and systems theory have been allowed to slide rather quietly into
place, the logico-deductive outlook has been the most loudly
announced and hotly defended – possibly because, of the whole
'new archaeological' front, it is the most vulnerable sector.

Essentially, the proponents of this viewpoint believe that
archaeology must adopt a logico-positivist philosophy of science
and employ the explanatory procedures which are an integral
part of this philosophy. These procedures are logico-deductive
in nature and have as their object the confirmation of 'covering'
or general laws. As Albert C. Spaulding has said: 'The view
which I find convincing is attractively simple: there is only one
kind of serious explanation, the nomological or covering-law
explanation.'[58]

The principal philosopher of science who has championed such a view and who is most often cited by Spaulding, Fritz and Plog, Binford, and others is Carl Hempel. It is Hempel's contention that the only valid kind of explanation involves covering or general laws.[59] Probabilistic procedures do not produce 'explanations.'

This, however, raises the question as to whether there is only one kind of explanation or a variety of explanations. Positivist philosophers, such as Hempel and Oppenheim, hold to the first view while idealist philosophers, such as Collingwood, Croce, Dilthey, and Dray, hold to the latter. The former would argue that if history and social science are to be considered as sciences, then their manner of arriving at explanations should be identical to that of the physical sciences. The latter would hold that there is a separable philosophy of history with its own explanatory procedures.[60] They would further maintain that absolute laws of history which explain all cases and can predict the future cannot be discovered, although quantifiable probable explanations and predictions are possible.

American archaeology has not been traditionally concerned with these reaches of philosophy, and many archaeologists are ignorant of the vast literature which exists in the fields of the philosophies of science and history. As a result, many are probably unaware that among philosophers of science, who are concerned primarily with the 'hard' sciences, there is no agreement that the Hempelian view is the most tenable. But within the past decade there has been a steady attempt on the part of some 'new archaeologists' to 'sell' the Hempelian, positivist philosophical view of explanation. In fact, it is stated, according to some implicit value scheme, that deductive explanations are 'better' than others and are the only goal for which archaeologists should strive.[61] In doing this, a number of competing views have been ignored. For instance, there is no discussion, of any kind, of the writings, ideas, and philosophical positions of such men as W. H. Dray, Karl Popper, and others, many of whom have actually engaged in written dialogues and debates, in various philosophical journals and books, with Hempel on the matter of the validity of the covering-law model.[62] Indeed, such authors are not even cited so that the archaeological audience has tended to be left in ignorance of the full controversial philosophical context of the Hempelian model.

Spaulding has stated:

'Anthropology, like social science in general, can be contrasted with that other paradigm of science, classical mechanics. . . . Clearly anthropological explanations are characteristically probabilistic-statistical rather than deductive, and they are partial rather than complete. This is the penalty for dealing with anything so multidimensional and unwieldy as human behavior, and there is no easy remedy. Anthropologists are not forbidden, however, to struggle toward covering generalizations with greater powers of prediction and retrodiction.'[63]

His view is that probabilistic explanations are insufficient. But is this necessarily so? E. J. Meehan has cogently pointed out that the answer is no.

'If the deductive paradigm of explanation is accepted as the standard, the explanatory capacity of the social sciences is extremely limited. While this has long been recognized, the limitations have usually been taken as a sign of the weakness of social science rather than as an indication of the limited usefulness of the deductive paradigm. Perhaps the major reason for taking that position has been the assumed adequacy of the deductive paradigm as an account of the mode of inquiry actually pursued in physical science. The reasoning runs as follows: physical science has been successful; its success has been due to the strength of its explanations; its explanations are strong because they are deductive in form; other disciplines can be equally successful only if they can meet the same explanatory requirements. This line of reasoning elevates the deductive paradigm into a privileged position in the conduct of inquiry – where it becomes an albatross around the neck of the social scientist. For social science simply cannot meet the requirements for deductive explanations. We do not have, and we are unlikely to get, the "nomic empirical generalizations" or "empirical laws" that deductive explanations demand. It follows, if the deductive paradigm is accepted, that the social scientist's capacity to explain is severely restricted and is likely to remain so for the indefinite future.'[64]

He goes on to note that:

'The dilemma seems unresolvable until we realize that it depends on a set of hidden assumptions that are not necessarily valid. If the term "explanation" *must* be defined as it appears in the deductive paradigm – if no alternative definition is possible – the argument holds. Further, if the kind of activity that has led the physical sciences to success is truly defined by the deductive paradigm, and no other conceptualization will fit the practices of the scientists, then the conclusion that science is successful *because* its explanations fit the deductive pattern may not be a *non sequitur*. Both of these assumptions can be challenged.'[65]

Meehan then proceeds to introduce a 'systems paradigm' of explanation which he feels would be the most useful for the social sciences and perhaps for science in general. Explanatory systems paradigms could be 'fitted' to empirical systems models with known degrees of statistical probability. It is our view that this kind of explanatory procedure might be most useful in relation to the methodology of systems analysis that has been discussed above.

Following the model of scientific change proposed by Kuhn,[66] which sees scientific revolutions in terms of competing paradigms, it is obvious, as a number of archaeologists have pointed out, that American archaeology is currently witnessing a competition between basic theoretical and methodological paradigms. However, the situation is not as simple as some of the examples cited by Kuhn in which a competing paradigm is introduced into a developed discipline and eventually triumphs over a traditional paradigm. Archaeology is still an undeveloped or at best a developing science, and it is our belief that there are more than two competing paradigms (some of which are explicit, some implicit). In addition, there are competing paradigms on several levels, not simply on one general level. That is to say, there are differing methodological, theoretical, and logical paradigms whose interconnections are not presently clear. As we have already noted, the systems and evolutionary paradigms are currently triumphing over the older, static, normative models. In the writings of some 'new archaeologists,' a dichotomy has been set up between one general paradigm consisting of the evolutionary-systems 'package' enveloped in a logico-deductive 'wrapping' and a second consisting of a non-evolutionary-descriptive 'package' enclosed by an inductive 'wrapping.' It is our contention that there is a third paradigm consisting of the evolutionary-systems 'package' with a statistical-probabilistic 'wrapping' and that this paradigm will also become a strong competitor. Other obvious logical contenders may also emerge in the near future. We see no reason to accept the view that an evolutionary-systems approach necessitates a logico-deductive explanatory procedure.

In airing our views on this, we would make clear that we do not follow Bruce W. Trigger in his belief that there can be two kinds of anthropological archaeologies: one ideographic and one nomothetic.[67] We would argue, instead, that there should be one unified anthropological archaeology engaged in exploring a whole spectrum of models and procedures. In so doing, archaeologists will have to be explicit about their assumptions, models, and procedures if their colleagues are going to be able to appraise their paradigms and judge their explanations in the light of these. Certainly, the great emphasis of the 'new archaeology' on *explicit* procedures has been of real benefit to the archaeological discipline, as has been its emphasis on problem orientation and hypothesis testing. All of these things are now established in the mainstream of American archaeology.

But we believe it to be a mistake for any archaeologist to attempt to force this uniformity beyond reasonable bounds, to legislate the direction that American archaeology should take; and this seems to be what is being attempted by the insistence that the covering-law paradigm is the only 'scientific' one and the only one which will produce explanations.[68] As in other sciences, the paradigms that yield useful results will be the ones to triumph over their less successful competitors. Specifically, we would refer, in this connection, to Binford's article, 'Some Comments on Historical Versus Processual Archaeology,' in which he would reserve the term 'explanation' only for theories which have been tested deductively.[69] This article, which was written as a comment on one by the present authors,[70] takes the position that our inductive procedure (as used in this instance) will never lead to any meaningful explanation of the collapse of Maya civilization. Perhaps not, but, at the present moment, we feel that a statistical-probabilistic approach is just as likely to produce an acceptable explanation as a deductive one. Certainly the case is still open.

At the present stage of American archaeology, dogmatism is what we need least. Although some 'new archaeologists' undoubtedly feel a 'progressive' righteousness in the dogmatic championing of the positivist position, the long-term results may be retrogressive. A discipline deeply divided between polarized schools of thought (ideographic versus nomothetic) could easily suppress or delay the rise of productive 'middle-ground' thinking. In considering this we should not forget that another dogmatism, that of the anti-evolutionary, anti-environmentalist philosophies which long dominated American anthropology, did little service to American archaeology. In contrast, European prehistory of the same period, free from such a stultifying atmosphere, produced the seminal works of Gordon Childe and Grahame Clark. If history has its lessons, it might be well to reject that part of the 'new archaeology' that threatens to become the 'new dogmatism.'[71]

Some Recent Researches

Our consideration of the 'new archaeology' should go beyond discussion of theoretical principles and include at least a sampling of archaeological research in the explanatory vein. Although traditional Classificatory-Historical-style archaeology probably still predominates in the Americas, a great number of works have appeared since 1960 which are in the new mode. Most of these have been short articles, usually more or less balanced between substantive and theoretical presentation. There have been a very few monographs; but, importantly, a number of major projects are under way which embody the goals and orientations of the explanatory approach and which are known from partial publication or from preliminary statements. We must, of necessity, be brief and selective in our summary of this research. It is, for the most part, rather difficult to classify under convenient categories of discussion; but we will make an attempt to do so. In general, the archaeologist has asked questions about function and the nature of cultural change, and these questions have carried him into the social and ecological dimensions of culture. One such kind of question has been concerned with the recognition of individual and class status differences as these are revealed by archaeological data, especially the data of mortuary practices. Another kind of question has been directed to prehistoric residence patterns and their implications for kinship, as these may be inferred in artifactual, architectural, and settlement information. Other questions have been involved with cultural–environmental interrelationships or ecosystems and matters of subsistence. Still others, and perhaps the most exciting, have inquired into the complexities of cause that lie behind those fascinating 'quantum leaps' in human history that are sometimes called the 'agricultural' or 'urban revolutions' or the appearance of 'complex societies.'

We will begin with those studies that have been concerned with status differences in society. Quite fittingly, one of these has been summarized in Binford's classic 1962 article. In this research Binford was interested in explaining some peculiar variables in the prehistoric record of the Wisconsin Great Lakes region, especially with reference to an archaeological manifestation known as the 'Old Copper Culture.' The study is of particular interest for in it Binford incorporated Leslie White's views on cultural evolution, a general systems theory approach, and a deductive line of reasoning in testing the hypotheses he made about the Old Copper Culture.

This Old Copper Culture was known to be Archaic in date, but it was unique within Eastern North America in its possession of tools and weapons hammered out of nuggets of surface copper.[72] The problem posed by the Old Copper Culture was that its metal technology did not persist – at least in the form of heavy tools and points – into the later cultures of the area. Instead, these later cultures had reverted to stone implements. This appeared to contradict the evolutionary principle that more efficient tool types succeed those of less efficiency. Binford questioned the efficiency of the copper tools in question, citing White's energy potential theory of cultural evolution, and argued that the time needed for collecting surface copper and for making the artifacts greatly reduced this presumed 'efficiency.' He went on to suggest that these particular implements, rather than being essentially utilitarian, were 'socio-technic' items which functioned as achieved status symbols in an egalitarian society. A number of lines of evidence were developed to support this hypothesis. To begin with, the total cultural setting did, indeed, indicate that the Old Copper Culture, and the North American Archaic in general, had had an egalitarian social setting. Beyond this, the copper implements were relatively rare, were not of highly esoteric forms, and were virtually always found in graves. All of these things seemed to point to a symbolic function in a relatively simple society. That is, they were not common enough to have been general tools; but they were readily recognizable as symbolizing hunting, fishing, and woodworking activities. If they were symbols, the particular status an individual had achieved in the culture was not passed on to his descendants but ended at his death and was 'taken with him' to the after life. From a strictly technological standpoint, copper apparently was not prized highly enough for the culture to have developed mechanisms for retaining the metal within the sphere of the living and using it to refashion new tools. The failure of copper tools to be perpetuated in the later cultures of the region, such as the Adena and Hopewellian, could be taken to mean that these societies had moved away from the egalitarian norms of the Archaic, a supposition reinforced by the considerably more elaborate features of these cultures as revealed by archaeology. Whether Binford's explanation will stand as the correct one remains to be seen as more data come in on the Old Copper Culture; but he is quite right in saying that 'only within a systemic frame of reference could such an inclusive explanation be offered.'[73]

The great potential of burial and mortuary data for social inferences about past societies is an obvious one although it had long been neglected in American archaeology. William H. Sears was one of the first to point to it in his 1961 article 'The Study of Social and Religious Systems in North American Archaeology.'[74] More recently, Binford has examined the subject at greater length, and in world-wide perspective, in 'Mortuary Practices: Their Study and Potential.'[75] This latter article is one of a symposium volume on the subject,[76] which includes three Americanist papers on burials and their associations as these are seen at the respective sites of Etowah (Georgia), Moundville (Alabama), and Spiro

(Oklahoma) – three of the greatest town-and-ceremonial center sites of the Southeastern United States area. All of the authors are able to draw a number of inferences from their data in the deductive manner which Binford employed in his Old Copper Culture study. From Etowah, Lewis H. Larson, Jr., suggests a convincing social stratification as reflected in differences between mound and village interments. The remains in the mound appeared to be those of an upper class whose paraphernalia, duplicated with individuals of different age groups, is best interpreted as badges or symbols of office or class.[77] For Moundville, Christopher S. Peebles had somewhat comparable findings and interpretations: 'The model suggested from the archaeological remains is one of a complexly ranked and functionally specialized politico-religious organization as part of this cultural system.'[78] Actually, Peebles dealt with data from a number of other sites, and through statistical treatments of his data was able to indicate, within a high degree of probability, such entities as 'local communities,' 'local centers,' and a 'regional center,' the last being the apparent 'capital' of Moundville. Peebles's paper is as much methodological example as substantive report, and this is even more true of James Brown's on Spiro.[79] Both archaeologists use ethnographic data from historic source material on Southeastern Indian tribes as comparative checks on their archaeological findings, but there is also a conscious effort on the part of both to operate wholly within the archaeological realm in their primary considerations of the data and all of the relationships among these data. Brown does this in an especially formal manner. His objectives are to construct models for both archaeological (Spiro) and ethnological (Natchez, Choctaw) cultural systems and to compare these on a structural rather than a specific culture content basis. These attitudes toward the use of ethnographic data in analogy will be referred to again in the next section for they are very much a part of the 'new archaeology.'

Another use of burial data in social dimensional interpretation is that of William L. Rathje, as set out in his paper, 'Socio-Political Implications of Lowland Maya Burials: Methodology and Tentative Hypotheses.[80] Rathje examined the changes through time (from Late Preclassic to Late Classic, *ca.* 300 B.C.–A.D. 900) of Maya burial customs (amounts and nature of grave goods, nature of tomb or grave) as these related to age and sex and settlement location (ceremonial center, village hamlet, etc.), to make a strong case for a gradually increasing rigidity in class stratification. In a later paper he was able to incorporate his mortuary subsystem into an overall cultural system model that offered an explanatory hypothesis for the collapse of Maya civilization.[81]

Social organization, as reflected in residence patterns, is another theme that has attracted the attention of a number of younger scholars in the past decade. A leader in this has been J.J.F. Deetz. Deetz actually began his researches along this line in the late 1950s, and these culminated in a Ph.D. dissertation submitted in 1960. His best-known work, a monograph, *The Dynamics of Stylistic Change in Arikara Ceramics*, was based on the earlier thesis and was published in 1965.[82] In it Deetz analyzed a series of ceramic collections obtained from house ring excavations in sites documented as proto-historic-to-historic Plains Arikara. These analyses were made on a fine-grained attribute basis, and the numerous associations of these pottery decorative attributes, with each other and with house features, were provided through computer programming and analyses. It was Deetz's hypothesis that pottery decorative attributes would cluster in a distinctly non-random fashion in matrilocal households and that there would then be a trend from non-random to random as matrilocal residence broke down. Deetz's ceramic sequence through time bore out this kind of change, and the pottery change, in turn, appeared to correlate with a change from large to small house types. Supporting ethnohistoric information – that it was the Arikara women who made the pottery and that matrilocal residence quarters were larger than those of simple patrilocal families – provided the basic underlying assumptions for the study. Viewed as a whole, the two simultaneous aspects of change (in pottery and in house size) would seem to bear out Deetz's hypothesis; however, he adds, with caution, that while this suggests a systematic relationship it does not offer unequivocal proof.[83]

These concerns with prehistoric residence patterns, social organization, and social interaction are also seen in the writings of James N. Hill, William A. Longacre, Robert Whallon, and Mark Leone. Hill and Longacre, working in Southwestern Pueblo sites in eastern Arizona, have defined room and other architectural functions through statistical and materials analyses of pottery, artifacts, and pollen residues. The search of rooms or features of archaeological sites for artifacts or other data that might help identify the former purposes of these architectural remains is not new to archaeology; but a systematic examination of all recovered data to this end marks a departure from previous practices. After making a formal classification of the site's features, Hill then phrased a series of expectations or propositions that should be borne out by the analyses if his hypotheses about the functions of the various types of rooms and features were valid. Thus:

'The large rooms should contain a wider variety of materials than are found in other room-types, since the largest number of different kinds of activities were presumably performed in them.'

Or

'The small rooms, in addition to containing only a small number and variety of artifacts and manufacturing debris, should contain reasonably large quantities of the remains of stored food crops – especially corn and squash. . . . This evidence should be in the form of corn cobs, seeds, or pollen.[84]

Hill's hypotheses about the original uses of rooms and features were inspired by ethnographic analogies with historic and modern Hopi and Zuñi practices. These were largely confirmed by his tests, although some few were not, suggesting that there had been not altogether unexpected changes in site and feature functions in the thousand-year-long prehistoric-to-historic cultural continuum in the Puebloan Southwest.

Longacre, working with pottery design attributes, in the manner of Deetz, shows two major clusterings of these attributes in two distinct architectural assemblages of the same Puebloan site.[85] That each of these assemblages had its own *kiva*, or ceremonial chamber, suggested their original corporate nature. On the assumption that women of the culture made the pottery (borne out by ethnographic analogies from the same general region), these data, as in Deetz's Arikara work, argued for matrilocal residence and, probably, matrilocal clans. Of wider interest in Longacre's observations on this site in its general context is the fact that it marked a time in Southwestern prehistory in which small, apparently single-kin unit villages were being replaced by larger communities such as the one he investigated. This congregating of formerly dispersed populations into larger multi-unit sites can, in turn, be correlated with the onset of climatic stringencies which rendered the total environment less hospitable.

Whallon's studies of ceramic collections from prehistoric Iroquois sites in New York showed a high degree of attribute clusterings by site which, on the assumption that women made the pottery, tends to bear out the Deetz thesis of matrilocal residence for such archaeological situations.[86] In the Iroquois case such residence is, indeed, known from the slightly later historic horizon. On an intersite basis Whallon also discovered that, through time, there was an increasing stylistic uniformity in pottery within each site. This, he postulated, was to be correlated with an increasing lack of contact between sites (a trend verified from other lines of evidence) which resulted in a kind of ceramic decorative 'inbreeding.'

An intersite study in the Southwest by Mark Leone operated with the hypothesis that increasing dependence on agriculture led to community economic autonomy and to 'social distance' between communities.[87] Dependence upon agriculture was determined from variability of tools used in a village while social distance was measured by the evidence for greater or lesser endogamy within a village. This latter condition was appraised by variability in design and color attributes used on pottery found in the villages – a principle of the Deetz, Hill, Longacre, and Whallon studies. Both variables were found to co-vary positively, supporting Leone's thesis. This particular research, broader in scope than the previous ones, is very obviously aimed at cultural law which, in this case, might be stated as follows: unless other conditions (trade, major invasions, etc.) intervene, Neolithic-level economies result in community autonomy and in social distance.

While mortuarial customs and settlement and artifactual patternings have afforded variables by which to infer social status and residence and kin relationships, culture-and-environment interrelationships obviously have been the crucial ones in economic and demographic inferences. We are, to some extent, drawing artificial lines here, for the purposes of presentation, for all of these things are linked systemically. This linkage is, indeed, the main intellectual thrust of the 'new archaeology.' However, some research can be identified as definitely ecological. On the Mesoamerican scene, both W. T. Sanders and R. S. MacNeish have been pioneers in this regard. Sanders's interests along this line began as early as the 1950s,[88] and his Teotihuacan Valley (a branch of the Valley of Mexico) survey was carried out over many seasons, with interim reports,[89] and with the first of a series of final reports published in 1970.[90] The survey, carried out by Sanders and his colleagues, has been extraordinarily thorough, and, given its broad-gauged approach, promises to be one of the most impressive of all American archaeological researches. All this is especially interesting as it was in the Teotihuacan Valley that Manuel Gamio conducted another great survey almost fifty years before.[91] Both Gamio and Sanders were interested in the full gamut of human occupance of the valley; and the two reports will serve as a measure of the shifts in problem emphasis, theoretical concepts, and methods that have taken place in American archaeology and anthropology in the intervening decades. Sanders's preliminary reports run to several hundred pages and his procedures and results are quite involved so that these may only be touched upon here. In brief, he views culture as a complex of adaptive techniques to the problems of survival in a particular geographical region. While such adaptations may be primarily in the field of technology and subsistence, these, in turn, are systemically linked to all other aspects of culture. He looks upon environment not only as a permissive-restrictive factor in cultural development but, in the sense that it limits choice, as a directive factor. His view of the total ecological system is one that contains three semi-autonomous systems – culture, biota (flora-fauna), and physical environment. Each of these 'functions on the basis of discrete and separate processes'; yet there is interaction among them, and this interaction 'is one of the dominant stimuli that produces change in the cultural system.'[92] Sanders's ambitious objectives are, thus, to explain the changes that took place in the Valley of Teotihuacan in man's adaptations to his environment and all of the systemic effects that this technology-subsistence-environmental interaction produced. While Sanders's materialist-deterministic slant has been criticized by some Mesoamerican colleagues, there is general consensus that his interpretations, to date, go a long way toward elucidating cultural process in the Central Mexican Uplands from *ca.* 1000 B.C. to modern times.

MacNeish's attention has been directed to the threshold of village agriculture – the beginnings of settled life based on cultivation in Mesoamerica. He began this work in the dry caves of Tamaulipas in the late 1940s and in the 1950s where he demonstrated the early stages of maize domestication in preceramic, essentially food-collecting contexts.[93] Later, he shifted his geographical focus farther south into the 'heart' of Mesoamerica, exploring cave and open sites in the Tehuacan Valley of Puebla. It was here that he was able to push the first appearances of maize back to *ca.* 5000 B.C., at a time when that plant was either wild or in the very earliest stages of domestication. By bringing a variety of disciplines from the natural sciences to bear upon the problem, and by an imaginative plan of attack, MacNeish has been able to provide us with a number of community interaction models, each representative of a different time level and each diagramming the subsistence-settlement pattern relationships. Thus, 'semi-sedentary macrobands' lived in wet season fall camps, exploiting certain

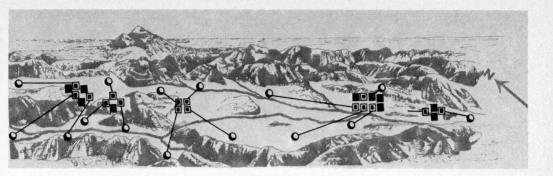

types of wild plant foods and carrying on a limited amount of plant cultivation. Such 'macrobands' then split up into dry season 'microbands' which followed other food-getting pursuits for that period. At a certain point in time (*ca.* 1500 B.C.) this kind of semi-sedentary living was superseded by the establishment of the first permanent villages and little ceremonial centers.[94]

In a different environmental context – the Pacific Coast of Guatemala – Michael D. Coe and Kent Flannery have made a similar ecosystem study involving the varied but integrated exploitation of a number of 'microenvironmental' niches as these bear on the problem of the first permanent villages in that region.[95]

Turning his attention to the Mexican Highlands, and drawing upon MacNeish's work and his own in the Valley of Oaxaca, Kent Flannery then went beyond subsistence-settlement diachronic models to offer an explanation of the detailed processes involved in these changes. This article, 'Archaeological Systems Theory and Early Mesoamerica,' published in 1968, is, to our thinking, the best example of the archaeology of the Explanatory Period now in print.[96] Drawing upon both archaeological and ethnological information, Flannery reconstructs the 'procurement systems' (actually subsystems of an overall subsistence system) of the late (*ca.* 5000–2000 B.C.) preceramic and pre-agricultural phases of the

122 Diagram showing relationships between seasonal communities and subsistence scheduling in the Tehuacan Valley of Mexico. The Coxcatlan and early Abejas phases here represented are later preceramic complexes. Community pattern: Semi-sedentary macrobands that had wet-season fall camps ▣, or annual camps ■ , but often separated into dry-season microband camps ◐ . (After MacNeish, 1964a)

123 Diagrammatic representation of micro-environments and food resources available to the early inhabitants of the Pacific coast of Guatemala. (After Coe and Flannery, 1967)

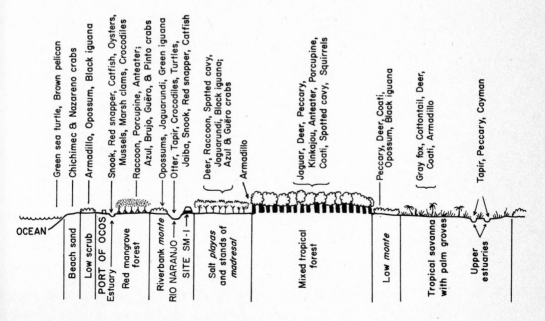

Mexican Uplands. These 'procurement systems' included the gathering of things like the maguey plant, cactus fruits, and wild grasses, and the hunting of deer and other animals. Such procurement activities were 'regulated' by nature's seasonality and by culture's scheduling. As Flannery says:

'Seasonality and scheduling . . . were part of a "deviation-counter-acting" feedback system. They prevented intensification of any one procurement system to the point where the wild genus was threatened; at the same time, they maintained a sufficiently high level of procurement efficiency so that there was little pressure for change . . .
'Under conditions of fully-achieved and permanently-maintained equilibrium, prehistoric cultures might never have changed. That they did change was due at least in part to the existence of positive feedback or "deviation-amplifying processes . . ."
'These Maruyama (1963: 164) describes as "all processes of mutual causal relationships that amplify an insignificant or accidental initial kick, build up deviation and diverge from the initial condition . . ."
'Such "insignificant or accidental initial kicks" were a series of genetic changes which took place in one or two species of Meso-american plants which were of use to man. The exploitation of these plants had been a relatively minor procurement system compared with that of maguey, cactus fruits, deer, or tree legumes, but positive feedback following these initial genetic changes caused one minor system to grow out of all proportion to the others, and eventually to change the whole ecosystem of the Southern Mexican Highlands.'[97]

This, in a nutshell, is the most convincing hypothesis about the immediate causes of the 'agricultural revolution,' in the Mexican Highlands of the fifth-to-third millennium B.C. that has been offered. More than any other single short paper, it points to the potential of the Explanatory Period which we are just entering.

Other ecosystem researches that deserve mention are those of Stuart Struever,[98] working with Woodland cultures in the Illinois Valley, of Ezra Zubrow, in his consideration of 'Carrying Capacity and Dynamic Equilibrium in the Prehistoric Southwest,'[99] and an examination, by Binford, of 'Post-Pleistocene Adaptations' on a world-wide basis, with the development of a series of hypotheses about the stage threshold crossings or 'quantum leaps' from Paleolithic-to-Mesolithic and from the latter to village agriculture.[100]

The ecosystem model and ecological explanations have been applied by some American archaeologists to that other great transformation of human history, the shift from simpler agricultural societies to civilizations. With such a model, they would see a sequence of events in which a technological improvement in dealing with the environment – specifically, canal irrigation – so increased food production that population boomed. This, in turn, created other greater economic capacities and needs, and all of these demographic pressures and other complexities eventually gave rise to the state and civilization.[101] Others, while admitting the importance of all of this, are not convinced that the triggering mechanism necessarily always lies in an ecological relationship

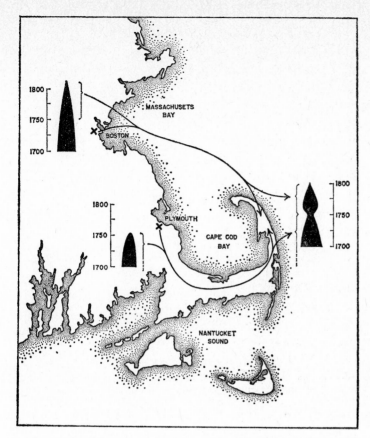

124 Changes in tombstone style in eastern Massachusetts during the 18th century. James Deetz's use of historic archaeology to test archaeological assumptions and hypotheses has been one of the important advances of the Explanatory Period (After Deetz, 1968b)

and would prefer to see a greater role assigned to ideology.[102] Still others have offered explanations which involve a complex systemic interplay of trade, ideology, and social prestige as offering the most convincing model of the rise of civilization and the truly complex society or state.[103] In all of this there is the question of definitions as well as the arguments about process. What is the meaning of the elusive term 'civilization'? While some authorities are willing to apply the name to such early elaborate ceremonial center-oriented cultures as Olmec or Chavin, others would prefer to associate the term and concept with the rise of formal urbanism as at Teotihuacan. The long-term program of René F. Millon and associates, in the mapping and close-up functional study of the great Teotihuacan site, has been of real importance in turning archaeologists' attention to these problems and providing basic data for their solution.[104]

One major branch of American archaeological research deserves separate mention here in view of its sudden upsurge in the 1960s. This is 'historical archaeology' or 'historic sites' archaeology. These terms refer to the subject matter of Post-Columbian times, involving either native peoples, Europeans, or both. As in Europe, the historical-archaeological field has been cultivated for a long time; but in the Americas, and especially in the United States, it has only recently come to claim its proper share of attention.[105] While most American 'historic sites' archaeologists have been primarily interested in historical particulars,[106] the influences of the Explanatory Period have also made themselves felt. For example, the work of Deetz and Dethlefsen on New England grave-stones has given archaeologists an excellent methodological check on seriational procedures.[107] In fact, according to Deetz, the great value of historical archaeology lies in just this ability to examine archaeological methods and theories in contexts of verifiable historical control and, in so doing, to refine concepts and procedures and to better understand processes of culture change.[108]

124

Ethnographic Analogy and Archaeology

We have referred to American archaeology's close linkage with ethnology and ethnography throughout its history. The interrelationships of the data of prehistory and ethnohistory were the crux of Cyrus Thomas's attack on the 'Mound-Builder' versus Indian problem. The direct-historical approach pointed the way to specific ethnic identifications of archaeological complexes in the Classificatory-Historical Period, and Strong, Steward, and others called for more systematic and intensive uses of ethnographic analogy in the functional and contextual interpretations of archaeological data. As American archaeology moves into the Explanatory Period ethnographic analogy retains a vital role. We have seen its uses in the ceramic-social organizational studies of Deetz, Longacre, and others; and Sanders's Teotihuacan Valley investigation relies heavily upon the data of ethnohistory as these pertain to the former populations in Central Mexico seen by the 16th century Spanish. In general, a positive attitude toward ethnographic analogy is still held by many or most American archaeologists who see in such 'specific historical' analogies the only way of reconstructing the historical, particularistic qualities of past cultures. At the same time ethnographic analogy – or certain uses and limitations of it – have come under some attack by 'new archaeologists.' To put this debate in proper perspective it is necessary to first say something about analogy in archaeology in general.

To begin with, analogy in archaeology is the metaphysic by which the residues of human behavior are translated into the original terms of that behavior (insofar as possible). It is the first step in archaeology. Hypotheses about the past cannot be framed without it, nor can inductive or deductive reasoning be brought into play to test these hypotheses until the analogies have been made. There are two kinds of analogy available to the archaeologist. One of these is the kind to which we have just referred, 'specific historical' analogy or what is more commonly called 'ethnographic analogy.' It operates within a specific historical context – for example, the continuum of the Southwestern North American Puebloan cultural tradition, from prehistoric-to-historic times, or the Teotihuacan-Toltec-historic Aztec continuum of central Mexico. Such 'specific historical' or ethnographic analogy stands in contrast to the other kind of analogy, 'general comparative' analogy. 'General comparative' analogy is also 'ethnographic' in the sense that its points of reference are located in observed human behavior, but its interpretations of the past are projected through broadly comparative and essentially universalistic observations and generalizations about human cultural behaviour rather than being derived from the narrow confines of a 'specific historical' context.[109]

In a recent article entitled 'Major Aspects of the Interrelationship of Archaeology and Ethnology,' K.-C. Chang has discussed these two kinds of analogy in some detail, and has emphasized the vital importance of ethnographic analogy to the archaeologist.[110] In a commentary on Chang's article, Binford, as a spokesman of the 'new archaeology,' has taken a somewhat different view.[111] He argues that to rely wholly or even primarily upon such 'specific historical' analogies is to seriously limit the archaeologist in his abilities to see the past in processual terms – as the raw material for the eventual formulation of cultural laws. In our detailing of this argument it should be made clear that Binford is not, *per se*, opposed to all uses of ethnographic or 'specific historical' analogy.[112] His position is, rather, that it is useful as an adjunct in archaeological interpretation and as a pool of information to be drawn upon in framing hypotheses about particular past cultures; but it cannot be considered as an essential key to explanation of process. The latter, he says, must be approached by the archaeologist on his own terms, and by this he means through the uses of 'general comparative' analogy.

In contrast to Binford's position, Keith M. Anderson has written:

'Careful analysis and comparison of archaeological remains, the use of vigorous analytical techniques, and statistical manipulation may lead to precise definition of significant and comparable technological elements. However, these techniques do not, by themselves, interpret prehistory. Such interpretation depends upon ethnographic analogy.'

And, very directly addressed to the 'new archaeology,' he adds:

'Knowledge of systemic relations between components of technology and the rest of culture is necessary to make inferences concerning the use of particular artifacts. However, there are limitations to the exactness of a systemic model.'[113]

As we see it, much of this disagreement over the value of ethnographic or 'specific historical' analogy derives from a difference in emphasis on the objectives of archaeology. If one favors a 'reconstruction' of a specific past, with interpretations of the functions of artifacts found in a Southwestern Pueblo ruin or of the meaning of gods of the Teotihuacan murals, then Anderson is correct. Such interpretations must derive from ethnohistory or ethnographic analogies. But if, instead, one eschews the 'reconstruction of the past' as the prime goal of archaeology, as Binford does, then 'specific historical' analogy is much less important and, indeed, can be quite limiting. However, we cannot accuse either Chang or Anderson of a disinterest in process.[114] Nor would the authors of this history be satisfied with an archaeology that was entirely particularizing. But we would not go along all the way with Binford's assertion that archaeologists today are self-contained to formulate verifiable hypotheses to explain archaeological observations.[115] At least we question whether these hypotheses would be very pertinent or meaningful. Is the perspective of technico-ecological interaction sufficient to explain all that it is important to know about past cultures? We would say no. Anderson puts it well in his statement:

'Logical analysis of form depends as much on perception of the object, which is conditioned by cultural background, as by any universal principles.'[116]

It is our feeling – given the uncertainties which surround the record of the past – that we will come to grips with process in greater certainty by the fullest possible utilization and comprehension of 'specific historical' contexts, both archaeological and ethnographic, in conjunction with 'general comparative' analogies. The most meaningful hypotheses of explanation will be framed in this light.

Retrospect, Appraisal, and Prospects for the Future

In this history we have attempted to recount how American archaeology had its beginnings in an era of speculation about the new-found world and its inhabitants, how within this ambience of speculation there was always a hard element of fact-searching, and how this element provided the basis for what we have called the Classificatory-Descriptive Period of the archaeological discipline. Indeed, a formal discipline only emerged at this time, toward the middle of the 19th century; and this emergence of an American archaeology was, of course, vitally influenced by prior European developments. These European developments are best seen in Denmark, in England, and in France, with Thomsen's 'Three-Age' system of archaeological classification, with Boucher de Perthes's demonstration of Pleistocene Paleolithic cultures, by archaeological researches in England, and, finally, by the revolution in all scientific thought produced by Darwin's theory of evolution.

American archaeology then followed a course of its own, one in which the prehistory of the New World continents was seen to be an aspect of a larger subject which also subsumed the ethnography, ethnology, and ethnohistory of the American Indian. Proper chronological perspective on American archaeological cultures did not become a major concern until after World War I. For various reasons stratigraphy, the prime method of archaeological chronology, lagged in Americanist studies. It was not effectively employed until about 1914, the point in our history when our Classificatory-Descriptive Period, one concerned essentially with description and classification of remains, gave way to what we have designated as the Classificatory-Historical Period, when chronology became the prime order of the day. Great advances were made in chronological and chronological-geographical distributional ordering in the early part of the Classificatory-Historical Period, from 1914 to 1940, and in some American areas local site and regional chronologies were linked together to effect 'area syntheses,' the ultimate goal of the American archaeology of that time. But this ultimate goal came to be seen as too limited, and restrictive, and American archaeologists, under the stimulus of some social-anthropological colleagues, grew restive under these restrictions. They began to ask questions about cultural context and function and even to speculate, if dimly, about the processes of culture change. These trends characterized the latter half of our Classificatory-Historical Period, from about 1940 until 1960, although in this time they were expressed by a relative minority of the American archaeological profession. The main stream of archaeological research remained in chronological-distributional ordering, and notable advances continued in this mainstream.

Out of these concerns with context and function still other trends emerged in American archaeology. These have come rapidly to the fore, insofar as archaeological theory and methodology are concerned, after 1960, and we have seen this date as marking a division between our Classificatory-Historical Period and a new period which we are calling the Explanatory. The innovations of the Explanatory Period have been dubbed by some as the 'new archaeology.' The watchword of the 'new archaeology' is process – the explanation of culture change or, as its proponents would say, the explanation of the variability that is observed in the archaeological record.

In a sense, archaeology has come full circle, or, to follow an evolutionary conceit, a full spiral has been completed in the progressive development of American archaeology. The 'proto-archaeologists' of the Speculative Period were concerned with explanation (in their definition of that term) of the wondrous phenomena of the New World and its peoples, but they were doomed to do no more than speculate. Then, in the wake of the rising tide of 19th century science, an orderly archaeology came into being. It eventually mastered the dimension of chronology, and from there it went on to contextual reconstruction of past cultures and functional description. More recently, there has been a theoretical and methodological synthesis in American archaeology in which the once discredited theory of cultural evolution has been made viable and applicable through general systems models. This systemic outlook should serve archaeology well and keep its research in the mainstream of the social sciences and of the other sciences in general. For as a member of another social science has observed:

'The perspectives of a systems analysis serve to link all of the sciences, natural and social, help to make communication among them possible and rewarding, and generate common kinds of problems that interdisciplinary discussion can help to resolve.'[117]

It is our belief that with this new theoretical-methodological synthesis American archaeology stands poised for a great stride forward. For the first time, archaeologists are now in a position not only to speculate but to have some hope of reasonable verification of their speculations (or hypotheses) on the nature and causes of culture change. Nor do we mean to limit this observation to American archaeology alone. Archaeology on these continents remains 'American' only in its particularities of subject matter. Inquiries into the whys and wherefores of the rise and fall of civilization and the methodological approaches devised to serve these inquiries are clearly of world-wide scope and are being so conceived by an increasing number of archaeologists.

The rate of change in American archaeology, and in world-wide archaeology, has accelerated so quickly in these last few years, and even in this very last decade, that it is hazardous to attempt to predict what the discipline will be like in another few decades. Here in the New World it is certain that substantive knowledge, of a descriptive-chronological sort, will be greatly augmented, as will all sorts of materials analyses as more and more developments from other sciences are brought to bear on archaeology. On the practical and administrative side, it is safe to say that as field programs incorporate multi-disciplinary aids, and as an increasing number of questions are asked by the archaeologists about their data, the archaeologist will become, perforce, the coordinator of the efforts of many others. Special laboratory and institutional facilities, which unfortunately do not exist at the present time, will have to be developed for a variety of investigations and for data-banking.[118] In all of this inevitable proliferation it can only be hoped that the archaeologist of the future will manage to be a thinking and imaginative individual and not become a cog in a machine.

Another practical concern is that of the archaeologist's general social responsibility. In a growing and increasingly intercommunicative world the archaeologist can no longer proceed in the *laissez-faire* manner of the past. Archaeologists will have to be willing to cooperate fully with local governments in adherence to and enforcement of laws governing antiquities;[119] and in those countries of the New World where such protective laws do not generally exist, as in the United States, they should work for them. If we, and the archaeologists who follow us, do not do these things, then the prehistoric resources of the Americas will soon be despoiled and exhausted.[120] Nor will the American archaeologist be able to stop with this. As he is now beginning to realize, he cannot ignore the relevance of his work to the feelings of various native peoples. It will be incumbent upon him to consider these feelings in relation to the preparation of museum exhibits and in the excavation of sites on Indian lands.

To return to the theoretical and methodological levels, which have been the central concern of this history, we repeat that the outlook is bright. There are some difficulties, but we predict they will be surmounted. One hazard which American archaeology now faces is an over-emphasis on polemical rhetoric at the expense of substantive contribution. We believe that the discipline has now moved beyond the need to be 'sold' on the goals of processual investigation.[121] If we may go back to our analogy of that fabulous animal the 'talking dog,' we think that the creature has demonstrated his power of speech; he must now look more to the content of his message.

Another difficulty is in presentation. It is true that archaeologists are attempting to talk about things they have not been concerned with before. New concepts and new terminologies are needed. At the same time, there is a discouraging opacity in much that has been written recently. Statistical manipulations have their place, but it is always reassuring to the reader to intersperse these with occasional references to people, places, and things – to the human scale.

Finally, and more serious, we hope that American archaeology will not become locked in an excessive rigidity in theoretical and methodological thinking. We have referred to this before, in connection with inductive and deductive reasoning, with ethnographic analogy, and with hypothesis formulation. We would also add here that a flexibility of thought should be maintained with regard to assumptions about cultural processes and the primacy of one cultural subsystem over others in culture change.[122] As yet we know so very little. Most of us feel that culture evolves, but we still do not know just how and in what circumstances. These, indeed, are the great questions of archaeology and of culture history in the broad sense. They are extraordinarily difficult and complex questions. We cannot begin to answer them. There is abroad now, however, a new optimism about the possibility of their solution, and this is good. Still, we must remind ourselves that there is a fine line between optimism and self-congratulation. Given the vagaries, fortuities, and complexities that are present in any record of a mute past, modesty is always a becoming stance for the archaeologist.

Notes on the Text

Chapter One

1 Archaeology is most usually spelled with *ae* (as separate letters or as a ligature), and this spelling will be followed here; however, some American archaeologists and institutions substitute *e*.
2 Trigger (1970); Spaulding (1968); Clarke (1968, pp. 12–14); Chapter Six of this book.
3 Daniel (1950, 1964, 1967, 1968); Clark (1939); Bibby (1956); Lynch and Lynch (1968); Clarke (1968, pp. 4–11).
4 Rowe (1965).
5 Trigger (1968b).
6 Rowe (1962a).
7 This idea of human social and cultural evolution is much older than the mid 19th century (Harris 1968, pp. 29–31).
8 Trigger (1968b).
9 Clark (1939, Chapter I).
10 This is not meant to exclude Europeans or other inhabitants of the Old World who happened to arrive in the New World prior to 1492. Thus the Viking presence, now documented in Newfoundland *ca.* A.D. 1000, is certainly within the compass of American archaeology as would be any Asiatics (such as Jomon voyagers from Japan *ca.* 3000 B.C.) who may or may not have reached the coasts of South or Middle America.
11 See Willey (1968) or Hallowell (1960).
12 For such syntheses of substantive archaeology of the Americas see Willey (1966–71) or Jennings (1968).
13 Some works in the 19th century, such as Haven's *Archaeology of the United States* (1856) or Winsor's *Narrative and Critical History of North America*, Vol. I: *Aboriginal America* (1889), trace through the development of theoretical thinking about American antiquities and aborigines to their respective times.
14 One of us (Willey) was a student in the course and, subsequently, taught it at Columbia in 1942–43. See also Strong (1952). Mention should also be made here of a Harvard course, 'History of American Archaeology,' offered in 1960–65 by Stephen Williams (Belmont and Williams, 1965).
15 Schwartz (1968, also 1967).
16 Willey (1968). Other articles or books which deserve special mention for reviews of American archaeological (and anthropological) development are: Nelson (1933); Hallowell (1960); F. Johnson (1961); Wilmsen (1965); Silverberg (1968); and Lyon (1969).
17 Gamio's (1913) pioneering work was carried out in 1911, at the urging of A.M. Tozzer and Franz Boas. Nelson's fieldwork (1914, 1916) was carried out 1912–15.

Chapter Two

1 For supplementary reading, see Belmont and Williams (1965); Hallowell (1960); Haven (1856); Silverberg (1968); Wauchope (1962); Willey (1968); Wilmsen (1965); Winsor (1889); Huddleston (1967); and S. Williams (1964).
2 Hole and Heizer (1969, pp. 181–3).
3 Hallowell (1960, p. 74).
4 Silverberg (1968).
5 '*Speculate*: to form conjectures regarding anything without experiment;' from *Funk and Wagnall's New College Standard Dictionary* (1956).
6 Atwater (1820).
7 See Wilmsen (1965, p. 176).
8 Deloria (1969) and Josephy (1970).
9 Rowse (1959).
10 Crone (1969, p. 176).
11 A misnomer deriving from Columbus's belief that he had landed in India.
12 Nelson (1933, pp. 88–9).
13 Spinden (1933, p. 220).
14 Hallowell (1960, p. 4).
15 Hanke (1951 and 1949).
16 Huddleston (1967) argues that it did not become popular until the latter part of the 16th century and that many writers to whom this theory is attributed, such as Las Casas, did not believe in it.
17 Huddleston (1967, pp. 38–41).
18 Adair (1775).
19 Kingsborough (1831–48).
20 Wauchope (1962, pp. 30–1).
21 De Groot (1963), de Laet (1643, 1644), and Horn (1652) as cited in Spinden (1933).
22 Beals (1957); also Wilmsen (1965, p. 173), and Huddleston (1967, Chapter II).
23 Wauchope (1962, p. 85).
24 J.E.S. Thompson (1958, p. 92).
25 Treulein (1949, p. 161) as quoted in Ives (1956, p. 420); also see Wilmsen (1965, p. 173).
26 The Moundbuilder versus Indian debate only began in earnest in the 19th century.
27 Galatin (1845, p. 177).
28 Wilmsen (1965, p. 173).
29 For further discussion of the many wild speculations as to the origins of the American Indians, see Robert Wauchope (1963).
30 'Mesoamerica' includes central and southern Mexico and northern Central America (see Willey, 1966, p. 85 for more exact definition.)
31 The Peruvian coast and highlands and the adjacent highlands of Bolivia (Willey, 1971).
32 The Mixtec codices would be just one example (see Spores, 1967).
33 Leon-Portilla (1969, p. 119).
34 Sahagun (1950–63), the Anderson–Dibble edition (in English and Aztec).
35 Fray Diego Duran (1964), the Hayden–Horcasitas edition (in English).
36 Garcilaso de la Vega (1966), the Livermore edition (in English).
37 Landa (1941), the Tozzer edition (in English).

38 Landa (1941, pp. 276–82).
39 Landa (1941, p. vii).
40 Casas (1909), in Spanish.
41 Casas (1927), in Spanish.
42 Hanke (1951, Chapter III).
43 Hanke (1951, p. 62).
44 Hanke (1951, pp. 70–1).
45 Huddleston (1967, pp. 23–4).
46 Du Pratz (1758).
47 Clavijero (1817), the Cullen edition (in English).
48 Robertson (1777).
49 Bartram (1791).
50 Silverberg (1968, p. 26).
51 Thomas (1894).
52 Silverberg (1968, p. 57).
53 There were also Spaniards who thought of the Indians as savages; nevertheless, there appear to have been general attitudinal differences between the Spanish and the English, as well as the French (Spencer, Jennings, Jesse, *et al.*, 1965, pp. 496–7).
54 Obviously, the question was basically the same, since it was not supposed that there were any predecessors to the Moundbuilders in North America.
55 Garcilaso de la Vega (1951), the Varner edition (in English).
56 Elvas, Gentleman of (1907), in English.
57 Webster, the famous lexicographer, later retracted this opinion (Shetrone 1930, p. 14).
58 Kalm (1772); also see Nelson (1933, p. 90).
59 Zeisberger (1910).
60 Carver (1779).
61 Barton (1787; 1797; 1799).
62 Bartram (1791).
63 Madison (1803).
64 Harris (1805).

65 Stoddard (1812).
66 Brackenridge (1813).
67 Haywood (1823).
68 Rafinesque (1824).
69 Barton (1799, p. 188).
70 Barton (1797); also see Wilmsen (1965, p. 174).
71 Silverberg (1968, pp. 33–42).
72 Silverberg (1968, Chapter 2).
73 Belmont and Williams (1965).
74 Parsons (1793), (in a letter written in 1786); Heart (1793).
75 Shetrone (1930, pp. 9–13).
76 Silverberg (1968, p. 30).
77 Clinton (1820).
78 Gallatin (1836).
79 Harrison (1839).
80 Silverberg (1968, p. 83).
81 Silverberg (1968, pp. 106–9).
82 Sargent (1799).
83 Hyer (1837).
84 Taylor (1838).
85 Ashley Montagu (1942).
86 Humboldt (1811).
87 Pollock (1940, p. 183).
88 Walckenaër, de Larenaudière, and Jomard (1836); also see Pollock (1940, p. 184).
89 Waldeck (1838).
90 Dupaix (1834).
91 See Ian Graham (1963).
92 Lund (1842) (as discussed in Nelson, 1933, p. 90).
93 Wauchope (1962, pp. 50–3).
94 Jefferson (1944, p. 222).
95 As early as the 16th century, explorations with ancient ruins as their object were undertaken; but Palacio's trip (1840) to Copan, and Del Rio's (1822) to Palenque had little import for, or impact on, the growth of American archaeology.

96 Jefferson (1944, pp. 222–4).
97 Lehmann-Hartleben (1943, p. 163).
98 Wheeler (1956, p. 6).
99 Wheeler (1956, p. 6).
100 Lehmann-Hartleben (1943, p. 163).
101 Sargent: American Philosophical Society (1799, p. xxxvii).
102 Sargent: American Philosophical Society (1799, p. xxxvii).
103 Sargent: American Philosophical Society (1799, p. xxxviii).
104 As Wheeler (1956, p. 43) has said referring to Jefferson's excavations: 'Unfortunately, this seed of a new scientific skill fell upon infertile soil.'
105 Shipton (1945, pp. 164–5).
106 Shipton (1945, p. 165).
107 Wissler (1943, p. 195); Silverberg (1968, p. 59).
108 Shipton (1967, p. 35).
109 Hallowell (1960, p. 79).
110 Mitra (1933, p. 99).
111 Atwater (1820).
112 See Silverberg (1968, p. 74).
113 Although McCulloh saw military service in Ohio (Silverberg 1968, p. 58), he was basically armchair-bound (McCulloh, 1829).
114 McCulloh (1829).
115 Haven (1856, p. 48); quoted in Mitra (1933, p. 104).
116 Thomas (1894, p. 600); quoted in Silverberg (1968, p. 58) and Hallowell (1960, p. 81).
117 Wissler (1942, p. 201).
118 Washburn (1967, p. 106).
119 Goetzmann (1966, p. 232).

1 Among the useful general sources for this period are: Belmont and Williams (1965); Clewlow (1970); Goetzmann (1967); Hallowell (1960); Haven (1856); Haynes (1900); Morgan and Rodabaugh (1947); Pollock (1940); Silverberg (1968); Thomas (1898); Willey (1968); Wilmsen (1965).
2 Haven (1856; p. 149), for example, could state unequi-

vocally, in the beginning of the period, that there were no antiquities in the Oregon Territory. By the end of the period, such a statement would have been impossible.
3 Thomas (1894).
4 Haven (1856, p. 122).
5 Squier (1848).
6 Washburn (1967, p. 153).
7 Whittlesey in Squier and Davis (1848, pp. 41–2).
8 Squier (1849).

9 Lapham (1855).
10 Haven (1856).
11 Fewkes (1897, p. 751).
12 Schoolcraft (1854, pp. 135–6).
13 An index (F. S. Nichols, 1954) is now available.
14 See McKusick's monograph on one particular society (the Davenport Academy of Sciences, Iowa).
15 Pidgeon (1853).
16 Lubbock (1865).

Chapter Three

17 Baldwin (1872).
18 Foster (1873).
19 Larkin (1880).
20 Bancroft (1882).
21 Nadaillac (1884).
22 Silverberg (1968, pp. 159–60).
23 Freeman (1965).
24 McKusick (1970, pp. 2–3).
25 Haynes (1900, p. 32); Peet (1892–1905).
26 Hallowell (1960, p. 54).
27 Hallowell (1960, p. 84).
28 Darrah (1951); Judd (1967).
29 Judd (1967, pp. 18–19).
30 Henshaw (1883).
31 Thomas (1894, p. 528).
32 The lack of adequate temporal typologies of artifacts led Thomas (1885, p. 70) to support his otherwise well-founded case by arguing against any great time depth.
33 Jennings (1968, p. 33).
34 Thomas (1898).
35 See Brew (1968) for a fuller discussion of the founding of the Peabody Museum.
36 Wyman (1868a; 1875).
37 Morlot (1861).
38 Jones (1864); Wyman (1868b) and Schumacher (1873) even call the shell-heaps 'kjökken-möddings.'
39 It should be noted that even earlier on both Charles Lyell and F. W. Putnam (1883, 1899) expressed similar views; see also Dexter (1966a, p. 152).
40 Walker (1883); Bullen (1951).
41 For a biography of Putnam see Tozzer (1935).
42 Dexter (1966b).
43 Dexter (1966a).
44 Dexter (1965); Morgan and Rodabaugh (1947, p. 6).
45 See, for example, Putnam (1886).
46 Abbott (1876).
47 See, for example, Richards (1939).
48 Haynes (1889).
49 Gibbs's (1862) 'Instructions for Archaeological Investigations in the United States,' in the *Annual Report of the Smithsonian Institution for 1861*, clearly shows these European influences.
50 Whitney (1872).
51 See, especially, Holmes (1903).

52 Holmes (1892); Hough (1916, p. 195).
53 Clewlow (1970); but cf. Jennings (1968, p. 34).
54 See Schultz (1945) for further details on Hrdlička's career.
55 Hrdlička (1925).
56 Schultz (1945, pp. 312–13).
57 Roberts (1940, p. 52).
58 Clewlow (1970, p. 32).
59 W. H. Goetzmann (1959, 1967).
60 Goetzmann (1967, pp. 255–6, 325–6); Emory (1848).
61 Judd (1968).
62 Cushing (1890).
63 Bandelier (1892); Hewett (1906); Hough (1903).
64 For examples, see Moore (1896, 1902, 1910).
65 Moorehead (1892); also (1922) on Maine and (1928) on Cahokia.
66 Moorehead (1910).
67 Mills (1906, 1907); Schwartz (1967, pp. 26ff.).
68 Thomas (1894).
69 Thruston (1890); Schwartz (1967, p. 26).
70 On general evolutionary grounds, Mills (1907) felt that the more complex-looking Hopewell culture was later than the Fort Ancient culture. He even tried to use some stratigraphic data to bolster this contention.
71 Dall (1877, p. 47).
72 Dall (1877, pp. 49–51).
73 For background on Dall's life, see Merriam (1927).
74 Uhle (1907).
75 Uhle (1907, p. 8).
76 Uhle (1907, p. 39).
77 Uhle (1907, p. 39).
78 Nelson (1909, 1910).
79 See Rowe (1962).
80 Kroeber (1909, p. 15).
81 Rowe (1962, pp. 399–400).
82 Von Hagen (1947).
83 Catherwood (1844).
84 Stephens (1837, 1838, 1839).
85 Pollock (1940, p. 185).
86 Charnay (1887).
87 Wauchope (1962, pp. 7–21).
88 Maudslay (1889–1902); Thomas (1899).
89 Maler (1901; 1903; 1908).
90 Bastian (1876); Habel (1878).

91 See Pollock (1940, p. 190); Sapper (1895).
92 Gann (1900).
93 Edward H. Thompson (1897; 1898; 1904).
94 Batres (1906); Nuttall (1910).
95 Holmes (1895–97).
96 Gordon (1896, 1902); also see Saville (1892).
97 Tozzer, a student of Putnam's and an early Harvard Ph.D., trained a whole generation of students in Middle American archaeology (Phillips, 1955).
98 Tozzer (1911, 1913); Hewett (1912, 1916); Morley (1913); Pollock (1940, pp. 191–2); Merwin and Vaillant (1932).
99 J. E. S. Thompson (1958b, p. 43).
100 Förstemann (1906); Ian Graham (1971); Joseph T. Goodman (1897, 1905) made similar discoveries, but it is not completely clear how independent these were of the work of Förstemann.
101 Landa (1864); see also Landa (1941) for an annotated translation by Tozzer.
102 Brinton (1882, 1885).
103 Prescott (1843); also see Landa (1941).
104 Morgan (1876); Bandelier (1877, 1878, 1879).
105 Joyce (1914).
106 Spinden (1913).
107 Tschudi (1869).
108 Castelnau (1852).
109 Wiener (1880).
110 Middendorf (1893–95).
111 Squier (1877).
112 Markham (1856, 1871, 1892, 1910).
113 Reiss and Stübel (1180–87).
114 Bandelier (1910).
115 See Rowe (1954) for a discussion of Uhle's career and influence. The significance of much of Uhle's work was not made known until Kroeber and others worked over the Uhle notes and collections a good many years later (Kroeber, 1925a, 1925b, 1926, 1927; Kroeber and Strong, 1924a, 1924b; Gayton, 1927; Gayton and Kroeber, 1927).
116 Stübel and Uhle (1892).
117 Uhle (1903).
118 Uhle had formulated

his chronology by 1900; but he referred to it again in later publications (1903, 1910, 1913a, 1913b).

119 Uhle (1910, 1913a, 1913b); Kroeber (1926).

120 Since Uhle's time it has been recognized that the more probable center for the radiation of Tiahuanaco-like influences to coastal Peru was the site of Huari, near Ayacucho (Menzel, 1964).

121 Uhle (1916, 1919, 1922a).

122 Rowe (1954, p. 15).

123 González Suárez (1878, 1892, 1910).

124 Dorsey (1901).

125 Saville (1907–10).

126 Verneau and Rivet (1912–22).

127 Uhle (1922b, 1923).

128 Rowe (1954, fly-leaf quotation from Uhle).

129 Rowe (1954, pp. 54–5).

130 Rowe (1954, Appendix A – Uhle lectures). Rowe's opinion of the influence of cultural evolutionary thinking on Uhle is not as favourable as ours.

131 Erland von Nordenskiöld (1913).

132 Ambrosetti (1906).

133 Ambrosetti (1897, 1902, 1906, 1908).

134 Debenedetti (1910, 1912).

135 Boman (1908).

136 Rosen (1904, 1924).

137 Torres (1907, 1911).

138 Outes (1897, 1905, 1907).

139 Ameghino (1911, 1915); Hrdlička et al. (1912).

140 Bollaert (1860).

141 Restrepo (1895).

142 Marcano (1889).

143 Steinen (1904).

144 Fewkes (1907, 1912d).

145 Joyce (1916).

146 Squier (1852, 1853).

147 Holmes (1888).

148 MacCurdy (1911).

149 Hartman (1901, 1907); see also Rowe (1959b) for an appraisal of Hartman.

150 Derby (1879).

151 Hartt (1871, 1885).

152 Farabee (1921).

153 Steere (1927).

154 Goeldi (1900).

155 Ihering (1895).

156 See Mattos (1946) for bibliography on this.

157 Joyce (1912).

158 Rau (1876); Rau (1879) also made some early observations on a tablet from Palenque, Chiapás, Mexico.

159 Wilson (1899).

160 Fowke (1896).

161 See Trigger (1968b, p. 529).

162 Henry (1875, p. 335).

163 Holmes (1903).

164 Thruston (1890).

165 Mason (1895, 1905).

166 Wissler (1914).

167 Mills (1907).

168 Squier and Davis (1848).

169 Hough (1916).

170 Cushing (1886).

171 For these objectives see Wright et al. (1909, p. 114). The Boasian attitude can also be seen in the evaluations of various archaeological luminaries by Robert H. Lowie (1956); see also Boas (1940).

172 Harris (1968).

173 Boas (1913) was one of those who encouraged Gamio to make stratigraphic excavations in the Valley of Mexico.

Chapter Four

1 See Rowe (1962a, pp. 399–400); also Kroeber (1909).

2 Gamio (1913); Boas (1913); Tozzer (1915). J. A. Graham (1962) observes that Engerrand, who was trained primarily as a geologist, had just returned to Mexico from Europe where he had seen recent geological and archaeological excavations and that it is possible that he passed these ideas along to Boas.

3 Holmes (1885).

4 R. E. W. Adams (1960).

5 See Spier (1931); Woodbury (1960a, 1960b). It should be emphasized, again, that neither Gamio nor Nelson were the first to observe and record cultural superposition in archaeological sites. In the Southwestern area, alone, other archaeologists, including Richard Wetherill (see Prudden, 1897), J. W. Fewkes (1912), and Byron Cummings (1910), had made these superpositional discoveries prior to Nelson's or Gamio's work; however, in none of these

instances was gradual cultural change plotted by means of stratigraphy.

6 Nelson (1909, 1910).

7 Uhle's work of 1902 was published in 1907. Kroeber's negative opinion of the results came out in 1909. See Rowe (1962a, pp. 399–400).

8 Nelson (1914, 1916).

9 Bandelier (1892).

10 Hewett (1906).

11 Nelson (1916, p. 161).

12 Nelson (1916, p. 162).

13 In the 1920s and early 1930s there were some retrospective reflections on the importance of chronology and stratigraphy in American archaeology (for examples, see Tozzer, 1926, 1927; Spinden, 1933); these were more enthusiastic than those of *ca.* 1914.

14 Kidder (1915).

15 Kidder (1924, 1931). The 1931 report was written in collaboration with C. A. Amsden.

16 Kidder (1924, 1931).

17 Kidder (1931, pp. 6–7).

18 Schmidt (1928).

19 Gladwin (1928); Winifred and H. S. Gladwin (1929, 1935); Gladwin et al. (1937).

20 Haury (1932, 1936a, 1936b, 1940); also sections in Gladwin et al. (1937).

21 Roberts (1929, 1931, 1932).

22 Martin, Roys, and Von Bonin (1936); Martin, Rinaldo, and Kelly (1940).

23 Vaillant (1930, 1931, 1937). Kroeber (1925c) attempted stratigraphic digging in the Valley of Mexico 'Archaic' sites in 1924. He had little success with sequence in the digging, but through seriation of several site collections of pottery he was able to establish a rough chronology of complexes or phases.

24 Bennett (1934).

25 Collins (1937, 1940); see also de Laguna (1934).

26 Ford (1935, 1936, pp. 257–8).

27 Webb and De Jarnette (1942) is the best published

example; however, W. S. Webb's influence on South-eastern excavations dates back to the 1930s.

28 A very 'stratigraphy-conscious' article is one by Willey (1939).

29 Woodbury (1960a, 1960b). Uhle's (1907) California shell-mound digging had been by natural strata.

30 Wheeler (1954, p. 53).

31 Kidder (1931, pp. 9–10).

32 Haury in Gladwin *et al.* (1937, pp. 22–5).

33 Vaillant (1930, pp. 19–30).

34 See Heizer's (1959, ed., p. 282) comments and see also R. H. Thompson's (1955) review of Wheeler (1954).

35 For further details of stratigraphic excavations the reader is referred to Heizer (1959, ed., pp. 214–343).

36 Dunnell (1970); Rouse (1967).

37 Rowe (1961).

38 Rouse (1967); Daniel (1950).

39 Rowe (1962b).

40 Rouse (1967); see also Petrie (1899, 1904).

41 Kroeber (1916).

42 Dunnell (1970).

43 Kroeber (1916, p. 15).

44 Spier (1917).

45 Spier (1917, p. 282).

46 Spier (1917, p. 326).

47 Nelson (1920).

48 Roberts (1939).

49 Kroeber and Strong (1924a). Other publications in this series of studies based on the Uhle collections include: Kroeber and Strong (1924b); Kroeber (1925a, 1925b, 1926); Strong (1925); Gayton (1927); Gayton and Kroeber (1927).

50 Kroeber and Strong (1924a, p. 96).

51 Strong (1925).

52 Collins (1937).

53 Personal communication from J. A. Ford to G. R. Willey in the late 1930s.

54 Ford (1936).

55 For example, as expressed by Rouse (1967) and Dunnell (1970).

56 Ford (1938).

57 Spier (1931).

58 Kroeber (1919).

59 Ford (1962).

60 Rouse (1939).

61 See, for example, Rouse (1941).

62 Although Rouse (1960) was writing a good many years later his distinction can certainly be applied in retrospect.

63 Rouse (1960).

64 Lothrop (1926).

65 Lothrop (1926, see pp. 392–417).

66 Such chronologies were not established until many years later (see M. D. Coe and Baudez, 1961 and Baudez, 1963).

67 Lothrop (1926, pp. 105–6).

68 See Winifred and H. S. Gladwin (1928a, 1928b, 1930). It should be pointed out, however, that the binomial system of pottery taxonomy was formulated, as a scheme, in the First Pecos Conference on Southwestern Archaeology, held at Pecos, New Mexico in 1927 (Kidder, 1927).

69 Winifred and H. S. Gladwin (1931); Haury (1936b); Sayles (1936).

70 Winifred and H. S. Gladwin (1930). These pottery type procedures were further formulated in the Southwestern conferences, at Pecos, again, in 1929, and at Gila Pueblo, Arizona, in 1930 (Hargrave, 1932).

71 Winifred and H. S. Gladwin (1930).

72 Colton and Hargrave (1937).

73 Colton and Hargrave (1937, p. 4).

74 Ford (1936).

75 Ford, (1938, ed).

76 Ford (1938, ed.). Although Ford is best described as the editor of this report, there can be little doubt, in view of the phraseology and idea content, that this and the following quote are directly from him.

77 Ford (1938, ed.).

78 See Krieger (1944).

79 These first type descriptions were prepared by W. C. Haag.

80 Vaillant (1930, 1931). Vaillant's pottery figurine classification was formal and structured but essentially descriptive.

81 Bennett (1934).

82 Smith (1936a, 1936b, 1955).

83 Kidder (1927).

84 Kidder (1924).

85 For instance, those of Roberts (1935, 1937).

86 Winifred and H. S. Gladwin (1934).

87 Winifred and H. S. Gladwin (1934).

88 Gladwin was generally careful not to place linguistic or ethnic tags on archaeological complexes (Winifred and H. S. Gladwin, 1934). The 'Caddoan Root' designation was a temporary exception.

89 McKern (1939).

90 Winifred and H. S. Gladwin (1934). Shetrone, as early as 1920, proposed that Ohio Valley culture complexes should be recognized and classified according to their typologies (see Griffin, 1959). A comparative discussion of the Pecos, Gladwin, McKern, and Colton Classifications may be consulted in McGregor (1941, pp. 57–68).

91 The classic work on the *Kulturkreislehre* school is Graebner (1911), but there is an informative review of the school and its approach in Kluckhohn (1936).

92 His best summary statement on the method and his views of it were published a little later (Imbelloni, 1945).

93 See Menghin (1957). The author of *Weltgeschichte der Steinzeit* (1931) did not begin work in the Americas until after World War II.

94 Wedel (1938).

95 Parker (1916).

96 Ritchie (1932, 1938).

97 Collins (1927); Ford (1936); Stirling (1940).

98 Strong (1935). See also Strong (1927), for combined ethnologic and archaeologic research done under Kroeber's encouragement at the University of California. Steward (1937) also wrote along similar lines under Kroeber's influence.

99 Especially A. T. Hill.

100 See Wedel (1936, 1938, 1940); Strong (1940).

101 Strong (1933).

102 Steward (1942).

103 Strong (1935) regretted that his Nebraska work had been done largely before the Midwestern scheme had been made known, and he attempted to fit his cultures into the scheme; however, this added nothing to Nebraska culture history that had not been achieved by the Direct Historical Approach.

104 Tello's early general works were published in 1923 and 1929. A later synthesis of 1942 follows along the same lines although by this date Tello was able to bring the Chavin concept into sharper focus. Previously, it had been a part of a larger, vaguer construct called 'Archaic Andean' culture.

105 Means's great work was published in 1931; however, his interpretation was fairly well set as expressed in an article published in 1917.

106 Kroeber (1927).

107 Wendell C. Bennett (1934, 1936, 1939).

108 Larco Hoyle (1938–40, 1941).

109 Kroeber (1944).

110 Kidder (1924).

111 He called these 'areas.' They would correspond to what are now more usually referred to as 'regions' within a major culture area (Willey, 1966–71).

112 McGregor (1941, pp. 69–85); Bannister (1963).

113 McGregor (1941, p. 322).

114 Roberts (1935, 1937).

115 Gladwin (1937, Vol. 2).

116 Sayles and Antevs (1941); but the Cochise culture had been brought to the attention of other Southwestern archaeologists in the 1930s.

117 McGregor (1941, p. 67).

118 As of that time there were two Maya-Christian calendrical correlations, the 11.16.0.0.0 (also known as the 'Goodman-Thompson-Martinez Correlation') and the 12.9.0.0.0 (also known as the 'Spinden Correlation'). See J. E. S. Thompson (1937). Radiocarbon dates favor the 11.16.0.0.0 correlation which would place the Classic Maya dates in the span of about A.D. 270–890; the 12.9.0.0.0 correlation would move this chronology back by about 260 years.

119 Spinden (1928).

120 Ricketson and Ricketson (1937); J. E. S. Thompson (1939).

121 See Kidder (1940) for a summary.

122 See Caso (1938) for one of the later preliminary reports on Monte Alban.

123 Vaillant (1927).

124 Vaillant (1935).

125 Vaillant (1941, pp. 1–27, Table I). See also the chronological chart (Table X) in *The Maya and Their Neighbors*, C. L. Hay *et al.*, 1940, which was prepared by Kroeber, in conjunction with Vaillant.

126 Deuel (1935).

127 Parker (1922); Ritchie (1938).

128 Strong (1935).

129 Setzler (1940).

130 Ford and Willey (1941).

131 This is a quite distinct usage of the term from that applied by Spinden (1928).

132 Griffin (1946).

133 Mathiassen (1927); Jenness (1928); de Laguna (1934); Collins (1937).

134 Jenness (1933); Birket-Smith (1936); Mathiassen (1937).

135 Collins (1940).

136 Rouse (1939).

137 Heizer and Fenenga (1939); Heizer (1941).

138 See, for example, the summary articles by Márquez Miranda (1946a, 1946b); Lothrop (1946); Casanova (1946); Aparicio (1948); Willey (1946); Serrano (1946). Bird's (1946a) article on northern Chile, based upon his own stratigraphic digging (Bird, 1943), is an exception.

139 Bird (1938, 1946b).

140 For examples, Kidder II (1940) or Vaillant (1932).

141 Lothrop (1940).

142 Phillips (1940); Brew (1940).

143 Kroeber (1940, Table XI).

144 Kroeber (1930); Kidder (1936).

145 Spinden (1917).

146 Vaillant (1934).

147 Erland von Nordenskiöld (1921, 1931).

148 Gladwin (1937 – the volume 2 of the 'Snaketown' report) was one notable exception. He felt that Old World contacts with New World later cultures were clear and strong. Contrast his views with those of Kidder (1936).

149 Figgins (1927).

150 Howard (1935).

151 Roberts (1935b).

152 Roberts (1940).

153 See Roberts (1940) for bibliographic references to these various complexes.

154 For example, see Ricketson and Ricketson (1937).

155 See Cole and Deuel (1937).

156 See Webb and DeJarnette (1942) or Lewis and Kneberg (1946). Although the dates on these particular reports are slightly later than 1940, much of the fieldwork upon which they are based was done in the 1930s.

1 Strong (1936). It is undoubtedly significant that Strong, although primarily an archaeologist, had published in ethnology (Strong, 1927).

2 Martin, Lloyd, and Spoehr (1938); Martin and Rinaldo (1939); J. W. Bennett (1943).

3 Steward and Setzler (1938). This article was published in *American Antiquity*, the journal of the Society for American Archaeology whose founding in 1935, was a signal event in the growth of American archaeology.

4 Steward (1938).

5 Steward (1937a).

6 Steward (1937b).

7 Kluckhohn (1940); see also Kluckhohn (1939).

8 Hay *et al.* (1940).

9 Kluckhohn and Reiter, eds. (1939).

10 Kluckhohn (1940, p. 47).

11 Linton (1936).

12 Cole and Deuel (1937).

13 Martin, Lloyd, and Spoehr (1938).

Chapter Five

14 Rouse (1939, p. 16). Rouse was a student of the ethnologist Cornelius Osgood, who was much interested in material culture typology from both ethnological (Osgood, 1940) and archaeological (Osgood, 1942) perspectives.

15 J. W. Bennett (1943). Bennett received his graduate education at the University of Chicago, where Radcliffe-Brown, an influential proponent of the functionalist approach, had taught.

16 Lewis and Kneberg (1941).

17 Keur (1941).

18 Wedel (1941).

19 J. W. Bennett (1944b).

20 Waring and Holder (1945); their ideas were known in Southeastern archaeological circles before that time.

21 J. W. Bennett (1943, p. 213).

22 Linton (1944).

23 J. W. Bennett (1944a).

24 Vaillant (1932); Phillips (1940). Later, however, Vaillant (1940) did consider Meso-american-Southeastern relationships in a functional light.

25 W. C. Bennett (1945).

26 Willey (1948).

27 Taylor (1948).

28 Taylor (1948, pp. 34–5).

29 Taylor (1948, p. 39).

30 Taylor (1948, p. 67).

31 Taylor (1948, p. 48).

32 Representative works: J. E. S. Thompson (1939, 1940).

33 Representative works: Haury (1934, 1940).

34 Representative works: Roberts (1929, 1931, 1939).

35 Representative works: Webb and De Jarnette (1942); Webb and Snow (1945).

36 Representative work: Griffin (1943).

37 It is important to note that Taylor (1948, p. 170) was quite positively influenced by the British archaeologist, Grahame Clark (1939, 1940).

38 Taylor (1948, p. 157).

39 Willey (1953a); however, Willey was influenced by Taylor in his pursuit of the Virú Valley settlement studies (Willey, 1953b). See Woodbury (1954) for a critical review of Taylor.

40 Ford, ed. (1938); see also Krieger (1944).

41 Ford (1952).

42 Ford (1952, p. 314).

43 Ford (1952, p. 318).

44 Spaulding (1953a).

45 Spaulding (1953b). Earlier uses of statistics in pottery American studies (Strong, 1925; Willey, 1943; Brainerd, 1951; Robinson, 1951) had been primarily concerned with chronological ordering.

46 Ford (1954a, 1954b, 1954c); Spaulding (1954a, 1954b); see also Spaulding (1960).

47 R. H. Thompson (1958); Rouse (1953a, 1960); Wheat, Gifford and Wasley (1958), and the Peruvian studies of Rowe (1962c) and his associates (Menzel, Rowe, and Dawson, 1964) in which attempts have been made to relate form and meaning in art. On the Ford side of the argument see a statement by Brew (1946).

48 See Wheat, Gifford, and Wasley (1958); Gifford (1960); Sabloff and Smith (1969).

49 Rouse (1939, 1960); Lathrap (1962); Wright (1967); Dunnell (1971).

50 The best example of this is an article, by A. C. Spaulding (1960).

51 Phillips and Willey (1953); Willey and Phillips (1955); Willey and Phillips (1958).

52 See Spaulding (1957) and Swanson (1959) for critical comments.

53 Willey and Phillips (1958, p. 5).

54 Willey and Phillips (1958, p. 5).

55 Phillips and Willey (1953); see also Willey (1953a).

56 Willey (1953c).

57 Lathrap, ed. (1956).

58 Lathrap, ed. (1956, p. 26).

59 R. H. Thompson, ed. (1956).

60 For the culture 'tradition' concept see Willey (1945) and Goggin (1949).

61 Wauchope (1966).

62 There are very few post-1960 references cited in Wauchope's bibliography and none that could be said to pertain to the 'new' archaeology of the 1960s. Binford (1968a, p. 14),

for example, notes that Wauchope's definition of cultural process differs from that accepted in the 1960s.

63 Griffin (1956) and Cressman (1956) are among the archaeologists; Kroeber (1948); White (1949), Goldschmidt (1959); and Sahlins and Service, eds. (1960) are among the ethnologists-social anthropologists.

64 For Griffin and Cressman see above note; see also Caldwell (1958).

65 Caldwell (1958).

66 See Willey (1946b) for an early summary and description of the Virú Valley project; subsequent publications on the project, in addition to Willey (1953b) are: Strong and Evans (1952); Bird (1948); W. C. Bennett (1950); Collier (1955); Ford (1949); Ford and Willey (1949); and Holmberg (1950).

67 Willey (1953b); however, O. G. Ricketson, Jr. had been concerned with Maya settlement size, in connection with population estimates, and this work forms a chapter of the Uaxactun site monograph (Ricketson and Ricketson, 1937).

68 Willey (1953b, p. 1).

69 D. E. Thompson (1964a, 1964b), a graduate student of Willey's, did a settlement survey of the Casma Valley; see also Patterson and Lanning (1964).

70 Willey et al. (1965).

71 Willey, ed. (1956).

72 Meggers, ed. (1956).

73 Chang (1958).

74 Chang (1958, p. 324).

75 Nicholson (1958); see also Rouse (1968) and Chang (1968).

76 Willey (1968b).

77 See Trigger (1963, 1967, 1968a); K. C. Chang, ed. (1968); Sears (1961); Mayer-Oakes (1961); Millon (1967); Sanders (1949, 1962); and Naroll (1962).

78 Kroeber (1939).

79 Sabloff and Willey (1967).

80 Vayda and Rappaport (1968); it is noteworthy that Steward's 'cultural ecology' did not really embrace a holistic, truly ecological approach.

81 See Daniel (1950, pp. 302–8) for a concise historical discussion of environmental concerns in European archaeology. See also Crawford (1912, 1921); Fox (1923, 1932); and Clark (1936, 1952, 1953, 1954). The general lack of influence on American archaeology by cultural geography is noted by Haag (1957) and surely was a factor in the differences in development between European and American archaeology. However, a few individual geographers, such as Sauer (1952) have had some influence on the discipline.

82 Helm (1962, p. 631).

83 As Meighan (1959, p. 404) has stated: 'The study of archaeology may be seen as largely a natural science when dealing with the earliest or simplest technological levels, whereas as cultures become more complex, the archaeologist may utilize more and more of the humanities.'

84 Wedel (1941, 1953).

85 Haury *et al.* (1950).

86 Frederick Johnson (1942, 1949, ed.). For recent summaries of the contributions of this type of interdisciplinary study see Brothwell and Higgs, eds. (1969).

87 Jennings (1957); Haag (1957); Quimby (1954, 1960a, 1960b); see also Helm (1962) for additional references.

88 E. W. Gifford (1916).

89 Cook (1946, 1950). Heizer (1960) offers a full discussion and numerous references; see also Heizer (1955).

90 See Manners, ed. (1964) for further discussions of Steward's role in the development of American anthropology.

91 See Vayda and Rappaport (1968) for criticisms of Steward's work.

92 Steward (1949a).

93 Steward (1955b).

94 Wittfogel (1957).

95 Steward (1947, 1948a); cf. Rouse (1953b, 1956, 1964a) and Sturtevant (1960).

96 Armillas (1948, 1951); Armillas, Palerm and Wolf (1956); Sanders and Price (1968). The influence of V. Gordon Childe is evident in Armillas's thinking.

97 Palerm (1955); Wolf and Palerm (1955); Palerm and Wolf (1957).

98 White (1949). J. A. Ford maintained an adherence to White's evolutionary theories, but he never expressed this beyond the formulation that change was inevitable and, essentially, regularized in the fashion that could be observed in the unimodal pottery development charts. With particular reference to our present context of cultural-environment studies, Helm (1962, pp. 638–9) has stated:
'The Whitean school . . . is anti-pathetic, in its sweeping universalism, to the empirical tradition that has fostered the ecological approach in anthropology.'
If one substitutes 'environmental,' as we have used that concept in this chapter, for 'ecological,' then Helm's statement would be more acceptable as regards developments in the 1940–60 period. However, as the 1960s have shown, White's students have been in the forefront of the development of a systemic, ecological approach to archaeology.

99 Meggers (1954, 1955, 1957).

100 W. R. Coe (1957); Hirshberg and Hirshberg (1957); Altschuler (1958).

101 Sabloff (1972); also Ferdon (1959).

102 Meggers and Evans (1957); Evans and Meggers (1960).

103 Barth (1950, p. 339). See also Barth's (1948) article on the determinative influences of environment on southern South American cultures.

104 Meighan *et al.* (1958, p. 131).

105 See Heizer (1953); Rowe (1953); the essays in Griffin, ed. (1951); Hole and Heizer (1969, Chs. 9–13); and Brothwell and Higgs (1969).

106 Daniel (1950, p. 287).

107 Libby (1955); Willis (1969).

108 The debate still goes on as to how much earlier than 10,000 B.C. man first arrived; but most American archaeologists would now put the figure at more than 20,000 years ago (see Willey, 1966–71, Vol. I, Ch. 2, Vol. II, Ch. 2).

109 See Willey (1968a).

110 Jennings (1957, 1964).

111 Drucker, Heizer, and Squier (1959).

112 See Willis (1969) and Allibone (1970).

113 Bannister (1969).

114 See Friedman, Smith, and Clark (1969) and R. M. Cook (1969). In addition, a relatively new technique called 'thermoluminescence,' which can date pottery directly, has yet to make a contribution but appears to have much potential (see Hall, 1969). For bone analyses see Cook and Heizer (1953); Cook and Ezra-Cohn (1959); Cook (1960); and Oakley (1969).

115 Bryan and Ray (1940); Haury *et al.* (1950, pp. 75–126); Heizer (1951); Mangelsdorf and Smith (1949); see also Heizer (1953).

116 Heizer (1953, pp. 6–14).

117 Fisk (1944); Phillips, Ford, and Griffin (1951).

118 Especially, Shepard (1956).

119 For example, Howel Williams (1956); Williams and Heizer (1969).

120 See the recent papers in Brill, ed. (1971).

121 Shippee (1932).

122 Ford and Willey (1949).

123 As early as 1930, by Judd (1931).

124 Meighan (1950); Rowe (1953, pp. 912–13).

125 Aitken (1969); Rainey and Ralph (1966).

126 Brainerd (1951); Robinson (1951); Spaulding (1953, 1960).

127 See a pamphlet by Johnson, Kidder, Webb, and Brew (1945). These archaeologists composed the first Committee for the Recovery of Archaeological Remains, an organization which still continues in the interests of salvage archaeology.
While much of salvage archaeology has been concerned with sites in government domain and in areas of prospective flooding, the concept has also spread to archaeological rescue in connection

with highways and the oil pipelines of private companies, with state and private monies provided for archaeological research. For further references on United States salvage archaeology see Stephenson (1963); Jennings (1963); Frederick Johnson (1966); King (1971). While most salvage archaeology in the New World has been in the United States some comparable work has been done under Canadian and under Mexican auspices.

128 Hodge, ed. (1907–10).

129 Steward, ed. (1946–50).

130 Wauchope, ed. (1964–70), now in process of publication.

131 Under the editorship of W. C. Sturtevant.

132 One of the largest archaeological budgets of any national government is that of Mexico where, of course, archaeological research and restoration have played an important part in tourism.

133 Full referencing of these findings and interpretations, or others so briefly reviewed in this chapter, are not possible here; see Willey (1966–71) and Jennings (1968) for further bibliographic references.

134 Especially, see Krieger (1964) and Haynes (1964).

135 See the various articles in Irwin-Williams, ed. (1968).

136 Mirambell (1967); MacNeish (1969, 1970).

137 Willey (1966–71); Jennings (1968).

138 See Lanning's (1967) general summary of Peruvian archaeology for discussion and further references; see also Engel (1966).

139 See, for example, Rowe (1963).

140 Menzel (1964).

141 Lumbreras (1971); T. C. Patterson (1971).

142 See Lanning (1967). A significant discovery of this Initial Period was the monumental construction at Kotosh, in the Peruvian Highlands (Izumi and Sono, 1963; Izumi, 1971).

143 Bennett and Bird (1949, with a 1964 edition); Bushnell (1956, with a 1963 edition); Mason (1957); Lanning (1967).

144 See Meggers (1966) for additional references. The first Evans and Meggers Ecuadorian work was published in 1957; Estrada's first monograph came out in 1954.

145 Reichel-Dolmatoff began significant publication in the early 1950s; the book in question dates as 1965a.

146 Sequence work in Panama began with Willey and McGimsey (1954); later M. D. Coe and Claude Baudez (1961) made important contributions to chronology in Costa Rica. For area syntheses see Stone (1958); Haberland (1959); and Baudez (1970).

147 Rouse (1964b) is a recent and representative statement.

148 Rouse and Cruxent (1963).

149 Meggers and Evans (1957); see also Evans and Meggers (1960) for work in British Guiana.

150 Lathrap (1958, 1970, 1971).

151 Hilbert (1968).

152 See the publications by the Programa Nacional de Pesquisas Arqueológicas (1967–69).

153 See Lathrap (1970).

154 A previous attempt at chronological ordering and area synthesis for Northwestern Argentina was that of Bennett, Bleiler, and Sommer (1948), an exercise based on the literature, on museum collections, and seriational principles. For Gonzalez's cave excavations see especially 1960; for his work in the 'Diaguita region' see 1961.

155 Gonzalez (1963).

156 Menghin (1957) would be a representative work. Menghin's chronological ordering often derived as much from a world-embracing theory of cultural succession (*Kulturkreise*) as from solid stratigraphy.

157 See, e.g. Bormida (1968) and Cigliano (1962).

158 Emperaire, Laming-Emperaire, and Reichlen (1964).

159 Stirling (1943); Drucker (1952); Drucker, Heizer, and Squier (1959); Coe (1968); Bernal (1969).

159a Thompson (1950). The recent controversial 'translations' of Knorozov (1967) should also be mentioned. Some Maya scholars (see Proskouriakoff's Preface to Knorozov's work) feel that the Russian hieroglyphic specialist may not be wholly wrong.

159b Proskouriakoff (1963, 1964). In this connection see also Berlin (1958), for his work on 'emblem glyphs,' and Kelley (1962).

159c Caso (1947).

160 See Millon (1967); Sanders and Price (1968).

161 Jiménez Moreno (1959); Sabloff and Willey (1967).

162 MacNeish (1958, 1967).

163 Kirchhoff (1943).

164 Krickeberg (1956); Covarrubias (1957); Jiménez Moreno (1959); Peterson (1959); MacNeish (1964); Piña Chan (1967); Disselhoff (1967); Haberland (1969); M. D. Coe (1962, 1966); Morley (1946); Thompson (1954); and Brainerd and Morley (1956). This list is not complete as it does not include many Mesoamerican articles of a general synthetic nature, such as those in the *Handbook of Middle American Indians* (see Wauchope, ed. 1964–70), nor does it include many books which are essentially picture albums although containing some archaeological information.

165 Armillas (1948); Bernal (1959); Sanders and Price (1968).

166 Di Peso (1963); Di Peso et al. (1956); Schroeder (1957, 1965).

167 Irwin-Williams (1968).

168 As to area syntheses, the two best known are Wormington (1961) and MacGregor (1965), the latter being a revision of his earlier 1941 book.

169 See appropriate sections in Willey (1966–71, Vol. I); Jennings (1968); or Griffin's (1967) summary article. See Fitting (1968) for an account of some of the factors of this shift from Early Lithic (Paleo-Indian) to Archaic cultures; see also Haag (1961).

170 See Caldwell (1959, 1964).

171 The following is only a sampling, scattered over the East, geographically, and also scattered, chronologically, over the 1940–71 period: Webb and DeJarnette (1942); Lewis and Kneberg (1946); Willey (1949); Newell and Krieger (1949); Phillips, Ford, and Griffin (1951); Bell and Baerreis (1951); Mayer-Oakes (1955); J. L. Coe (1964); Ritchie (1965); Fitting (1970); see also the collection of regional summary articles in Griffin, ed. (1952).

172 The most recent comprehensive article on the whole area is Griffin (1967).

173 Wedel (1961); Lehmer (1971).

174 See Meighan (1961 and 1965) and Heizer (1964) for a general overview. For California see also Warren (1967); for the Great Basin see Jennings (1957); Jennings and Norbeck (1955); W. L. d'-Azevedo *et al.*, eds. (1966); for the Northwest Coast see Cressman *et al.* (1960) and Laguna (1956); for the Plateau see Cressman *et al.* (1960); Butler (1961); Borden (1961); Sanger (1967); and Warren (1968).

175 See MacNeish (1964b).

176 Larsen and Rainey (1948); Larsen (1961); Giddings (1960, 1964); Anderson (1968, 1970); see also Meldgaard (1962) and Bandi (1969).

177 Martin, Quimby, and Collier (1947).

178 Canals Frau (1950, 1955). Canals Frau, although not strictly in the Argentine *Kulturkreislehre* group, showed marked pan-diffusionistic tendencies.

179 Alcina Franch (1965, publication date, but with an earlier copyright date of 1958).

180 Wauchope (1954); Willey (1955a, 1955b, 1958).

181 Willey and Phillips (1955, 1958). See also an article by Willey (1960b), which follows an evolutionary organization, and one by Armillas (1956) which does so in part.

182 Steward (1947, 1948b, 1949b).

183 Steward and Faron (1959).

184 Sanders and Merino (1970).

185 Wormington (1957).

186 Kubler (1962).

187 Spencer and Jennings *et al.* (1965).

188 Meggers and Evans, eds. (1963).

189 Jennings and Norbeck, eds. (1964).

190 Jennings (1968).

191 Willey (1966–71). For a briefer historical treatment see Willey (1960a). See also two very recent general syntheses by Schobinger (1969) and by Bosch-Gimpera (1971).

192 Ford (1969).

193 For example, Rudenko (1961).

194 See Bushnell and McBurney (1959) for a negative view; see Müller-Beck (1966) or Chard (1963) for positive ones. A recent survey of the question is also in Griffin (1960).

195 See the Arctic references in note 176.

196 Heine-Geldern (1954, 1959a, 1959b, 1966).

197 See Phillips (1966). A recent article by Clair C. Patterson (1971) presents a strong argument against the Trans-Pacific diffusion of metallurgical techniques (casting, gilding, etc.) to Peru from Asia as Heine-Geldern (1954) had argued. See also Riley *et al.* eds. (1971) for articles presenting both sides of the issue.

198 Meggers, Evans, and Estrada (1965); (Willey, 1966–71, see Vol. II, Ch. 5).

199 See Rowe (1966) for a strong negative reaction.

200 Ekholm (1964); Ford (1969).

201 Willey (1966–71, Vol. II, Ch. 5).

202 Kroeber (1944).

203 Willey (1945).

204 Willey (1948).

205 See Parsons (1957) and Meggers and Evans (1961) for some specific applications; see also Willey and Phillips (1958, pp. 29–34) and Rouse (1955).

206 Willey (1945, p. 53).

207 Gladwin and Gladwin (1934).

208 Goggin (1949).

209 Kirchhoff (1943).

210 W. C. Bennett (1948).

211 Martin and Rinaldo (1951).

212 Rouse (1954).

213 See also Rouse (1957).

214 Willey and Phillips (1955, 1958); R. H. Thompson, ed. (1956); Caldwell (1958); Willey (1966–71).

215 Caldwell (1964). The British archaeologist, Christopher Hawkes (1954), has defined what he calls a 'diffusion sphere' which is similar to the interaction sphere although not quite the same.

216 The 'Southeastern Ceremonial Complex' or 'Southern Cult' data of Waring and Holder (1945) might be subsumed under the interaction sphere concept although the horizon style definition might also apply.

217 See our comments in Chapter One. See also Harris (1968, p. 28) and Clarke (1970, pp. 4–14), as well as Morgan (1877).

218 Steward (1938).

219 Steward (for examples, 1948a, 1949a).

220 The later book by Steward and Faron (1959), which was based on the *Handbook*, expresses this even more clearly.

221 Steward (1949a).

222 Steward (1948b).

223 See also Willey (1950).

224 Published in Tax, *et al.*, eds. (1953, p. 247).

225 Kidder (1924, 1927).

226 Ford and Willey (1941).

227 See Strong (1948); Willey (1948); Larco Hoyle (1948); Bennett and Bird (1949); Bushnell (1956). The Uhle-Kroeber Peruvian 'horizon' scheme, which we have described in Chapter Four, did not have these stage qualities; and Rowe's (1960) chronology for the area derives directly from theirs.

228 Armillas (1948).

229 Willey and Phillips (1958).

230 See Swanson (1959) and Miller (1959).

231 For examples, McKern (1956) and Evans and Meggers (1958).

232 Hester (1962) and Rouse (1964c).

Chapter Six

1 See Harris (1968) for extended discussion and references.
2 See White (1949) for a collection of writings by him up to that date.
3 Willey and Phillips (1958, p. 200).
4 Willey and Phillips (1958, pp. 70–1).
5 See South (1955) and Haag (1959) for criticism of Willey and Phillips (and others) on this count.
6 Meggers (1955, p. 121).
7 Meggers (1955, p. 129).
8 Meggers, ed. (1956).
9 For example, Ford (1962).
10 Quimby (1960a).
11 Haag (1959).
12 Willey (1960b); see also Willey's (1961) review of Sahlins and Service (1960) in which he questions the nature of causality in evolution as expressed by the writers of the essays.
13 Braidwood (1948, 1952).
14 Childe (1934, 1936, 1943) and, especially, his *Social Evolution* (1951). Childe is best known to American archaeologists as an evolutionist although much of his writing was in a vein of modified diffusionism.
15 Braidwood (1959).
16 R. McC. Adams (1960).
17 Wittfogel (1957).
18 R. McC. Adams (1966).
19 Steward (1966).
20 See the exchange between Opler (1961) and Meggers (1961).
21 See, especially, White (1959).
22 Harris (1968).
23 Binford (1968a, p. 27).
24 Binford and Binford, eds. (1968).
25 W. W. Taylor (1969, p. 383).
26 Binford (1968a, p. 27).
27 Clarke (1968, see Ch. 2).
28 Caldwell (1959); see Wissler (1917) for an earlier use of the term, 'new archaeology.'
29 Binford (1962, 1963, 1964, 1965, 1967a, 1967b, 1968a, 1968b, 1968c, 1968d).
30 Binford received graduate anthropological-archaeological training at the University of Michigan and has

taught, subsequently, at the Universities of Chicago, California at Santa Barbara, California at Los Angeles, and New Mexico.
31 H. G. Johnson (1971).
32 Binford (1962).
33 Binford (1962, p. 218).
34 Hardesty (1971); see also Vayda and Rappaport (1968).
35 Sanders (1956); MacNeish (1958, 1964a); MacNeish (1967).
36 Yarnell (1964); Cleland (1966); also McPherron (1967). The overall project was organized by James B. Griffin.
37 For preliminary reports, see Flannery, Kirkby, Kirkby, and Williams (1967); Flannery (1968b); Flannery and Schoenwetter (1970).
38 See especially Flannery (1968a); see also Flannery (1965, 1967a, 1967b, 1969); Coe and Flannery (1964, 1967); and Hole, Flannery, and Neely (1968).
39 Tansley (1935).
40 Odum (1953); a new edition (Odum 1971) has recently appeared.
41 Bates (1953).
42 See F. C. Evans (1956); also Odum (1963, pp. 3–4) and Boughey (1971).
43 See Vayda and Rappaport (1968, pp. 493–4); also Trigger (1971) on the importance of open systems analysis. Rappaport's New Guinea study (1968), is the best social-anthropological example of ecosystem analysis to which the archaeologist can look for analogies to his own research.
44 Bertalanffy (1950); Wiener (1954, 1961); also the articles in Buckley, ed. (1968) and Emery, ed. (1969).
45 Flannery (1968a); see also Doran (1970) for an introduction to systems theory and archaeology.
46 Clarke (1968); see also comments by Rouse (1970), Mayer-Oakes (1970), Moberg (1970), and Hymes (1970), along with the reply by Clarke (1970). Another development with British antecedents, is the growing use of locational analysis (see Haggett, 1965).

47 Hole and Heizer (1966, 1969).
48 Binford (1965).
49 See Caldwell (1964); also see Struever (1968a) on 'activity areas.'
50 Cowgill (1967a, 1967b, 1968); Tugby (1969).
51 See Ascher and Ascher (1963); Kuzara, Mead, and Dixon (1966); Hole and Shaw (1967); Cowgill (1968); Hodson (1969, 1970); Dunnell (1970); Gelfand (1971); also Freeman and Brown (1964); Deetz (1965); Hill (1966); Longacre (1968), among others. Longacre (1970) contains a general discussion of the subject.
52 Binford (1962).
53 See Doran (1970).
54 K. V. Flannery, lecture at Harvard University, May 1971.
55 Longacre (1970, p. 132).
56 See the cautionary article by Brothwell (1969).
57 See, especially, Binford (1968a, 1968d); Fritz and Plog (1970); Spaulding (1968).
58 Spaulding (1968, p. 34).
59 See Hempel (1966).
60 See Dray (1964).
61 See, for example, Spaulding (1968).
62 Dray (1957, 1964) and Popper (1961); see also The essays in Gardiner, ed. (1958).
63 Spaulding (1968, p. 36).
64 Meehan (1968, pp. 2–3).
65 Meehan (1968, p. 3).
66 Kuhn (1962).
67 Trigger (1970).
68 As seems to be the position in a new book, *Explanation in Archaeology, An Explicitly Scientific Approach*, by Watson, LeBlanc, and Redman (1971).
69 Binford (1968d).
70 Sabloff and Willey (1967).
71 We wish to acknowledge the critical aid of C. C. Lamberg-Karlovsky in the preparation of this section, although the views expressed here are our own and not necessarily his.
72 For a description of the Old Copper Culture see Wittry and Ritzenthaler (1956).

73 Binford (1962, p. 224).
74 Sears (1961).
75 Binford (1971).
76 Brown, ed. (1971).
77 Larson (1971).
78 Peebles (1971).
79 Brown (1971).
80 Rathje (1970).
81 Rathje (1971, Ms.).
82 Deetz's (1960) dissertation, thus, precedes Binford's 1962 article, and Deetz deserves credit as an independent pioneer of 'new archaeology' apart from the University of Chicago group led by Binford. See Deetz (1965, 1968a).
83 See, especially, Deetz (1968a).
84 Hill (1968, p. 120; see also 1966). Hill, Longacre, and Leone all have worked in Southwestern archaeology with Paul S. Martin who, as we have noted, was one of the first to express dissatisfactions with traditional archaeology.
85 Longacre (1968; see also 1964, 1966).
86 Whallon (1968); see Allen and Richardson (1971) for a critical review of the use of such concepts as the 'matrilocal residence' and 'clans' by the 'new archaeologists.'
87 Leone (1968).
88 Sanders (1956).
89 Sanders (1962, 1965).
90 Sanders *et al.* (1970).
91 Gamio (1922).
92 Sanders (1965, p. 193).
93 MacNeish (1958).
94 MacNeish (1964a; also 1967).

95 Coe and Flannery (1964, 1967).
96 Flannery (1968a).
97 Flannery (1968a, p. 79).
98 Struever (1968a).
99 Zubrow (1971).
100 Binford (1968c).
101 See, for instance, Sanders (1968) or Sanders and Price (1968).
102 See, for instance, M.D. Coe (1968a, 1968b) or Willey (1962, 1971).
103 These ideas have been developed in various ways with Olmec and Maya data by Flannery (1968b); Rathje (1971); and M.C. Webb (1964). See also Willey and Shimkin (1971).
104 Millon (see especially the summary articles, 1967, 1970).
105 A 'Society for Historical Archaeology,' with a journal, *Historical Archaeology*, was founded in the United States in 1967.
106 See, for example Noel Hume (1969) or the majority of the articles in the above-mentioned journal.
107 Deetz and Dethlefsen (1965, 1971) and Deetz (1966).
108 Deetz (1968b); see also Schuyler (1970).
109 See Willey in Tax, *et al.*, eds. (1953, p. 252) for these definitions. Ascher (1961) has referred to 'general comparative' analogy as the 'new analogy,' and to 'specific historical' analogy as the 'old analogy.' Actually, 'general comparative' analogy may be

the older of the two – at least with reference to many 19th century studies with their strong evolutionary (and universalistic) orientations.
110 Chang (1967b).
111 Binford (1967a); see also Binford's (1968a) later observations on the subject.
112 See his use of ethnographic analogy in the context of Mississippi Valley archaeology (Binford, 1967b).
113 K.M. Anderson (1969).
114 See, for example, Chang (1958) and, especially (1967a) for this archaeologist's concern with process.
115 Binford (1967a, 1968a).
116 K.M. Anderson (1969).
117 Easton (1965, p. xiii).
118 Struever (1968b); Lamberg-Karlovsky (1970).
119 R.McC. Adams (1971); also see the resolutions against illicit antiquities traffic which were approved by the Society for American Archaeology in May 1971, and published in *American Antiquity*, Vol. 36, No. 3, pp. 253–4.
120 McGimsey (1971).
121 This is not to say that all American archaeologists are 'sold' on the 'new archaeology.' See Bayard (1969) for a more or less total rejection of it. Swartz (1967) offers a more temperate critique, by implication, in a well balanced presentation of archaeological objectives.
122 A most promising article, in this regard, is one by Kushner (1970).

Photographic Acknowledgments

The photographs used for the undermentioned illustrations are reproduced by courtesy of:

American Museum of Natural History, 107; America Foundation, Dragoon, Arizona, 104; Arizona State Museum, 116; Michael D. Coe, 109; William R. Coe, 113; D.L. De Jarnette, 95, 96; Alfred Guthe, 98; Robert F. Heizer, 110; J.D. Jennings, 115; M.A.S.C.A., University Museum, University of Pennsylvania, 106; B.J. Meggers and C. Evans, 118; René Millon, 111; Museum für Völkerkunde und Vorgeschichte, Hamburg, 62, 82; National Anthropological Archives, Smithsonian Institution, 17, 18, 25, 26, 27, 39; Peabody Museum, Harvard University, 30, 31, 32, 34, 35, 37, 38, 43, 53, 54, 56, 57, 58, 59, 60, 83, 90, 93, 112; Servicio Aerofotográfico Nacional, Peru, 105; Smithsonian Institution, 92; Stuart Struever, 121; E.N. Wilmsen, 91.

Bibliography

ABBOT, CHARLES C. 'On the Discovery of Supposed Paleolithic Implements from the Glacial Drift in the Valley of the Delaware River, near Trenton, New Jersey,' *Tenth Annual Report, Trustees of the Peabody Museum*, vol. 2, 30–43. Cambridge, Mass., 1877.

ADAIR, JAMES. *The History of the American Indian, particularly those nations adjoining to the Mississippi, east and west Florida, Georgia, South and North Carolina, and Virginia; containing an account of their origins, language, manners . . . and other particulars sufficient to render it a complete Indian system . . . also an appendix . . . with a new map of the country referred to in the history.* London, 1775.

ADAMS, RICHARD E. W. 'Manuel Gamio and Stratigraphic Excavation,' *American Antiquity*, vol. 26, no. 1, 99. Salt Lake City, 1960.

ADAMS, ROBERT McC. 'Some Hypotheses on the Development of Early Civilizations,' *American Antiquity*, vol. 21, no. 3, 227–32. Salt Lake City, 1956.

'The Evolutionary Process in Early Civilizations,' in *Evolution After Darwin*, Sol Tax, ed., vol. 2, 153–68. Chicago, 1960.

The Evolution of Urban Society. Early Mesopotamia and Prehispanic Mexico. Chicago, 1966.

Editorial, 'Illicit International Traffic in Antiquities,' *American Antiquity*, vol. 36, no. 1, ii–iii. Salt Lake City, 1971.

AITKEN, MÁRTIN J. 'Magnetic Location,' in *Science in Archaeology*, revised edition, D. Brothwell and E. Higgs, eds., 681–94. London and New York, 1969.

ALCINA FRANCH, J. *Manual de Arqueología Americana.* Madrid, 1965.

ALLEN, WILLIAM L. and RICHARDSON, JAMES B. III. 'The Reconstruction of Kinship from Archaeological Data: the concepts, methods, and the feasibility,' *American Antiquity*, vol. 36, no. 1, 41–53. Salt Lake City, 1971.

ALLIBONE, T. E., *The Impact of the Natural Sciences on Archaeology*, Joint Symposium of the Royal Society and British Academy. London, 1970.

ALTSCHULER, MILTON. 'On the Environmental Limitations of Mayan Cultural Development,' *Southwestern Journal of Anthropology*, vol. 14, no. 2, 189–98. Albuquerque, 1958.

AMBROSETTI, JUAN B. 'La Antigua Ciudad de Quilmes (Valle Calchaqui),' *Boletín Instituto Geografía Argentino*, vol. 17, 33–70. Buenos Aires, 1897.

'El Sepulcro de "La Paya" ultimamente descubierto en los Valles Calchaquíes (Provincia de Salta),' *Arqueología Argentina*, vol. 1, ser. 3, 119–48. Buenos Aires, 1902.

'Exploraciones Arqueológicas en la Pampa Grande (Prov. de Salta),' *Revista de la Universidad de Buenos Aires*, vol. 6, no. 1. Buenos Aires, 1906.

'Exploraciones Arqueológicas en la Ciudad Prehistórica de "La Paya" (Valle Calchaquí, Provincia de Salta),' *Revista de la Universidad de Buenos Aires*, vol. 8, no. 3. Buenos Aires, 1908.

AMEGHINO, FLORENTINO. 'Une Nouvelle Industrie Lithique,' *Anales del Museo Nacional de Buenos Aires*, vol. 13, ser. 3, 189–204. Buenos Aires, 1911.

La Antiguedad de los Hombres en El Plata, Obras Completas y Correspondencia de Florentino Ameghino, vol. 3. La Plata, 1915.

ANDERSON, DOUGLAS D. 'A Stone Age Campsite at the Gateway to America,' *Scientific American*, vol. 218, no. 6, 24–33. New York, 1968.

'Akmak: an early archaeological assemblage from Onion Portage, Northwest Alaska,' *Acta Arctica*, vol. 16. Copenhagen, 1970.

ANDERSON, KEITH M. 'Ethnographic Analogy and Archaeological Interpretation,' *Science*, vol. 163, no. 3863, 133–8. Washington, D.C., 1969.

APARICIO, FRANCISCO DE. 'The Archaeology of the Parana River,' in *Handbook of South American Indians*, Julian H. Steward, ed., vol. 3, 57–67, Bureau of American Ethnology, Bulletin 143. Washington, D.C., 1948.

ARMILLAS, PEDRO. 'A Sequence of Cultural Development in Meso-America,' in *A Reappraisal of Peruvian Archaeology*, W. C. Bennett, ed., Society for American Archaeology, Memoir 4, 105–12. Menasha, 1948.

'Tecnología, Formaciones Socio-económicas y Religión en Mesoamérica,' in *The Civilizations of Ancient America*, Sol Tax, ed., vol. 1, 19–30. Chicago, 1951.

'Cronología y Periodificación de la Historia de la America Precolumbina,' *Journal of World History*, vol. 3, no. 2, 463–503. Paris, 1956.

ARMILLAS, PEDRO, PALERM, ANGEL, and WOLF, ERIC R. 'A Small Irrigation System in the Valley of Teotihuacan,' *American Antiquity*, vol. 21, no. 4, 396–99. Salt Lake City, 1956.

ASCHER, ROBERT. 'Analogy in Archaeological Interpretation,' *Southwestern Journal of Anthropology*, vol. 17, no. 4, 317–25. Albuquerque, 1961.

ASCHER, MARCIA and ASCHER, ROBERT. 'Chronological Ordering by Computer,' *American Anthropologist*, vol. 65, no. 5, 1045–52. Menasha, 1963.

ATWATER, CALEB. 'Description of the Antiquities Discovered in the State of Ohio and Other Western States,' *Transactions and Collections of the American Antiquarian Society*, vol. 1, 105–267. Worcester, 1820.

d'AZEVEDO, WARREN et al., eds. *The Current Status of Anthropological Research in the Great Basin: 1964*, Desert Research Institute, Social Sciences and Humanities Publications, no. 1. Reno, 1966.

BANCROFT, HUBERT H. *The Native Races.* San Francisco, 1882.

BANDELIER, ADOLPH F. 'On the Art of War and Mode of Warfare of the Ancient Mexicans,' *Report of the Peabody Museum*, vol. 2, 95–161. Cambridge, 1877.

'On the Tenure and Distribution of Lands, and the Customs with respect to Inheritance, Among the Ancient Mexicans,' *Eleventh Report of the Peabody*

Museum, 385–448. Cambridge, Mass., 1878.

'On the Social Organization and Mode of Government of the Ancient Mexicans,' *Twelfth Report of the Peabody Museum*, vol. 2, 557–669. Cambridge, Mass., 1880.

'Report on the Ruins of the Pueblo of Pecos,' *Papers of the Archaeological Institute of America*, America Series, vol. 1, 37–133. London, 1881.

'Final Report of Investigations Among the Indians of the Southwestern United States,' *Papers of the Archaeological Institute of America*, vol. 4, 1–591. Cambridge, Mass., 1892.

The Islands of Titicaca and Koati. New York, 1910.

BANDI, HANS-GEORG. *Eskimo Prehistory*, translated by Ann E. Keep, Studies in Northern Peoples No. 2, Univ. of Alaska Press, College, Alaska, 1969.

BANNISTER, BRYANT. 'Dendrochronology,' in *Science in Archaeology*, D. Brothwell and E. Higgs, eds. 161–76. London and New York, 1963.

'Dendrochronology,' in *Science in Archaeology*, revised edition, D. Brothwell and E. Higgs, eds., 191–205. London and New York, 1969.

BARTH, FREDRIK. 'Cultural Development in Southern South America: Yahgan and Alakaluf vs. Ona and Tehuelche,' *Acta Americana*, vol. 6, 192–9. Mexico, D.F., 1948.

'Ecologic Adaptation and Cultural Change in Archaeology,' *American Antiquity*, vol. 15, no. 4, 338–9. Menasha, 1950.

BARTON, BENJAMIN S. *Observations on Some Parts of Natural History*. London, 1787.

New Views of the Origin of the Tribes and Nations of America. Philadelphia, 1797.

Fragments of the Natural History of Pennsylvania, Part I. Philadelphia, 1799.

BARTRAM, WILLIAM. *Travels Through North and South Carolina, Georgia, east and west Florida, the Cherokee Country, the Extensive Territories of the Muscogulges or Creek Confederacy and the Country of the Chactaws*. Philadelphia, 1791.

BASTIAN, ADOLPH. 'Die Monumente in Santa Lucia Cotzumalhuapa,' *Zeitschrift für Ethnologie*, vol. 8, 322–6, 403–4. Berlin, 1876.

BATES, MARSTON. 'Human Ecology,' in *Anthropology Today*, prepared under the Chairmanship of A.L. Kroeber, 700–13. Chicago, 1953.

BATRES, LEOPOLDO. *Teotihuacán ó la Ciudad Sagrada de los Tolteca*. Mexico, D.F., 1906.

BAUDEZ, CLAUDE F. 'Cultural Development in Lower Central America,' in *Aboriginal Cultural Development in Latin America: an interpretative review*, B.J. Meggers and C. Evans, eds., 45–54. Washington, D.C., 1963.

Central America, Archaeologia Mundi. Geneva and London, 1970.

BAYARD, DONN T. 'Science, Theory, and Reality in the "New Archaeology",' *American Antiquity*, vol. 34, no. 4, 376–84. Salt Lake City, 1969.

BEALS, RALPH L. 'Father Acosta on the First Peopling of the New World,' *American Antiquity*, vol. 23, no. 2, 182–3. Salt Lake City, 1957.

BELL, ROBERT E. and BAERREIS, DAVID A. 'A Survey of Oklahoma Archaeology,' *Bulletin of the Texas Archaeological and Paleontological Society*, vol. 22, 7–100. Lubbock, 1951.

BELMONT, JOHN S. and WILLIAMS, STEPHEN. *The Foundations of American Archaeology*. Mimeographed, Cambridge, Mass., 1965.

BENNETT, JOHN W. 'Recent Developments in the Functional Interpretation of Archaeological Data,' *American Antiquity*, vol. 9, no. 2, 208–19. Menasha, 1943.

'Middle American Influences on Cultures of the Southeastern United States,' *Acta Americana*, vol. 2, 25–50. Washington, D.C., 1944a.

'The Interaction of Culture and Environment in the Smaller Societies,' *American Anthropologist*, vol. 46, no. 4, 461–78. Menasha, 1944b.

'Empiricist and Experimental Trends in Eastern Archaeology,' *American Antiquity*, vol. 11, no 3, 198–200. Menasha, 1946.

BENNETT, WENDELL. C. 'Excavations at Tiahuanaco,' *Anthropological Papers of the American Museum of Natural History*, vol. 34, pt. 3, 359–494. New York, 1934.

'Excavations in Bolivia,' *Anthropological Papers of the American Museum of Natural History*, vol. 35, pt. 4, 329–507. New York, 1936.

'Archaeology of the North Coast of Peru,' *Anthropological Papers of the American Museum of Natural History*, vol. 37, pt. 1, 1–153. New York, 1939.

'Interpretations of Andean Archaeology,' *Transactions of the New York Academy of Sciences*, series 2, vol. 7, 95–9. New York, 1945.

'The Peruvian Co-tradition,' in *A Reappraisal of Peruvian Archaeology*, W.C. Bennett, ed., Society for American Archaeology, Memoir 4, 1–7. Menasha, 1948.

The Gallinazo Group, Virú Valley, Peru, Yale University Publications in Anthropology, no. 43. New Haven, 1950.

BENNETT, WENDELL C. and BIRD, JUNIUS B. *Andean Culture History*, American Museum of Natural History Handbook Series, no. 15. New York, 1949.

BENNETT, WENDELL C., BLEILER, EVERETT F., and SOMMER, FRANK H. *Northwest Argentine Archaeology*, Yale University Publications in Anthropology, no. 38. New Haven, 1948.

BERLIN, HEINRICH. 'El Glifo "emblema" en las Inscripciones Mayas,' *Journal de la Société des Américanistes*, vol. 47, 111–19. Paris, 1958.

BERNAL, IGNACIO. 'Evolución y Alcance de las Culturas Mesoamericanas,' in *Esplendor del México Antiguo*, R. Noriega, C. Cook de Leonard, and J.R. Moctezuma, eds., vol. 1, 97–126. Mexico, D.F., 1959.

The Olmec World, translated by Doris Heyden and Fernando Horcasitas. Berkeley and Los Angeles, 1969.

BERTALANFFY, LUDWIG VON. 'The Theory of Open Systems in Physics and Biology,' *Science*, vol. 111, 23–9. Lancaster, 1950.

BIBBY, GEOFFREY. *The Testimony of the Spade*. New York, 1956.

BINFORD, LEWIS R. 'Archaeology as Anthropology,' *American Antiquity*, vol. 28, no. 2, 217–25. Salt Lake City, 1962.

'"Red Ochre" Caches from the Michigan Area: a possible case of cultural drift,' *Southwestern Journal of Anthropology*, vol. 19, no. 1, 89–108. Albuquerque, 1963.

'A Consideration of Archaeological Research Design,' *American Antiquity*, vol. 29, no. 4, 425–41. Salt Lake City, 1964.

'Archaeological Systematics and the Study of Cultural Process,' *American Antiquity*, vol. 31, no. 2, 203–10. Salt Lake City, 1965.

'Comment on K.C. Chang's "Major Aspects of the Interrelationship of Archaeology and Ethnology",' *Current Anthropology*, vol. 8, no. 3, 234–5. Chicago, 1967a.

'Smudge Pits and Hide Smoking: the use of analogy in archaeological Reasoning,' *American Antiquity*, vol. 32, no. 1–13. Salt Lake City, 1967b.

'Archaeological Perspectives,' in *New Perspectives in Archaeology*, S.R. Binford and L.R. Binford, eds., 5–33. Chicago, 1968a.

'Methodological Considerations of the Archaeological Use of Ethnographic Data,' in *Man the Hunter*, R.B. Lee and I. Devore, eds., 268–73. Chicago, 1968b.

'Post-Pleistocene Adaptations,' in *New Perspectives in Archaeology*, S.R. Binford and L.R. Binford, eds., 313–41. Chicago, 1968c.

'Some Comments on Historical Versus Processual Archaeology,' *Southwestern Journal of Anthropology*, vol. 24, no. 3, 267–75. Albuquerque, 1968d.

'Mortuary Practices: Their Study and Potential,' in *Approaches to the Social Dimensions of Mortuary Practices*, J.A. Brown, ed., Society for American Archaeology, Memoir 25, 58–67. Washington, D.C., 1971.

BINFORD, SALLY R. and BINFORD, LEWIS R., eds. *New Perspectives in Archaeology*. Chicago, 1968.

BIRD, JUNIUS B. 'Antiquity and Migrations of the Early Inhabitants of Patagonia,' *The Geographical Review*, vol. 28, no. 2, 250–75. New York, 1938.

'Excavations in Northern Chile,' *Anthropological Papers of the American Museum of Natural History*, vol. 38, pt. 4a, 171–318. New York, 1943.

'The Cultural Sequence of the North Chilean Coast,' *Handbook of South American Indians*, Julian H. Steward, ed., vol. 2, 587–94, Bureau of American Ethnology, Bull. 143. Washington, D.C., 1946a.

'The Archaeology of Patagonia,' *Handbook of South American Indians*, Julian H. Steward, ed., vol. 1, 17–24, Bureau of American Ethnology, Bulletin 143. Washington, D.C., 1946b.

'Preceramic Cultures in Chicama and Virú,' in *A Reappraisal of Peruvian Archaeology*, W.C. Bennett, ed., 21–8, Society for American Archaeology, Memoir 4. Menasha, 1948.

BIRKET-SMITH, KAJ. *The Eskimos*. London, 1936.

BLOM, FRANS F. 'The Maya Ball-game *pok-ta-pok*,. *Middle American Research Institute*, Publication 4, no. 13, 485–530. New Orleans, 1932.

BOAS, FRANZ. 'Archaeological Investigations in the Valley of Mexico by the International School, 1911–12,' *18th International Congress of Americanists*, pt. 1, 176–9. London, 1913.

Race, Language, and Culture. New York, 1940.

BOLLAERT, WILLIAM. *Antiquarian, Ethnological, and Other Researches in New Granada, Equador, Peru, and Chile*. London, 1860.

BOMAN, ERIC. *Antiquités de la Région Andine de la République Argentine et du Désert d'Atacama*. Paris, 1908.

BORDEN, CHARLES E. 'Fraser River Archaeological Project, Progress Report, April 20, 1961,' *Anthropology Papers of the National Museum of Canada*, no. 1, 1–6. Ottawa, 1961.

BÓRMIDA, MARCELO. 'Arqueología de las Altas Cotas de La Costa Norpatagónica,' *37th International Congress of Americanists*, vol. 3, 345–74. Buenos Aires, 1968.

BOSCH-GIMPERA, PEDRO. *L'America Precolombiana. Nuova Storia Universale Dei Popoli e Delle Civilta*, vol. 7. Torino, 1971.

BOUGHEY, A.S. *Man and Environment; an introduction to human ecology and evolution*. New York, 1971.

BRACKENRIDGE, HENRY M. 'On the Population and Tumuli of the Aborigines of North America,' in a letter from H.M. Brackenridge, Esq. to Thomas Jefferson, read October 1. Baton Rouge, 1813.

BRAIDWOOD, ROBERT J. *Prehistoric Man*, Chicago Natural History Museum Popular Series in Anthropology, no. 37. Chicago, 1948.

The Near East and the Foundations for Civilization, Condon Lectures, Oregon State System for Higher Education. Eugene, 1952.

'Archaeology and the Evolutionary Theory,' *Evolution and Anthropology: a centennial appraisal*, 76–89. Washington, D.C., 1959.

BRAIDWOOD, ROBERT J. and WILLEY, GORDON R., eds. *Courses Toward Urban Life*, Viking Fund Publications in Anthropology, no. 32. Chicago, 1962.

BRAINERD, GEORGE W. 'The Place of Chronological Ordering in Archaeological Analysis,' *American Antiquity*, vol. 16, no. 4, 301–13. Salt Lake City, 1951.

BREW, JOHN O. 'Mexican Influence upon the Indian Cultures of the Southwestern United States in the Sixteenth and Seventeenth Centuries,' in *The Maya and Their Neighbors*, C.L. Hay et al., eds., 341–8. New York, 1940.

'The Uses and Abuses of Taxonomy,' *Archaeology of Alkali Ridge, Southeastern Utah*, Papers of the Peabody Museum, vol. 21, 44–66. Cambridge, Mass., 1946.

One Hundred Years of Anthropology, John O. Brew, ed. Cambridge, Mass., 1968.

BRILL, ROBERT H., ed. *Science and Archaeology*. Cambridge, Mass., 1971.

BRINTON, DANIEL G. *The Maya Chronicles*, Brinton's Library of Aboriginal American Literature, no. 1. Philadelphia, 1882.

The Annals of the Cakchiquels, Brinton's Library of Aboriginal American Literature, no. 6. Philadelphia, 1885.

BROTHWELL, DON R. 'Stones, Pots and People,' in *Science in Archaeology*, D. Brothwell and E. Higgs, eds., 669–80. London and New York, 1969.

BROTHWELL, DON R. AND HIGGS, E., eds. *Science in Archaeology*, revised edition. London and New York, 1969.

BROWN, J. A. 'The Dimensions of Status in Burials at Spiro,' in *Approaches to the Social Dimensions of Mortuary Practices*, J.A. Brown, ed., Society for

American Archaeology, Memoir 25, 92–112. Washington, D.C., 1971.

Approaches to the Social Dimensions of Mortuary Practices, J.A. Brown, ed., Society for American Archaeology, Memoir 25. Washington, D.C., 1971.

BRYAN, KIRK, and RAY, LOUIS R. *Geologic Antiquity of the Lindenmeier Site in Colorado,* Smithsonian Institution Miscellaneous Collection, vol. 99, no. 2. Washington, D.C., 1940.

BUCKLEY, WALTER, ed. *Modern Systems Research for the Behavioral Scientist; a sourcebook.* Chicago, 1968.

BULLEN, RIPLEY P. 'S.T. Walker, an early Florida Archaeologist,' *Florida Anthropologist,* vol. 4, 46–9. Gainesville, 1951.

BUSHNELL, GEOFFREY H. *Peru,* Ancient Peoples and Places Series, G. Daniel, ed. 2nd ed., London and New York, 1963.

BUSHNELL, GEOFFREY H. and McBURNEY, C.B.M. 'New World Origins Seen from the Old World,' *Antiquity,* vol. 33, 93–101. London, 1959.

BUTLER, B. ROBERT. *The Old Cordilleran Culture in the Pacific Northwest,* Occasional Papers of the Idaho State University Museum, no. 5. Pocatello, 1961.

CALDWELL, JOSEPH R. *Trend and Tradition in the Prehistory of the Eastern United States,* Illinois State Museum Scientific Papers, vol. 10, and the American Anthropological Association, Memoir 88. Springfield and Menasha, 1958.

'The New American Archaeology,' *Science,* vol. 129, no. 3345, 303–7. Lancaster, 1959.

'Interaction Spheres in Prehistory,' in *Hopewellian Studies,* J.R. Caldwell and R.L. Hall, eds., Illinois State Museum Scientific Papers, vol. 12, 133–43. Springfield, 1965.

CANALS FRAU, SALVADOR. *Prehistoria de América.* Buenos Aires, 1950.

Las Civilizaciones Prehispánicas de América. Buenos Aires, 1955.

CARR, ROBERT F. and HAZARD, JAMES E. *Map of the Ruins of Tikal, El Peten, Guatemala,* University of Pennsylvania Museum Monographs, Tikal Report no. 11. Philadelphia, 1961.

CARVER, JONATHAN. *Travels through the Interior Parts of North America in the Years 1766, 1767, and 1768.* Dublin, 1779.

CASANOVA, EDUARDO. 'The Cultures of the Puna and the Quebrada of Humuhuaca,' in *Handbook of South American Indians,* Julian H. Steward, ed., vol. 2, 619–32, Bureau of American Ethnology, Bulletin 143. Washington, D.C., 1946.

CASAS, BARTOLOMÉ DE LAS. *Apologética Historia de las Indias,* M. Serrano y Sanz, ed. Madrid, 1909.

Historia de las Indias, Gonzalo de Raparaz, ed., 3 vols. Madrid, 1927.

Apologética Historia Sumaria, edition prepared by Edmundo O'Gorman. Madrid, 1967.

CASO, ALFONSO. *Exploraciones en Oaxaca, Quinta y Sexta Temporadas, 1936–1937,* Pan American Institute of Geography and History, Publication 34. Tacubaya, 1938.

'Calendario y Escritura de las Antiguas Culturas de Monte Alban,' in *Obras Completas de Miguel Othón de Mendizábal.* Mexico, D.F., 1946.

CASTELNAU, FRANCIS DE. *Expédition dans les Parties Centrales de l'Amérique du Sud, Troisième Partie: Antiquités des Incas et Autres Peuples Anciens.* Paris, 1854.

CATHERWOOD, FREDERICK. *Views of Ancient Monuments in Central America, Chiapas, and Yucatan.* London, 1844.

CHANG, KWANG-CHIH. 'Study of the Neolithic Social Grouping: Examples from the New World,' *American Anthropologist,* vol. 60, no. 2, 298–334. Menasha, 1958.

Rethinking Archaeology. New York, 1967a.

'Major Aspects of the Interrelationship of Archaeology and Ethnology,' *Current Anthropology,* vol. 8, no. 3, 227–43. Chicago, 1967b.

Settlement Archaeology, K.C. Chang, ed. Palo Alto, 1968.

'Toward a Science of Prehistoric Society,' in *Settlement Archaeology,* K.C. Chang, ed., 1–9. Palo Alto, 1968.

CHARD, CHESTER S. 'The Old World Roots: review and speculations,' *University of Alaska Anthropological Papers,* vol. 10, no. 2, 115–21. College, 1963.

CHARNAY, DÉSIRÉ. *The Ancient Cities of the New World.* New York, 1887.

CHILDE, V. GORDON. *The Most Ancient East.* London, 1934.

Man Makes Himself. London, 1936.

What Happened in History. London and New York, 1943.

Social Evolution. London, 1951.

CIGLIANO, E.M. *El Ampajanguense,* Instituto de Antropologia, Universidad Nacional de Litoral. Rosario, 1962.

CLARK, J. GRAHAME D. *The Mesolithic Settlement of Northern Europe.* Cambridge, 1936.

Archaeology and Society. London, 1939.

Prehistoric England. London, 1940.

Prehistoric Europe; the Economic Basis. London, 1952, reprinted 1972.

'The Economic Approach to Prehistory,' *Proceedings of the British Academy,* vol. 39, 215–38. London, 1953.

Excavations at Star Carr. Cambridge, 1954.

CLARKE, DAVID L. *Analytical Archaeology.* London, 1968.

'Reply to the comments on *Analytical Archaeology,*' *Norwegian Archaeological Review,* vol. 34, nos. 3–4, 25–34. Oslo, 1970.

CLAVIJERO, FRANCISCO J. *The History of Mexico,* translated by Charles Cullen. Philadelphia, 1817.

CLELAND, CHARLES E. *The Prehistoric Animal Ecology and Ethnology of the Upper Great Lakes Region,* University of Michigan Museum Anthropological Papers, no. 29. Ann Arbor, 1966.

CLEWLOW, C. WILLIAM, and HRDLIČKA, ALEŠ. 'Some Thoughts on the Background of Early Man,' *Kroeber Anthropological Society Papers,* vol. 42, 26–46. Berkeley, 1970.

CLINTON, DE WITT. *A Memoir on the Antiquities of the Western Parts of the State of New York.* Albany, 1820.

COE, JOFFRE L. *The Formative Cultures of the Carolina Piedmont,* Transactions, American Philosophical Society, vol. 54, pt. 5. Philadelphia, 1964.

COE, MICHAEL D. *Mexico*, Ancient Peoples and Places Series, G. Daniel, ed. London and New York, 1962.

The Maya, Ancient Peoples and Places Series, G. Daniel, ed. London and New York, 1966.

'San Lorenzo and the Olmec Civilization,' *Proceedings, Dumbarton Oaks Conference on the Olmec*, 41–78. Washington, D.C., 1968a.

America's First Civilization. New York, 1968b.

COE, MICHAEL D. and BAUDEZ, CLAUDE F. 'The Zoned Bichrome Period in Northwestern Costa Rica,' *American Antiquity*, vol. 26, no. 4, 505–15. Salt Lake City, 1961.

COE, MICHAEL D. and FLANNERY, KENT V. 'Microenvironments and Mesoamerican Prehistory,' *Science*, vol. 143, no. 3607, 650–4. Washington, D.C., 1964.

Early Cultures and Human Ecology in South Coastal Guatemala, Smithsonian Contributions to Anthropology, vol. 3. Washington, D.C., 1967.

COE, WILLIAM R. 'Environmental Limitation on Maya Culture: a reexamination,' *American Anthropologist*, vol. 59, 328–35. Menasha, 1957.

'Tikal: ten years of study of a Maya ruin in the lowlands of Guatemala,' *Expedition*, vol. 8, no. 1, 50–6. Philadelphia, 1965.

COLE, FAY-COOPER and DEUEL, THORNE. *Rediscovering Illinois*, University of Chicago Publications in Anthropology. Chicago, 1937.

COLLIER, DONALD. *Cultural Chronology and Change as Reflected in the Ceramics of the Virú Valley, Peru*, Chicago Natural History Museum, Fieldiana: Anthropology, vol. 43. Chicago, 1955.

COLLINS, HENRY B., JR. 'Potsherds from Choctaw Village Sites in Mississippi,' *Journal of the Washington Academy of Sciences*, vol. 17, no. 10, 259–63. Washington, D.C., 1927.

Archaeology of St. Lawrence Island, Alaska, Smithsonian Miscellaneous Collections, vol. 96, no. 1. Washington, D.C., 1937.

'Outline of Eskimo Prehistory,' *Essays in Historical Anthropology*, Smithsonian Miscellaneous Collections, vol. 100, 533–92. Washington, D.C., 1940.

COLTON, HAROLD S. and HARGRAVE, LYNDON L. *Handbook of Northern Arizona Pottery Wares*, Museum of Northern Arizona Bulletin, no. 11. Flagstaff, 1937.

COOK, ROBERT M. 'Archaeomagnetism,' in *Science in Archaeology*, revised edition D. Brothwell and E. Higgs, eds., 76–87. London and New York, 1969.

COOK, SHERBURNE F. 'A Reconsideration of Shellmounds with Respect to Population and Nutrition,' *American Antiquity*, vol. 12, no. 1, 50–3. Menasha, 1946.

'Physical Analysis as a Method for Investigating Prehistoric Habitation Sites,' *University of California Archaeological Survey Report*, no. 7, 2–5. Berkeley, 1950.

'Dating Prehistoric Bone by Chemical Analysis,' in *Viking Fund Publications in Anthropology*, no. 28, 223–45. New York, 1960.

COOK, SHERBURNE F. and EZRA-COHN, H.C. 'An Evaluation of the Fluorine Dating Method,' *Southwestern Journal of Anthropology*, vol. 15, no. 3, 276–90. Albuquerque, 1959.

COOK, SHERBURNE F. and HEIZER, ROBERT F. 'Archaeological Dating by Chemical Analysis of Bone,' *Southwestern Journal of Anthropology*, vol. 9, no. 2, 231–8. Albuquerque, 1953.

COVARRUBIAS, MIGUEL. *Indian Art of Mexico and Central America*. New York, 1957.

COWGILL, GEORGE L. 'Computer Applications in Archaeology,' *American Federation of Information Processing Societies Conference Proceedings*, vol. 31, 331–7. Washington, D.C., 1967.

'Computers and Prehistoric Archaeology,' in *Computers in Humanist Research*, E.A. Bowles, ed., 47–56. Englewood Cliffs, 1967.

'Archaeological Applications of Factor, Cluster, and Proximity Analyses,' *American Antiquity*, vol. 33, no. 3, 367–75. Salt Lake City, 1968.

CRAWFORD, O.G.S. 'The Distribution of Early Bronze Age Settlements in Britain,' *Geographical Journal*, vol. 40, no. 3, 183–217. London, 1912.

Man and His Past. London, 1921.

CRESSMAN, LUTHER S. 'Man in the World,' in *Man, Culture, and Society*, H.L. Shapiro, ed., 139–67. New York, 1956.

CRESSMAN, LUTHER S. *et al*. *Cultural Sequences at the Dalles, Oregon*, Transactions, American Philosophical Society, vol. 50, pt. 10. Philadelphia, 1960.

CRONE, GERALD R. *The Discovery of America*. New York, 1969.

CUMMINGS, BYRON. 'The Ancient Inhabitants of the San Juan Valley,' *Bulletin of the University of Utah*, vol. 3, no. 3, pt. 2. Salt Lake City, 1910.

CUSHING, FRANK H. 'A Study of Pueblo Pottery as Illustrative of Zuñi Culture Growth,' *Bureau of American Ethnology, 4th Annual Report*, 467–521. Washington, D.C., 1886.

'Preliminary Notes on the Origin, Working Hypothesis and Primary Researches of the Hemenway . . . Expedition,' *Seventh International Congress of Americanists*, 151–94. Berlin, 1890.

DALL, WILLIAM H. 'On Succession in the Shell-heaps of the Aleutian Islands,' U.S. Department of the Interior, *Contributions to North American Ethnology*, vol. 1, 41–91. Washington, D.C., 1877.

DANIEL, GLYN E. *A Hundred Years of Archaeology*. London, 1950.

The Idea of Prehistory. Harmondsworth, 1964.

The Origins and Growth of Archaeology. Harmondsworth, 1967.

'One Hundred Years of Old World Prehistory, in *One Hundred Years of Anthropology*, J.O. Brew, ed., 57–96. Cambridge, Mass., 1968.

DARRAH, WILLIAM C. *Powell of the Colorado*. Princeton, 1951.

DEBENEDETTI, SALVADOR. 'Exploración Arqueológica en los Cementerios Prehistoricos de la Isla de Tilcara,' *Revista de la Universidad de Buenos Aires*, vol. 6. Buenos Aires, 1910.

'Influencias de la Cultura de Tiahuanaco en la Region del Noroeste Argentino,' *Revista de la Universidad de Buenos Aires*, vol. 17, 326–52. Buenos Aires, 1912.

DEETZ, JAMES J. F. *An Archaeological Approach to Kinship Change in Eighteenth Century Arikara Culture*, Ph.D. dissertation, Harvard University. Cambridge, Mass., 1960.

The Dynamics of Stylistic Change in Arikara Ceramics, University of Illinois Series in Anthropology, no. 4. Urbana, 1965.

'The Inference of Residence and Descent Rules from Archaeological Data,' in *New Perspectives in Archaeology*, S. R. Binford and L. R. Binford, eds., 41–9. Chicago, 1968a.

'Late Man in North America: Archaeology of European Americans,' in *Anthropological Archaeology in the Americas*, B. J. Meggers, ed., 121–30. Washington, D.C., 1968b.

DEETZ, JAMES J. F. and DETHLEFSEN, EDWIN. 'The Doppler Effect and Archaeology: a consideration of the spatial aspects of seriation,' *Southwestern Journal of Anthropology*, vol. 21, 196–206. Albuquerque, 1965.

'Some Social Aspects of New England Colonial Mortuary Art,' in *Approaches to the Social Dimensions of Mortuary Practices*, J. A. Brown, ed., Society for American Archaeology, Memoir 25, 30–8. Washington, D.C., 1971.

DELORIA, VINE, JR. *Custer Died for Your Sins: and an Indian manifesto*. London, 1969.

DEL RIO, ANTONIO, and CABRERA, PAUL F. *Description of the Ruins of an Ancient City, discovered near Palenque, in the Kingdom of Guatemala, in Spanish America;* followed by *Teatro Critico Americano*. London, 1822.

DERBY, ORVILLE A. 'Artificial Mounds of the Island of Marajó, Brazil,' *American Naturalist*, vol. 13, no. 4, 224+. Salem, 1879.

DETHLEFSEN, EDWIN, and DEETZ, JAMES J. F. 'Death's Heads, Cherubs, and Willow Trees: experimental archaeology in Colonial cemeteries,' *American Antiquity*, vol. 31, no. 4, 502–11. Salt Lake City, 1966.

DEUEL, THORNE. 'Basic Cultures of the Mississippi Valley,' *American Anthropologist*, vol. 37, no. 3, 429–45. Menasha, 1935.

DEXTER, RALPH W. 'Contributions of Frederic Ward Putnam to Ohio Archaeology,' *Ohio Journal of Science*, vol. 65, no. 3, 110–17. Columbus, 1965.

'Frederick Ward Putnam and the Development of Museums of Natural History and Anthropology in the United States.' *Curator*, vol. 9, no. 2, 151–5. New York, 1966a.

'Putnam's Problems Popularizing Anthropology,' *American Scientist*, vol. 54, no. 3, 315–32. Easton, 1966b.

DI PESO, CHARLES C. 'Cultural Development in Northern Mexico,' in *Aboriginal Cultural Development in Latin America: an interpretative review*, B. J. Meggers and C. Evans, eds. Smithsonian Miscellaneous Collection, vol. 146, no. 1, 1–16. Washington, D.C., 1963.

DI PESO, CHARLES C. et al. *The Upper Pima of San Cayetano del Tumacacori; an archaeological reconstruction of the Ootam of Pimeria Alta*, Amerind Foundation, Publication 7. Dragoon, 1956.

DISSELHOFF, HANS-DIETRICH. *Geschichte der Altamerikanischen Kulturen*. 2. Revised and enlarged edition. Munich, 1967.

DORAN, JAMES. 'Systems Theory, Computer Simulations, and Archaeology,' *World Archaeology*, vol. 1, no. 3, 289–98. London, 1970.

DORSEY, G. A. 'Archaeological Investigations on the Island of La Plata, Ecuador,' *Field Columbian Museum Anthropological Series*, vol. 2, no. 5. 245–80. Chicago, 1901.

DRAY, WILLIAM H. *Laws and Explanation in History*. Oxford, 1957.

Philosophical Analysis and History, W. H. Dray, ed. New York, 1966.

Philosophy of History. Englewood Cliffs, 1967.

DRUCKER, PHILLIP. *La Venta, Tabasco; a study of Olmec Ceramics and Art*, Bureau of American Ethnology, Bulletin 153. Washington, D.C., 1952.

DRUCKER, PHILLIP, HEIZER, ROBERT F., and SQUIER, ROBERT J. *Excavations at La Venta, Tabasco, 1955*, Bureau of American Ethnology, Bulletin 170. Washington, D.C., 1959.

DUNNELL, ROBERT C. 'Seriation Method and its Evaluation,' *American Antiquity*, vol. 35, no. 3, 305–19. Salt Lake City, 1970.

'Sabloff and Smith's "The Importance of Both Analytic and Taxonomic Classification in the Type-variety System",' *American Antiquity*, vol. 36, no. 1, 115–18. Washington, D.C., 1971

DUPAIX, GUILLAUME. *Antiquités Mexicaines; relation des trois expéditions du Capitaine Dupaix, ordonnées en 1805, 1806, et 1807 . . . par MM. Baradère de St. Priest*. Paris, 1834.

DURÁN, FRAY DIEGO. *The Aztecs; the history of the Indies of New Spain*, translated by Doris Heyden and Fernando Horcasitas. New York, 1964.

EASTON, DAVID. *Framework for Political Analysis*. Englewood Cliffs, 1965.

EKHOLM, GORDON F. 'Transpacific Contacts,' in *Prehistoric Man in the New World*, J. D. Jennings and E. Norbeck, eds., 489–510. Chicago, 1964.

EMPERAIRE, JOSÉ M., LAMING-EMPERAIRE, ANNETTE and REICHLEN, HENRI. 'La grotte Fell et autres sites de la región volcanique de la Patagonie chilienne,' *Journal de la Société des Américanistes*, vol. 52, 169–254. Paris, 1964.

ELVAS, GENTLEMAN OF. 'The Narrative of the expedition of Hernando de Soto,' in *Spanish Explorers in the Southern United States*, Theodore H. Lewis, ed., 127–272. New York, 1907.

EMERY, F. E., ed. *Systems Thinking*. New York, 1969.

EMORY, WILLIAM H. 'Notes of a Military Reconnaissance from Fort Leavenworth, in Missouri, to San Diego, in California, Including Parts of the Arkansas, Del Norte, and Gila Rivers,' 30th Congress, 1st session, *Senate Executive Docket 7*. Washington, D.C., 1848.

ENGEL, FRÉDÉRIC. 'Le complexe précéramique d'El Paraiso (Pérou),' *Journal de la Société des Américanistes*, vol. 55, no. 1, 43–96. Paris, 1967.

ESTRADA, EMILIO. *Ensayo Preliminar Sobre la Arqueologia del Milagro, Guayaquil*, Museo Victor Emilio Estrada, Guayaquil, 1954.

Prehistoria de Manabí, Publicaciones del Museo Victor Emilio Estrada, no. 4. Guayaquil, 1957.

EVANS, CLIFFORD, and MEGGERS, B. J. 'Formative Period Cultures in the Guayas Basin, Coastal Ecuador,' *American Antiquity*, vol. 22, no. 3, 235–46. Salt Lake City, 1957.

Archaeological Investigations in British Guiana, Bureau

of American Ethnology, Bulletin 177. Washington, D.C., 1960.

EVANS, FRANCIS C. 'Ecosystem as the Basic Unit in Ecology,' *Science*, vol. 123, 1127–8. Lancaster, 1956.

FARABEE, WILLIAM C. 'Exploration at the Mouth of the Amazon,' *Museum Journal of the University Museum*, vol. 12, no. 13, 142–61. Philadelphia, 1921.

FERDON, EDWIN N., JR. 'Agricultural Potential and the Development of Cultures,' *Southwestern Journal of Anthropology*, vol. 15, 1–19. Albuquerque, 1959.

FEWKES, JESSE W. 'Anthropology,' in *The Smithsonian Institution, 1846–1896*, G.B. Goode, ed., 745–72. Washington, D.C., 1897.

'The Aborigines of Porto Rico and Neighboring Islands,' *Bureau of American Ethnology, 25th Annual Report*. Washington, D.C., 1907.

'A Prehistoric Island Culture Area of America,' *Bureau of American Ethnology, 34th Annual Report*, 1–281. Washington, D.C., 1912a.

'Casa Grande, Arizona,' *Bureau of American Ethnology, 28th Annual Report*, 25–179. Washington, D.C., 1912b.

FIGGINS, JESSE D. 'The Antiquity of Man in America,' *Natural History*, vol. 27, no. 3, 229–39. New York, 1927.

FISK, H. N. *Summary of the Geology of the Lower Alluvial Valley of the Mississippi River,* Mississippi River Commission, War Department, Corps of Engineers. Washington, D.C., 1944.

FITTING, JAMES E. 'Environmental Potential and the Post-glacial Readaptation in Eastern North America,' *American Antiquity*, vol. 33, no. 4, 441–5. Salt Lake City, 1968.

The Archaeology of Michigan; a guide to the prehistory of the Great Lakes Region. Garden City, 1970.

FLANNERY, KENT V. 'The Ecology of Early Food Production in Mesopotamia,' *Science*, vol. 147, no. 3663, 1247–56. Washington, D.C., 1965.

'Culture History vs. Cultural Process: a debate in American archaeology,' *Scientific American*, vol. 217, 119–22. New York, 1967a.

'Vertebrate Fauna and Hunting Patterns,' in *The Pre-history of the Tehuacan Valley*, vol. 1, *Environment and Subsistence*, D.S. Byers, ed., 132–77. Austin, 1967b.

'Archaeological Systems Theory and Early Mesoamerica,' in *Anthropological Archaeology in the Americas*, B.J. Meggers, ed., 67–87. Washington, D.C., 1968a.

'The Olmec and the Valley of Oaxaca: a model for inter-regional interaction in Formative times,' in *Dumbarton Oaks Conference on the Olmec*, E.P. Benson, ed., 79–110. Washington, D.C., 1968b.

'Origins and Ecological Effects of Early Domestication in Iran and the Near East,' in *The Domestication and Exploitation of Plants and Animals*, G.W. Dimbleby and P.J. Ucko, eds., 73–100. London and Chicago, 1969.

FLANNERY, KENT V., *et al.* 'Farming Systems and Political Growth in Ancient Oaxaca,' *Science*, vol. 158, no. 3800, 445–54. Washington, D.C., 1967.

FLANNERY, KENT V. and SCHOENWETTER, JAMES. 'Climate and Man in Formative Oaxaca,' *Archaeology*, vol. 23, no.2, 144–52. New York, 1970.

FORD, JAMES A. *Ceramic Decoration Sequence at an Old Indian Village Site, Near Sicily Island, Louisiana*, Anthropological Study no. 1, Department of Conservation, Louisiana State Geological Survey. New Orleans, 1935.

Analysis of Indian Village Site Collections from Louisiana and Mississippi, Anthropological Study no. 2, Department of Conservation, Louisiana State Geological Survey. New Orleans, 1936.

'A Chronological Method Applicable to the Southeast,' *American Antiquity*, vol. 3, no. 3, 260–64. Menasha, 1938.

'Report of the Conference on Southeastern Pottery Typology,' Ceramic Repository, Museum of Anthropology, University of Michigan, mimeograph. Ann Arbor, 1938.

'Cultural Dating of Prehistoric Sites in the Virú Valley, Peru', *Anthropological Papers of the American Museum of Natural History*, vol. 43, pt. 1. New York, 1949.

'Measurements of Some Prehistoric Design Developments in the Southeastern States,' *Anthropological Papers of the American Museum of Natural History*, vol. 44, pt. 3. New York, 1952.

Letter, 'Spaulding's Review of Ford,' *American Anthropologist*, vol. 56, 109–12. Menasha, 1954a.

'Comment on A.C. Spaulding, "Statistical Techniques for the Discovery of Artifact Types",' *American Antiquity*, vol. 19, no. 4, 390–91. Salt Lake City, 1954b.

'On the Concept of Types,' *American Anthropologist*, vol. 56, 42–53. Menasha, 1954c.

A Quantitative Method for Deriving Cultural Chronology, Pan American Union Technical Manual, no. 1. Washington, D.C., 1962.

A Comparison of Formative Cultures in the Americas; diffusion or the psychic unity of man?, Smithsonian Institution Contributions to Anthropology, vol. 11. Washington, D.C., 1969.

FORD, JAMES A., PHILLIPS, PHILIP, and HAAG, WILLIAM G. *The Jaketown Site in West-central Mississippi*, Anthropological Papers of the American Museum of Natural History, vol. 45, pt. 1. New York, 1955.

FORD, JAMES A. and WILLEY, GORDON R. 'An Interpretation of the Prehistory of the Eastern United States,' *American Anthropologist*, vol. 43, no. 3, 325–63. Menasha, 1941.

The Virú Valley: background and problems, Anthropological Papers of the American Museum of Natural History, vol. 43, pt. 1. New York, 1949.

FÖRSTEMANN, ERNST W. 'Commentary on the Maya Manuscripts in the Royal Public Library of Dresden,' *Papers of the Peabody Museum*, vol. 4, no. 2, 49–266. Cambridge, Mass., 1906.

FOSTER, JOHN W. *Prehistoric Races of the United States.* Chicago, 1873.

FOWKE, GERARD. 'Stone Art,' *Bureau of American Ethnology, 13th Annual Report*, 47–184. Washington, D.C., 1896.

FOX, SIR CYRIL *The Archaeology of the Cambridge Region.* Cambridge, 1932.

'The Personality of Britain,' *Man*, vol. 32, 202+. London, 1932.

FREEMAN, JOHN F. 'University Anthropology: early departments in the United States,' *Papers of the*

Kroeber Anthropological Society, vol. 32, 78–90. Berkeley, 1965.

FREEMAN, L. G. JR., and BROWN, J. A. 'Statistical Analysis of Carter Ranch Pottery,' in *Chapters in the Prehistory of Eastern Arizona, II*, P. S. Martin, et al., eds., Chicago Museum of Natural History, Fieldiana: Anthropology, vol. 55, 126–54. Chicago, 1964.

FRIEDMAN, I., SMITH, R. L., and CLARK, D. 'Obsidian Dating,' in *Science in Archaeology*, revised edition D. Brothwell and E. Higgs, eds., 62–75. London and New York, 1969.

FRITZ, JOHN M. and PLOG, FRED T. 'The Nature of Archaeological Explanation,' *American Antiquity*, vol. 35, no. 4, 405–12. Salt Lake City. 1970.

GALLATIN, ALBERT. 'A Synopsis of the Indian Tribes within the United States east of the Rocky Mountains, in the British and Russian Possessions in North America,' *Archaeologia Americana*, vol. 2, 1–422. Cambridge, Mass., 1836.

'Notes on the Semi-civilized Nations of Mexico, Yucatan, and Central America,' *Transactions of the American Ethnological Society*, vol. 1. New York, 1845.

GAMIO, MANUEL. 'Arqueologia de Atzcapotzalco, D. F. Mexico,' *Proceedings, Eighteenth International Congress of Americanists*, 180–87. London, 1913.

La Poblacion del Valle de Teotihuacan, 3 vols. Mexico, 1922.

GANN, THOMAS W. F. 'Mounds in Northern Honduras,' *Bureau of American Ethnology, 19th Annual Report*, pt. 2, 655–92. Washington, D.C., 1900.

GARCIA DE PALACIO, DIEGO. 'Description de la province de Guatemala, Envoyée au Roi d'Espagne en 1576, par le licencié Palacios,' in *Recueil de Documents et Mémoires Originaux sur l'Histoire des Possesiones Espagnoles*, H. Ternaux-Compana, ed. Paris, 1840.

GARCILASO DE LA VEGA. *The Florida of the Inca; a history of the Adelantado, Hernando de Soto, Governor and Captain General of the Kingdom of Florida, and other Heroic Spanish and Indian Cavaliers*, translated by John Grier Varner and Jeannette Johnson Varner. Austin, 1951.

Royal Commentaries of the Incas, 2 vols, translated with an introduction by Harold V. Livermore. Austin, 1966.

GARDINER, PATRICK, ed. *Theories of History*. Glencoe, 1959.

GAYTON, ANNA H. 'The Uhle Collections from Nievería,' *University of California Publications in American Archaeology and Ethnology*, vol. 21, no. 8, 305–29. Berkeley, 1927.

GAYTON, ANNA H. and KROEBER, ALFRED L. 'The Uhle Pottery Collections from Nazca,' *University of California Publications in American Archaeology and Ethnology*, vol. 24, no. 1, 1–21. Berkeley, 1927.

GIBBS, GEORGE. 'Instructions for Archaeological Investigations in the United States,' *Smithsonian Institution Annual Report for 1861*, 392–6. Washington, D.C., 1862.

GIDDINGS, JAMES L. 'The Archaeology of Bering Strait,' *Current Anthropology*, vol. 1, no. 2, 121–38. Chicago. 1960.

The Archaeology of Cape Denbigh. Providence, 1964.

GELFAND, ALAN E. 'Seriation Methods for Archaeological Materials,' *American Antiquity*, vol. 36, no. 3, 263–74. Salt Lake City, 1971.

GIFFORD, EDWARD W. 'Composition of California Shellmounds,' *University of California Publications in American Archaeology and Ethnology*, vol. 12, no. 1, 1–29. Berkeley, 1916.

GIFFORD, JAMES C. 'The Type-variety Method of Ceramic Classification as an Indicator of Cultural Phenomena,' *American Antiquity*, vol. 25, no. 3, 341–47. Salt Lake City, 1960.

GLADWIN, HAROLD S. *Excavations at Casa Grande, Arizona*, Papers of the Southwest Museum, no. 2. Los Angeles, 1928.

Excavations at Snaketown, vol. 2, *Comparisons and Theories*, Medallion Papers, no. 26. Globe, 1937.

GLADWIN, WINIFRED and GLADWIN, HAROLD S. *A Method for the Designation of Ruins in the Southwest*, Medallion Papers, no. 1. Pasadena, 1928a.

The Use of Potsherds in an Archaeological Survey of the Southwest, Medallion Papers, no. 2. Pasadena, 1928b.

The Red-on-Buff Culture of the Gila Basin, Medallion Papers, no. 3. Globe, 1929.

A Method for the Designation of Southwestern Pottery Types, Medallion Papers, no. 7, Globe, 1930.

Some Southwestern Pottery Types. Series II, Medallion Papers, no. 10. Globe, 1931.

A Method for the Designation of Cultures and Their Variations, Medallion Papers, no. 15. Globe, 1934.

The Eastern Range of the Red-on-Buff Culture, Medallion Papers, no. 16. Globe, 1935.

GLADWIN, HAROLD S. et al. *Excavations at Snaketown: material culture*, Medallion Papers, no. 25, vol. 1. Globe, 1937.

GOELDI, EMILIO A. *Excavacoes Archeologicas en 1895*, pt. 1, Mem. Museu Paraense de Historia Natural e Ethnografia, Paraense, 1900.

GOETZMANN, WILLIAM H. *Army Exploration in the American West, 1803–1863*. New Haven, 1959.

Exploration and Empire. New York, 1967.

GOGGIN, JOHN M. 'Cultural Traditions in Florida Prehistory,' in *The Florida Indian and His Neighbors*, J. W. Griffin, ed., 13–44. Winter Park, 1949.

GOLDSCHMIDT, WALTER R. *Man's Way: a preface to the understanding of human society*. Cleveland, 1959.

GONZALEZ, ALBERTO R. 'La Estratigrafia de la Gruta de Intihuasi (Prov. de San Luis, R. A.) y sus Relaciones con Otros Sitios Preceramicos de Sudamérica,' *Revista del Instituto de Antropología*, vol. 1, 5–302, Córdoba, 1960.

'The La Aguada Culture of Northwestern Argentina,' in *Essays in Precolumbian Art and Archaeology*, S. K. Lothrop and others, eds., 389–420. Cambridge, Mass., 1961.

'Cultural Development in Northwestern Argentina,' in *Aboriginal Cultural Development in Latin America: an interpretative review*, B. J. Meggers and C. Evans, eds., Smithsonian Miscellaneous Collection, vol. 140, no. 1, 103–18. Washington, D.C., 1963.

GONZÁLEZ SUÁREZ, FEDÉRICO. *Estudio Histórico sobre los Cañaris, Antiguos Habitantes de la Provincia del Azuay, en la Republica del Ecuador*. Quito, 1878.

Los Aborigenes de Imbabura y del Carchi. Quito, 1910.

GOODMAN, JOSEPH T. 'The Archaic Maya Inscriptions,' in *Biologia Centrali Americana*, A.P. Maudslay, ed., pt. 8, Appendix to vol. 1. London, 1897.

'Maya Dates,' *American Anthropologist*, vol. 7, 642–47. Menasha, 1905.

GORDON, GEORGE B. *Prehistoric Ruins of Copan, Honduras*. Cambridge, Mass., 1896.

The Hieroglyphic Stairway; ruins of Copan, Memoirs of the Peabody Museum, vol. 1, no. 6. Cambridge, Mass., 1902.

GRAEBNER, FRITZ. *Methode der Ethnologie*. Heidelberg, 1911.

GRAHAM, IAN. 'Juan Galindo, Enthusiast,' *Estudios de Cultura Maya*, vol. 3, 11–36. Mexico, D.F., 1963.

'Introduction and Catalogue,' in *The Art of Maya Hieroglyphic Writing*, Peabody Museum, Cambridge, Mass., 1971.

GRAHAM, JOHN A. 'George C. Engerrand in Mexico, 1907–1917,' *Bulletin of Texas Archaeological Society*, vol. 32, 19–31. Austin, 1962.

GRIFFIN, JAMES B. *The Fort Ancient Aspect: its cultural and chronological position in Mississippi Valley archaeology*. Ann Arbor, 1943.

'Culture Change and Continuity in Eastern United States,' in *Man in Northeastern North America*, F. Johnson, ed., 37–95. Andover, 1946.

Essays on Archaeological Methods, James B. Griffin, ed., Anthropological Papers of the University of Michigan Museum of Anthropology, no. 8. Ann Arbor, 1951.

Archaeology of Eastern United States, James B. Griffin, ed. Chicago, 1952.

'The Study of Early Cultures,' in *Man, Culture, and Society*, H.L. Shapiro, ed., 22–48. New York, 1956.

'The Pursuit of Archaeology in the United States,' *American Anthropologist*, vol. 61, 379–88. Menasha, 1959.

'Some Prehistoric Connections Between Siberia and America,' *Science*, vol. 131, no. 3403, 801–12. Washington, D.C., 1960.

'Eastern North American Archaeology: a summary,' *Science*, vol. 156, no. 3772, 175–91. Washington, D.C., 1967.

GROOD, HUGO DE. *Desertatio de Origini Gentium Americanarum*. Amsterdam and Paris, 1643.

HAAG, WILLIAM G. 'Recent Work by British Archaeologists, *Annals of the Association of American Geographers*, vol. 43, 298–303. Albany, 1957.

'The Status of Evolutionary Theory in American Archaeology,' in *Evolution and Anthropology; a centennial appraisal*, 90–105. Washington, D.C., 1959.

'Twenty-five Years of Eastern Archaeology,' *American Antiquity*, vol. 27, no. 1, 16–23. Salt Lake City, 1961.

HABERLAND, WOLFGANG. *Archäologische Untersuchungen in Südost-Costa Rica*, Acta Humboldtiana, Series Geographica et Ethnographica, no. 1. Wiesbaden, 1959.

'Die Kulturen Meso-Und Zentral-Amerikas,' in *Handbuch der Kulturgeschichte*, 3–192. Frankfurt, 1969.

HAGEN, VICTOR W. *Maya Explorer: John Lloyd Stephens and the lost cities of Central American and Yucatán*. Norman, 1947.

HAGGETT, PETER. *Locational Analysis in Human Geography*. London, 1965.

HALL, E.T. 'Dating Pottery by Thermoluminescence,' in *Science in Archaeology*, revised edition D. Brothwell and E. Higgs, eds., 106–8. London and New York, 1969.

HALLOWELL, A.I. 'The Beginnings of Anthropology in America,' in *Selected Papers from the American Anthropologist, 1888–1920*, Frederica de Laguna, ed., 1–90. Evanston, 1960.

HANKE, LEWIS. *The Spanish Struggle for Justice in the Conquest of America*. Philadelphia, 1949.

Bartolomé de las Casas; an interpretation of his life and writings. The Hague, 1951.

HARDESTY. DONALD L. 'The Ecosystem Model, Human Energetics and the Analysis of Environmental Relations,' *The Western Canadian Journal of Archaeology*, vol. 2, no. 2, 1–17. Edmonton, 1971.

HARGRAVE, LYNDON L. *Guide to Forty Pottery Types from Hopi Country and the San Francisco Mountains, Arizona*, Museum of Northern Arizona, Bulletin 1. Flagstaff, 1932.

HARRIS, MARVIN. *The Rise of Anthropological Theory*. New York, 1968.

HARRIS, THADDEUS M. *The Journal of a Tour into the Territory Northwest of the Alleghany Mountains; made in the spring of the year 1803*. Boston, 1805.

HARRISON, WILLIAM H. 'A Discourse on the Aborigines of the Ohio Valley,' in *Transactions of the Historical and Philosophical Society of Ohio*, vol. 1, pt. 2. Cincinnati, 1839.

HARTMAN, CARL V. *Archaeological Researches in Costa Rica*. Stockholm, 1901.

Archaeological Researches on the Pacific Coast of Costa Rica, Memoirs of the Carnegie Museum, vol. 3, no. 1. Pittsburgh, 1907.

HARTT, CHARLES F. 'The Ancient Indian Pottery of Marajó, Brazil,' *American Naturalist*, vol. 5, 259–71. New York, 1871.

'Contribuições para a Ethnologia do Valle do Amazonas,' *Archivos do Museu Nacional*, vol. 6, 1–174. Rio de Janeiro, 1885.

HAURY, EMIL W. *Roosevelt:9:6, a Hohokam Site of the Colonial Period*, Medallion Papers, no. 11. Globe, 1932.

The Canyon Creek Ruin . . . of the Sierra Ancha, Medallion Papers, no. 14. Globe, 1934.

The Mogollon Culture of Southwestern New Mexico, Medallion Papers, no. 20. Globe, 1936a.

Some Southwestern Pottery Types, Series IV, Medallion Papers, no. 19. Globe, 1936b.

Excavation in the Forestdale Valley, East-central Arizona, University of Arizona Social Science Bulletin, no. 12. Tucson, 1940.

HAURY, EMIL W. et al. *The Stratigraphy and Archaeology of Ventana Cave, Arizona*. Albuquerque and Tucson, 1950.

HAVEN, SAMUEL F. *Archaeology of the United States*, Smithsonian Contributions to Knowledge, vol. 8, art. 2. Washington, D.C., 1856.

HAWKES, C.F.C. 'Archaeological Theory and Method: some suggestions from the Old World,'

American Anthropologist, vol. 56, no. 1, 155–68. Menasha, 1954.

HAY, CLARENCE L. *et al. The Maya and Their Neighbors.* New York, 1940.

HAYNES, CALEB V. 'Fluted Projectile Points: their age and dispersion,' *Science*, vol. 145, no. 3639, 1408–13. Washington, D.C., 1964.

HAYNES, HENRY W. 'The Prehistoric Archaeology of North America,' in *Narrative and Critical History of America*, Justin Winsor, ed. Boston, 1889.

'Progress·of American Archaeology during the Past Ten Years,' *Journal of the Archaeological Institute of America*, ser. 2, vol. 4, 17–39. Norwood, 1900.

HAYWOOD, JOHN. *The Natural and Aboriginal History of Tennessee, up to the first settlements therein by the white people, in the year 1768.* Nashville, 1823.

HEART, JONATHAN. 'Account of Some Remains of Ancient Work on the Muskingun, with a plan of these works,' *Columbian Magazine*, vol. 1, 425–27. Philadelphia, 1787.

'Observations on the Ancient Mounds,' in *Topographical Description of the Western Territory*, Gilbert Imlay, ed. New York, 1793.

HEINE-GELDERN, ROBERT VON. 'Die Asiatische Herkunft der Südamerikanischen Metalltechnik,' *Paideuma*, vol. 5, 347–423. Frankfurt am Main, 1954.

'Representations of the Asiatic Tiger in the Art of the Chavin Culture: a proof of early contacts between China and Peru,' *Actas del 33rd Congreso Internacional de Americanistas*, 321–26. San José, 1959a.

'Chinese Influence in Mexico and Central America: the Tajin Style of Mexico and the Marble Vases from Honduras,' *Actas del 33rd Congreso Internacional de Americanistas*, 207–10. San José, 1959b.

'The Problem of Transpacific Influences in Mesoamerica,' in *Handbook of Middle American Indians*, R. Wauchope *et al.*, eds., vol. 4, 277–96. Austin, 1966.

HEIZER, ROBERT F. 'The Direct-Historical Approach in California Archaeology,' *American Antiquity*, vol. 7, no. 2, 98–122+. Menasha, 1941.

'Preliminary Report on the Leonard Rockshelter Site, Pershing County, Nevada,' *American Antiquity*, vol. 17, no. 2, 89–98. Salt Lake City, 1951.

'Long-range Dating in Archaeology,' in *Anthropology Today*, edited under the chairmanship of A. L. Kroeber, 3–42. Chicago, 1953.

'Primitive Man as an Ecologic Factor,' *Papers of the Kroeber Anthropological Society*, no. 13, 1–31. Berkeley, 1955.

The Archaeologist at Work, Robert F. Heizer, ed. New York, 1959.

'Physical Analysis of Habitation Residues,' in *Viking Fund Publications in Anthropology*, no. 28, 93–142. New York, 1960.

'The Western Coast of North America,' in *Prehistoric Man in the New World*, J. D. Jennings and E. Norbeck, eds., 117–48. Chicago, 1964.

HEIZER, ROBERT F. and FENENGA, FRANKLIN. 'Archaeological Horizons in Central California,' *American Anthrop.*, vol. 41, 378–99. Menasha, 1939.

HELM, JUNE. 'The Ecological Approach to Anthropology,' *American Journal of Anthropology*, vol. 67, no. 6, 630–39. Chicago, 1962.

HEMPEL, CARL G. *Philosophy of Natural History.* Englewood Cliffs, 1966.

HENRY, JOSEPH. Editorial comment, *Annual Report of the Smithsonian Institution for 1874*, 335. Washington, D.C., 1875.

HENSHAW, HENRY W. 'Animal Carvings from the Mounds of the Mississippi Valley,' *U.S. Bureau of American Ethnology, 2nd Annual Report 1880/1881*, 4–35. Washington, D.C., 1883.

HESTER, JAMES J. 'A Comparative Typology of New World Cultures,' *American Anthropologist*, vol. 64, no. 5, 1001–15. Menasha, 1962.

HEWETT, EDGAR L. '*Antiquities of the Jemez Plateau, New Mexico*,' U.S. Bureau of American Ethnology, Bulletin 32. Washington, D.C., 1906.

HILBERT, PETER P. *Archäologische Untersuchungen am Mittleren Amazonas.* Berlin, 1968.

HILL, JAMES N. 'A Prehistoric Community in Eastern Arizona,' *Southwestern Journal of Anthropology*,' vol. 22, no. 1, 9–30. Albuquerque, 1966.

'Broken K Pueblo; patterns of form and function,' in *New Perspectives in Archaeology*, S. R. Binford and L. R. Binford, eds., 103–43. Chicago, 1968.

HIRSCHBERG, RICHARD and HIRSCHBERG, JOAN F. 'Meggers' Law of Environmental Limitation on Culture,' *American Anthropologist*, vol. 59, 890–92. Menasha, 1957.

HODGE, FREDERICK W., ed. *Handbook of American Indians North of Mexico*, 2 pts., Bureau of American Ethnology, Bulletin 30. Washington, D.C., 1907–10.

HODSON, FRANK R. 'Classification by Computer,' in *Science in Archaeology*, revised edition, D. Brothwell and E. Higgs, eds., 649–60. London and New York, 1969.

'Clusters Analysis and Archaeology: some new developments and applications,' *World Archaeology*, vol. 1, no. 3, 299–320. London, 1970.

HOLE, FRANK, FLANNERY, KENT V. and NEELY, JAMES. *Prehistoric and Human Ecology of the Deh Luran Plain*, Memoirs of the University of Michigan Museum of Anthropology, no. 1. Ann Arbor, 1968.

HOLE, FRANK, and HEIZER, ROBERT F. *An Introduction to Prehistoric Archaeology.* New York, 1966, 2nd ed. 1969.

HOLE, FRANK, and SHAW, MARY. *Computer Analysis of Chronological Seriation*, Rice University Studies, vol. 53, no. 3. Houston, 1967.

HOLMBERG, ALLEN R. 'Virú: remnant of an exalted people,' *Patterns for Modern Living*, 367–416. Chicago, 1950.

HOLMES, WILLIAM H. 'Evidences of the Antiquity of Man on the Site of the City of Mexico,' *Transactions of the Anthropological Society of Washington*, vol. 3, 68–81. Washington, D.C., 1885.

'Ancient Art of the Province of Chiriquí,' *Bureau of American Ethnology, 6th Annual Report 1884/85*, 3–187. Washington, D.C., 1888.

'Modern Quarry Refuse and the Paleolithic Theory,' *Science*, vol. 20, 295–7. Lancaster, 1892.

Archaeological Studies Among the Ancient Cities of Mexico, Field Columbian Museum Anthropological Series, vol. 1, no. 1. Chicago, 1895–7.

'Aboriginal Pottery of the Eastern United States,'

Bureau of American Ethnology, 20th Annual Report. Washington, D.C., 1903.

'Areas of American Culture Characterization Tentatively Outlined as an aid in the study of the Antiquities,' *American Anthropologist*, vol. 16, no. 3, 413–46. Lancaster, 1914.

HORN, GEORGE. *De Originibus Americanis*. Leyden, 1652.

HOUGH, WALTER. 'Archaeological Field Work in Northeastern Arizona,' *U.S. National Museum Annual Report for 1901*, 279–358. Washington, D.C., 1903.

'Experimental Work in American Archaeology and Ethnology,' in *Holmes Anniversary Volume*, 194–97. Washington, D.C., 1916.

'William Henry Holmes,' *American Anthropologist*, vol. 35, 752–64. Menasha, 1933.

HOWARD, E. B. 'Evidence of Early Man in America,' *The Museum Journal*, vol. 24, 53–171. Philadelphia, 1935.

HRDLIČKA, ALEŠ et al. *Early Man in South America*, Bureau of American Ethnology, Bulletin 52. Washington, D.C., 1912.

'The Origin and Antiquity of the American Indian,' *Annual Report of the Smithsonian Institution for 1923*, 481–94. Washington, D.C., 1925.

HUDDLESTON, LEE E. *Origins of the American Indians; European concepts, 1492–1729*. Austin, 1967.

HUMBOLDT, ALEXANDER VON. *Political Essay on the Kingdom of New Spain*. London, 1811.

Researches Concerning the Institutions and Monuments of the Ancient Inhabitants of America, translated by H. M. Williams. London, 1814.

HUME, IVOR N. *Historical Arch.* New York, 1969.

HYER, N. F. 'Ruins of the Ancient City of Aztalan,' *Milwaukee Advertiser*, February 25, 1837. Milwaukee.

HYMES, DELL H. 'Comments on *Analytical Archaeology*,' *Norwegian Archaeological Review*, vol. 34, nos. 3–4, 16–21. Oslo, 1970.

IHERING, HERMANN VON. 'A Civilisacão Prehistorica do Brazil Meridional,' *Revista do Museu Paulista*, vol. 1, 34–159. São Paulo, 1895.

IMBELLONI, JOSÉ. 'Culturas y Geografía, Culturas y Raza,' *Acta Venezolana*, vol. 1 129–40. Caracas, 1945.

IRWIN-WILLIAMS, CYNTHIA. 'Archaic Culture History in the Southwestern United States,' in *Early Man in Western North America*, Eastern New Mexico University Contributions to Anthropology, vol. 1, no. 4, 48–54. Portales, 1968.

Early Man in Western North America, Cynthia Irwin-Williams, ed., Eastern New Mexico University Contributions to Anthropology. Portales, 1968.

IVES, RONALD L. 'An Early Speculation Concerning the Asiatic Origin of the American Indian,' *American Antiquity*, vol. 21, no. 4, 420–21. Salt Lake City, 1956.

IZUMI, SEIICHI. 'A Viewpoint Based on Material from the Kotosh Site,' *Dumbarton Oaks Conference on Chavín*, E. P. Benson, ed., 49–72. Washington, D.C., 1971.

IZUMI, SEIICHI, and SONO, TOSHIHIKO. *Andes 2: excavations at Kotosh, Peru, 1960*. Tokyo, 1963.

JEFFERSON, THOMAS. *The Life and Selected Writings of Thomas Jefferson*, Adrienne Koch and William Reden, eds. New York, 1944.

JENNESS, DIAMOND. 'Archaeological Investigations in Bering Strait,' *Annual Report of the National Museum of Canada for 1926*. Ottawa, 1928.

'The Problem of the Eskimo,' in *The American Aborigines, Their Origin and Antiquity*, D. Jenness, ed., 373–96. Toronto, 1933.

JENNINGS, JESSE D. *Danger Cave*, Society for American Archaeology, Memoir 14. Salt Lake City, 1957.

'Administration of Contract Emergency Archaeological Programs,' *American Antiquity*, vol. 28, no. 3, 282–85. Salt Lake City, 1963.

'The Desert West,' in *Prehistoric Man in the New World*, J. D. Jennings, and E. Norbeck, eds., 149–74. Chicago, 1964.

Prehistory of North America. New York, 1968.

JENNINGS, JESSE D. and NORBECK, EDWARD. 'Great Basin Prehistory: a review,' *American Antiquity*, vol. 21, no. 1, 1–11. Salt Lake City, 1955.

Prehistoric Man in the New World. Chicago, 1964.

JIMÉNEZ MORENO, WIGBERTO. 'Síntesis de la Historia Pretolteca de Mesoamérica, in *Esplendor del México Antiguo*, Centro de Investigaciones Antropológicas de México, vol. 2, 1019–1108. Mexico, D.F., 1959.

JOHNSON, FREDERICK, ed. *The Boylston Street Fishweir*, Papers of the Robert S. Peabody Foundation for Archaeology, vol. 2. Andover, 1942.

The Boylston Street Fishweir II, Papers of the Robert S. Peabody Foundation for Archaeology, vol. 4, no. 1. Andover, 1949.

'A Quarter Century of Growth in American Archaeology,' *American Antiquity*, vol. 27, no. 1, 1–6. Salt Lake City, 1961.

'Archaeology in an Emergency,' *Science*, vol. 152, no. 3729, 1592–97. Washington, D.C., 1966.

JOHNSON, FREDERICK, et al. *Prehistoric America and the River Valley*, prepared by the Committee for the Recovery of Archaeological Remains. Andover, 1945.

JOHNSON, H. G. 'Revolution and Counter-revolution in Economics,' *Encounter*, vol. 36, no. 4, 23–33. London, 1971.

JONES, J. M. 'Recent Discoveries of Kjokkenmoddings,' *Anthropological Review and Journal of the Anthropological Society of London*, vol. 2, 223–6. London, 1864.

JOSEPHY, ALVIN M., JR. 'Indians in History,' *Atlantic*, vol. 225, no. 6, 67–72. Boston, 1970.

JOYCE, THOMAS A. *South American Archaeology*. London, 1912.

Mexican Archaeology. London, 1914.

Central American and West Indian Archaeology. London, 1916.

JUDD, NEIL M. 'Arizona's Prehistoric Canals, from the air,' *Explorations and Fieldwork of the Smithsonian Institution in 1930*, 157–66. Washington, D.C., 1931.

The Bureau of American Ethnology. Norman, 1967.

Men Met Along the Trail. Norman, 1968.

KALM, PETER. *Travels into North America*, 2nd ed. London, 1772.

KELLEY, DAVID H. 'Glyphic Evidence for a Dynastic Sequence at Quiriguá, Guatemala,' *American Antiquity*, vol. 27, no. 3, 323–35. Salt Lake City, 1962.

KEUR, DOROTHY L. *Big Bead Mesa*, Society for American Archaeology, Memoir 1. Menasha, 1941.

KIDDER, ALFRED V. 'Pottery of the Pajarito Plateau and Some Adjacent Regions in New Mexico,' *Memoirs of the American Anthropological Association*, vol. 2, pt. 6, 407–62. Lancaster, 1915.

An Introduction to the Study of Southwestern Archaeology, With a Preliminary Account of the Excavations at Pecos, Papers of the Southwestern Expedition, Phillips Academy, no. 1. New Haven, 1924.

'Southwestern Archaeological Conference,' *Science*, vol. 66, 489–91. Lancaster, 1927.

The Pottery of Pecos, vol. 1, Papers of the Southwestern Expedition, Phillips Academy. New Haven, 1931.

'Speculations on New World Prehistory,' in *Essays in Anthropology*, 143–52. Berkeley, 1936.

'Archaeological Problems of the Highland Maya,' in *The Maya and Their Neighbors*, C. L. Hay *et al.*, eds., 117–25. New York, 1940.

KIDDER, ALFRED II. 'South American Penetrations in Middle America,' in *The Maya and Their Neighbors*, C. L. Hay *et al.*, eds., 441–59. New York, 1940.

KING, THOMAS F. 'A Conflict of Values in American Archaeology,' *American Antiquity*, vol. 36, no. 3, 253–62. Washington, D.C., 1971.

KINGSBOROUGH, EDWARD. *Antiquities of Mexico*. London, 1831–48.

KIRCHHOFF, PAUL. 'Mesoamérica,' *Acta Americana*, vol. 1, 92–107. Mexico, D.F., 1943.

KLUCKHOHN, CLYDE. 'Some Reflections on the Method and Theory of the Kulturkreislehre,' *American Anthropologist*, vol. 38, no. 2, 157–96. Menasha, 1936.

'The Place of Theory in Anthropological Studies,' *Philosophy of Science*, vol. 6, no. 3, 328–44. Baltimore, 1939.

'The Conceptual Structure in Middle American Studies,' in *The Maya and Their Neighbors*, C. L. Hay *et al.*, eds., 41–51. New York, 1940.

KLUCKHOHN, CLYDE, and REITER, PAUL, eds. *Preliminary Report on the 1937 Excavations, Bc 50–51, Chaco Canyon, New Mexico*, University of New Mexico Anthropological Series, vol. 3, no. 2. Albuquerque, 1939.

KNOROZOV, Y. V. *Selected Chapters from the Writing of the Maya Indians*, translated by Sophie Coe, Russian Translation Series of the Peabody Museum, vol. 4. Cambridge, Mass., 1967.

KRICKEBERG, WALTER. *Altmexikanische Kulturen*. Berlin, 1956.

KRIEGER, ALEX D. 'The Typological Concept,' *American Antiquity*, vol. 9, 271–88. Menasha, 1944.

'Early Man in the New World,' in *Prehistoric Man in the New World*, J. D. Jennings, and E. Norbeck, eds., 23–84. Chicago, 1964.

KROEBER, ALFRED L. 'The Archaeology of California,' in *Putnam Anniversary Volume*, 1–42. New York, 1909.

'Zuñi Potsherds,' *Anthropological Papers of the American Museum of Natural History*, vol. 18, pt. 1, 7–37. New York, 1916.

'On the Principle of Order in Civilizations as Exemplified by Changes of Fashion,' *American Anthropologist*, vol. 21, no. 3, 235–63. Menasha, 1919.

'The Uhle Pottery Collections from Supe,' *University of California Publications in American Archaeology and Ethnology*, vol. 21, 235–64. Berkeley, 1925a.

'The Uhle Pottery Collections from Moche,' *University of California Publications in American Archaeology and Ethnology*, vol. 21, 191–234. Berkeley, 1925b.

'Archaic Culture Horizons in the Valley of Mexico,' *University of California Publications in American Archaeology and Ethnology*, vol. 17, 373–408. Berkeley, 1925c.

'The Uhle Pottery Collections from Chancay,' *University of California Publications in American Archaeology and Ethnology*, vol. 21, no. 7, 265–304. Berkeley, 1926.

'Coast and Highland in Prehistoric Peru,' *American Anthropologist*, vol. 29, 625–53. Menasha, 1927.

'Cultural Relations Between North and South America,' in *Proceedings of the 23rd International Congress of Americanists*, 5–22. New York, 1930.

'Cultural and Natural Areas of Native North America,' *University of California Publications in American Archaeology and Ethnology*, vol. 38, 1–242. Berkeley, 1939.

'Conclusions,' in *The Maya and Their Neighbors*, C. L. Hay *et al.*, eds., 460–90. New York, 1940.

Peruvian Archaeology in 1942, Viking Fund Publications in Anthropology, no. 4. New York, 1944.

Anthropology. New York, 1948.

KROEBER, ALFRED L. and STRONG, WILLIAM D. 'The Uhle Pottery Collections from Ica,' *University of California Publications in American Archaeology and Ethnology*, vol. 21, no. 3, 95–133. Berkeley, 1924a.

'The Uhle Collections from Chincha,' *University of California Publications in American Archaeology and Ethnology*, vol. 21, no. 1, 1–54. Berkeley, 1924b.

KUBLER, GEORGE. *The Art and Architecture of Ancient America. The Mexican, Maya, and Andean Peoples*. Baltimore, 1962.

KUHN, THOMAS S. *The Structure of Scientific Revolutions*. Chicago, 1962.

KUSHNER, GILBERT. 'A Consideration of Some Processual Designs for Archaeology as Anthropology,' *American Antiquity*, vol. 35, no. 2, 125–32. Salt Lake City, 1970.

KUZARA, RICHARD S., MEAD, GEORGE R., and DIXON, KEITH A. 'Seriation of Anthropological Data: a computer program for matrix-ordering,' *American Anthropolgist*, vol. 68, no. 6, 1442–55. Menasha, 1966.

LAET, JOHANNES DE. *Notae ad Dissertationem Hugonis Grotii de Origine Gentium Americanarum: et observationes aliquot ad meliorem indaginem difficillimae illius quaestionis*. Paris, 1643.

Responsis ad dissertationem secundum Hugonis Grotii. Amsterdam, 1644.

LAGUNA, FREDERICA DE. *The Archaeology of Cook Inlet, Alaska*. Philadelphia, 1934.

The Archaeology of Prince William Sound, Alaska,

University of Washington Publications in Anthropology, no. 13. Seattle, 1956.

LAMBERG-KARLOVSKY, C.C. 'Operations Problems in Archaeology,' *Bulletin of the American Anthropological Association*, vol. 3, no. 3, pt. 2, 111–14. Washington, D.C., 1970.

LANDA, DIEGO DE. *Relation de Choses de Yucatan de Diego de Landa*, translated by Charles E. Brasseur de Bourbourg. Paris, 1864.

Relación de las Cosas de Yucatán, a translation, Alfred M. Tozzer, ed., Papers of the Peabody Museum, vol. 18. Cambridge, Mass., 1941.

LANNING, E.P. *Peru before the Incas*. Englewood Cliffs, 1967.

LAPHAM, INCREASE A. *The Antiquities of Wisconsin*, Smithsonian Contributions to Knowledge, vol. 7, art. 4. Washington, D.C., 1855.

LARCO HOYLE, RAFAEL. *Los Mochicas*, 2 vols. Lima, 1938–1940.

Los Cupisniques. Lima, 1941.

Cronología Arqueólogica del Norte del Peru. Trujillo, 1948.

LARKIN, FREDERICK. *Ancient Man in America*. New York, 1880.

LARSEN, HELGE. 'Archaeology in the Arctic, 1935–60,' *American Antiquity*, vol. 27, no. 1, 7–15. Salt Lake City, 1961.

LARSEN, HELGE, and RAINEY, F.G. *Ipiutak and the Arctic Whale Hunting Culture*, Anthropological Papers of the American Museum of Natural History, vol. 42. New York, 1948.

LARSON, LEWIS H., JR. 'Archaeological Implications of Social Stratification at the Etowah Site, Georgia,' in *Approaches to the Social Dimensions of Mortuary Practices*, J.A. Brown, ed., Society for American Archaeology, Memoir 25, 58–67. Washington, D.C., 1971

LATHRAP, DONALD W., ed. 'An Archaeological Classification of Culture Contact Situations,' in *Seminars in Archaeology: 1955*, R. Wauchope, ed., Society for American Archaeology, Memoir 11, 1–30. Salt Lake City, 1956.

'The Cultural Sequence at Yarinacocha, Eastern Peru,' *American Antiquity*, vol. 23, no. 4, 379–88. Salt Lake City, 1958.

Yarinacocha: stratigraphic excavations in the Peruvian Montana, Ph.D. disseration, Harvard University. Cambridge, 1962.

The Upper Amazon, Ancient Peoples and Places Series, G. Daniel, ed. London and New York, 1970.

'The Tropical Forest and the Cultural Context of Chavín,' *Dumbarton Oaks Conference on Chavín*, E.P. Benson, ed., 73–100. Washington, D.C., 1971.

LEHMANN-HARTLEBEN, KARL. 'Thomas Jefferson, archaeologist,' *American Journal of Archaeology*, vol. 47, 161–63. Concord, 1943.

LEHMER, DONALD J. *Introduction to Middle Missouri Archaeology*, Anthropological Papers of the National Park Service, no. 1. Washington, D.C., 1971.

LEON-PORTILLA, MIGUEL. *Pre-Columbian Literatures of Mexico*. Norman, 1969.

LEONE, MARK P. 'Neolithic Economic Autonomy and Social Distance,' *Science*, vol. 162, no. 3858, 1150–51. Washington, D.C., 1968.

LE PAGE DU PRATZ, ANTOINE S. *Histoire de la Louisiane*, 3 vols. Paris, 1758.

LEWIS, THOMAS M.N. and KNEBERG, MADELINE. *The Prehistory of Chickamduga Basin in Tennessee*, Tennessee Anthrop. Papers, no. 1. Knoxville, 1941.

Hiwassee Island: an archaeological account of four Tennessee Indian peoples. Knoxville, 1946.

LIBBY, WILLARD F. *Radiocarbon Dating*, 2d ed. Chicago, 1955.

LINTON, RALPH. *The Study of Man*. New York, 1936.

'North American Cooking Pots,' *American Antiquity*, vol. 9, no. 4, 369–80. Menasha, 1944.

LONGACRE, WILLIAM A. 'Archaeology as Anthropology: a case study,' *Science*, vol. 144, no. 3625, 1454–1455. Washington, D.C., 1964.

'Changing Pattern of Social Integration: a prehistoric example from the American Southwest,' *American Anthropologist*, vol. 68, no. 1, 94–102. Menasha, 1966.

'Some Aspects of Prehistoric Society in East-central Arizona,' in *New Perspectives in Archaeology*, S.R. Binford and L.R. Binford, eds., 89–102. Chicago, 1968.

'Current Thinking in American Archaeology,' *Bulletin of the American Anthropological Association*, vol. 3, no. 3, pt. 2, 126–38. Washington, D.C., 1970.

LOTHROP, SAMUEL K. *Pottery of Costa Rica and Nicaragua*, 2 vols., Contributions from the Museum of the American Indian, Heye Foundation, vol. 8. New York, 1926.

'South America as Seen from Middle America,' in *The Maya and Their Neighboes*, C.L. Hay *et al.*, eds., 417–29. New York, 1940.

'The Diaguita of Chile,' in *Handbook of South American Indians*, Julian H. Steward, ed., vol. 2, 633–36, Bureau of American Ethnology, Bulletin 143. Washington, D.C., 1946.

LOWIE, ROBERT H. 'Reminiscences of Anthropological Currents in America Half a Century Ago,' *American Anthropologist*, vol. 58, no. 6, 995–1016. Menasha, 1956.

LUBBOCK, SIR JOHN. *Prehistoric Times*. London, 1865.

LUMBRERAS, LUIS G. 'Towards a Re-evaluation of Chavín,' *Dumbarton Oaks Conference on Chavín*, E.P. Benson, ed., 1–28. Washington, D.C., 1971.

LUND, P.W. 'Blik poa Brasiliens Dyreverden, etc.,' *Det Kongelige Danske Videnskabernes Selskabs Naturvidenskabelige og Mathematiske Afhandlinger, Niende Dul*, 195–6. Copenhagen, 1842.

LYNCH, BARBARA D. and LYNCH, THOMAS F. 'The Beginnings of a Scientific Approach to Prehistoric Archaeology in 17th and 18th Century Britain,' *Southwestern Journal of Anthropology*, vol. 24, no. 1, 33–65. Albuquerque, 1968.

LYON, PATRICIA J. 'Anthropological Activity in the United States, 1865–1879,' *The Kroeber Anthropological Society Papers*, no. 40, 8–37. Berkeley, 1969.

McCULLOH, JAMES H., JR. *Researches Philosophical and Antiquarian Concerning the Aboriginal History of America*. Baltimore, 1829.

MacCURDY, GEORGE G. *A Study of Chiriquian Antiquities*, Memoirs of the Connecticut Academy of Sciences, vol. 3. New Haven, 1911.

McGimsey, Charles R. III, 'Archaeology and the Law,' *American Antiquity*, vol. 36, no. 2, 125–26. Salt Lake City, 1971.

McGregor, John C. *Southwestern Archaeology*. New York, 1941.

Southwestern Archaeology, 2nd ed. Urbana, 1965.

McKern, William C. 'The Midwestern Taxonomic Method as an Aid to Archaeological Study,' *American Antiquity*, vol. 4, 301–13. Menasha, 1939.

'On Willey and Phillips' "Method and Theory in American Archaeology",' *American Anthropologist*, vol. 58, 360–61. Menasha, 1956.

McKusick, Marshall. *The Davenport Conspiracy*, Office of the State Archaeologist, Report no. 1. Iowa City, 1970.

MacNeish, Richard S. *Preliminary Archaeological Investigations in the Sierra de Tamaulipas, Mexico*, Transactions, American Philosophical Society, vol. 48, pt. 6. Philadelphia, 1958.

'Ancient Mesoamerican Civilization,' *Science*, vol. 143, no. 3606, 531–37. Washington, D.C., 1964a.

Investigations in the Southwest Yukon: part II, Archaeological Excavation, Comparisons and Speculations, Papers of the R. S. Peabody Foundation for Archaeology, vol. 6, no. 1. Andover, 1964b.

'A Summary of the Subsistence,' in *Prehistory of the Tehuacan Valley*, D. S. Byers, ed., 290–309. Austin, 1967.

First Annual Report of the Ayacucho Archaeological-Botanical Project, R. S. Peabody Foundation. Andover, 1969.

The Prehistory of the Tehuacan Valley, R. S. MacNeish et al., eds. Austin, 1967.

MacNeish, Richard S., Nelken-Turner, Antoinette, and Cook, Angel Garcia. *Second Annual Report of the Ayacucho Archaeological-Botanical Project*, R. S. Peabody Foundation. Andover, 1970.

McPherron, Alan, *The Juntenen Site and the Late Woodland Prehistory of the Upper Great Lakes Area*, Anthropological Papers of the University of Michigan Museum of Anthropology, no. 30. Ann Arbor, 1967.

Madison, James. 'A Letter on the Supposed Fortification of the Western Country from Bishop Madison of Virginia to Dr. Barton,' *Transactions of the American Philosophical Society*, vol. 6. Philadelphia, 1803.

Maler, Teobert. *Researches in the Central Portion of the Usumatsintla Valley*, Memoirs of the Peabody Museum, vol. 2, no. 2. Cambridge, Mass., 1901.

Researches in the Central Portion of the Usumatsintla Valley. Cambridge, Mass., 1903.

Explorations of the Upper Usumatsintla and Adjacent Region: Altar de Sacrificios, Seibal, Itsimte-Sacluk, Cankuen, Memoirs of the Peabody Museum, vol. 4, no. 1. Cambridge, Mass., 1908.

Mangelsdorf, Paul C. and Smith, C. Earle. 'New Archaeological Evidence on Evolution in Maize,' *Botanical Museum Leaflets*, Harvard University, vol. 13, no. 8, 213–47, Cambridge, Mass., 1949.

Manners, Robert A., ed. *Process and Pattern in Culture; essays in honor of Julian H. Steward*. Chicago, 1964.

Marcano, G. 'Ethnographie Précolombienne du Venezuela, Vallées d'Aragua et de Caracas,' *Mémoires d'Anthropologie*, ser. 2, vol. 4, 1–86. Paris, 1889.

Markham, Sir Clements R. *Cuzco: a journey to the ancient capital of Peru*. London, 1856.

'On the Geographical Positions of the Tribes which Formed the Empire of the Yncas,' *Journal of the Royal Geographical Society*, vol. 41, 281–338. London, 1871.

A History of Peru. Chicago, 1892.

The Incas of Peru. London, 1910.

Márquez Miranda, Fernando. 'The Diaguita of Argentina,' in *Handbook of South American Indians*, Julian H. Steward, ed., vol. 2, 637–54, Bureau of American Ethnology, Bulletin 143. Washington, D.C., 1946a.

'The Chaco-Santiagueño Culture,' in *Handbook of South American Indians*, Julian H. Steward, ed., vol. 2, 655–60, Bureau of American Ethnology, Bulletin 143. Washington, D.C., 1946b.

Martin, Paul S., Lloyd, Carl, and Spoehr, Alexander. 'Archaeological Works in the Ackman-Lowry Area, South-western Colorado, 1937,' *Field Museum of Natural History Anthropological Series*, vol. 23, no. 2, 217–304. Chicago, 1938.

Martin, Paul S., Quimby, George I. and Collier, Donald. *Indians Before Columbus*. Chicago, 1947.

Martin, Paul S. and Rinaldo, John. 'Modified Basket Maker Sites, Ackman-Lowry Area, South-western Colorado, 1938.' *Field Museum of Natural History Anthropological Series*, vol. 23, no. 3, 305–499. Chicago, 1939.

'The Southwestern Co-tradition,' *Southwestern Journal of Anthropology*, vol. 7, 215–29. Albuquerque, 1951.

Martin, Paul S., Rinaldo, John, and Kelly, Marjorie. 'The Su Site, Excavations at a Mogollon Village, Western New Mexico, 1939,' *Field Museum of Natural History Anthropological Series*, vol. 32, no. 1. Chicago, 1940.

Martin, Paul S., Roys, Lawrence, and von Bonin, Gerhardt. 'Lowry Ruin in Southwestern Colorado,' *Field Museum of Natural History Anthrop. Series*, vol. 23, no. 1. Chicago, 1936.

Maruyama, Mogoroh. 'The Second Cybernetics: deviation-amplifying mutual causal processes,' *American Scientist*, vol. 51, no. 2, 164–79. Champaign, 1963.

Mason, J. Alden. *The Ancient Civilizations of Peru*. Baltimore, 1957.

Mason, Otis T. 'Influence of Environment upon Human Industries or Arts,' *Annual Report of the Smithsonian Institution for 1895*, 639–65. Washington, D.C., 1895.

'Environment,' in *Handbook of American Indians*, F. W. Hodge, ed., 427–30, Bureau of American Ethnology, Bulletin 30. Washington, D.C., 1905.

Mathiassen, Therkel. *Archaeology of the Central Eskimos*, Report of the 5th Thule Expedition, 1921–4, vol. 4. Copenhagen, 1927.

'The Eskimo Archaeology of Greenland,' *Annual Report of the Smithsonian Institution for 1936*, 397–404. Washington, D.C., 1937.

Mattos, Anibal. 'Lagoa Santa Man,' in *Handbook of South American Indians*, Julian H. Steward, ed., vol. 1, 399–400, Bureau of American Ethnology, Bulletin 143. Washington, D.C., 1946.

MAUDSLAY, ALFRED P. 'Archaeology,' *Biologia Centrali Americana*, 4 vols. London, 1889–1902.

MAYER-OAKES, WILLIAM J. *Prehistory of the Upper Ohio Valley; an introductory study*, Carnegie Museum Anthropological Series, no. 2. Pittsburgh, 1955.

'A Developmental Concept of Pre-Spanish Urbanization in the Valley of Mexico.' *Middle American Research Records*, vol. 2, no. 8, 167–75. New Orleans, 1961.

'Comments on *Analytical Archaeology*,' *Norwegian Archaeological Review*, vol. 34, nos. 3–4, 12–16. Oslo, 1970.

MEANS, PHILIP A. 'A Survey of Ancient Peruvian Art,' *Transactions of the Connecticut Academy of Arts and Sciences*, vol. 21, 315–24. New Haven, 1917.

Ancient Civilizations of the Andes. New York, 1931.

MEEHAN, EUGENE J. *Explanation in Social Science, a system paradigm.* Homewood, 1968.

MEGGERS, BETTY J. 'Environmental Limitation on the Development of Culture,' *American Anthropologist*, vol. 56, no. 5, 801–24. Menasha, 1954.

'The Coming of Age of American Archaeology,' in *New Interpretations of Aboriginal American Culture History*, 116–29. Washington, D.C., 1955.

'Functional and Evolutionary Implications of Community Patterning,' in *Seminars in Archaeology: 1955*, R. Wauchope, ed., Society for American Archaeology, Memoir 11, 129–57. Salt Lake City, 1956.

'Environment and Culture in the Amazon Basin: an appraisal of the theory of environmental determinism,' in *Studies in Human Ecology*, Angel Palerm et al., eds., Pan American Union Social Sciences Monograph, no. 3, 71–90. Washington, D.C., 1957.

'Field Testing of Cultural Law: a reply to Morris Opler,' *Southwestern Journal of Anthropology*, vol. 17, no. 14, 352–54. Albuquerque, 1961.

Ecuador, Ancient Peoples and Places Series, G. Daniel, ed. London and New York, 1966.

MEGGERS, BETTY J. and EVANS, CLIFFORD. *Archaeological Investigations at the Mouth of the Amazon*, Bureau of American Ethnology, Bulletin 167. Washington, D.C., 1957.

'Review of "Method and Theory in American Archaeology",' *American Antiquity*, vol. 24, no. 2, 195–96. Salt Lake City, 1958.

'An Experimental Formulation of Horizon Styles in the Tropical Forest Area of South America,' in *Essays in Pre-Columbian Art and Archaeology*, S. K. Lothrop et al., eds., 372–88. Cambridge, Mass., 1961.

Aboriginal Cultural Development in Latin America: An Interpretative Review, Smithsonian Miscellaneous Collection, vol. 146, no. 1. Washington, D.C., 1963.

MEGGERS, BETTY J., EVANS, CLIFFORD, and ESTRADA, EMILIO. *Early Formative Period of Coastal Ecuador*, Smithsonian Contributions to Anthropology, vol. 1. Washington, D.C., 1965.

MEIGHAN, CLEMENT W. 'Excavations in Sixteenth Century Shellmounds at Drake's Bay, Marin County,' *Reports of the California Archaeological Survey*, no. 9, 27–32. Berkeley, 1950.

'The Little Harbor Site, Catalina Island: an example of ecological interpretation in archaeology,' *American Antiquity*, vol. 24, no. 4, 383–405. Salt Lake City, 1959.

'The Growth of Archaeology in the West Coast and the Great Basin, 1935–60,' *American Antiquity*, vol. 27, no. 1, 33–8. Salt Lake City, 1961.

'Pacific Coast Archaeology,' in *The Quaternary of the United States*, H. E. Wright, Jr. and D. G. Frey, eds., 7th Congress of the International Association for Quaternary Research, 709–22. Princeton, 1965.

MEIGHAN, CLEMENT W. *et al.* 'Ecological Interpretation in Archaeology,' *American Antiquity*, vol. 24, no. 1, 1–23, no. 2, 131–50. Salt Lake City, 1958.

MELDGAARD, JÖRGEN A. 'On the Formative Period of the Dorset Culture,' in *Prehistoric Cultural Relations Between the Arctic and Temperate Zones of North America*, J. M. Campbell, ed., 92–95, Arctic Institute of North America Technical Paper no. 11. Montreal, 1962.

MENGHIN, OSWALD F. A. *Weltgeschicte der Steinzeit*. Vienna, 1931.

'Das Protolithikum in Amerika,' *Acta Praehistorica*, no. 1. Buenos Aires, 1957.

MENZEL, DOROTHY, 'Style and Time in the Middle Horizon,' *Ñawpa Pacha*, no. 2, 1–106. Berkeley, 1964.

MENZEL, DOROTHY, ROWE, JOHN, and DAWSON, LAWRENCE E. *The Paracas Pottery of Ica, a study in style and time*, University of California Publications in American Archaeology and Ethnology, vol. 50. Berkeley, 1964.

MERRIAM, C. HART. 'William Healy Dall,' *Science*, vol. 65, no. 1684, 345–47. Lancaster, 1927.

MERWIN, RAYMOND E. and VAILLANT, GEORGE C. *The Ruins of Holmul, Guatemala*, Memoirs of the Peabody Museum, vol. 3, no. 2. Cambridge, Mass., 1932.

MIDDENDORF, E. W. *Peru*, 3 vols. Berlin, 1893–5.

MILLER, TOM. 'Evolutionism and History in American Archaeology,' *Tebiwa*, vol. 2, no. 2, 55–6. Pocatello, 1959.

MILLON, RENÉ F. 'Teotihuacán,' *Scientific American*, vol. 216, no. 6, 38–48. New York, 1967.

'Teotihuacán: completion of maps of giant ancient city in the Valley of Mexico,' *Science*, vol. 170, 1077–82. Washington, D.C., 1970.

MILLS, WILLIAM C. 'Baum Prehistoric Village,' *Ohio State Archaeological and Historical Quarterly*, vol. 16, no. 2, 113–93. Columbus, 1906.

'Explorations of the Edwin Harness Mound,' *Ohio State Archaeological and Historical Quarterly*, vol. 25, no. 3, 262–398. Columbus, 1907.

MIRAMBELL SILVA, LORENA, 'Excavaciones en un sitio pleistocénico de Tlapacoya, México,' *Boletín del Instituto Nacional de Anthropolgía e Historia*, no. 29, 37–41. Mexico, D.F., 1967.

MITRA, PANCHANAN. *A History of American Anthropology*. Calcutta, 1933.

MOBERG, CARL-AXEL. 'Comments on *Analytical Archaeology*,' *Norwegian Archaeological Review*, vol. 34, nos. 3–4, 21–24. Oslo, 1970.

MONTAGUE, M. F. ASHLEY. 'Earliest Accounts of the Association of Human Artifacts with Fossil Mammals in North America,' *Science*, vol. 95, 380–81. Lancaster, 1942.

MOORE, CLARENCE B. 'Certain Sand Mounds of the St. John's River, Florida', *Journal of the Academy of Natural Sciences of Philadelphia*, vol. 10. Philadelphia, 1894.

'Certain River Mounds of Duval County, Florida', *Journal of the Academy of Natural Sciences of Philadelphia*, vol. 10. Philadelphia, 1896.

'Certain Aboriginal Remains of the Northwest Florida Coast,' pt. 2, *Journal of the Academy of Natural Sciences of Philadelphia*, vol. 12. Philadelphia, 1902.

'Antiquities of the St. Francis, White and Black Rivers, Arkansas,' *Journal of the Academy of Natural Sciences of Philadelphia*, vol. 14. Philadelphia, 1910.

MOOREHEAD, WARREN K. *Primitive Man in Ohio.* New York, 1892.

The Stone Age in North America, 2 vols. Boston, 1910.

A Report on the Archaeology of Maine, Publications of the Department of Archaeology, Phillips Academy. Publication 5. Andover, 1922.

The Cahokia Mounds, University of Illinois Bulletin, vol. 26, no. 4. Urbana, 1928.

MORGAN, LEWIS H. 'Montezuma's Dinner,' *North American Review*, vol. 122, 265–308. Boston, 1876.

Ancient Society. New York, 1877.

MORGAN, RICHARD G. and RODABAUGH, JAMES H. *Bibliography of Ohio Archaeology*, Ohio State Archaeological and Historical Society. Columbus, 1947.

MORLEY, SYLVANUS. G. 'Excavations at Quirigua, Guatemala,' *National Geographic Magazine*, vol. 24, 339–61. Washington, D.C., 1913.

The Ancient Maya, 1st ed. Stanford, 1946.

MORLEY, SYLVANUS G. and BRAINERD, G.W. *The Ancient Maya*, 3rd ed. Stanford, 1956.

MORLOT, A. VON. 'General Views on Archaeology,' *Annual Report of the Smithsonian Institution for 1860*, 284–343. Washington, D.C., 1861.

MÜLLER-BECK, HANSJÜRGEN. 'Paleohunters in America: origins and diffusions,' *Science*, vol. 152, no. 3726, 1191–1210. Washington, D.C., 1966.

NADAILLAC, JEAN FRANÇOIS, MARQUIS DE. *Prehistoric America*, translated by N. d'Anvers, W.H. Dall, ed. New York and London, 1884.

NAROLL, RAOUL S. 'Floor Area and Settlement Population,' *American Antiquity*, vol. 27, no. 4, 587–9. Salt Lake City, 1962.

NELSON, NELS C. 'Shellmounds of the San Francisco Bay Region,' *University of California Publications in American Archaeology and Ethnology*, vol. 7, no. 4, 319–48. Berkeley, 1909.

'The Ellis Landing Shellmound,' *University of California Publications in American Archaeology and Ethnology*, vol. 7, no. 5, 357–426. Berkeley, 1910.

'Pueblo Ruins of the Galisteo Basin,' *Anthropological Papers of the American Museum of Natural History*, vol. 15, pt. 1. New York, 1914.

'Chronology of the Tano Ruins, New Mexico,' *American Anthropologist*, vol. 18, no. 2, 159–80. Lancaster, 1916.

'Notes on Pueblo Bonito,' in *Pueblo Bonito*, G.H. Pepper, ed., Anthropological Papers of the American Museum of Natural History, vol. 27. New York, 1920.

'The Antiquity of Man in America in the Light of Archaeology,' in *The American Aborigines, their origin and antiquity*, D. Jenness, ed., 85–130. Toronto, 1933.

NETTO, LADISLÁU. 'Investigacoes Sobre a Archeologia Brazileira,' *Archivos do Museo Nacional*, vol. 6, 257–555. Rio de Janeiro, 1885.

NEWELL, H. PERRY, and KRIEGER, ALEX D. *The George C. Davis Site, Cherokee County, Texas*, Society for American Arch., Memoir 5. Menasha, 1949.

NICHOLS, FRANCES S., compiler. *Index to Schoolcraft's 'Indian Tribes of the United States,'* Bureau of American Ethnology, Bulletin 152. Washington, D.C., 1954.

NICHOLSON, HENRY B. 'Settlement Pattern Analysis in Contemporary American Archaeology,' *American Anthropologist*, vol. 60, no. 6, 1189–92. Menasha, 1958.

NORDENSKIÖLD, ERLAND VON. 'Urnengräber und Mounds im Bolivianischen Flachlande,' *Baessler Archives*, vol. 3, 205–55. Berlin, 1913.

Comparative Ethnographical Studies IV: the Copper and Bronze Ages in South America. Göteborg, 1921.

Origin of the Indian Civilizations in South America, Comparative Ethnographical Studies, no. 9. Göteborg, 1931.

NORDENSKIÖLD, GUSTAF VON. *The Cliff Dwellers of the Mesa Verde, Southwestern Colorado; their pottery and implements*, translated by D.L. Morgan. Stockholm, 1893.

NUTTAL, ZELIA. 'The Island of Sacrificios,' *American Anthropologist*, vol. 12, 257–95. Lancaster, 1910.

OAKLEY, KENNETH P. 'Analytical Methods of Dating Bones,' in *Science in Archaeology*, revised edition D. Brothwell and E. Higgs, eds., 35–45. London and New York, 1969.

ODUM, EUGENE P. *Fundamentals of Ecology*. Philadelphia and London, 1953.

Ecology. New York, 1963.

Fundamentals of Ecology, 3rd ed. Philadelphia and London, 1971.

OPLER, MORRIS E. 'Cultural Evolution, Southern Athapaskans, and Chronology in Theory,' *Southwestern Journal of Anthropology*, vol. 17, no. 1, 1–20. Albuquerque, 1961.

OSGOOD, CORNELIUS. *Ingalik Material Culture*, Yale University Publications in Anthropology, no. 22. New Haven, 1940.

The Ciboney Culture of Cayo Redondo, Cuba, Yale University Publications in Anthropology, no. 25. New Haven, 1942.

OUTES, FELIX F. 'La Edad de la Piedra en Patagonia,' *Anales del Museo Nacional de Buenos Aires*, vol. 12, 203–575. Buenos Aires, 1905.

'Arqueología de San Blas, Provincia de Buenos Aires,' *Anales del Museo Nacional de Buenos Aires*, vol. 14, 249–75. Buenos Aires, 1907.

Los Querandies. Buenos Aires, 1897.

PALERM, ANGEL. 'The Agricultural Basis of Urban Civilization in Mesoamerica,' in *Irrigation Civilizations: a comparative study*, Pan American Union Social Sciences Monograph, no. 1, 28–42. Washington, D.C., 1955.

PALERM, ANGEL, and WOLF, E. R. 'Ecological Potential and Cultural Development in Mesoamerica,' in *Studies in Human Ecology*, Pan American Union Social Sciences Monograph, no. 3, 1–37. Washington, D.C., 1957.

PARKER, ARTHUR C. *Excavations in an Erie Indian Village and Burial Site at Ripley, Chautaqua County, New York*, New York State Museum, Bulletin 117. Albany, 1907.

Archaeological History of New York, New York State Museum, Bulletins 235–8. Albany, 1922.

PARSONS, LEE A. 'The Nature of Horizon Markers in Middle American Archaeology,' *Anthropology Tomorrow*, vol. 5, no. 2, 98–121. Chicago, 1957.

PARSONS, SAMUEL H. *Discoveries Made in the Western Country*, Memoirs of the American Academy of Arts and Sciences, vol. 2. Boston, 1793.

PATTERSON, CLAIR C. 'Native Copper, Silver, and Gold Accessible to Early Metallurgists,' *American Antiquity*, vol. 36, no. 3, 286–321. Washington, D.C., 1971.

PATTERSON, T. C. 'Chavín: an interpretation of its spread and influence,' *Dumbarton Oaks Conference on Chavín*, E. P. Benson, ed., 29–48. Washington, D.C., 1971.

PATTERSON, T. C. and LANNING, E. P. 'Changing Settlement Patterns on the Central Peruvian Coast,' *Ñawpa Pacha*, vol. 2, 113–23. Berkeley, 1964.

PEEBLES, C. S. 'Moundville and Surrounding Sites: some structural consideration of mortuary practices II,' in *Approaches to the Social Dimensions of Mortuary Practices*, J. A. Brown, ed., Society for American Archaeology, Memoir 25, 68–91. Washington, D.C., 1971.

PEET, STEPHEN D. *Prehistoric America*, 5 vols. Chicago, 1892–1905.

PETERSON, FREDERICK. A. *Ancient Mexico*. New York, 1959.

PETRIE, SIR W. M. FLINDERS. 'Sequences in Prehistoric Remains,' *Journal of the Royal Anthropological Institute of Great Britain and Ireland*, vol. 29, 295–301. London, 1899.

Methods and Aims in Archaeology. London, 1904.

PHILLIPS, PHILIP. 'Middle American Influences on the Archaeology of the Southwestern United States,' in *The Maya and Their Neighbors*, C. L. Hay et al., eds., 349–67. New York, 1940.

'Alfred Marsten Tozzer, 1877–1954,' *American Antiquity*, vol. 21, no. 1, 72–80. Salt Lake City, 1955.

'The Role of Transpacific Contacts in the Development of New World Pre-Columbian Civilizations,' in *Handbook of Middle American Indians*, R. Wauchope et al., eds., vol. 4, 296–319. Austin, 1966.

PHILLIPS, PHILIP, FORD, JAMES A. and GRIFFIN, JAMES B. *Archaeological Survey in the Lower Mississippi Alluvial Valley, 1940–47*, Papers of the Peabody Museum, vol. 25. Cambridge, Mass., 1951.

PHILLIPS, PHILIP, and WILLEY, GORDON R. 'Method and Theory in American Archaeology: an operational basis for culture-historical integration,' *American Anthropologist*, vol. 55, 615–33. Menasha, 1953.

PIDGEON, WILLIAM. *Traditions of De-coo-dah. And Antiquarian Researches*. New York, 1853.

PIGGOTT, STUART. 'Prehistory and Evolutionary Theory,' in *Evolution After Darwin*, S. Tax, ed., vol. 2, 85–98. Chicago, 1960.

PIÑA CHAN, ROMAN. *Una Visión del México Prehispánico*, Instituto de Investigaciones Historicas, Universidad Nacional Autónoma de México, Serie de Culturas Mesoamericanos, no. 1. Mexico, 1967.

POLLOCK, HARRY E. D. 'Sources and Methods in the Study of Maya Architecture,' in *The Maya and Their Neighbors*, C. L. Hay et al., eds., 179–201. New York, 1940.

POMO DE AYALA, FELIPE GUAMAN. *Nueva Corónica y Buen Gobierno (Codex Peruvien Illustré)*. Paris, 1936.

POPPER, KARL R. *The Poverty of Historicism*, 2nd ed. London, 1961.

POWELL, JOHN W. 'Introduction,' *Annual Report of the Bureau of Ethnology to the Secretary of the Smithsonian Institution*, vol. 1. Washington, D.C., 1879/80.

PRESCOTT, WILLIAM H. *History of the Conquest of Mexico*. New York, 1843.

PROGRAMA NACIONAL DE PESQUISAS ARQUEOLÓGICAS. *Resultados Preliminares do Primeiro, Segundo, e Terceiro Anos*, Publicaçãos Avulsas, nos. 6, 10, 13. Belem, 1967–69.

PROSKOURIAKOFF, TATIANA. 'Historical Data in the Inscriptions of Yaxchilan, Part I,' Universidad Nacional Autónoma de México, *Estudios de Cultura Maya*, vol. 3, 149–67. Mexico, D.F., 1963.

'Historical Data in the Inscription of Yaxchilan, Part II,' Universidad Nacional Autónoma de México, *Estudios de Cultura Maya*, vol. 4, 177–201. Mexico, D.F., 1964.

PRUDDEN, THEOPHIL M. 'An Elder Brother to the Cliff-Dwellers,' *Harper's New Monthly Magazine*, vol. 95, June, 56–63. New York, 1897.

PUTNAM, FREDERIC W. 'The First Notice of the Pine Grove or Forest River Shellheap,' *Bulletin of the Essex Institute*, vol. 15, 86–92. Salem, 1883.

'On Methods of Archaeological Research in America,' *Johns Hopkins University Circular*, vol. 5, no. 49, 89. Baltimore, 1886.

'A Problem in American Anthropology,' *Proceedings of the American Association for the Advancement of Science*, vol. 48, 1–17. Easton, 1899.

'The Serpent Mound of Ohio,' *Century Illustrated Magazine*, vol. 39, April, 871–88. New York, 1890.

QUIMBY, GEORGE I. 'Cultural and Natural Areas Before Kroeber,' *American Antiquity*, vol. 19, 317–31. Salt Lake City, 1954.

'Habitat, Culture, and Archaeology,' in *Essays in the Science of Culture*, G. E. Dole and R. L. Carneiro, eds., 380–89. New York, 1960a.

Indian Life in the Upper Great Lakes, 11,000 B.C. to A.D. 1800. Chicago, 1960b.

RAFINESQUE, CONSTANTINE S. *Ancient History or Annals of Kentucky*. Frankfort, 1824.

RAINEY, FROELICH G. and RALPH, ELIZABETH K. 'Archaeology and its New Technology,' *Science*, vol. 153, no. 3743, 1481–91. Washington, D.C., 1966.

RAPPAPORT, ROY A. *Pigs for the Ancestors; ritual in the ecology of a New Guinea people*. New Haven, 1968.

RATHJE, WILLIAM L. 'Socio-Political Implications of Lowland Maya Burials: Methodology and Tentative Hypotheses,' *World Archaeology*, vol. 1, no. 3, 359–74. London, 1970.

'The Origin and Development of Lowland Classic Maya Civilization,' *American Antiquity*, vol. 36, no. 3, 275–85. Washington, D.C., 1971.

'Classic Maya Development and Denouement,' to be published in the symposium volume, *The Collapse of Ancient Maya Civilization: a new assessment*, T. P. Culbert, ed. Albuquerque, 1972.

RAU, CHARLES. *The Archaeological Collection of the United States National Museum, in charge of the Smithsonian Institution*, Smithsonian Contributions to Knowledge, vol. 22, no. 4. Washington, D.C., 1876.

The Palenque Tablet in the United States National Museum, Washington, D.C., Smithsonian Contributions to Knowledge, vol. 22, art. 5. Washington, D.C., 1879.

REICHEL-DOLMATOFF, GERARDO. *Colombia*, Ancient Peoples and Places Series, G. Daniel, ed., London and New York, 1965a.

Excavaciones Arqueológicas en Puerto Hormiga (Departamento de Bolívar), Publicaciones de la Universidad de Los Andes, Antropología 2. Bogotá, 1965b.

REISS, WILHELM, and STÜBEL, ALPHONS. *The Necropolis of Ancón in Peru*, 3 vols. Berlin, 1880–87.

RESTREPO. VICENTE. *Los Chibchas antes de la Conquista Española*. Bogotá, 1895.

RICHARDS, HORACE G. 'Reconsideration of the Dating of the Abbott Farm Site at Trenton, New Jersey,' *American Journal of Science*, vol. 237, no. 5, 345–54. New Haven, 1939.

RICKETSON, OLIVER G., JR. and RICKETSON, EDITH B. *Uaxactun, Guatemala, Group E: 1926–1931*, Carnegie Institution of Washington, Publication 477. Washington, D.C., 1937.

RILEY, CARROLL L. *et al.*, eds., *Man Across the Sea: problems of pre-Columbian contacts*. Austin, 1971.

RITCHIE, WILLIAM A. 'The Algonkin Sequence in New York,' *American Anthropologist*, vol. 34, 406–14. Menasha, 1932.

'A Perspective of Northeastern Archaeology,' *American Antiquity*, vol. 4, no. 2, 94–112. Menasha, 1938.

The Archaeology of New York State. Garden City, 1965.

ROBERTS, FRANK H.H. JR. *Shabik'eshchee Village, a late Basketmaker site in the Chaco Canyon, New Mexico*, Bureau of American Ethnology, Bulletin 92. Washington, D.C., 1929.

The Ruins of Kiatuthlanna, eastern Arizona, Bureau of American Ethnology, Bulletin 100. Washington, D.C., 1931.

The Village of the Great Kivas on the Zuñi Reservation, New Mexico, Bureau of American Ethnology, Bulletin 111, Washington, D.C., 1932.

A Survey of Southwestern Archaeology,' *American Anthropologist*, vol. 37, no. 1, 1–33. Menasha, 1935a.

A Folsom Complex: preliminary report on investigations at the Lindenmeier Site in northern Colorado, Smithsonian Miscellaneous Collections, vol. 94, no. 4. Washington, D.C., 1935b.

'Archaeology in the Southwest,' *American Antiquity*, vol. 3, no. 1, 3–33. Menasha, 1937.

Archaeological Remains in the Whitewater District, eastern Arizona, Bureau of American Ethnology, Bulletin 121. Washington, D.C., 1939.

'Developments in the Problem of the North American Paleo-Indian,' in *Essays in Historical Anthropology in North America*, Smithsonian Miscellaneous Collections, vol. 100, 51–116. Washington, D.C., 1940.

ROBERTSON, WILLIAM. *The History of America*, 2 vols. London, 1777.

ROBINSON, W.S. 'A Method for Chronologically Ordering Archaeological Deposits,' *American Antiquity*, vol. 16, no. 4, 293–300. Salt Lake City, 1951.

ROSEN, ERIC VON. *Archaeological Researches on the Frontier of Argentina and Bolivia in 1901–1902*. Stockholm, 1904.

Popular Account of Archaeological Research During the Swedish Chaco-Cordillera Expedition, 1901–1902. Stockholm, 1924.

ROUSE, IRVING. *Prehistory in Haiti, A Study in Method*, Yale University Publications in Anthropology, no. 21. New Haven, 1939.

Culture of the Ft. Liberté Region, Haiti, Yale University Publications in Anthropology, no. 24. New Haven, 1941.

'The Strategy of Culture History,' in *Anthropology Today*, A.L. Kroeber *et al.*, eds., 57–76. Chicago, 1953a.

The Circum-Caribbean Theory, an archaeological test,' *American Anthropologist*, vol. 55, 188–200. Menasha, 1953b.

'On the Use of the Concept of Area Co-tradition,' *American Antiquity*, vol. 19, no. 3, 221–25. Salt Lake City, 1954.

'On the Correlation of Phases of Culture,' *American Anthropologist*, vol. 57, no. 4, 713–22. Menasha, 1955.

'Settlement Patterns in the Caribbean Area,' in *Prehistoric Settlement Patterns in the New World*, G.R. Willey, ed., Viking Fund Publications in Anthropology, no. 23, 165–72. New York, 1956.

'Culture Area and Co-tradition,' *Southwestern Journal of Anthropology*, vol. 13, 123–33. Albuquerque, 1957.

'The Classification of Artifacts in Archaeology,' *American Antiquity*, vol. 25, no. 3, 313–23. Salt Lake City, 1960.

'The Caribbean Area,' in *Prehistoric Man in the New World*, J. Jennings and E. Norbeck, eds., 389–417. Chicago, 1964a.

'Prehistory in the West Indies,' *Science*, vol. 144, no. 3618, 499–514. Washington, D.C., 1964b.

'Archaeological Approaches to Cultural Evolution,' in *Explorations in Cultural Anthropology*, Ward H. Goodenough, ed., 455–68. New York, 1964c.

'Seriation in Archaeology,' in *American Historical Anthropology, essays in honor of Leslie Spier*, C.L. Riley and W.W. Taylor, eds., 153–95. Carbondale, 1967.

Prehistory, Typology, and the Study of Society,' in *Settlement Archaeology*, K.C. Chang, ed. 10–30. Palo Alto, 1968.

'Comments on *Analytical Archaeology*,' *Norwegian*

Archaeological Review, vol. 34, nos. 3–4, 4–12. Oslo, 1970.

ROUSE, IRVING, and CRUXENT, JOSÉ M. *Venezuelan Archaeology*, Yale University Caribbean Series, no. 6. New Haven, 1963.

ROWE, JOHN H. 'Technical Aids in Anthropology: a historical survey,' in *Anthropology Today*, A.L. Kroeber *et al.*, eds., 895–940. Chicago, 1953.

Max Uhle, 1856–1944; a memoir of the father of Peruvian archaeology, University of California Publications in American Archaeology and Ethnology, vol. 46, no. 1. Berkeley, 1954.

'Archaeological Dating and Cultural Process,' *Southwestern Journal of Anthropology*,' vol. 15, no. 4, 317–24. Albuquerque, 1959a.

'Carl Hartman and his Place in the History of Archaeology,' *33rd International Congress of Americanists*, vol. 2, 268–79. San José, 1959b.

'Cultural Unity and Diversification in Peruvian Archaeology,' in *Men and Cultures*, A.F. Wallace, ed., Selected Papers of the 5th International Congress of Anthropological and Ethnological Sciences, 627–31. Philadelphia, 1960.

'Stratigraphy and Seriation,' *American Antiquity*, vol. 26, no. 3, 324–30. Salt Lake City, 1961.

'Alfred Louis Kroeber, 1876–1960,' *American Antiquity*, vol. 27, no. 3, 395–415. Salt Lake City, 1962a.

'Worsaae's Law and the Use of Grave Lots for Archaeological Dating,' *American Antiquity*, vol. 28, no. 2, 129–37. Salt Lake City, 1962b.

Chavín Art . . . New York, 1962c.

'Stages and Periods in Archaeological Interpretation,' *Southwestern Journal of Anthropology*, vol. 18, no. 1, 40–54. Albuquerque, 1962d.

'Urban Settlements in Ancient Peru,' *Ñawpa Pacha*, vol. 1, no. 1, 1–27. Berkeley, 1963.

'The Renaissance Foundations of Anthropology,' *American Anthropologist*, vol. 67, no. 1, 1–20. Menasha, 1965.

'Diffusionism and Archaeology,' *American Antiquity*, vol. 31, no. 3, 334–38. Salt Lake City, 1966.

ROWSE, A.L. *The Elizabethans and America*. London and New York, 1959.

RUDENKO, SERGEI I. 'The Ust'-Kanskaia Paleolithic Cave Site, Siberia,' *American Antiquity*, vol. 27, no. 2, 203–15. Salt Lake City, 1961.

SABLOFF, JEREMY A. 'Major Themes in the Past Hypotheses of the Collapse,' to appear in *The collapse of Classic Maya civilization*, T.P. Culbert, ed. Albuquerque, 1972 (in the press).

SABLOFF, JEREMY A. and SMITH, ROBERT E. 'The Importance of Both Analytic and Taxonomic Classification in the Type-variety System,' *American Antiquity*, vol. 34, no. 3, 278–85. Salt Lake City, 1969.

SABLOFF, JEREMY A. and WILLEY, GORDON R. 'The Collapse of Maya Civilization in the Southern Lowlands: a consideration of history and process,' *Southwestern Journal of Anthropology*, vol. 23, no. 4, 311–36. Albuquerque, 1967.

SAHAGÚN, FRAY BERNARDINO DE. *Florentine Codex; general history of the things of New Spain*, translated by Charles E. Dibble and Arthur J.O. Anderson, Monographs of the School of American Research and the Museum of New Mexico no. 14, pts. 2, 6, 8–13. Santa Fé, 1950–53.

SAHLINS, M.D. and SERVICE, ELMAN R., eds. *Evolution and Culture*. Ann Arbor, 1960.

SANDERS, WILLIAM T. *The 'Urban Revolution' in Central Mexico*, undergraduate honors thesis, Harvard University. Cambridge, Mass., 1949.

Tierra y Agua, Ph.D. dissertation, Harvard University. Cambridge, Mass., 1956.

Teotihuacan Valley Project, 1960–61, Mexico, Pennsylvania State University, mimeograph. University Park, 1962.

The Cultural Ecology of the Teotihuacan Valley. University Park, Pennsylvania, 1965.

'Hydraulic Agricultures, Economic Symbiosis and the Evolution of States in Central Mexico,' in *Anthropological Archaeology in the Americas*, B.J. Meggers, ed., 88–107. Washington, D.C., 1968.

SANDERS, W.T. and MERINO, JOSEPH. *New World Prehistory; archaeology of the American Indian*, Foundations of Modern Anthropology Series. Englewood Cliffs, 1970.

SANDERS, W.T. and PRICE, BARBARA J. *Mesoamerica, the evolution of civilization*, Random House Studies in Anthropology. New York, 1968.

SANDERS, W.T. *et al. The Natural Environment, contemporary occupation and 16th century population of the valley*, The Teotihuacan Valley Project, Final Report, vol. 1, Pennsylvania State University Department of Anthropology Occasional Papers, no. 3. University Park, 1970.

SANGER, DAVID. 'Prehistory of the Pacific Northwest Plateau as Seen from the Interior of British Columbia,' *American Antiquity*, vol. 32, no. 2, 186–98. Salt Lake City, 1967.

SAPPER, KARL. 'Altindianische Ansiedlungen in Guatemala und Chiapas,' *Publications of the Königlichen Museum für Völkerkunde*, vol. 4, 13–20. Berlin, 1895.

SARGENT, WINTHROP. 'A Letter from Colonel Winthrop Sargent to Dr. Benjamin Smith Barton Accompanying Drawings and Some Accounts of Certain Articles, which were taken out of an ancient tumulus, or grave in the Western Country,' *Transactions of the American Philosophical Society*, vol. 4, 173–6. Philadelphia, 1799.

SAUER, CARL O. *Agricultural Origins and Dispersals*. New York, 1952.

SAVILLE, MARSHALL H. 'Explorations on the Main Structure of Copan, Honduras,' *Proceedings of the American Association for the Advancement of Science*, no. 41, 271–5. Salem, 1892.

The Antiquities of Manabí, Ecuador, 2 vols., Contributions to South American Archaeology, Heye Foundation. New York, 1907–10.

SAYLES, EDWIN B. *Some Southwestern Pottery Types, Series V*, Medallion Papers, no. 21. Globe, 1936.

SAYLES, EDWIN B. and ANTEVS, ERNST. *The Cochise Culture*, Medallion Papers, no. 29. Globe, 1941.

SCHMIDT, ERICH F. *Time-relations of Prehistoric Pottery Types in Southern Arizona*, Anthropological Papers of the American Museum of Natural History, vol. 30, pt. 5. New York, 1928.

SCHOBINGER, JUAN. *Prehistoria de Suramérica*, Nueva Colección Labor, no. 95, Barcelona, 1969.

SCHOOLCRAFT, HENRY R. *Historical and Statistical Information Respecting the History, Condition, and Prospects of the Indian Tribes of the United States, Part IV*. Philadelphia, 1854.

SCHROEBER, ALBERT H. 'The Hakataya Cultural Tradition,' *American Antiquity*, vol. 23, no. 2, 176–8. Salt Lake City, 1957.

'Unregulated Diffusion from Mexico into the Southwest Prior to A.D. 700,' *American Antiquity*, vol. 30, no. 3, 297–309. Salt Lake City, 1965.

SCHULTZ, ADOLPH H. 'Biographical Memoir of Aleš Hrdlička,' *Biographical Memoirs of the National Academy of Sciences*, vol. 23, Memoir 12, 305–38. Washington, D.C., 1945.

SCHUMACHER, PAUL. 'Remarks on the Kjokkenmoddings on the Northwest Coast of America,' *Annual Report of the Smithsonian Institution for 1873*, 354–62. Washington, D.C., 1874.

SCHUYLER, ROBERT L. 'Historical and Historic Sites Archaeology as Anthropology: basic definitions and relationships,' *Historical Archaeology*, vol. 4, 83–89. Bethlehem, 1970.

SCHWARTZ, DOUGLAS W. *Conceptions of Kentucky Prehistory*. Lexington, 1967.

'North American Archaeology in Historical Perspective,' *Actes du XIᵉ Congrès International d'Histoire de Sciences*, vol. 2, 311–15. Warsaw and Cracow, 1968.

SEARS, WILLIAM H. 'The Study of Social and Religious Systems in North American Archaeology,' *Current Anthropology*, vol. 2, no. 3, 223–31. Chicago, 1961.

SERRANO, ANTONIO. 'The Sambaquís of the Brazilian Coast,' *Handbook of South American Indians*, Julian H. Steward, ed., vol. 1, 401–7, Bureau of American Ethnology, Bulletin 143. Washington, D.C., 1946.

SETZLER, FRANK M. 'Archaeological Perspectives in the Northern Mississippi Valley,' *Essays in Historical Anthropology*, Smithsonian Miscellaneous Collections, vol. 100, 253–90. Washington, D.C., 1940.

SHEPARD, ANNA O. *Ceramics for the Archaeologist*, Carnegie Institution of Washington Publication, no. 609. Washington, D.C., 1956.

SHETRONE, HENRY C. 'The Culture Problem in Ohio Archaeology,' *American Anthropologist*, vol. 22, no. 2, 144–72. Menasha, 1920.

The Mound-builders. New York, 1930.

SHIPPEE, ROBERT. 'The "Great Valley of Peru" and other Aerial Photographic Studies by the Shippee-Johnson Peruvian Expedition,' *The Geographical Review*, vol. 22, no. 1, 1–29. New York, 1932.

SHIPTON, CLIFFORD K. 'The American Antiquarian Society,' *The William and Mary Quarterly*, 3rd series, vol. 2, April, 164–72. Williamsburg, 1945.

'The Museum of the American Antiquarian Society,' in *A Cabinet of Curiosities*, W.M. Whitehall, ed., 35–48. Charlottesville, 1967.

SILVERBERG, ROBERT. *Mound Builders of Ancient America; the archaeology of a myth*, Greenwich, New York, 1968.

SMITH, ROBERT E. *Preliminary Shape Analysis of Uaxactun Pottery*, Special Publications of the Carnegie Institution. Washington, D.C., 1936a.

Ceramics of Uaxactun; a preliminary analysis of decorative technics and designs, Special Publications of the Carnegie Institution. Washington, D.C., 1936b.

Ceramic Sequence at Uaxactun, Guatemala, 2 vols., Middle American Research Series, Publication 20. New Orleans, 1955.

SOUTH, STANLEY A. 'Evolutionary Theory in Archaeology,' *Southern Indian Studies*, vol. 7, 10–32. Chapel Hill, 1955.

SPAULDING, ALBERT C. 'Review of "Measurements of Some Prehistoric Design Developments in the Southeastern States"', by J.A. Ford, *American Anthropologist*, vol. 55, 588–91. Menasha, 1953a.

'Statistical Techniques for the Discovery of Artifact Types,' *American Antiquity*, vol. 18, no. 4, 305–13. Salt Lake City, 1953b.

'Reply to Ford,' *American Antiquity*, vol. 19, no. 4, 391–3. Salt Lake City, 1954a.

'Reply (to Ford),' *American Anthropologist*, vol. 56, 112–14. Menasha, 1954b.

'Review of "Method and Theory in American Archaeology"', by G.R. Willey and P. Phillips, *American Antiquity*, vol. 23, no. 1, 85–87. Salt Lake City, 1957.

'The Dimensions of Archaeology,' in *Essays in the Science of Culture*, G.E. Dole and R.L. Carneiro, eds., 437–56. New York, 1960.

'Explanation in Archaeology,' in *New Perspectives in Archaeology*, S.R. Binford and L.R. Binford, eds., 33–41. Chicago, 1968.

SPENCER, ROBERT F. *et al., eds. The Native Americans*. New York, 1965.

SPIER, LESLIE. *An Outline for a Chronology of Zuñi Ruins*, Anthropological Papers of the American Museum of Natural History, vol. 18, pt. 3. New York, 1917.

'N.C. Nelson's Stratigraphic Technique in the Reconstruction of Prehistoric Sequences in Southwestern America,' in *Methods in Social Science*, S.A. Rice, ed., 275–83. Chicago, 1931.

SPINDEN, HERBERT J. *A Study of Maya Art*, Memoirs of the Peabody Museum, vol. 6. Cambridge, Mass., 1913.

'The Origin and Distribution of Agriculture in America,' *Proceedings, 19th International Congress of Americanists*, 269–76. Washington, D.C., 1917.

Ancient Civilizations of Mexico and Central America, American Museum of Natural History Handbook Series, no. 3. New York, 1928.

'Origin of Civilizations in Central America and Mexico,' in *The American Aborigines, their origin and antiquity*, D. Jenness, ed., 217–46. Toronto, 1933.

SPORES, RONALD M. *The Mixtec Kings and Their People*. Norman, 1967.

SQUIER, EPHRAIM G. 'Observations on the Aboriginal Monuments of the Mississippi Valley,' *Transactions of the American Ethnological Society*, vol. 2, 131–207. New York, 1948.

Aboriginal Monuments of New York, (later revised under title *Antiquities of the State of New York*), Smithsonian Contributions to Knowledge, vol. 2. Washington, D.C., 1849.

Nicaragua; its people, scenery, monuments . . ., 2 vols. New York and London, 1852.

'Observations on the Archaeology and Ethnology of Nicaragua,' *Transactions of the American Ethnological Society*, vol. 3, 83–158. New York, 1853.

Peru: incidents of travel and exploration in the Land of the Incas. New York, 1877.

SQUIER, EPHRAIM G. and DAVIS, E. H. *Ancient Monuments of the Mississippi Valley*, Smithsonian Contributions to Knowledge, vol. 1. Washington, D.C., 1848.

STEERE, J. B. *The Archaeology of the Amazon*, University of Michigan Official Publications, vol. 29, no. 9, Report of the Associate Director of the Museum of Anthropology, University of Michigan. Ann Arbor, 1927.

STEINEN, KARL VON DEN. 'Ausgrabungen am Valenciasee,' *Globus*, vol. 86, no. 77, 101–8. Hildburghausen, 1904.

STEPHENS, JOHN L. *Incidents of Travel in Egypt, Arabia Petraea and the Holy Land*, 2 vols. New York, 1837.

Incidents of Travel in Greece, Turkey, Russia and Poland, 2 vols. New York, 1838.

Incidents of Travel in Central America, Chiapas and Yucatan, 2 vols. New York, 1841.

Incidents of Travel in Yucatan, 2 vols. New York, 1843.

STEPHENSON, ROBERT L. 'Administrative Problems of the River Basin Surveys,' *American Antiquity*, vol. 28, no. 3, 277–81. Salt Lake City, 1963.

STERNS, FREDERICK H. 'A Stratification of Cultures in Eastern Nebraska,' *American Anthropologist*, vol. 17, no. 1, 121–7. Lancaster, 1915.

STEWARD, JULIAN H. *Ancient Caves of the Great Salt Lake Region*, Bureau of American Ethnology, Bulletin 116. Washington, D.C., 1937a.

'Ecological Aspects of Southwestern Society,' *Anthropos*, vol. 32, 87–104. Vienna, 1937b.

Basin-plateau Aboriginal Sociopolitical Groups, Bureau of American Anthropology, Bulletin 120, 1–3+. Washington, D.C., 1938.

'The Direct Historical Approach to Archaeology,' *American Antiquity*, vol. 7, no. 4, 337–43. Menasha, 1942.

The Handbook of South American Indians, 6 vols., Julian H. Steward, ed., Bureau of American Ethnology, Bulletin 143. Washington, D.C., 1946–50.

'American Culture History in the Light of South America,' *Southwestern Journal of Anthropology*, vol. 3, 85–107. Albuquerque, 1947.

'Culture Areas of the Tropical Forests,' in *Handbook of South American Indians*, Julian H. Steward, ed., vol. 3, 883–99, Bureau of American Ethnology, Bulletin 143, Washington, D.C., 1948a.

'A Functional-Developmental Classification of American High Cultures,' in *A Reappraisal of Peruvian Archaeology*, W. C. Bennett, ed., Society for American Archaeology, Memoir 4, 103–4. Menasha, 1948b.

'Cultural Causality and Law: A Trial Formulation of the Development of Early Civilizations,' *American Anthropologist*, vol. 51, 1–27. Menasha, 1949a.

'South American Cultures: an interpretative summary,' in *Handbook of South American Indians*, Julian H. Steward, ed., vol. 5, 669–772, Bureau of American Ethnology, Bulletin 143. Washington, D.C., 1949b.

Irrigation Civilizations: a comparative study, Julian H. Steward, ed., Pan American Union Social Science Monographs no. 1. Washington, D.C., 1955a.

Theory of Culture Change. Urbana, 1955b.

'Toward Understanding Cultural Evolution,' *Science*, vol. 153, 729–30. Washington, D.C., 1966.

STEWARD, JULIAN H. and FARON, L. C. *Native Peoples of South America*. New York, 1959.

STEWARD, JULIAN H. and SETZLER, FRANK M. 'Function and Configuration in Archaeology,' *American Antiquity*, vol. 4, no. 1, 4–10. Salt Lake City, 1938.

STIRLING, MATTHEW W. 'The Historic Method as Applied to Southeastern Archaeology,' in *Essays in Historical Anthropology of North America*, Smithsonian Miscellaneous Collections, vol. 100, 117–24. Washington, D.C., 1940.

Stone Monuments of Southern Mexico, Bureau of American Ethnology, Bulletin 138. Washington, D.C., 1943.

STODDARD, AMOS. *Sketches, Historical and Descriptive, of Louisiana*. Philadelphia, 1812.

STONE, DORIS Z. *Introduction to the Archaeology of Costa Rica*. San José, 1958.

STRONG, WILLIAM D. 'The Uhle Pottery Collections fron Ancón,' *University of California Publications in American Archaeology and Ethnology*, vol. 21, 135–90. Berkeley, 1925.

'An Analysis of Southwestern Society,' *American Anthropologist*, vol. 29, 1–61. Menasha, 1927.

'The Plains Culture Area in the Light of Archaeology,' *American Anthropologist*, vol. 35, no. 2, 271–87. Menasha, 1933.

An Introduction to Nebraska Archaeology, Smithsonian Miscellaneous Collections, vol. 93, no. 10. Washington, D.C., 1935.

'Anthropological Theory and Archaeological Fact,' in *Essays in Anthropology*, R. H. Lowie, ed., 359–68. Berkeley, 1936.

'From History to Prehistory in the Northern Great Plains,' in *Essays in Historical Anthropology of North America*, Smithsonian Miscellaneous Collections, vol. 100, 353–94. Washington, D.C., 1940.

'Cultural Epochs and Refuse Stratigraphy in Peruvian Archaeology,' in *A Reappraisal of Peruvian Archaeology*, W. C. Bennett, ed., 93–102, Society for American Archaeology, Memoir 4. Menasha, 1948.

'The Value of Archaeology in the Training of Professional Anthropologists,' *American Anthropologist*, vol. 54, 318–21. Menasha, 1952.

STRONG, WILLIAM D. and EVANS, CLIFFORD, JR. *Cultural Stratigraphy in the Virú Valley, Northern Peru: the Formative and Florescent epochs*, Columbian Studies in Archaeology and Ethnology, vol. 4. New York, 1952.

STRUEVER, STUART. 'Woodland Subsistence Settlement Systems in the Lower Illinois Valley,' in *New Perspectives in Archaeology*, S. R. Binford and L. R. Binford, eds., 285–312. Chicago, 1968a.

'Problems, Methods and Organization: a disparity in the growth of archaeology,' in *Anthropological Archaeology in the Americas*, 131–51. Washington, D.C., 1968b.

STÜBEL, ALPHONS and UHLE, MAX. *Die Ruinenstaette*

von Tiahuanaco im Hochlande des alten Peru. Leipzig, 1892.

STURTEVANT, WILLIAM C. *The Significance of Ethnological Similarities Between Southeastern North America and the Antilles,* Yale University Publications in Anthropology, no. 64. New Haven, 1960.

SWANSON, EARL H., JR. 'Theory and History in American Archaeology,' *Southwestern Journal of Anthropology,* vol. 15, 120–24. Albuquerque, 1959.

SWARTZ, B.K., JR. 'A Logical Sequence of Archaeological Objectives,' *American Antiquity,* vol. 32, no. 4, 487–98. Salt Lake City, 1967.

TANSLEY, A.G. 'The Use and Abuse of Vegetational Concepts and Terms,' *Ecology,* vol. 16, 284–307. Durham, 1935.

TAX, SOL, *et al.,* eds. *An Appraisal of Anthropology Today,* supplement to *Anthropology Today,* A.L. Kroeber, ed. Chicago, 1953.

TAYLOR, RICHARD C. 'Notes Respecting Certain Indian Mounds and Earthworks in the Form of Animal Effigies, chiefly in the Wisconsin Territory, U.S.,' *American Journal of Science and Art,* vol. 34, 88–104. New Haven, 1838.

TAYLOR, WALTER, W., JR. *A Study of Archaeology,* Memoir Series of the American Anthropological Association, no. 69. Menasha, 1948.

'Review of *New Perspectives in Archaeology,*' S.R. Binford and L.R. Binford, eds., *Science,* vol. 165, 382–4. Washington, D.C., 1969.

TELLO, JULIO C. ' Vira-Kocha,' *Inca,* vol. 1, 93–320, 583–606. Lima, 1923.

Antiguo Peru; primera epoca, Editado por la Comisión Organizadora del Segundo Congreso Sudamericano de Turismo. Lima, 1929.

'Origin y Desarrollo de las Civilizaciones Prehistóricas Andinas,' *Actas y Trabajos Cientificos, 27th International Congress of Americanists,* vol. 1, 589–720. Lima, 1942.

'Discovery of the Chavín Culture in Peru,' *American Antiquity,* vol. 9, 135–60. Salt Lake City, 1943.

THOMAS, CYRUS. 'Who Were the Moundbuilders?' *American Antiquarian and Oriental Journal,* no. 2, 65–74. Chicago, 1885.

Report of the Mound Explorations of the Bureau of Ethnology. Washington, D.C., 1894.

Introduction to the Study of North American Archaeology. Cincinnati, 1898.

'Maudslay's Archaeological Work in Central America,' *American Anthropologist,* vol. 1, no. 3, 552–61. Menasha, 1899.

THOMPSON, DONALD E. 'Formative Period Architecture in the Casma Valley, Peru,' *Actas y Memorias, 35th International Congress of Americanists,* vol. 1, 205–12. Mexico, D.F., 1964a.

'Postclassic Innovations in Architecture and Settlement Patterns in the Casma Valley, Peru,' *Southwestern Journal of Anthropology,* vol. 20, no. 1, 91–105. Albuquerque, 1964b.

THOMPSON, EDWARD H. *The Chultunes of Labna, Yucatan,* Memoirs of the Peabody Museum, vol. 1, no. 3. Cambridge, Mass., 1897.

'Ruins of Xkichmook, Yucatan,' *Field Columbian Museum Anthropological Series,* vol. 2, no. 3, 209–29. Chicago, 1898.

Archaeological Researches in Yucatan, Memoirs of the Peabody Museum, vol. 3, no. 1. Cambridge, Mass., 1904.

THOMPSON, J.E.S. 'Maya Chronology; the correlation question,' *Publications of the Carnegie Institution of Washington,* no. 456, 51–104. Washington, D.C., 1937.

Excavations at San José, British Honduras, Publications of the Carnegie Institution of Washington, no. 506. Washington, D.C., 1939.

Late Ceramic Horizons at Benque Viejo, British Honduras, Publications of the Carnegie Institution of Washington, no. 528. Washington, D.C., 1940.

Maya Hieroglyphic Writing: an introduction, Publications of the Carnegie Institution of Washington, no. 589. Washington, D.C., 1950.

The Rise and Fall of Maya Civilization. Norman, 1954.

Thomas Gage's Travels in the New World, J.E.S. Thompson, ed. Norman, 1958a.

'Research in Maya Hieroglyphic Writing,' in *Middle American Anthropology,* G.R. Willey, ed., 43–60. Washington, D.C., 1958b.

THOMPSON, RAYMOND H. 'Review of *Archaeology from the Earth,*' R.E.M. Wheeler, *American Antiquity,* vol. 21, no. 2, 188–9. Salt Lake City, 1955.

'An Archaeological Approach to the Study of Cultural Stability,' R.H. Thompson, ed., in *Seminars in Archaeology: 1955,* R. Wauchope, ed., Society for American Archaeology, Memoir 11, 31–58. Salt Lake City, 1956.

Modern Yucatecan Maya Pottery Making, Society for American Archaeology, Memoir 15. Salt Lake City, 1958.

THRUSTON, GATES P. *The Antiquities of Tennessee.* Cincinnati, 1890.

TORRES, LUIS M. 'Arqueología de la Cuenca del Rio Paraná,' *Revista del Museo de La Plata,* vol. 14, 53–122. Buenos Aires, 1907.

Los Primitivos Habitantes del Delta del Paraná, Universidad Nacional de La Plata Biblioteca Centenaria, vol. 4. Buenos Aires, 1911.

TOZZER, ALFRED M. 'A Preliminary Study of the Prehistoric Ruins of Tikal, Guatemala,' *Memoirs of the Peabody Museum,* vol. 5, no. 2, 93–135. Cambridge, Mass., 1911.

'A Preliminary Study of the Prehistoric Ruins of Nakum, Guatemala,' *Memoirs of the Peabody Museum,* vol. 5, no. 3, 137–201. Cambridge, Mass., 1913.

'Report of the Director of the International School of Archaeology and Ethnology in Mexico for 1913–1914,' *American Anthropologist,* vol. 17, no. 2, 391–5. Lancaster, 1915.

'Chronological Aspects of American Archaeology,' *Proceedings of the Massachusetts Historical Society,* vol. 59, 283–91. Boston, 1926.

'Time and American Archaeology,' *Natural History,* vol. 27, no. 3, 210–21. New York, 1927.

'Frederic Ward Putnam,' *National Academy of Sciences Biographical Memoirs,* vol. 16, no. 4. Washington, D.C., 1935.

TREUTLEIN, T.E., trans. *Pfefferkorn's Description of the Province of Sonora,* Coronado Quarto Centennial Publications, 1540–1940. Albuquerque, 1949.

TRIGGER, BRUCE G. 'Settlement as an Aspect of Iroquoian Adaptation at the Time of Contact,' *American Anthropologist*, vol. 65, no. 1, 86–101. Menasha, 1963.

'Settlement Archaeology – its goals and promise,' *American Antiquity*, vol. 32, no. 2, 149–61. Salt Lake City, 1967.

'The Determinants of Settlement Patterns,' in *Settlement Archaeology*, K.C. Chang, ed., 53–78. Palo Alto, 1968a.

'Major Concepts of Archaeology in Historical Perspective,' *Man*, vol. 3, no. 4, 527–41. London, 1968b.

'Aims in Prehistoric Archaeology,' *Antiquity*, vol. 44, no. 173, 26–37. Cambridge, 1970.

'Archaeology and Ecology,' *World Archaeology*, vol. 2, no. 3, 321–36. London, 1971.

TSCHUDI, JOHANN. *Reisen Durch Süd-Amerika*, 5 vols. Leipzig, 1869.

TUGBY, DONALD J. 'Archaeology and Statistics,' in *Science in Archaeology*, revised edition, D. Brothwell and E. Higgs, eds., 635–48. London and New York, 1969.

UHLE, MAX. *Pachacamac*. Philadelphia, 1903.

The Emeryville Shellmound, University of California Publications in American Archaeology and Ethnology, vol. 7, no. 1. Berkeley, 1907.

'Ueber die Frühkulturen in der Umgebung von Lima,' *16th International Congress of Americanists*, 347–70. Vienna, 1910.

'Die Muschelhügel von Ancón, Peru,' *18th International Congress of Americanists*, 22–45. London, 1913a.

'Die Ruinen von Moche,' *Journal de la Société des Americanistes de Paris*, vol. 10, 95–117. Paris, 1913b.

'Sobre la Estación Paleolítica de Taltal,' *Publicaciones del Museo de Etnología*, vol. 31–50. Santiago, 1916.

'La Arqueología de Arica y Tacna,' *Boletín de la Sociedad Ecuatoriana de Estudios Historicos Americanos*, vol. 3, nos. 7 and 8, 1–48. Quito, 1919.

Fundamentos Etnicos y Arqueología de Arica y Tacna, 2nd ed. Quito, 1922a.

'Influencias Mayas en el Alto Ecuador,' *Boletín de la Academia Nacional de Historia*, vol. 4, nos. 10 and 11, 205–46. Quito, 1922b.

'Civilizaciones Mayoides de la Costa Pacífica de Sudamérica,' *Boletín Academia Nacional de Historia* vol. 6, 87–92. Quito, 1923.

VAILLANT, GEORGE C. 'The Chronological Significance of Maya Ceramics,' Ph.D. thesis, Harvard University. Cambridge, Mass., 1927.

Excavations at Zacatenco, Anthropological Papers of the American Museum of Natural History, vol. 32, pt. 1. New York. 1930.

Excavations at Ticoman, Anthropological Papers of the American Museum of Natural History, vol. 32, pt. 2. New York, 1931.

Some Resemblances in the Ceramics of Central and North America, Medallion Papers, no. 12. Globe, 1932.

'The Archaeological Setting of the Playa de Los Muertos Culture,' *Maya Research*, vol. 1, no. 2, 87–100. New York, 1934.

'Chronology and Stratigraphy in the Maya Area,' *Maya Research*, vol. 2, no. 2, 119–43. New York, 1935.

'History and Stratigraphy in the Valley of Mexico,. *Scientific Monthly*, vol. 44, 307–24. New York, 1937.

'Patterns in Middle American Archaeology,' in *The Maya and Their Neighbors*, C.L. Hay *et al.*, eds., 295–305. New York, 1940.

Aztecs of Mexico. Garden City, 1941.

VAILLANT, SUZANNAH B. and VAILLANT, GEORGE C. *Excavations at Gualupita*, Anthropological Papers of the American Museum of Natural History, vol. 35, no. 6, New York, 1934.

VAYDA, ANDREW P. and RAPPAPORT, ROY A. 'Ecology, Cultural and Noncultural,' in *Introduction to Cultural Anthropology*, J.A. Clifton, ed., 477–97. Boston, 1968.

VERNEAU, RENE, and RIVET, PAUL. *Ethnographie Ancienne de l'Equateur*, 2 vols. Paris, 1912–22.

WALCKENAËR, DE LARENAUDIÈRE, and JOMARD. 'Rapport sur le Concours Relatif à la Géographie et aux Antiquités de l'Amérique Centrale,' *Bulletin de la Société de Géographie*, 2nd series, vol. 5, 253–91. Paris, 1836.

WALDECK, JEAN FRÉDÉRIC MAXIMILIAN, COUNTE DE. *Voyage pittoresque et archéologique dans la province d' Yucatan (Amérique Centrale), pendant les années 1834 et 1836*. Paris, 1838.

WALKER, S.T. 'Mounds, Shellheaps, Ancient Canal, etc., Florida,' *Annual Report of the Smithsonian Institution for 1881*, 685. Washington, D.C., 1883.

WARING, ANTONIO J., JR. and HOLDER, PRESTON. 'A Prehistoric Ceremonial Complex in the Southeastern United States,' *American Anthropologist*, vol. 47, no. 1, 1–34. Menasha, 1945.

WARREN, CLAUDE N. 'The San Dieguito Complex: a review and hypothesis,' *American Antiquity*, vol. 32, no. 2, 168–86. Salt Lake City, 1967.

The View from Wenas: a study in Plateau prehistory, Occasional Papers of the Idaho State University Museum, no. 24, Pocatello, 1968.

WASHBURN, WILCOMB E. 'Joseph Henry's Conception of the Purpose of the Smithsonian Institution,' in *A Cabinet of Curiosities*, W.N. Whitehall, ed., 106–66. Charlottesville, 1967.

WATSON, PATTY JO, LEBLANC, S.A., and REDMAN, CHARLES L. *Explanation in Archaeology, An Explicitly Scientific Approach*. New York, 1971.

WAUCHOPE, ROBERT. 'Implications of Radiocarbon Dates from Middle and South America,' *Middle American Research Records*, vol. 2, no. 2, 19–39. New Orleans, 1954.

Handbook of Middle American Indians, R. Wauchope, ed., 9 vols. (to date), University of Texas Press, Austin, 1964–70.

Lost Tribes and Sunken Continents. Chicago, 1962.

Archaeological Survey of Northern Georgia . . . Memoirs of the Society for American Archaeology, Memoir 21. Salt Lake City, 1966.

WEBB, MALCOLM C. *The Post-Classic Decline of the Peten Maya: an interpretation in the light of a general theory of state society*, Ph.D. dissertation, University of Michigan. Ann Arbor, 1964.

WEBB, WILLIAM S. and DE JARNETTE, DAVID L. *An Archaeological Survey of Pickwick Basin in the Adjacent Portions of the States of Alabama, Mississippi, and Tennessee*, Bureau of American Ethnology, Bulletin 129. Washington, D.C., 1942.

WEBB, WILLIAM S. and SNOW, C. E. *The Adena People*, University of Kentucky Report in Anthropology and Archaeology, vol. 6. Lexington, 1945.

WEDEL, WALDO R. *An Introduction to Pawnee Archaeology*, Bureau of American Ethnology, Bulletin 112. Washington, D.C., 1936.

The Direct-Historical Approach in Pawnee Archaeology, Smithsonian Miscellaneous Collections, vol. 97, no. 7. Washington, D.C., 1938.

'Culture Sequence in the Central Great Plains,' in *Essays in Historical Anthropology of North America*, Smithsonian Miscellaneous Collections, vol. 100, 291–352. Washington, D.C., 1940.

Environment and Native Subsistence Economies in the Central Great Plains, Smithsonian Miscellaneous Collections, vol. 100, no. 3. Washington, D.C., 1941.

'Some Aspects of Human Ecology in the Central Plains, *American Anthropologist*, vol. 55, 499–514. Menasha, 1953.

Prehistoric Man on the Great Plains. Norman, 1961.

WHALLON, ROBERT, JR. 'Investigations of Late Prehistoric Social Oraganization in New York State,' in *New Perspectives in Archaeology*, S.R. Binford and L. R. Binford, eds., 223–44. Chicago, 1968.

WHEAT, JOE BEN, GIFFORD, JAMES C. and WASLEY, WILLIAM. 'Ceramic Variety, Type Cluster, and Ceramic System in Southwestern Pottery Analysis,' *American Antiquity*, vol. 24, no. 1, 34–47. Salt Lake City, 1958.

WHEELER, Sir MORTIMER. *Archaeology from the Earth*. Oxford, 1954.

WHITE, LESLIE A. *The Science of Culture: a study of man and civilization*. New York, 1949.

The Evolution of Culture. New York, 1959.

WHITNEY, JOSIAH D. *Cave in Calaveras County, California*, Annual Report of the Smithsonian Institution for 1867. Washington, D.C., 1872.

WIENER, CHARLES. *Pérou et Bolivie*. Paris, 1880.

WIENER, NORBERT, *The Human Use of Human Beings: cybernetics and society*. New York, 1954.

Cybernetics, 2nd ed. Cambridge, 1961.

WILLEY, GORDON R. 'Ceramic Stratigraphy in a Georgia Village Site,' *American Antiquity*, vol. 5, no. 2, 140–47. Menasha, 1939.

'A Supplement to the Pottery Sequence at Ancón,' in *Archaeological Studies in Peru*, W.D. Strong, G.R. Willey, and J.M. Corbett, eds., Columbia University Studies in Archaeology and Ethnology, vol. 1, no. 4, 119–211. New York, 1943.

'Horizon Styles and Pottery Traditions in Peruvian Archaeology,' *American Antiquity*, vol. 11, 49–56. Menasha, 1945.

'The Archaeology of the Greater Pampa,' in *Handbook of South American Indians*, Julian H. Steward, ed., vol. 1, 25–46, Bureau of American Ethnology, Bulletin 143. Washington, D.C., 1946a.

'The Virú Valley Program in Northern Peru,' *Acta Americana*, vol. 4, no. 4, 224–38. Washington, D.C., 1946b.

'A Functional Analysis of "Horizon Styles" in Peruvian Archaeology,' in *A Reappraisal of Peruvian Archaeology*, W. C. Bennett, ed., 8–15, Society for American Archaeology, Memoir 4. Menasha, 1948.

Archaeology of the Florida Gulf Coast, Smithsonian Miscellaneous Collections, vol. 113. Washington, D.C., 1949.

'Growth Trends in New World Cultures,' in *For the Dean: anniversary volume for Byron Cummings*, 223–47. Santa Fé, 1950.

'Archaeological Theories and Interpretation: New World,' in *Anthropology Today*, A.L. Kroeber et al., eds., 361–85. Chicago, 1953a.

Prehistoric Settlement Patterns in the Virú Valley, Peru, Bureau of American Ethnology, Bulletin 155. Washington, D.C., 1953b.

'A Pattern of Diffusion-Acculturation,' *Southwestern Journal of Anthropology*, vol. 9, 369–84. Albuquerque, 1953c.

'The Interrelated Rise of the Native Cultures of Middle and South America,' in *New Interpretations of Aboriginal American Culture History*, 75th Anniversary Volume, Anthropological Society of Washington, 28–45. Washington, D.C., 1955a.

'The Prehistoric Civilizations of Nuclear America,' *American Anthropologist*, vol. 57, no. 3, 571–93. Menasha, 1955b.

Prehistoric Settlement Patterns in the New World, Viking Fund Publications in Anthropology, no. 23. New York, 1956.

'Estimated Correlations and Dating of South and Central American Culture Sequences,' *American Antiquity*, vol. 23, no. 4, 353–78. Salt Lake City, 1958.

'New World Prehistory,' *Science*, vol. 131, no. 3393, 73–83. Washington, D.C., 1960a.

'Historical Patterns and Evolution in Native New World Cultures,' in *Evolution After Darwin*, S. Tax, ed., vol. 2, 111–41. Chicago, 1960b.

'Review of *Evolution and Culture*,' M.D. Sahlins and E.R. Service, eds., *American Antiquity*, vol. 26, no. 3, 441–3. Salt Lake City, 1961.

'The Early Great Styles and the Rise of the Pre-Columbian Civilizations,' *American Anthropologist*, vol. 64, no. 1, 1–14. Menasha, 1962.

An Introduction to American Archaeology, 2 vols. Englewood Cliffs, 1966–71.

'One Hundred Years of American Archaeology,' in *One Hundred Years of Anthropology*, J.O. Brew, ed., 29–56. Cambridge, Mass., 1968a.

'Settlement Archaeology: an appraisal,' in *Settlement Archaeology*, K.C. Chang, ed., 208–26. Palo Alto, 1968b.

'Commentary on: The Emergence of Civilizations in the Maya Lowlands,' in *Observations on the Emergence of Civilization in Mesoamerica*, R.F. Heizer and J.A. Graham, eds., 97–112, Contributions of the University of California Archaeological Research Facility, no. 11. Berkeley, 1971.

WILLEY, GORDON R. *et al. Prehistoric Maya Settlements in the Belize Valley*, Papers of the Peabody Museum, vol. 54. Cambridge, Mass., 1965.

WILLEY, GORDON R. and MCGIMSEY, CHARLES R. *The Monagrillo Culture of Panama*, Papers of the

Peabody Museum, vol. 49, no. 2. Cambridge, Mass., 1954.

WILLEY, GORDON R. and PHILLIPS, PHILIP. 'Method and Theory in American Archaeology, II: historical-developmental interpretations,' *American Anthropologist*, vol. 57, 723–819. Menasha, 1955.

Method and Theory in American Archaeology. Chicago, 1958.

WILLEY, GORDON R. and SHIMKIN, D.B. 'The Collapse of Classic Maya Civilization in the Southern Lowlands: a symposium summary statement,' *Southwestern Journal of Anthropology*, vol. 27, no. 1, 1–18. Albuquerque, 1971.

WILLIAMS, HOWEL. 'Petrographic Notes on Tempers of Pottery from Chupicuaro, Cerro del Tepelcate and Ticoman, Mexico,' *Transactions of the American Philosophical Society*, vol. 45, no. 5, 576–80. Philadelphia, 1956.

WILLIAMS, HOWEL and HEIZER, ROBERT F. 'Sources of Rocks Used in Olmec Monuments,' *Contributions of the University of California Archaeological Research Facility*, no. 1, 1–40. Berkeley, 1965.

WILLIAMS, STEPHEN. *Anthropology 139: archaeology of Eastern North America*, Harvard University, Department of Anthropology, on file in the Peabody Museum Library. Cambridge, Mass., 1964.

WILLIS, ERIC H. 'Radiocarbon Dating,' in *Science in Archaeology*, revised edition, D. Brothwell and E. Higgs, eds., 46–57. London and New York, 1969.

WILLOUGHBY, CHARLES CLARK. 'Pottery of the New England Indians,' *Putnam Anniversary Volume*, 83–101. New York, 1909.

WILMSEN, EDWIN N. 'An Outline of Early Man Studies in the United States,' *American Antiquity*, vol. 31, no. 2, 172–92. Salt Lake City, 1965.

WILSON, THOMAS. 'Chipped Stone Classifications,' *Report of the U.S. National Museum for 1897*, 887–944. Washington, D.C., 1899.

WINSOR, JUSTIN, ed. 'The Progress of Opinion Respecting the Origin and Antiquity of Man in America,' in *Narrative and Critical History of America*, vol. 1, 369–412. Boston, 1889.

WISSLER, CLARK. 'Material Cultures of the North American Indians,' *American Anthropologist*, vol. 16, no. 3, 447–505. Lancaster, 1914.

'The New Archaeology,' *The American Museum Journal*, vol. 17, 100–1. New York, 1917.

The American Indian, 3rd ed. New York, 1938.

'The American Indian and the American Philosophical Society,' *Proceedings of the American Philosophical Society*, vol. 86, 189–204. Philadelphia, 1942.

WITTFOGEL, KARL A. *Oriental Despotism*. New Haven, 1957.

WITTRY, WARREN L. and RITZENTHALER, ROBERT E. 'The Old Copper Complex: an archaic manifestation in Wisconsin,' *American Antiquity*, vol. 21, no. 3, 244–54. Salt Lake City, 1956.

WOLF, ERIC R. and PALERM, ANGEL. 'Investigation in the Old Acolhua Domain, Mexico,' *Southwestern Journal of Anthropology*, vol. 11, no. 3, 265–81. Albuquerque, 1955.

WOODBURY, RICHARD B. 'Review of *A Study of Archaeology*,' *American Antiquity*, vol. 19, no. 3, 292–6. Salt Lake City, 1954.

'Nels C. Nelson and Chronological Archaeology,' *American Antiquity*, vol. 25, no. 3, 400–1. Salt Lake City, 1960a.

'Nelson's Stratigraphy,' *American Antiquity*, vol. 26, no. 1, 98–99. Salt Lake City, 1960b.

WORMINGTON, H. MARIE. *Ancient Man in North America*, 4th ed., Denver Museum of Natural History Popular Series, no. 4. Denver, 1957.

Prehistoric Indians of the Southwest, 5th ed., Denver Museum of Natural History Popular Series, no. 7. Denver, 1961.

WORSAAE, JENS J. A. *Danmarks Oldtid Oplyst ved Oldsager og Gravhøie*. Copenhagen, 1843.

WRIGHT, JAMES V. 'Type and Attribute Analysis: their application to Iroquois culture history,' *Proceedings of the 1965 Conference on Iroquois Research*, 99–100. Albany, 1967.

WRIGHT, JOHN H. *et al.* 'Report of the Committee on Archaeological Nomenclature,' *American Anthropologist*, vol. 11, 114–19. Lancaster, 1909.

WYMAN, JEFFRIES. 'An Account of the Fresh-water Shell-heaps of the St. Johns River, Florida,' *American Naturalist*, vol. 2, nos. 8 and 9, 393–403, 449–63. Boston, 1868a.

'An Account of Some Kjoekken, Moeddings, or Shell-heaps, in Maine and Massachusetts,' *American Naturalist*, vol. 1, 561–84. Boston, 1868b.

'Fresh-water Shell Mounds of the St. John's River, Florida,' *Memoirs of the Peabody Academy of Science*, no. 4, 3–94. Salem, 1875.

YARNELL, RICHARD A. *Aboriginal Relationships Between Culture and Plant Life in the Upper Great Lakes Basin*, Anthropological Papers of the Museum of Anthropology of the University of Michigan, no. 23. Ann Arbor, 1964.

ZEISBERGER, DAVID. 'History of the Northern American Indians,' A. B. Hulbert and W. N. Schwarze, eds., *Ohio Archaeological and Historical Quarterly*, vol. 19, 1–189. Columbus, 1910.

Index

Italic numerals refer to the captions and cite the illustration number